U.S. Navy Auxiliary Vessels

U.S. Navy Auxiliary Vessels

A History and Directory from World War I to Today

Ken W. Sayers

McFarland & Company, Inc., Publishers
Jefferson, North Carolina

LIBRARY OF CONGRESS CATALOGUING-IN-PUBLICATION DATA

Names: Sayers, Ken W., author.
Title: U.S. Navy auxiliary vessels : a history and directory
from World War I to today / Ken W. Sayers.
Description: Jefferson, North Carolina : McFarland & Company, Inc.,
Publishers, 2019 | Includes bibliographical references and index.
Identifiers: LCCN 2019013656 | ISBN 9781476672564
(paperback. : acid free paper) ∞
Subjects: LCSH: United States. Navy—Transportation—History. |
Cargo ships—United States—Registers. | Government vessels—
United States—Registers. | Government vessels—United States—History.
Classification: LCC VC533 .S29 2019 | DDC 359.3/20973—dc23
LC record available at https://lccn.loc.gov/2019013656

BRITISH LIBRARY CATALOGUING DATA ARE AVAILABLE

ISBN (print) 978-1-4766-7256-4
ISBN (ebook) 978-1-4766-3532-3

© 2019 Ken W. Sayers. All rights reserved

*No part of this book may be reproduced or transmitted in any form
or by any means, electronic or mechanical, including photocopying
or recording, or by any information storage and retrieval system,
without permission in writing from the publisher.*

Front cover: The aircraft carrier USS *Nimitz* (CVN 68) and guided missile
cruiser USS *Princeton* (CG 59) are engaged in an underway replenishment with
the fast combat support ship USS *Bridge* (AOE 10) steaming between them
in the Arabian Gulf in April 2003 (United States Navy photograph)

Printed in the United States of America

*McFarland & Company, Inc., Publishers
Box 611, Jefferson, North Carolina 28640
www.mcfarlandpub.com*

For Richard C. Marshall, and the officers,
sailors and civilian mariners who have served
on board the Navy's auxiliary ships

Acknowledgments

You can't produce a book like this alone. Most certainly I needed the assistance of other people and I was lucky to be aided along the way by some wonderful men and women—in and out of uniform.

A.D. Baker III, who edited *Combat Fleets of the World* for the U.S. Naval Institute from 1977 to 2003, was instrumental in getting this project underway. Widely known for his columns, articles, and detailed illustrations of Navy ships, Dave encouraged me to do this book, later suggested the publisher, and finally lent me some photographs from his own archives. I also drew from several of his superb *Naval History* articles on various auxiliary ships. Over the years, Dave has always been ready and most willing to lend a helping hand to me, and I greatly appreciate it.

Lieutenant Commander Lauren E. Cole, director of the Navy Office of Information East, obtained vital Department of the Navy support for this book. Lieutenants Chika U. Onyekanne and Mary L. Sanford, public affairs officers at the Naval History and Heritage Command (NHHC), along with David J. Colamaria, photo archivist at NHHC, enabled me to acquire the 200 images you see in these pages. And Jillian K. Morris, deputy director of congressional and public affairs at the Military Sealift Command, and Colleen E. O'Rourke, public affairs team lead at the Naval Sea Systems Command, provided valuable information about the MSC command structure and a new class of naval auxiliary vessels.

But without Charles L. Perdue at McFarland none of this would have been possible. It has been my good fortune to have had Charlie as a collaborator from the beginning. He not only provided a welcoming home for the project but also helped shape its architecture and structure, and has been an insightful and engaging editor from beginning to end. I am very grateful to him and to Rhonda Herman, McFarland's president, for their support.

Table of Contents

Acknowledgments vi
Preface 1
Glossary 3
Introduction 9

1 • Combat Logistics and Fleet Support Ships 23
2 • Support Ships 139
3 • Directory of U.S. Navy Auxiliary Ships 214

Bibliography 341
Index 349

Preface

I have always been interested in ships, particularly those of the United States Navy. I have read extensively about them, photographed them, written articles and books about them, and even served on board one—a Butler-class destroyer escort.

In recent years that interest has tended to focus on the lesser known, unusual, atypical and uncommon vessels in the Navy. I have visited various Reserve Fleet anchorages just to see vintage ships that were decommissioned and mothballed many years before I was commissioned. I have lectured about unclassified miscellaneous (IX) ships, a novel category that includes unique vessels such as "Old Ironsides," a former German heavy cruiser, Dewey's flagship at Manila Bay, a prize ship from the Spanish-American War, and a paddlewheel aircraft carrier that operated on the Great Lakes during World War II. I have authored a book about a four-masted luxury yacht once owned by the richest woman in the United States that was later manned by Coast Guardsmen as a weather ship during the Battle of the Atlantic. So even as libraries and book stores have provided numerous volumes about the usual popular suspects—battleships, aircraft carriers and submarines—my eyes and pen have focused instead on the underappreciated and often ignored members of the Navy's behind-the-scenes supporting cast—the equivalent of the fleet's extras, stage hands and roadies.

This book originates from and reflects that interest. It was written to inform and illuminate the irreplaceable role played by all of the auxiliary ships that have served the fleet since World War I right up to the present day. It defines, describes and documents the various auxiliary vessels used by today's Navy to deliver fuel, food, ammunition, parts and equipment to U.S. warships while they are forward-deployed and most often underway. It also discusses a variety of auxiliary ships that provide specialized support and services—such as salvage, towing, surveying, special missioning, logistical prepositioning, and high-speed transport—to the Navy and the other branches of the armed forces. It documents many of the law enforcement, humanitarian and disaster relief operations performed by auxiliary ships. And this volume provides a comprehensive accounting of auxiliary ship types that are no longer in active service, such as decommissioned ammunition ships and destroyer tenders. In all, more than 4,200 current and former naval vessels are covered in various levels of detail.

That extensive content was derived and assembled from hundreds of hours of research in a number of books and periodicals in my own collection and from numerous online sources, all of which are cited in detail in the bibliography. For readers desiring to dig even a little deeper about a specific vessel or a given ship type, the bibliography identifies what I found to be the six best repositories of such information. Seek further and ye shall find.

These pages contain considerable information about and illustrations of the 130 different types of ships that have been classified as auxiliary vessels in the last 100 years. With the sheer number of hulls in that population, it is not possible to include individual data and historical narrative for every one of those vessels within the confines of a single volume. As a result, some of the data and information must be compressed and abbreviated, and presented collectively rather than individually. Nevertheless, the book's coverage remains both wide and deep.

As the Navy is an acronym- and jargon-rich organization, a glossary of abbreviations and terms leads off this volume. In the introduction that follows, readers will find an account of the historical role and performance of auxiliary ships in the U.S. Navy, along with a discussion of the technologies, operational techniques and trends that have influenced that role and performance.

Chapter 1 covers nearly 400 combat logistics and fleet support vessels in 13 different classifications that currently provide underway replenishment and general support to fleet units and combatant forces. Chapter 2 includes more than 360 auxiliary vessels in 14 different classifications that today support the Navy's combatants and shore-based establishment, but which are not directly involved with warships and are not considered part of the battle force inventory. The third chapter is devoted to more than 3,500 ships, boats and other vessels classified in 103 auxiliary hull types that are no longer in active service because they have been retired, sold off, scrapped, or transferred to other countries and agencies. Chapter 3 also includes listings of defunct Navy auxiliary classifications that were never actually applied to specific vessels.

The ship listings in all three chapters are arranged in alphabetical order by their hull classification symbols, i.e., typically a two-to-three letter abbreviation representing the ship type (as in AD for destroyer tender, AE for ammunition ship, and so on). Specific hull numbers are assigned to individual specific ships by attaching one or more sequential numbers to the hull classification symbol (as in AD 1 for USS *Dixie*, AD 2 for USS *Melville*, and so on). This volume adheres to the current Navy style of leaving a space between the abbreviation and hull number rather than inserting the hyphen which was used for many years (e.g., AD 1 rather than AD-1).

In the Chapter 1 and Chapter 2 listings of the vessels constituting a given ship type, a bracketed abbreviation follows the vessel's name (as in "AGS 1 *Pathfinder* [SS]"). That abbreviation indicates the vessel's most recent status, e.g., active or transferred or sold for scrap. The introductory material of each chapter defines its status abbreviations.

Following the chapters, readers will find a complete bibliography of the various sources used in preparing the content of this volume, along with suggested key sources for those who might wish to explore this subject later.

Finally, I hope that this work appropriately recognizes, highlights and encourages greater appreciation for the thousands of auxiliary ships whose singular and collective contributions helped to make the U.S. Navy the premier sea service it has been and remains today. And I hope, too, as you read on, that you will enjoy the voyage and come to share my enthusiasm for these remarkable ships and their crews.

Glossary

Special Terms

The following terms and names are used throughout this volume, and refer to specific administrative processes affecting a naval vessel's official status and the government organizations involved in those processes.

Acquired—The date on which the vessel came into the Navy's custody or ownership.

Christening—The ceremony usually preceding the launch during which a newly constructed ship is publicly named and her bow struck with a bottle of champagne.

Commissioning—The ceremony or act of placing a Navy ship in active service.

Decommissioning—The ceremony or act of removing a Navy ship from active service.

Disposed—Once a vessel has been struck (see below), it is removed from the Navy's legal custody—that is, disposed of—by one of several possible methods, including: scrapping, transfer to MARAD (see below), foreign transfer, use in an experiment, expenditure as a target, donation, conversion to a historic memorial, transfer to other government/non-government agencies or entities, or outright sale.

In Service—The date on which the vessel formally begins its naval service; usually refers to MSC (see below) vessels and analogous to commissioning.

Laid down—The formal date on which construction of a ship begins, i.e., the laying down of its keel.

Launch—Transferring a ship to the water; herein generally refers to the date on which a newly constructed vessel enters the water for the first time.

Maritime Administration (MARAD)—The U.S. agency that succeeded the U.S. Maritime Commission (see below). MARAD maintains the inactive National Defense Reserve Fleet (NDRF) (see below) as a ready source of ships for use during national emergencies and it logistically supports the military when needed. Some naval ships or service craft are maintained and laid up at MARAD facilities on a temporary basis when the Navy cannot accommodate the vessels at its own inactive ship maintenance facilities. During this period, the Navy pays MARAD for the pier space.

Maritime Commission (MC)—An independent agency created by the Merchant Marine Act of June 29, 1936, to further develop and maintain a merchant marine for the promotion of U.S. commerce and defense. The Maritime Commission was abolished on May 24, 1950, and its functions were assigned to the Federal Maritime Board and the U.S. Maritime Administration.

Military Sea Transportation Service (MSTS)—The first single managing agency for the U.S. Department of Defense's ocean transportation needs. It was renamed Military Sealift Command (MSC) in 1970.

Military Sealift Command (MSC)—The former MSTS, it is responsible for providing sealift and ocean transportation for all armed forces branches as well as for other government agencies. Navy-owned ships operated by civilian crews in the MSC have the prefix "USNS" (U.S.

Naval Ship) before their names and a "T" prefix appended to their hull numbers, as in T-AH 19.

National Defense Reserve Fleet (NDRF)—Established by the 1946 Merchant Ship Sales Act, the NDRF is maintained by MARAD and serves as a reserve of inactive ships for national defense and emergencies. At its height in 1950 the NDRF consisted of 2,277 ships in eight anchorages; in more recent times the NDRF has held approximately 100 vessels in three anchorages.

Naval Sea Systems Command (NAVSEA)—The organization responsible for the design, construction, delivery, maintenance, and disposal of the Navy's ships and ship systems. Its four inactive ship maintenance facilities retain some 52 decommissioned ships—including seven auxiliary vessels—awaiting disposal.

Ready Reserve Force (RRF)—A component of the NDRF first established in 1976 to provide vessels for the rapid deployment of military equipment and materials. The RRF consists of approximately 46 vessels.

Struck—The Navy uses the term "stricken" to designate the formal removal by the Secretary of the Navy (upon the recommendation of the Chief of Naval Operations) of a ship from the official list of Navy vessels. The official list has been known since 1942 as the Vessel Register, and since 1962 as the Naval Vessel Register (NVR). "Stricken" or struck is a legal action preliminary to "Disposal."

United States Shipping Board (USSB)—An organization established during World War I to build and operate merchant ships to support the U.S. war effort; later succeeded by the U.S. Maritime Commission (see above).

War Shipping Administration (WSA)—When the War Shipping Administration was established in 1942, it took over many functions of the Maritime Commission, including operation of the merchant marine, while shipbuilding activity remained under the MC. These functions were returned to the Maritime Commission after September 1, 1946.

Abbreviations and Terminology

Multiple definitions for the same hull classification symbol reflect changes over time in the Navy's nomenclature for that ship type.

AB—Crane ship
Abaft—Behind, toward the stern
ABD—Advanced base dock
Abeam—Directly abreast off the side of a ship
ABSD—Advanced base sectional dock
AC—Collier
ACS—Crane ship
ACM—Auxiliary minelayer
ACV—Auxiliary aircraft carrier
AD—Destroyer tender
ADG—Degaussing vessel or degaussing ship
AE—Ammunition ship
AF—Storeship or provision store ship or store ship
AFD—Auxiliary floating dock
AFDB—Auxiliary floating dry dock—big or large auxiliary floating dry dock or large auxiliary floating dry dock (non–self-propelled)
AFDC—Auxiliary floating dry dock—little (concrete)
AFDL—Auxiliary floating dry dock—little or auxiliary floating dock—lengthened or small auxiliary dry dock or small auxiliary floating dry dock (non–self-propelled)
AFDM—Auxiliary floating dry dock—medium or medium auxiliary floating dry dock or medium auxiliary floating dry dock (non–self-propelled)
AFS—Combat store ship
AFSB—Afloat forward staging base
AG—Miscellaneous auxiliary vessel
AGB—Icebreaker
AGC—Amphibious force flagship
AGDE—Escort research ship
AGDS—Auxiliary deep submergence support ship
AGEH—Hydrofoil research ship
AGER—Environmental research ship
AGF—Miscellaneous command ship
AGFF—Frigate research ship or auxiliary general frigate
AGHS—Patrol combatant support ship
AGM—Missile range instrumentation ship
AGMR—Major communications relay ship
AGOR—Oceanographic research ship

Glossary

AGOS—Ocean surveillance ship
AGP—Motor torpedo boat tender or patrol craft tender
AGR—Radar picket ship
AGS—Surveying ship
AGSC—Coastal surveying ship
AGSE—Submarine escort ship
AGSL—Satellite launching ship
AGSS—Miscellaneous auxiliary submarine or auxiliary research submarine
AGTR—Technical research ship
AH—Hospital ship
AHLC—Heavy salvage lift craft
AK—Cargo ship
AKA—Attack cargo ship or amphibious cargo ship
AKB—Auxiliary cargo barge or lighter ship
AKD—Cargo ship dock
AKE—Dry cargo and ammunition ship
AKF—Auxiliary cargo float-on/float-off ship
AKI—General store ship issue
AKL—Light cargo ship
AKN—Net cargo ship
AKR—Vehicle cargo ship
AKS—Stores issue ship or general stores issue ship
AKV—Aircraft transport or aircraft cargo ship or cargo ship and aircraft ferry
AM—Minesweeper
AMc—Coastal minesweeper
AMCM—Airborne mine countermeasures
AN—Net tender or net laying ship
ANL—Net laying ship
AO—Oiler or fleet replenishment oiler
AOE—Fast combat support ship
AOG—Gasoline tanker
AOR—Area of Responsibility
AOR—Replenishment oiler
AOSS—Submarine oiler
AOT—Transport oiler
AP—Transport
APA—Attack transport
APB—Self-propelled barracks ship
APc—Coastal transport (small)
APC—Small coastal transport
APD—High-speed transport
APF—Administrative flagship
APG—Supporting gunnery ship
APH—Transport fitted for evacuation of wounded or wounded evacuation transport or evacuation transport
APL—Labor transport or barrack ship or non-self-propelled barracks craft
APM—Mechanized artillery transport
APN—Non-mechanized artillery transport
APR—Transport rescue vessel or rescue transport
APS—Transport submarine
APSS—Submarine transport
APV—Airplane transport or transport and aircraft ferry
AR—Repair ship
ARb—Base repair ship
ARB—Battle damage repair ship
ARC—Cable repairing ship
ARD—Non-self-propelled auxiliary repair dock or auxiliary repair dry dock
ARD(BS)—Bathyscaphe support auxiliary dry dock
ARDC—Auxiliary repair dock—concrete or concrete auxiliary repair dock
ARDM—Non-self-propelled medium auxiliary repair dry dock or medium auxiliary repair dock
ARG—Internal combustion engine repair ship
ARH—Heavy-hull repair ship
ARL—Landing craft repair ship or repair ship—small
ARM—Heavy-machinery repair ship
ARS—Salvage ship or rescue and salvage ship
ARSD—Salvage lifting vessel
ARST—Salvage craft tender
ARV—Aircraft repair ship
ARVA—Aircraft repair ship (aircraft)
ARVE—Aircraft repair ship (engine)
ARVH—Aircraft repair ship (helicopter)
AS—Submarine tender
ASR—Submarine rescue vessel or submarine rescue ship
ASSP—Transport submarine
ASW—Antisubmarine warfare
AT—Ocean-going tug or fleet tug

Glossary

ATA—Ocean-going tug—auxiliary or auxiliary ocean tug

ATB—Tank-barge mechanically connected to a tug

ATF—Ocean tug—fleet or fleet tug or fleet ocean tug

ATO—Ocean tug—old

ATR—Ocean tug—rescue

ATS—Salvage tug or salvage and rescue ship

ATS(X)—Towing, salvage and rescue ship (interim designation)

AV—Heavier-than-air aircraft tender or large seaplane tender or aircraft tender or seaplane tender

Availability—A period of repair, maintenance, upkeep or overhaul usually either in a shipyard or alongside a tender

AVB—Advanced aviation base ship or aviation logistics support ship

AVC—Catapult lighter

AVD—Seaplane tender—destroyer

AVG—Aircraft escort vessel

AVM—Guided missile ship

AVP—Small seaplane tender

AVR—Aircraft rescue vessel

AVS—Aviation supply ship

AVT—Auxiliary aircraft transport or auxiliary aircraft landing training ship

AW—Distilling ship

AZ—Lighter-than-air aircraft tender

BARS—Salvage ship built in the United States intended for service in the Royal Navy

BB—Battleship

Beam—Maximum width of a ship or boat

bhp—Brake horsepower (for diesel engines)

BM—Monitor

Bow—The front of a ship or boat

Bulkhead—A vertical structure or wall separating compartments on a ship

Cal.—caliber

CARAT—Cooperation afloat readiness and training

CC—Command ship

CENTCOM—U.S. Central Command

CG—Guided missile cruiser

CIWS—Close-in weapon system

CM—Minelayer

Complement—The officers and crew of a naval vessel

CV—Aircraft carrier

CVA—Attack aircraft carrier

CVE—Escort aircraft carrier

CVHE—Helicopter escort aircraft carrier

CVL—Light aircraft carrier

CVN—Nuclear-powered aircraft carrier

CVS—ASW aircraft carrier

CVT—Training carrier

CVU—Utility aircraft carrier

DANFS—Dictionary of American Naval Fighting Ships

DD—Destroyer

DDG—Guided missile destroyer

DDR—Radar picket destroyer

DE—Destroyer escort or escort ship

Displacement—The weight of water that a ship displaces when it is floating; thus a measurement of the ship's weight (including its contents)

DMZ—Demilitarized Zone

DOD—U.S. Department of Defense

DSRV—Deep submergence rescue vehicle

EPF—Expeditionary fast transport

ESB—Expeditionary sea base

ESD—Expeditionary transfer dock

Fantail—The area on the main deck at the stern of a vessel

FAST—Fast automated shuttle transfer

FDL—Fast deployment logistics ship

FF—Frigate

FFG—Guided missile frigate

FS—Freight and supply ship (Army)

HADR—Humanitarian assistance and disaster relief

hp—Horsepower

HST—High speed transport

HSV—High speed vessel

ID—Prefix for identification number assigned to civilian vessels considered for Navy use between 1917 and 1941.

ihp—Indicated horsepower

INSURV—Navy Board of Inspection and Survey

Glossary

IX—Unclassified miscellaneous vessel
JHSV—Joint high speed vessel
JLOTS—Joint logistics over the shore
Keel—The structural member of a ship at the bottom of a hull, i.e., the vessel's backbone or spine
Knot—A measurement of speed equal to about 1.151 miles an hour
LASH—Lighter aboard ship
LaWS—Laser weapon system
LCAC—Air cushion landing craft
LCC—Amphibious command ship or command ship
LCM—Mechanized landing craft
LCU—Utility landing craft
LCVP—Landing craft vehicles/personnel
LHA—Amphibious assault ship (general purpose)
LHD—Amphibious assault ship (multi-purpose)
LKA—Amphibious cargo ship
LMSR—Large, medium-speed roll-on/roll-off ship
LPA—Amphibious transport
LPD—Amphibious transport dock
LPR—Small amphibious transport
LPSS—Amphibious transport submarine
LSD—Dock landing ship
LSM—Medium landing ship
LST—Tank landing ship
LSV—Vehicle landing ship
MCM—Mine countermeasures ship
Mk—Mark
MLP—Mobile landing platform
MPS—Maritime prepositioning ship
MSC—Military Sealift Command
MSTS—Military Sea Transportation Service
MT—Motor tanker (diesel)
MV or M/V—Motor Vessel (diesel)
NAS—Naval Auxiliary Service
NASA—National Aeronautics and Space Administration
NAVSEA—Naval Sea Systems Command
NDRF—National Defense Reserve Fleet
NISMF—Naval inactive ship maintenance facility
NOAA—National Oceanic and Atmospheric Administration
NOTS—Naval Overseas Transportation Service
NTS—Naval Transportation Service
NVR—Naval Vessel Register
OPDS—Offshore petroleum distribution system
OSV—Offshore supply vessel
PCS—Patrol craft sweeper
PG—Patrol gunboat
Pilot—A person qualified to guide and direct the movement of a ship in and out of a port or harbor
Port—Left
PY—Patrol yacht
RHIB—Rigid-hull inflatable boat
RIMPAC—Rim of the Pacific exercise
RO/RO—Roll-on/roll-off
ROS—Reduced operating status
RRF—Ready Reserve Fleet or Ready Reserve Force
S2S—Skin-to-skin; two ships immediately alongside each other
SecNav—Secretary of the Navy
SES–Surface effect ship
shp—Shaft horsepower
SIGINT—Signals intelligence
SLBM—Sea-launched ballistic missile
SOSUS—Sound surveillance system
SS—Submarine
SSBN—Nuclear-powered ballistic missile submarine
SSN—Nuclear-powered attack submarine
SP—Section Patrol; prefix for identification number assigned to civilian vessels considered for Navy use during World War I
SS—Steam ship
SSP—Submarine transport
Starboard—Right
Stern—The back of a ship or boat
STREAM—Standard tensioned replenishment alongside method
SURTASS—Surveillance towed array sensor system
TF—Task Force
TS or T/S—Training ship
Transom—The flat surface forming the stern of a ship or boat

UAV—Unmanned aerial vehicle
UNOLS—University national oceanographic laboratory system
UNREP—Underway replenishment
USACS—U.S. Army Cable Ship
USAID—United States Agency for International Development
USAMP—U.S. Army Mine Planter
USCG—United States Coast Guard
USC&GS—U.S. Coast & Geodetic Survey
USSB—United States Shipping Board
UUV—Unmanned underwater vehicle
VERTREP—Vertical replenishment
WAGB—U.S. Coast Guard icebreaker
WAGC—U.S. Coast Guard amphibious force flagship
WAT—U.S. Coast Guard auxiliary tug
WATF—U.S. Coast Guard fleet tug
WestPac—Western Pacific Ocean
WMEC—U.S. Coast Guard medium endurance cutter
WSA—War Shipping Administration
YAG—Miscellaneous auxiliary
YAGR—Ocean radar station ship or radar picket ship
YDG—Degaussing vessel
YHLC—Heavy salvage lift craft
YMS—Motor minesweeper
YN—Net tender (boom)
YOG—Self-propelled gasoline barge
YP—Patrol craft

MC/MARAD Design Classifications

The first letter indicates ship type: C for cargo; P for passenger; R for refrigerator; S for special type; T for tanker; and VC for Victory-cargo.

The second letter indicates propulsion: M for motor (diesel); ME2 for motor, 2 shafts (diesel); MET for diesel-electric with two shafts; S for steam; S2 for steam, two shafts; SE for turbo-electric; SE2 for turbo-electric, two shafts; ST for steam, 2 shafts.

The third letter indicates specific ship design.

(See "List of MC Designs with Descriptions," http://shipscribe.com/shiprefs/mc/DsnList.html, for specifics.)

Introduction

Napoleon Bonaparte had the right idea. "An army marches on its stomach," he once remarked, meaning that without adequate provisioning and supply, land forces cannot travel or fight over extended distances. Similarly, a navy cannot operate far from its homeports, shipyards and supply depots for very long unless its ships and crews are properly maintained and sustained wherever they are deployed. And for the United States Navy, much of its vital resupply, replenishment and other material support is provided in distant waters by a relatively small fleet of naval auxiliary ships.

Some Auxiliary History

The U.S. Navy's use of auxiliary vessels dates back to its earliest years. In 1799, for example, the Navy Department employed the chartered schooner *Elizabeth* to transport supplies from Philadelphia to the United States Frigate *Constitution* which was patrolling off the coast of Saint-Domingue (Haiti).[1] *Elizabeth* was taken in tow by the frigate, and small boats (tenders) were used to shuttle the schooner's cargo over to *Constitution*. This 18th century event is considered the Navy's first underway replenishment (UNREP), and it enabled the legendary "Old Ironsides" to remain on station for 347 days during her 366-day deployment in the Caribbean Sea.[2]

Early in the 19th century the Navy used at least a dozen vessels—including *Franklin, Alert, Tom Bowline, Relief, Fredonia,* and the aptly named *Supply*—as store ships to carry supplies, and operated four others—including *Rescue, Fenimore Cooper* and *John P. Kennedy*—as tenders.[3]

During the American Civil War of 1861–1865, the U.S. Navy utilized numerous vessels to support the warships enforcing the Union's blockade of Confederate ports as well as those protecting merchant vessels at sea. These auxiliaries worked as transports, supply ships, picket boats, dispatch vessels, floating barracks, and tug boats. The Navy even acquired an ice breaker for duty during the conflict. Owned and lent by the city of Philadelphia in April 1861, *Ice Boat* (also known as *Refrigerator* and *Release*) operated in the Potomac River between Virginia and Maryland, occasionally engaged Confederate batteries on the Virginia shore and helped to defend Washington, D.C.[4] But because the Navy had not yet acquired the ability to replenish its warships while they were underway, Union steamships on Civil War blockade duty had to leave their stations periodically to refuel in port. As a consequence, a Royal Navy admiral later estimated that the Union

Navy's blockade of the South had only been about 75 percent effective since at any given time a quarter of the ships were in port refueling.[5]

Thus, one of the Navy's primary logistical challenges in the second half of the 19th century was to routinely provide coal for its steam-powered ships. The service initially employed contracted colliers to carry and deliver the coal to shore-based coaling stations along the U.S. coasts, where warships could replenish their supplies either while moored at a pier or from lighters when anchored. Later, the Navy commissioned 17 of its own auxiliary colliers (designated as ACs) to handle the coal transport and delivery mission (see Chapter 3). Either way, for the sailors and mariners involved, coaling was a dirty, time consuming, all-hands business. During the Spanish-American War of 1898, the Navy encountered the same problem it had faced during the Civil War as its blockade enforcers off Cuba had to steam 45 miles away from their stations to re-coal, thus weakening the U.S. blockade of the Spanish fleet. These two wartime experiences led to various experiments and innovations in the early 1900s for transferring fuel and cargo at sea. (See Technology, Techniques and Trends below.)

Following the 1898 American victory over Spain, the geographical reach of the United States extended beyond the country's east and west coasts to the waters of the Caribbean Basin and out to the more distant Pacific Ocean islands, including the Philippines. Since the U.S. Navy would have to patrol and someday possibly fight again in those seas, the service found that it needed dedicated vessels to service and support the warships that would be operating far from home. Similarly, the Navy also required specialized auxiliaries to serve as tenders for the new types of combatant vessels, such as submarines and destroyers, which were being commissioned early in the 20th century. It first tried to meet this growing need for support vessels by converting some civilian colliers and merchant ships into naval auxiliaries. And it later converted some of its own ships into auxiliaries. For example, the Navy colliers USS *Ontario* and USS *Vestal* were converted into repair ships, and some auxiliary cruisers, such as USS *Dixie*, USS *Prairie* and USS *Buffalo*, were repurposed as destroyer tenders.

But even at that, just before the United States entered World War I in April 1917, the Navy's auxiliary ship force was still comparatively modest, consisting of six destroyer tenders, three submarine tenders, two repair ships, two hospital ships, two transports, and some colliers, oilers and tug boats.[6] However, during the 19 months in which the United States fought in "the Great War" both the combatant fleet and the auxiliary force underwent a rapid expansion (see Chart 1 below). The number of destroyers and submarines nearly doubled, while the Navy acquired more than 560 colliers, cargo ships, tankers, transports, salvage ships and tugs for temporary service in 1917–1918.[7]

In the first two decades following World War I the Navy's inventory of vessels used to maintain and repair its men-of-war consisted of approximately 23 active duty destroyer tenders, submarine tenders, seaplane tenders and repair ships, plus fewer than six others laid up in reserve. As Thomas and Trent Hone point out in their detailed examination of the Navy in the 1919–1939 period, there hadn't been significant change in these auxiliary assets between 1922 and 1937. The six destroyer tenders (ADs) that had been in commission in 1922 were still operating in 1937 and the two newest ADs serving in 1937 had been commissioned 13 years earlier. Five of the six submarine tenders in commission in 1937 had joined the fleet in 1922; the other arrived in 1926. Two of the three 1937 active duty repair ships began their careers in 1909 and 1910; the youngest had been commissioned in 1924. Four store ships in service in 1937 had been serving the fleet since 1922, as had

The salvage tug USS *Favorite* (ID-1385) was purchased by the Navy in January 1918, commissioned the next month and sent to France for wartime duty as a salvage vessel. She was decommissioned in April 1920 (U.S. Navy photograph).

the three colliers then existent. Their 18 oiler (tanker) counterparts had been active in 1922, as had all five cargo ships, two ammunition ships, two transports, and a hospital ship. Put another way, "the auxiliary force was allowed to age. Successive Chiefs of Naval Operations in the 1930s tried to persuade President Roosevelt to replace many of these aging vessels but he refused—until he got a 20 percent increase in ship authorizations in 1938."[8]

Fortunately, by the end of 1939 the fleet was undergoing a transformation as a result of the Naval Expansion Act of May 1938. Congress had appropriated Fiscal Year 1940 funding for new auxiliaries, including three 18-knot tankers. As the fleet expanded, the Navy ordered new specialized auxiliary ships, such as the Dixie-, Fulton- and Vulcan-class tenders, the Curtiss- and Barnegat-class seaplane tenders, Navaho-class fleet tugs, and Aloe-class net tenders. By comparison, whereas in September 1937 the Navy counted 75 vessels as active duty auxiliaries, by December 1941, when the United States entered World War II, there were already 210 auxiliary ships in active service.[9]

The global conflict in which the Navy fought following the Japanese attack on Pearl Harbor obviously required and produced an enormous increase in both its combatant and auxiliary forces. Between December 1941 and August 1945, for example, the number of battleships grew from 17 to 23, fleet carriers went from seven to 28, escort carriers from one to 23, cruisers from 37 to 72, destroyers from 171 to 377, frigates from none to 361, submarines from 112 to 232, mine warfare ships from 135 to 586, amphibious warfare ships from none to 2,547, and patrol vessels from 100 to 1,204. Not only was there a monumental increase in warships but there also was a corresponding expansion in the fleet's operating areas. As the Navy conducted an unprecedented "two ocean" war in the Atlantic and Pacific and beyond, its ships steamed at ever increasing distances from the major bases, shipyards, dry docks, and facilities that had furnished "beans and bullets," repairs, fuel, parts and supplies in peacetime. The Navy had to be able to deliver those critical items and capabilities in the faraway waters and remote islands where its combatant vessels were battling in 1942–1945. And those factors, of course, necessitated a parallel build up in the auxiliary force. It grew more than 400 percent, from 210 active duty vessels in 1941 to 1,267 four years later (see Chart 1). Moreover the growth in auxiliaries occurred not just in the *number* of such ships but also in the various *kinds* of ships.

Whereas up to World War II the auxiliary force was comprised of just a few basic types, such as destroyer and submarine tenders, oilers and cargo ships, during the war a whole host of highly specialized, unique and diverse vessels was commissioned to serve the fleet in a variety of new roles. For example, the Navy acquired degaussing vessels, amphibious force flagships, motor torpedo boat tenders, net cargo ships and tenders, gasoline tankers, small coastal transports, wounded evacuation transports, battle damage repair ships, internal combustion engine repair ships, landing craft repair ships, and distilling ships, among others. (See Chapter 3 for a comprehensive listing of these and other veteran auxiliaries.)

Not only did the Navy commission new auxiliary ships built as such from the keel up but it also derived many of its wartime auxiliaries by converting various civilian Maritime Commission cargo ship hulls and some of its own tank landing ships (LSTs) into various species of tenders. (By the time the Japanese surrendered in August 1945, the Navy was operating more than 130 self-propelled tenders and more than 70 additional non-self-propelled barges used as auxiliaries.)[10]

Beginning immediately after the war, the Navy decommissioned, mothballed and disposed of hundreds of combatant and support vessels between 1945 and 1950, and the active duty auxiliary ship force dropped from 1,267 vessels to just 218. But those deactivations and disposals found the Navy somewhat shorthanded in June 1950 when North Korea invaded its southern neighbor. As the United States joined in the United Nations effort to repel the invasion, the Navy had to quickly reactivate and put to sea some of

The landing craft repair ship USS *Egeria* (ARL 8) was converted from the former tank landing ship USS LST 136 in 1944. She is seen here off Baltimore, Maryland, in April 1944 shortly before her deployment to the Pacific theater (U.S. Navy photograph).

the very same auxiliary ships it had laid up only a few years earlier. In order to both support Task Force 77 operating off the Korean coast and transport U.S. Army and Marine troops and their equipment and supplies to the fighting ashore, the Navy increased its active auxiliary ship force from 218 to 309 ships between June 1950 and June 1952 (see Chart 1). During the three-year conflict, more than 95 percent of all U.S. troops and combat cargo was delivered to Korea by ship. In fact, the Navy's Military Sea Transportation Service carried more than 52 million tons of cargo and 22 million tons of petroleum, oil and lubricants to Korea.[11]

In the 1960s, as the United States incrementally increased its involvement in the Vietnam conflict, a number of auxiliary ships were pulled out of the mothball fleet and put back into active service. For example, the hospital ship USS *Repose* (AH 16), which had been laid up in 1954, was recommissioned in October 1965 for wartime duty. During her deployment in Southeast Asia she cared for more than 9,000 battlefield casualties. The transport USNS *General LeRoy Eltinge* (T-AP 154), first commissioned in February 1945, was restored to active duty in May 1965 and carried nearly 2,500 troops to Southeast Asia. The cargo ship and aircraft ferry USNS *Card* (T-AKV 40), a World War II veteran, was removed from the Reserve Fleet in Beaumont, Texas, in 1963 and used to carry helicopters from the U.S. East Coast to Saigon. (She was sunk there on May 3, 1964, but refloated two weeks later, and returned to service on December 11, 1964.) The former seaplane tender USS *Albemarle* (AV 5) was converted in 1965 into a floating aeronautical maintenance facility for Army helicopters, renamed USNS *Corpus Christi Bay* (T-ARVH 1), and sent to Vietnam in 1966. During the Vietnam war the small repair ships USS *Askari* (ARL 30), *India* (ARL 37), *Satyr* (ARL 23) and *Sphinx* (ARL 24), all formerly in mothballs, were summoned back to duty to provide maintenance and support to riverine warfare boats and small craft, while USS *Krishna* (ARL 38) served as a mother ship for Navy and Coast Guard patrol boats engaged in Operation Market Time.

On the other hand, some of the auxiliaries that participated in the war were only in their very first years in naval service. For example the fast combat support ship USS *Sacramento* (AOE 1), which had been commissioned in March 1964, was assigned to Task Force 73 (the U.S. Seventh Fleet's Logistics Support Force) in the mid–1960s and delivered her cargoes to aircraft carriers and other combatants at Yankee Station off the coast of Vietnam. During her first deployment, *Sacramento* serviced 294 ships, transferred 35 million gallons of fuel, more than 1,100 tons of provisions, and 670 tons of ammunition over a four-month stretch.

In all, 99 percent of the ammunition and fuel and 95 percent of the supplies, vehicles and construction resources was delivered to Vietnam by sea.[12] Between 1965 and 1969, the Navy's Military Sea Transportation Service (MSTS) carried nearly 54 million tons of combat equipment and supplies, and nearly eight million tons of fuel for use in the conflict. Some 16 transports were employed for the buildup of U.S. forces in country. During the war the Navy's Service Squadron 3, which operated as Task Force 73, sustained and provisioned 100 deployed combatant vessels with ammunition, petroleum products, supplies and repairs. Task Force 73 also furnished parts, communications, towing, salvage, and medical support to the Navy's warships operating off Vietnam.[13]

During the Gulf War of 1990–1991, the auxiliary ships of the Military Sealift Command (MSC) delivered more than 12 million tons of vehicles, helicopters, ammunition, dry cargo, fuel, and other supplies and equipment for U.S. and coalition forces engaged in Operations Desert Shield and Desert Storm. More than 230 government-owned and

The small repair ship USS *Krishna* (ARL 38) is anchored off the island of Phu Quoc in South Vietnam in 1966 while serving as a joint Navy-Coast Guard operations and communications center (U.S. Navy photograph).

chartered ships were employed in that effort. MSC's combat stores ships, fast combat support ships, oilers, replenishment fleet tankers, and ammunition ships replenished and supported the Navy's carrier task groups and individual warships in the Red Sea, Persian Gulf and North Arabian Sea during the conflict. After the war, MSC reversed the logistics flow to the battlefield by using 456 ships to withdraw 1.9 million tons of tanks, armored personnel carriers, helicopters, ammunition and other materiel from the operational theater.[14]

These examples, and those in the chapters that follow, illustrate the durability, versatility and utility of the Navy's auxiliary force. They demonstrate how naval auxiliary ships provide on-time logistics and strategic sealift and perform specialized missions anywhere in the world's oceans, every day and all day throughout the year. None of that would have been possible without the constant evolution in operating methods, ship types and force structure employed by the auxiliary ship community.

Technology, Techniques and Trends

Over the years the technologies and operational techniques utilized by the Navy's auxiliary vessels have changed, sometimes in dramatic ways. One obvious change was the transformation in marine propulsion systems first from wind to steam-power, and later from coal-burning to oil-fired boilers. At the turn of the last century, coal was hauled onto naval ships in baskets, canvas bags and metal buckets, and then moved via chutes to below-deck coal bunkers.

In 1904 a new fuel transfer system developed by Stephen Miller was tried on the battleship USS *Illinois* (BB 7) by which the battleship would tow a coal-carrying collier from at a distance of 400 yards and haul aboard a trolley carrying 3,500 pounds of coal

Crewmen on the battleship USS *Maine* (BB 10) ca. 1904 are preparing to handle a large bag of coal transferred over from a collier on her port side (U.S. Navy photograph).

from the collier. This and similar experiments ended in 1914 when oil took the place of coal as the Navy's fuel source.

In 1917 the Navy oiler USS *Maumee* (AO 2) implemented an experimental fuel transfer method devised by her executive officer, Lieutenant Chester W. Nimitz. His plan called for the oiler to tow a destroyer moored alongside while both vessels were underway, and to pump oil to the destroyer via hoses rigged between the two ships (see AO section in Chapter 1 for additional information). On May 28, 1917, *Maumee* refueled six destroyers in about ten and a half hours, and went on to refuel 34 destroyers over the next three months. This new method is regarded as a landmark in the history of naval underway replenishment (UNREP) operations. Three decades later, Nimitz—by then a fleet admiral and the commander of allied forces in the Pacific Ocean area—said that "underway replenishment was the Navy's secret weapon" in defeating the Japanese military during World War II.

Nimitz's success was followed by other innovations in naval replenishment technologies, including the 1954 testing of a new span wire system to transfer supplies to ships underway; its replacement in 1960 by a more reliable ram-tensioned unit (pneumatic-hydraulic); the subsequent introduction of Fast Automated Shuttle Transfer (FAST) cargo handling stations in the 1960s by which high-speed trolleys and winches simplified the process of transferring ammunition and cargo to warships; and the Navy's current

Standard Tensioned Replenishment Alongside Method (STREAM), introduced in 1970. STREAM uses a hydraulic ram tensioner to keep a highline between the two ships taught even as the vessels roll and yaw in the sea. "Loads are hauled across with a trolley running along the tensioned highline. A sliding block raises the highline and the load on the UNREP ship. A sliding pad eye lowers the highline and the load on the combatant ship."[15] Using STREAM technology, auxiliaries can transfer loads as large as the heaviest missiles and aircraft engines, and achieve sustained transfer rates of two minutes per load. A new fuel and cargo delivery system called "Electric STREAM" (E-STREAM) has been tested ashore and underway, and found to be more reliable, easier to operate and maintain, and capable of increased transfer speeds. E-STREAM is to be deployed on new construction auxiliaries, starting with the USS John Lewis (T-AO 205)-class of fleet replenishment oilers (see Chapter 1).

The Navy's ability to deliver ammunition, supplies and materials to "customer" ships while underway was enhanced and expanded by another innovation in technique first adopted in the 1960s. To supplement and speed the delivery of cargo to a combatant steaming alongside, naval auxiliary ships began using helicopters to ferry palletized materials over to the customer vessel while simultaneously transferring other cargo using STREAM. The vertical replenishment (VERTREP) method of using rotary-wing aircraft also allows the supplying vessel to transfer cargos to multiple receiving ships even when they are operating some distance from the auxiliary.

Still other technological developments—some adopted from civilian use—include

On May 8, 2002, the fast combat support ship USNS *Seattle* (AOE 3) is transferring fuel to the aircraft carrier USS *John F. Kennedy* (CV 67) via hoses held in place by a tensioned highline (U.S. Navy photograph).

Introduction

A SH-60 Sea Hawk helicopter is carrying a pallet of supplies from the fleet replenishment oiler USNS *Kanawha* (T-AO 196) for delivery to the aircraft carrier USS *Theodore Roosevelt* (CVN 71) in the Atlantic Ocean on January 30, 2014 (U.S. Navy photograph).

roll-on/roll-off ships built with side ports and a stern ramp for the rapid loading and unloading of vehicles; heavy lift ships and lighter aboard ship (LASH) vessels that carry cargo bearing barges; and the offshore petroleum distribution system (OPDS) by which loaded tankers arriving off ports lacking suitable fuel handling infrastructure can transfer their cargo instead to an anchored OPDS vessel. That vessel, serving as a middleman, can in turn pump out more than two million gallons of the transferred fuel each day via flexible pipes running between the OPDS ship and the shore. (See Chapter 2 for information about these vessels.)

To meet its own unique needs, the Navy has developed and put in service in recent decades relatively new multi-product auxiliary ship types that incorporate in a single hull the various kinds of cargo heretofore carried by separate vessels.

As examples, ten combat store ships (AFS) were acquired between 1963 and 1984 to combine the capabilities of store ships (AF) and aviation store ships (AVS). They are no longer in the fleet, having been replaced by ammunition cargo ships (AKE). Similarly, the Navy's fast combat support ships (AOE) integrate in one hull the separate payloads of ammunition ships (AE), oilers (AO) and cargo ships (AK). This triple capability allows the AOE to replenish an aircraft carrier in three hours and one stop rather than the 10 hours the carrier would require to make stops at three different single-product ships. The AOEs joined the auxiliary force between March 1964 and March 1998, and today only two of the original nine AOEs are still in service. In addition, replenishment oilers (AOR) were acquired to combine the role of fleet oiler (AO) with a lesser capability as ammunition ships and combat stores ships (AKS). The AORs were commissioned between June 1969 and October 1976 and decommissioned between March 1993 and October 1995. Finally, ammunition cargo ships (AKE) were placed in service between June 2006 and October 2012 as replacements for the Kilauea (T-AE 26)-class ammunition ships and Mars (T-AFS 1)- and Sirius (T-AFS 8)-class combat store ships. The Navy's 14 AKEs are still in active service.

These innovations and evolutions in naval technology, operating methods and techniques have been paralleled by changes in the organization, composition and administration of naval auxiliaries. Prior to World War I the Naval Auxiliary Service (NAS) was comprised of 19 transports, supply ships, colliers and other vessels assigned to it by the Navy Department and manned by merchant marine officers and crews. When the United States entered the war in April 1917, NAS had some 230 officers and 1,100 enlisted personnel on active duty.[16] But NAS was disestablished that year and its ships became part of the wartime Naval Overseas Transportation Service (NOTS), and command of its vessels was exercised by commissioned Navy officers. During the war in Europe NOTS operated 450 vessels, with another 100 ships in the process of being acquired at the time of the November 1918 Armistice.[17] Those vessels carried nearly six million tons of cargo while assigned to NOTS.[18]

In World War II, four different government agencies—including what was then called the Naval Transportation Service—provided sea transportation for the armed forces. On December 15, 1948, the first U.S. Secretary of Defense, James V. Forrestal, directed that "all military sea transport including Army transports would be placed under Navy command." On July 9 of the next year, the Department of Defense established the Military Sea Transportation Service (MSTS) as the single organization responsible for DOD's sea transportation requirements. Three days later, Forrestal's successor, Louis A. Johnson, ordered that the U.S. Army's cargo and passenger vessels be transferred to the Navy. On October 1, 1949, MSTS began business and NTS was dissolved. The initial MSTS fleet consisted of six troop transports, three attack transports, 12 attack cargo ships, and 16 tankers—all commissioned vessels in the Navy and manned by Navy personnel.[19] At the same time, 57 government-owned and civilian-operated tankers under the aegis of the Navy's Chief of Naval Operations were added to the MSTS force. On March 1, 1950, 72 ships belonging to the Army Transport Service and operated by civilian merchant crews were also acquired by MSTS.

MSTS was renamed Military Sealift Command (MSC) on August 1, 1970. Like its predecessor organization, MSC plays a key role in the nation's defense and military operations. Case in point, as of 2013, MSC ships had delivered more than 25.7 billion gallons of fuel and transported more than 126.2 million square feet of combat equipment and supplies for U.S. and partner forces supporting the governments of Iraq and Afghanistan.[20]

Today the Military Sealift Command "controls" some 110–125 Navy-owned auxiliary ships and chartered civilian vessels. This fleet within the fleet performs in eight basic missions or programs as follows:

- Fleet Oiler (PM1)–consisting of approximately 15 fleet replenishment oilers that deliver a variety of fuels used in ship propulsion, aircraft operations and power generation;
- Special Mission (PM2)—about 22 ships that serve as operating platforms and provide services for various U.S. military and government missions;

- Prepositioning (PM3)—approximately 27 ships loaded with military equipment and supplies stationed in key ocean areas and readily available to deliver their cargos for use by the armed forces in various military and civil contingencies;
- Service Support (PM4)—vessels which provide the Navy with various services, including towing, rescue, salvage, submarine support, cable laying and repair, command and control and medical;
- Sealift (PM5)—a mix of government-owned and charted dry cargo ships and tankers to provide ocean transportation for the Department of Defense and other federal agencies;
- Fleet Ordnance & Dry Cargo (PM6)—some dozen vessels that replenish dry and refrigerated stores and ordnance for the Navy's combatant ships;
- Afloat Staging Command Support (PM7)—approximately four vessels serving as command ships, expeditionary sea bases, and cable laying and repair vessels; and
- Expeditionary Fast Transport (PM8)—about 10 high-speed vessels to provide rapid, intra-theater transport of troops and military equipment.

The individual names of MSC ships are preceded with the prefix "United States Naval Ship" (USNS) and are designated with a T-prefix before their hull number, as in USNS *Mercy* (T-AH 19). They are visually identifiable as MSC ships by the blue and gold bands on their stacks. Chartered civilian vessels working for MSC are individually named with one of the following four prefixes: GTS (for Gas Turbine Ship), MV (for Motor Vessel), RV (for Research Vessel), or SS (for Steamship).

During the 1960s, the Navy began to transfer its commissioned auxiliary ships to MSTS (and later MSC) operation, a trend that continued into recent decades. As those vessels, which previously had been termed "United States Ships" (USS), were decommissioned in the Navy, they became "United States Naval Ships" (USNS) with their prior hull numbers redesignated with a T- prefix. The regular Navy crews on those transferred auxiliaries were replaced by U.S. civil service or contract civilian mariners, so that today virtually all of the Navy's auxiliaries are commanded and operated by civilians. There are a few exceptions. Two submarine tenders stationed in Guam which although assigned to MSC remain in Navy commission and are operated by a combination of Navy and civilian MSC personnel (in what MSC calls a "hybrid" crew). Another exception is the expeditionary sea base USS *Lewis B. Puller* (ESB 3) which has a Navy captain in command and a permanently embarked joint Navy/MSC crew. *Puller* had begun her service in 2015 as an USNS ship designated as T-ESB 3 but when she deployed to the U.S. Fifth Fleet (U.S. Central Command) area of responsibility in August 2017, she was commissioned as a regular Navy ship and redesignated as ESB 3. A third exception are the two command ships. USS *Blue Ridge* (LCC 19) is a commissioned Navy vessel with an all–Navy complement whereas sister ship USS *Mount Whitney* (LCC 20) is operated by a joint Navy/MSC crew of approximately 320 personnel. The Navy contingent performs command, communications, and executive functions while the MSC civil service mariners perform in navigation, deck, engineering, laundry and mess functions. Finally, military and naval medical personnel staff the Navy's two hospital ships whenever they are fully activated and operated by MSC civilian crews, and several civilian-manned MSC ships carry small Navy communications detachments. All that said, there are today virtually no wholly Navy-manned auxiliary ships, whereas in the World War II era there were no civilians on board Navy auxiliary vessels.

Introduction

Chart 1

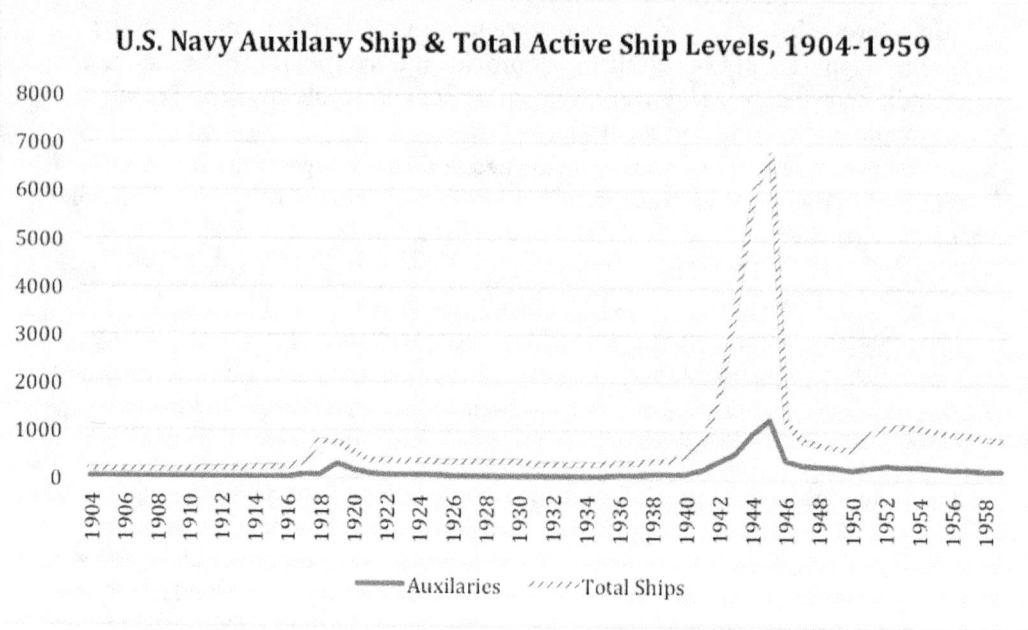

Chart 2

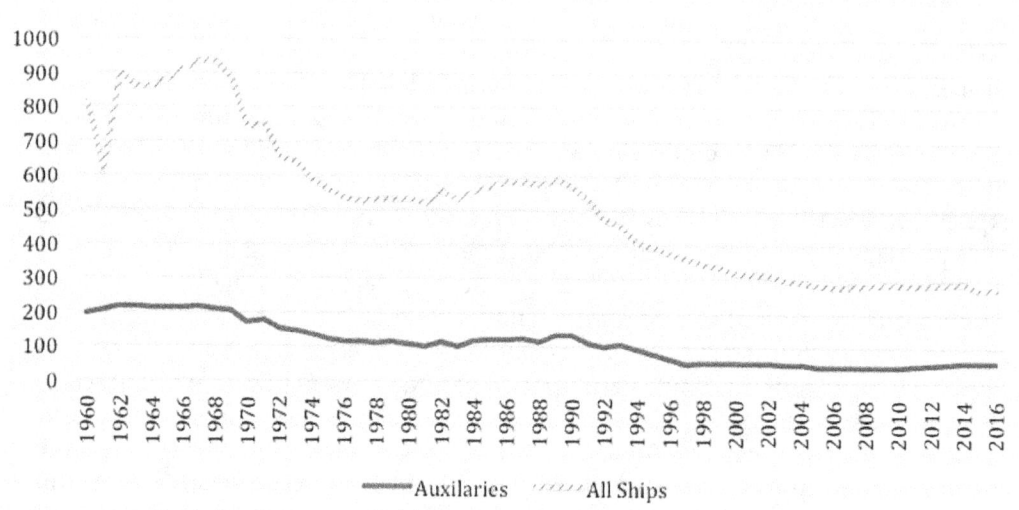

Source: "U.S. Ship Force Levels, 1886–Present," Naval History and Heritage Command.

Introduction

Another trend affecting the auxiliary force has been the reduction in its maintenance and repair capability afloat and ashore, especially in forward operating areas. Whereas the fleet once had some 200 tenders and repair ships of various types close at hand to support the Navy's deployed combatants, today are just two tenders on active duty. As a result, many warships needing substantial maintenance and repairs while overseas have to head to foreign or U.S. shipyards to obtain those services.

Over the years the number of active duty auxiliary ships has fluctuated as a result of economic and domestic politics along with international events, trends and requirements (see Charts 1 and 2, opposite).

Obviously, those numbers have increased in times of war and declined in times of peace. But clearly, with the heavy demands that are placed on the Navy of today—do more with fewer ships—the Navy's relatively small auxiliary ship force is now as vital and necessary as it ever was.

NOTES

1. *U.S. Navy Oilers and Tankers*, 2.
2. USS *Constitution* remains in commission today; see Chapter 2.
3. Silverstone, *The Sailing Navy, 1775–1854*, 62–3.
4. *U.S. Navy Oilers and Tankers*, 2.
5. Silverstone, *Civil War Navies, 1855–1883*, 79–94.
6. Silverstone, *U.S. Warships of World War II*, 281.
7. "United States Navy Temporary Auxiliary ships of World War I."
8. Hone and Hone, *Battle Line*, 174–5.
9. "U.S. Ship Force Levels, 1886-Present."
10. Baker, "The Navy's First God is No More," 12.
11. Marolda, *The U.S. Navy in the Korean War*, 228.
12. Marolda, *The U.S. Navy in the Vietnam War*, 233 and 239.
13. Marolda and Schneller, *Shield and Sword*, 102–3 and 383.
14. Marolda, *The U.S. Navy in the Vietnam War*, 233 and 239.
15. Miller, "Standby for Shotline," 77.
16. Whitted, "The Old Naval Auxiliary Service," 529.
17. Clephane, History of Naval Overseas Transportation Service, xix.
18. Silverstone, *The New Navy*, viii.
19. Mercogliano, "One Hundred Years in the Making."
20. "U.S. Navy's Military Sealift Command History."

Chapter 1

Combat Logistics and Fleet Support Ships

In its formal guidance for the classification of naval vessels, the Navy defines "other combatant classifications" as "ships which have the capability to provide support to fleet units."[1] Within that broad grouping, the Navy has established three major subsets of "other combatants": mine warfare, combat logistics, and fleet support, of which this volume considers the latter two as auxiliary ships.

Combat logistics vessels are described by the Navy as "auxiliary ships which have the capability to provide underway replenishment to fleet units" and include fleet replenishment oilers (AO), fast combat support ships (AOE), and dry cargo and ammunition ships (AKE).

Fleet support ships are described as "a group of ships designed to operate in the open ocean to provide general support to combatant forces." These vessels include command ships (LCC), submarine tenders (AS), surveillance ships (AGOS), salvage ships (ARS), fleet ocean tugs (ATF), towing, salvage and rescue ships (ATS), afloat forward staging bases (AFSB), dry cargo and ammunition ships (AKE),[2] expeditionary fast transports (EPF), expeditionary sea bases (ESB), and expeditionary transport docks (ESD).

Currently, there are some 400 vessels in 13 different "active" hull classifications comprising the fleet's combat logistics and fleet support ships. Each of those ship types are discussed below in alphabetical order of their hull classification symbols.

In the roster listings of each ship's name a bracketed letter indicates the vessel's most recently known status as follows: A = Active; B = Under construction; C = Converted or reclassified to another vessel type; D = Disposed of; K = Struck from the Naval Vessel Register; L = Deactivated and laid up, generally in the National Defense Reserve Fleet; OS = Out of government service; R = In stand-by/reserve/reduced manning condition; S = Sold to unknown buyer; SC = Sold or transferred to a civilian operator or entity; SS = Sold for scrapping; SX = Expended as target; T = Transferred or sold to another U.S. agency, institution or nation; X = Cancelled; and Z = Sunk or grounded/unsalvageable.

Notes

1. General Guidance for the Classification of Naval Vessels and Battle Force Counting Procedures" (SECNAV Instruction 5030.8C), June 14, 2016.
2. Includes AKEs designated to support the maritime prepositioning force.

Afloat Forward Staging Base (AFSB)[1]

In 2012 the Navy converted the amphibious transport dock USS *Ponce* (LPD 15) into an interim afloat forward staging base—AFSB(I)—to support mine countermeasure operations, coastal patrol activities, aircraft operations and various other missions. The conversion was in response to a long-standing request from the U.S. Central Command for a permanent forward-deployed sea base in the Persian Gulf region. A veteran LPD, *Ponce* had its scheduled 2012 decommissioning postponed as she was refitted for her new mission.

As an LPD *Ponce* had been armed with four twin 3-inch/50 guns but in her role as an AFSB, she was armed with two Mk 38 25-mm chain guns, two Phalanx CIWS guns, and eight .50-caliber machine guns. Her flight deck could operate helicopters up to CH-53 in size (e.g., two CH-46 Sea Knights or CH-53 Sea Stallions, or four UH-1 Hueys/AH-1 Super Cobras, or two AV-8B Harriers). The ship had accommodations for up to 90 naval staff personnel attached to an embarked flag officer, and her well deck could accommodate one LCU utility landing craft or two LCM-8 or four LCM-6 mechanized landing craft.

Ponce also served as a repair ship and was fitted with a machine shop, and metal, valve, hydraulic, and filter shops and a guest machine shop for embarked mine countermeasures, special forces, riverine, joint service, and partnership/coalition personnel. The ship could accommodate 350 or more embarked personnel, and contained more than 137 work stations in eight new mission spaces, all with video teleconference capability. Her large joint operations center provided access to six independent computer networks.[2]

USS *Ponce* operated overseas for five years (2012–2017) as a Navy AFSB(I) in the

A very young USS *Ponce* is underway on sea trials in Puget Sound, Washington, on June 7, 1971, just a few weeks after her launch and a month before she was commissioned (U.S. Navy photograph).

Military Sealift Command's Afloat Staging Command Support Program (PM7). The ship was commanded by a Navy captain and manned with a hybrid or composite crew of civilian mariners and uniformed Navy personnel.

Her mission was completed in the summer of 2017 when she was succeeded by USNS *Lewis B. Puller* (T-ESB 3), the first ship specifically purpose-built as an expeditionary sea base. *Ponce* has since been decommissioned, deactivated and laid up (see History below).

Following the practice of naming LPDs for cities honoring pioneers, USS *Ponce* was named for a city in Puerto Rico which honored the Spanish explorer Juan Ponce de Leon, the discoverer of Florida and the first governor of Puerto Rico. She retained that identity after her conversion into an interim afloat forward staging base.

The classification, nomenclature and designation for later AFSBs was changed on September 4, 2015, to expeditionary sea base [q.v.] (T-ESB).

AFSB Roster

AFSB(I), 15 *Ponce* [L/K]

Specifications

Length: 570 feet
Beam: 100 feet
Draft: 23 feet
Displacement: 16,591 tons (full load)
Propulsion: 2 De Laval steam turbines; 24,000 shp; 2 shafts
Speed: 21 knots
Personnel: 157 civilians & 292 Navy/military

History

USS *Ponce* was built by the Lockheed Shipbuilding and Construction Company in 1966–1971 as the 12th and last Austin-class amphibious transport dock (LPD). Her keel was laid down in Seattle, Washington, on October 31, 1966, and she was launched on May 20, 1970. *Ponce* was commissioned as LPD 15 on July 10, 1971, and assigned to the Atlantic Fleet amphibious force.

Her first deployment began in January 1973 when she operated in the Mediterranean as a unit of Amphibious Squadron 2. In June 1980 *Ponce* rescued 640 Cuban refugees in the Florida Straits who were fleeing the island nation in overcrowded boats. She supported American embassy personnel and Marines ashore in Beirut during the Lebanese civil war in April–August 1984. In addition, *Ponce* participated in various other humanitarian missions over the years, including: the evacuation of 1,100 people during the Liberian civil war in August 1990 (Operation Sharp Edge), assisting victims of Hurricane Andrew in Florida in the summer of 1992, supporting Operation Shining Hope's assistance to Kosovar refugees in 1999, and aiding victims of a magnitude 7.4 earthquake in Turkey that same year.

During Operation Iraqi Freedom in early 2003, USS *Ponce* served as the flagship of Mine Countermeasures Squadron 3 and with her attached coastal minehunters and aircraft helped clear the blocked Khawr Abd Allah estuary and port of Umm Qasr in southern Iraq.

On March 31, 2012, *Ponce* was reclassified as an interim afloat forward staging base (AFSB(I)) to be forward-deployed to support MH-53E Sea Dragon mine countermeasures helicopters along with patrol and small mine clearance vessels in the U.S. Fifth Fleet operating area. This new assignment must have come as quite a surprise as she had been previously scheduled to be decommissioned on March 30, 2012. But with the new orders in hand, she instead entered a commercial shipyard in February 2012 to be overhauled and modified for operation as an AFSB by a mixed civilian/Navy crew consisting of 165 civilian mariners of the Military Sealift Command and 55 uniformed Navy personnel. The yard work included replacing the ship's 40-year-old bridge equipment with modern commercial systems, and overhauling her main propulsion boilers, other engineering machinery and the galley.

Officially homeported in Norfolk, Virginia, and "owned" by Commander Naval Surface Forces, Atlantic, USS *Ponce* got underway on June 1, 2012, for her transit to the Persian Gulf. She was to spend the next five years in the Middle East demonstrating the utility of a hybrid Navy and civilian-specialist composite crew and participating with coalition partners in such exercises as Alligator Dagger and Artemis Trident, as well as executing boarding, search and seizure operations.

On April 8, 2013, the Navy announced that a new laser weapons system (LaWS) would be installed on *Ponce* for demonstration and system testing. Primarily developed as an experimental weapon to counter small boats and unmanned aerial vehicles (UAVs), LaWS was the first armament of its kind to be installed on a deployed Navy warship. Directed onto targets from a radar track obtained from a Mk 15 Phalanx Close-in Weapons System (CIWS), LaWS enabled the ship to destroy a variety of air and surface targets silently and undetected—at long distances and at the speed of light—at the cost of only about one dollar per shot. During the tests in the autumn of 2014, the LaWS hit a target on a high-speed boat, shot an unmanned aircraft out of the sky and destroyed other moving surface targets.

One month after she deployed from Virginia to the Fifth Fleet in the Persian Gulf region, USS *Ponce* (AFSB(I) 15) is entering port on July 6, 2012, conned by a local harbor pilot and assisted by a local tug (U.S. Navy photograph).

1. Combat Logistics and Fleet Support Ships

USS *Ponce* ended her long five-year deployment in 2017, transiting from the Persian Gulf to Norfolk between August 18 and September 27, with a stop in Yorktown, Virginia, to offload her ordnance at the Naval Weapons Station there. She was decommissioned in Norfolk on October 14, 2017, following which her civilian mariners steamed the vessel north to be berthed at the Navy's Inactive Ship Maintenance Facility (NISMF) in Philadelphia. While laid up there her name was struck from the Naval Vessel Register on November 13, 2017, in effect closing the Navy's book on the ship.

During the first 42 years of her service, USS *Ponce* completed 27 North Atlantic, Caribbean, Mediterranean, Indian Ocean and Persian Gulf deployments. Given her current age—now nearly a half-century old—and the acquisition of new purpose-built ESB sea bases, it is not likely she will ever be recalled to duty and deployed anywhere ever again.

Notes

1. Although the Navy's sole AFSB is no longer active and was retired in 2017, it is included in this chapter because the AFSB hull classification is still listed on both the current Naval Vessel Register and the Navy Secretary's formal guidance on the classification of naval vessels.
2. Stankus, "A Perspective from the Captain's Chair."

Ocean Surveillance Ships (AGOS)

Today's Navy is deploying five ocean surveillance ships (designated as T-AGOS) to collect underwater acoustic data utilizing a towed AN/UQQ-2 SURTASS array. SURTASS (an acronym for Surveillance Towed Array Sensor System) is used to detect submerged submarines in areas where the earlier seabed-installed Sound Surveillance System (SOSUS) is absent or inadequate. The UQQ-2 array is a long flexible structure containing multiple hydrophones which is towed by a 6,000-foot cable streamed by the ship. Data gathered from the SURTASS are initially processed on board the ship and then sent via satellite to facilities ashore for further processing and analysis and additional sharing with Navy antisubmarine units at sea.

The T-AGOS vessels are operated and maintained by civilian contractors for the Military Sealift Command (MSC) and are part of MSC's Special Mission (PM2) fleet. The ships also carry 15–20 Navy technical personnel. T-AGOS vessels are named for various attributes of capability, success and accomplishment.

The initial group of ocean surveillance ships belonged to the Stalwart class, consisting of T-AGOS 1 through T-AGOS 18. The first 12 of these monohull vessels were built by the Tacoma Boatbuilding Company in Tacoma, Washington, whereas T-AGOS 13–T-AGOS 18 were constructed by Halter Marine Services in New Orleans, Louisiana. The Stalwarts entered service between 1984 and 1990 and were removed from service between 1992 and 2004. Originally intended to monitor the movement of Soviet submarines, they lost much of their *reason d'etre* with the end of the Cold War and were subsequently retired and discarded (see Roster below for information on their post–Navy careers).

The Stalwart class was followed by the four-vessel Victorious class, consisting of T-AGOS 19 through T-AGOS 22. Built by McDermott Shipbuilding of Morgan City, Louisiana, the quartet was constructed on a small-waterplane, twin-hull (SWATH) design.

The ocean surveillance ship USNS *Loyal* (T-AGOS 22) began her service on July 1, 1993, and is seen here 14 years later on August 2, 2007. The view is from her bow looking back along the starboard side and it illustrates the unusual appearance of her twin hulls and overall boxy configuration (U.S. Navy photograph).

This catamaran-like hull form uses two fully submerged underwater hulls with structures rising out of the water to support the ship's superstructure. Such an arrangement provides a SWATH ship with a greater stability in turbulent sea states as well as a large working deck area abaft the deck house.

The contract for the first of these vessels—USNS *Victorious* (T-AGOS 19)—was awarded in November 1988, and options for the next three (T-AGOS 20–T-AGOS 22)— were exercised in October 1988. The four ships were placed in service between August 1991 and July 1993, assigned to the Pacific Fleet area of operations, and remain on active duty today.

The final group of ocean surveillance ships—the Impeccable class—was first planned to include four vessels. In the event, only one—USNS *Impeccable* (T-AGOS 23)—actually entered service. She had been ordered in March 1991 to be built to an enlarged SWATH ship design by American Ship Building Company (Tampa Shipyards) in Tampa, Florida. Problems with that yard led the Navy to transfer her while still under construction to a second builder (see History below). As a result, *Impeccable* did not enter service until 2001. The follow on Impeccable-class vessel (T-AGOS 24) was cancelled on November 1, 1991, and since then no further ocean surveillance ships have been procured. However, the February 2018 Navy Department long-range plan for naval vessel construction includes Fiscal Year 2022 funding of $344 million for a new ocean surveillance ship initially designated as T-AGOS(X) and Fiscal Year 2023 funding of $369 million for a second T-AGOS(X).

One illustration of the various ways in which the T-AGOS ships were employed earlier in this century was indicated in an August 17, 2000, MSC press announcement that it had awarded a three-year contract for more than $108 million to Maersk Line, Limited, of Norfolk, Virginia, to operate and maintain the 14 T-AGOS vessels existent at that time. While eight of the 14 vessels supported SURTASS operations, the other six had other duties: USNS *Stalwart* (T-AGOS 1), USNS *Indomitable* (T-AGOS 7) and USNS *Capable* (T-AGOS 16) supported counterdrug operations in the Caribbean and northern Pacific; USNS *Vindicator* (T-AGOS 3) and USNS *Persistent* (T-AGOS 6) supported U.S. Coast Guard counterdrug activities; and USNS *Invincible* (T-AGOS 10) supported the U.S. Air Force Electronic Systems Command by deploying a mobile surveillance and tracking radar system to monitor U.S. and foreign missile and weapons testing. Today, the five current T-AGOS ships are primarily tasked with monitoring Chinese submarine activity in the western Pacific.

T-AGOS Roster

T-AGOS 1	*Stalwart*[1] [T]		T-AGOS 14	*Worthy*[14] [T]
T-AGOS 2	*Contender*[2] [T]		T-AGOS 15	*Titan*[15] [T]
T-AGOS 3	*Vindicator*[3] [T]		T-AGOS 16	*Capable*[16] [T]
T-AGOS 4	*Triumph*[4] [L]		T-AGOS 17	*Tenacious*[17] [T]
T-AGOS 5	*Assurance*[5] [T]		T-AGOS 18	*Relentless*[18] [T]
T-AGOS 6	*Persistent*[6] [T]		T-AGOS 19	*Victorious*[19] [A]
T-AGOS 7	*Indomitable*[7] [T]		T-AGOS 20	*Able*[20] [A]
T-AGOS 8	*Prevail*[8] [C/A]		T-AGOS 21	*Effective* [A]
T-AGOS 9	*Assertive*[9] [T]		T-AGOS 22	*Loyal* [A]
T-AGOS 10	*Invincible*[10] [C/A]		T-AGOS 23	*Impeccable*[21] [A]
T-AGOS 11	*Audacious*[11] [T]		T-AGOS 24	*Integrity*[22] [X]
T-AGOS 12	*Bold*[12] [T]		(no number)	*Cory Chouest*[23] [OS]
T-AGOS 13	*Adventurous*[13] [T]			

SELECTED SPECIFICATIONS

Stalwart class: T-AGOS 1–T-AGOS 18

Length: 224 feet (overall)
Beam: 43 feet
Draft: 15 feet
Displacement: 2,285 tons (full load)
Propulsion: 4 Caterpillar D-398B diesel generators with General Electric motors; 3,200 bhp; 2 shafts
Speed: 11 knots (3 knots while towing SURTASS array)
Personnel: 19 civilians & 10 Navy

Victorious class: T-AGOS 19–T-AGOS 22

Length: 234.5 feet (overall)
Beam: 93.5 feet
Draft: 25 feet
Displacement: 3,384 tons (full load)
Propulsion: 4 Caterpillar-Kato 3512-TA diesel generators with 2 General Electric motors; 3,200 bhp; 2 shafts; 2 bow thrusters
Speed: 10 knots (3 knots while towing array)
Personnel: 19–22 civilians, 5 technicians & up to 15 Navy

Impeccable class: T-AGOS 21
Length: 281.5 feet (overall)
Beam: 95.8 feet
Draft: 26 feet
Displacement: 5,370 tons (full load)
Propulsion: 3 diesel generators, 2 Westinghouse motors; 5,000 shp; 2 shafts; 2 omni-thruster hydrojets
Personnel: 20 civilians, 5 technicians & up to 20 Navy

SELECTED HISTORIES

USNS *Indomitable* (T-AGOS 7)

- Built as a Stalwart-class ship by Tacoma Boatbuilding Company of Tacoma, Washington.
- Laid down on January 26, 1985, and launched on July 16 of that year.
- Delivered to the Navy on November 26, 1985, and placed in service with MSC four days later.
- SURTASS equipment removed in 1993 and AN/SPS-49 radar installed for use in counterdrug operations.
- Engaged in drug trafficking surveillance in the Caribbean Sea and Panama Canal area. "Played an integral role with MSC in the confiscation of billions of dollars of illegal narcotics, the capture of countless craft and airplanes, as well as numerous traffickers."[24]
- In March 2001 served as command ship for Coast Guard search and rescue mission off the western coast of Colombia; helped save 149 passengers from disabled Ecuadorian vessel *Fortuna*.
- Withdrawn from MSC service and struck on December 2, 2002.
- Transferred to National Oceanic and Atmospheric Administration (NOAA) on December 9, 2002.
- Renamed NOAAS *MacArthur II* (R 330) on May 20, 2003 and homeported in Seattle, Washington.
- Conducted oceanographic research in the eastern Pacific Ocean.
- Deactivated in 2011 and retired by NOAA on June 18, 2014.

USNS *Prevail* (T-AGOS 8)

- Built as a Stalwart-class ship by Tacoma Boatbuilding Company of Tacoma, Washington.
- Laid down on March 13, 1985, and launched on December 7, 1985.
- Delivered on March 4, 1986.
- Escorted submarines engaged in post-overhaul sea trials and replaced in that duty by USS *Gosport* (IX 517).
- Reclassified as an unclassified miscellaneous vessel and redesignated as IX 537 on October 17, 2003.
- Unofficially redesignated as a training support vessel (TSV 1) in 2003 and crewed under MSC contract by Trinity Ship Management.
- Based in Norfolk, Virginia, *Prevail* performs a variety of training missions, including operations security, threat simulation, electronics warfare service, cryp-

tologic training, and mine laying and retrieval operations. In this role, the ship is operated by 12 civilians and has accommodations for 39 personnel.

USNS *Victorious* (T-AGOS 19)
- Built as the lead ship of the Victorious class by McDermott Shipyards in Morgan City, Louisiana.
- Laid down on April 12, 1988, and launched on May 3, 1990.
- Placed in service with MSC on August 13, 1991.
- On March 4, 2009, a Chinese Bureau of Fisheries patrol vessel illuminated T-AGOS 19 with several sweeps of a high-beam searchlight while she was 120 miles off China's coast. The next day a Chinese Y-12 maritime patrol aircraft overflew the vessel numerous times.
- On May 1, 2009, while engaged in routine operations in international waters in the Yellow Sea 170 miles off China, *Victorious* was harassed by two Chinese fishing vessels, one of which closed to within 30 yards. Her crew sounded the ship's danger alarms and sprayed water at the Chinese vessels, which then departed.
- Currently assigned to MSC Special Mission (PM2) fleet and operates in the Asia-Pacific region.

USNS *Able* (T-AGOS 20)
- Built by McDermott Shipyards as a Victorious-class AGOS.
- Laid down on May 23, 1989, and launched on February 16, 1991.

On May 31, 2009, USNS *Able* is underway at a slow speed while a rigid-hull inflatable boat (RHIB) operates off her starboard quarter. This view illustrates the ship's special SURTASS-handling machinery and her catamaran-like twin hulls (U.S. Navy photograph).

- Placed in service with MSC on July 22, 1992.
- Removed from service in August 2004 and laid up at the Navy's Inactive Ship Maintenance Facility (NISMF) in Philadelphia.
- Withdrawn from NISMF in 2007 and sent to a commercial shipyard in Charleston, South Carolina, for installation of a Low-Frequency Active (LFA) system for submarine detection in shallow and coastal waters. The LFAS system supplements the vessel's AN/UQQ-2 SURTASS.
- Returned to service in 2008 and deployed to the western Pacific.

USNS *Impeccable* (T-AGOS 23)

- Built by Halter Marine Inc. as the first—and now only—Impeccable-class AGOS.
- Laid down on March 15, 1992, by American Ship Building Company in Tampa, Florida. Contractual problems with the builder halted construction of the ship when it was more than 60 percent completed and the unfinished vessel was transferred under tow in April 1995 to Halter Marine in Gulfport, Mississippi, to be finished. She was placed on the ways there on January 21, 1996.
- Launched on April 25, 1998, and placed in service with MSC on October 13, 2000.
- On March 5, 2009, a Chinese frigate crossed the ship's bow close aboard at a range of just 100 yards. Two days later, another Chinese vessel radioed *Impeccable*

The newest ocean surveillance ship—USNS *Impeccable* (T-AGOS 23)—is seen here in port on February 12, 2006. In March 2009 she had some dramatic encounters with various Chinese vessels in the South China Sea (U.S. Navy photograph).

charging that her operations were illegal and directing her to leave the area. On March 8, five Chinese vessels (an intelligence vessel, a fisheries patrol cutter, an oceanographic patrol ship and two small trawlers) surrounded *Impeccable* as she was steaming approximately 70 nautical miles off Hainan Island in international waters of the South China Sea. Two of the five closed within 50 feet. Despite being sprayed by fire hoses from *Impeccable*, the Chinese attempted to snag her SURTASS gear with poles but eventually she managed to maneuver free and departed the area. She returned the next day, this time escorted by the destroyer USS *Chung-Hoon* (DDG 93).
- On July 19, 2015, *Impeccable* rescued 11 fishermen from a floundering vessel in the South China Sea and transferred them to the Philippine Coast Guard in Subic Bay.

MV *Cory Chouest*[25]
- Built in 1974 as a 265-foot long North Sea oil support ship owned by Edison Offshore Support (ECO) of Cut Off, Louisiana.
- Chartered by MSC in 1989 and converted to include a 26-foot by 12-foot moon pool amidships. Equipped with a vertical line array, a multi-frequency horizontal line array receiver, analysis and processing suites, and extensive navigation and communication capabilities. For noise abatement purposes, Navy remounted all engines and generators. Vessel was fitted with laboratories and housing for up to 60 technicians and scientists.
- Conducted trials with SURTASS and Low Frequency Active (LFA) towed sonar array. Operated off west coast of Big Island of Hawaii. Monitored possible negative effects of sonar testing on marine life, especially humpback whales.
- On October 1, 1998, MSC issued a new long-term contract to charter the vessel through 2003.
- Returned to the owner in 2008. Subsequently offered for sale for $2.65 million; one report indicates the vessel is now off the market.

Notes

1. Delivered in April 1984, out of service in November 2002, transferred to MARAD in January 2004 and then transferred to the Maritime College of the State University of New York, and sold in 2011 to Stabbert Maritime as RV *Ocean Stalwart*.
2. Delivered in June 1984, out of service in October 1992, struck in December 1992, transferred by MARAD to U.S. Merchant Marine Academy and renamed TV *Kings Pointer*, and later transferred to Texas Maritime Academy in 2012 and renamed TV *General Rudder*.
3. Delivered in November 1984, out of service April 1993, transferred to USCG as USCGC *Vindicator* (WMEC 3), transferred by USCG to NOAA in 2002 and renamed NOAAS *Hi'ialakai* (R 334); homeported in Honolulu, Hawaii.
4. Delivered in February 1985, out of service June 1994; struck in January 1995, currently laid up in Suisan Bay group of NDRF providing "logistics support," i.e., cannibalized parts and materials.
5. Delivered in May 1985, out of service in March 1994, struck in January 1995, transferred to Portugal in September 1999 and renamed NRP *Amirante Gago Coutinho* (A523); still active.
6. Delivered in August 1985, out of service October 1994, struck in January 1995, acquired by Great Lakes Maritime Academy in 2002 and renamed TS *State of Michigan*; still active.
7. See Histories section for details.
8. *Ibid.*
9. Delivered in September 1986, out of service September 2003, transferred to NOAA in March 2004, and transferred to Seattle Maritime Academy in December 2008.
10. See Chapter 2, Missile Range Instrumentation Ships (AGM) section, for details.
11. Delivered in June 1989, struck in February 1997, transferred to Portugal December 1996 and renamed NRP *Dom Carlos I* (A 522); still active.

12. Delivered in October 1989, out of service March 2004, transferred to U.S. Environmental Protection Agency in March 2004 and renamed *Bold* (OSV 224), and sold in 2013 to Seattle Central Community College Maritime Academy.
13. Delivered in August 1988, out of service and transferred to NOAA June 1992, renamed NOAAS *Oscar Elton Sette* (R 335); still active and homeported in Honolulu. Hawaii.
14. Delivered in December 1988, out of service in March 1993, transferred to U.S. Army in 1995 for use as a missile range instrumentation ship (AGM) in the Marshall Islands.
15. Delivered in March 1989, out of service in August 1993, transferred to NOAA in August 1993 and renamed NOAAS *Ka'Imimoana* (R 333); retired in 2014.
16. Delivered in June 1989, out of service and transferred to NOAA in September 2004, renamed NOAAS *Okeanos Explorer* (R 337); active and homeported in North Kingston, Rhode Island.
17. Delivered in September 1989, out of service in June 1992, served with Naval Space and Warfare Systems Command 1992–1995, transferred in October 1996 to New Zealand as HMNZS *Resolution* (A 14); no longer active.
18. Delivered in January 1990, out of service March 1993, and transferred to NOAA as NOAAS *Gordon Gunter* (R 336); active and homeported in Pascagoula, Mississippi.
19. See Histories section for details.
20. *Ibid.*
21. *Ibid.*
22. Cancelled on November 1, 1991.
23.. See Histories section for details.
24. "MSC Transfers Special Mission Ship to National Oceanographic and Atmospheric Administration," MSC press release, December 12, 2002.
25. Information sourced from "Chouest." https://www.globalsecurity.org/military/systems/ship/chouest.htm.

Dry Cargo and Ammunition Ships (T-AKE)[1]

On December 1, 2017, the dry cargo and ammunition ship USNS *Alan Shepard* (T-AKE 3) is steaming alongside the amphibious assault ship USS *America* (LHA 6) just prior to conducting an underway replenishment in the Arabian Gulf. *America* is the flagship of an Amphibious Ready Group deployed in the Middle East (U.S. Navy photograph).

1. Combat Logistics and Fleet Support Ships

The Lewis and Clark–class dry cargo and ammunition ships (designated as T-AKE) were developed and placed in service to replace Kilauea (T-AE 26)-class ammunition ships [q.v.], and Mars (T-AFS 1)-class and Sirius (T-AFS 8)-class combat stores ships [q.v.]. They are intended to provide "effective fleet underway replenishment [UNREP] capability at the lowest life cycle cost."[2] The 689-foot T-AKEs have the largest cargo-carrying capacity and largest flight deck of any combat logistics ship now afloat. Their primary mission is to deliver cargo (consisting of ammunition, provisions, stores, spare parts, potable water and limited quantities of petroleum products) to deployed naval forces around the globe.

The Navy suggests that a T-AKE operating together with a Henry J. Kaiser (T-AO 187)-class fleet replenishment oiler [q.v.] can substitute for a T-AOE fast combat support ship [q.v.] Nevertheless some critics believe that the T-AKE does not adequately replicate the versatility of the T-AOE. They also argue that "with a minimal fuel capacity of 25,000 barrels, the T-AKE ... cannot satisfy the fuel requirements of an entire strike group. On the other hand, these ships do have a hardy stores and ammunition capacity of 5,298 short tons."[3] Their cargo capacity consists of 158,300 cubic feet of refrigerated supplies, 673,600 cubic feet of dry stores, 164,700 cubic feet of general cargo, 52,800 gallons of fresh water, and 24,900 barrels of fuel—altogether 63 percent more cargo space than previous AE and AFS vessels.

The 14 T-AKE 1-class dry cargo & ammunition ships were laid down between April 2004 and May 2011, and placed in service between June 2006 and October 2012. All 14 were built by National Steel and Shipbuilding Company of San Diego, California. They are crewed by some 124 civil service mariners of the Military Sealift Command (MSC) who operate and navigate the ships, 11 Navy personnel and a 36-person helicopter detachment which operates and maintains two Navy-flown MH-60S Seahawk helicopters. Some T-AKEs carry two SA.33J Puma or AS.332 Super Puma helicopters flown by contractors in lieu of the two Navy Seahawks. These rotary-wing aircraft are used in vertical replenishment (VERTREP) to ferry cargo from the T-AKE to her "customer" fleet ships.

The T-AKEs were built with eight internal cargo elevators, three port and two starboard kingposts for UNREP operations, along with four 10-ton capacity cranes.

USNS *Lewis and Clark* (T-AKE 1) and USNS *Sacagawea* (T-AKE 2) are assigned to the MSC Prepositioning Program (PM3) which stations ships carrying military equipment and supplies in distant ocean areas and enables regional combatant commanders to respond quickly to a crisis. Specifically these two AKEs are deployed to provide a selective offload of cargo for the resupply and sustainment of U.S. Marine forces ashore.

The other 12 dry cargo and ammunition ships (T-AKE 3–T-AKE 14) are assigned to the MSC Fleet Ordnance and Dry Cargo (PM6) program, i.e., the combat logistics force. Their job, along with two fast combat support ships (T-AOEs), is to replenish dry and refrigerated stores, as well as ordnance, of naval ships.

The ships are named for heroes, although the definition of "hero" in this instance does not encompass heroic wartime military and naval personnel but rather notable explorers, astronauts, aviators, scientists and civil rights leaders.

T-AKE Roster

T-AKE 1	*Lewis and Clark* [A]	T-AKE 3	*Alan Shepard*[4] [A]
T-AKE 2	*Sacagawea* [A]	T-AKE 4	*Richard E. Byrd* [A]

T-AKE 5   Robert E. Peary[5] [A]
T-AKE 6   Amelia Earhart[6] [A]
T-AKE 7   Carl Brashear [A]
T-AKE 8   Wally Schira[7] [A]
T-AKE 9   Matthew Perry[8] [A]
T-AKE 10 Charles Drew[9] [A]
T-AKE 11 Washington Chambers[10] [A]
T-AKE 12 William McLean [A]
T-AKE 13 Medgar Evers[11] [A]
T-AKE 14 Cesar Chavez[12] [A]

SPECIFICATIONS

Length: 689 feet
Beam: 105 feet
Draft: 30 feet
Displacement: 41,000 tons
Propulsion: Integrated electric propulsion (4 FM/MAN B&W diesel generators); 43,000 bhp; 1 shaft and bow thruster
Speed: 20 knots
Personnel: 129–197

SELECTED HISTORIES

USNS *Lewis and Clark* (T-AKE 1)

USNS *Lewis and Clark* (T-AKE 1) is arriving in Crete's Souda Bay in Greece on July 24, 2007, with a harbor patrol boat providing security off her port side (U.S. Navy photograph).

The keel of *Lewis and Clark* was laid down on April 22, 2004, in San Diego, California. She was launched by National Steel and Shipbuilding Company on May 21, 2005, and delivered to the Navy on June 20, 2006.

Six months later, on December 15–16, 2006, the ship performed her very first UNREP, with the aircraft carrier USS *Theodore Roosevelt* (CVN 71) as the recipient. By the summer of the following year, *Lewis and Clark* had deployed to the U.S. Central Command (CENTCOM) area of responsibility, arriving there on August 1, 2007. In September she spent a week delivering supplies to naval vessels at sea, followed by three days in Bahrain taking on new supplies, and then another week underway providing more than 500 pallets of cargo to the guided missile destroyer USS *James E. Williams* (DDG 95), amphibious assault ships USS *Kearsarge* (LHD 3) and USS *Bonhomme Richard* (LHD 6), amphibious transport docks USS *Ponce* (LPD 15) [see AFSB section above] and USS *Denver* (LPD 9), and dock landing ships USS *Gunston Hall* (LSD 44) and *Rushmore* (LSD 47).

Lewis and Clark returned to Norfolk, Virginia, from her freshman deployment on February 8, 2008. While deployed she had provided 73 underway and 28 in-port replenishments, delivered 5,856 pallets of food and supplies, and transferred almost 15 million gallons of fuel to two carrier strike groups and three expeditionary strike groups. Although T-AKEs carry 700,000 gallons of diesel fuel in their available stores, *Lewis and Clark* supplied 1.2 million gallons of fuel from her own bunkers to her customers. During that first deployment she also resupplied coalition naval forces from Pakistan, Germany, France, Australia and the United Kingdom.

On September 22, 2008, *Lewis and Clark* departed Norfolk on her second deployment, arriving in the U.S. Fifth Fleet (CENTCOM) area of operations on October 18.

Some of the days while the ship was deployed were more eventful than others. On May 5, 2009, for example, she was attacked by pirates off the coast of Somalia. Two pirate-manned skiffs pursued her for more than an hour, one getting to within 6,000 feet, while firing small arms at the ship without effect. The incident ended when the T-AKE increased speed and left the pirates behind. A year later, on November 20, 2010, *Lewis and Clark* was again fired on by pirates who were attacking the Chinese cargo vessel *Tai An Kou* about 100 nautical miles off the coast of Oman. The T-AKE and guided missile destroyer USS *Winston S. Churchill* (DDG 81) had responded to the Chinese ship's request for assistance. Both the DDG and the newly arrived Chinese frigate *Xuzhou* prompted the pirates to depart the area.

Lewis and Clark was in a position to assist in that incident because she had been engaged in replenishing U.S. and coalition ships participating in Combined Task Force 151 counter-piracy operations off the east coast of Africa in mid–2010. That role also enabled her to support disaster and humanitarian efforts following massive flooding in Pakistan that summer. After taking station in the Arabian Sea on August 11, the T-AKE transferred disaster-relief materials to the amphibious assault ship USS *Peleliu* (LHA 5) so that she in turn could transport them to Pakistan. Once every seven to ten days thereafter, *Lewis and Clark* returned to port, loaded aboard additional food, fuel and cargo, and then ferried those materials out to *Peleliu* in Pakistan, thereby enabling the LHA to remain continuously on the scene to aid the relief effort. In all, the ammunition and cargo ship's two SA-330J Puma helicopters were able to deliver more than 800 pallets of supplies and carried more than 50 people who were arriving to assist in the humanitarian operation. Such a mission was nothing new for *Lewis and Clark*; the ship had previously supplied Navy vessels providing aid and humanitarian assistance to Haiti early in 2010 following that country's major earthquake on January 12.

In March and April 2011 *Lewis and Clark* supported coalition maritime forces engaged in Operations Odyssey Dawn and Unified Protector to protect civilians in Libya.

As mentioned earlier, USNS *Lewis and Clark* has shifted from the MSC fleet ordnance and dry cargo (PM6) program to the prepositioning (PM3) program and is now assigned to Maritime Prepositioning Squadron 3 in the western Pacific. Her job is to provide U.S. Marine Corps forces in the region with a selective offload of cargo for resupply and sustainment ashore.

As an example of this newer role, she arrived at Tarawa, Republic of Kiribati, on October 24, 2015, to support Exercise Koa Moana (Ocean Warrior) 15–3. The Koa Moana series of exercises are designed to improve interoperability and military-to-military relations for U.S. and partner services in the Asia-Pacific area. In this particular instance, the exercise ran four months with participants from the Marines, Navy and Coast Guard as well as host nation participants from various Pacific island countries. During the exercise *Lewis and Clark* also paid a theater security visit both to Kiribati and Vanuatu.

USNS *Sacagawea* (T-AKE 2)

The dry cargo and ammunition ship USNS *Sacagawea* (T-AKE 2) is conducting underway replenishment in the Persian Gulf on March 18, 2008, with the amphibious assault ship USS *Tarawa* (LHA 1) on her port side (foreground) and amphibious dock landing ship USS *Germantown* (LSD 42) on her starboard side (U.S. Navy photograph).

- Laid down on June 7, 2005, and launched on June 24, 2006.
- Delivered on February 27, 2007.
- Departed on first deployment on December 11, 2007, bound for the U.S. Fifth Fleet area of operations.
- Participated in oil spill response drill at Port of Jebel Ali in United Arab Emirates on February 5, 2008.

1. Combat Logistics and Fleet Support Ships

- Rescued 10 Iraqi citizens from sinking coastal tanker MV *Nadi* in the central Arabian Gulf on February 22, 2008.
- During Operation Unified Response—disaster relief and humanitarian assistance following Haiti's January 12, 2010, magnitude 7.0 earthquake—*Sacagawea* delivered via UNREP more than 450 pallets of supplies to amphibious assault ship USS *Bataan* (LHD 5) on January 23. Followed up with UNREP delivery of 170 pallets of materials four days later. *Bataan* ferried the supplies ashore using her air cushion landing craft (LCAC), utility landing craft (LCUs) and helicopters.
- Performed VERTREP operations with guided missile frigates USS *Underwood* (FFG 36) and USS *Curts* (FFG 38) on July 5, 2012.
- Reassigned to the MSC Prepositioning (PM3) program as part of Maritime Prepositioning Squadron 3 in the western Pacific to provide logistical support to U.S. Marine Corps forces in the region.
- Between April 6 and April 11, 2013, conducted flight operations with MV-22B Osprey aircraft from Marine Medium Tiltrotor Squadron 265. These operations were the first time Ospreys had landed on a Maritime Prepositioning ship. The operations were part of Exercise Balikatan, an annual exercise involving U.S. and Philippine forces.
- During Balikatan and Exercise Freedom Banner in April–May 2013, *Sacagawea* delivered 170 pieces of Marine Corps cargo ashore via Navy watercraft for use by the III Marine Expeditionary Force in the Philippines.
- In Exercise Koa Moana 15–1 in 2015 took part in Balikatan and supported a Theater Security Cooperation mission in Saba, Malaysia. Later conducted Exercise Koa Moana 15–2 providing logistical support for Exercise Talisman Saber in Darwin, Australia, and TSC missions in Papa New Guinea and Timor-Leste.
- On September 7, 2016, offloaded more than 2,000 pallets of ordnance to a storage facility on the Joint base Charleston in South Carolina, prior to maintenance work in Jacksonville, Florida.
- Arrived in New Caledonia in the South Pacific on June 25, 2017, for Exercise Koa Moana 17. Carried various U.S.-based Marine units for participation in various exercise events in Kiribati, New Caledonia, Solomon Islands, Timor-Leste, Tonga, and Vanuatu.

USNS *Carl Brashear* (T-AKE 7)

- Laid down on November 2, 2007, and launched on September 18, 2008.
- Delivered and placed in service on March 3, 2009. Assigned to operate in the Pacific Ocean.
- Completed first sea trials on April 24, 2009.
- In mid–November 2009 provided logistic support to U.S. and Japanese warships during the ANNUALEX 21G exercise—the U.S. Seventh Fleet's largest annual exercise—off the coast of Okinawa, Japan.
- Participated in Operation Tomodachi ("Friend") to provide relief and aid following the March 11, 2011, magnitude 9.0 earthquake and subsequent tsunami 81 miles to the east of Sendai, Japan. *Carl Brashear* loaded more than 800 pallets of humanitarian cargo in Sasebo on March 20 and joined the Navy ships operating off northern Japan. She transferred fuel, shipboard supplies and 160 pallets of

In this view looking aft along the forecastle of the guided missile destroyer USS *Kidd* (DDG 100), the dry cargo and ammunition ship USNS *Carl Brashear* (T-AKE 7) is conducting an underway replenishment in the South China Sea on November 9, 2017 (U.S. Navy photograph).

humanitarian assistance and disaster relief supplies to the aircraft carrier USS *Ronald Reagan* (CVN 76), 30 pallets of supplies to the guided missile destroyer USS *Fitzgerald* (DDG 62) and 15 pallets to the cruiser USS *Cowpens* (CG 63) for delivery ashore.
- On September 29, 2012, departed the U.S. Fifth Fleet (CENTCOM) area of operations, bound for the Seventh Fleet in the western Pacific. While in the Middle East, *Carl Brashear* completed more than 50 UNREPs with U.S. and coalition ships.
- In 2013 provided logistics support to Exercise Trident Fury 13 in the Northwest Pacific. During the exercise delivered fuel and dry stores via UNREP to four Royal Canadian Navy ships, three Canadian Coast Guard ships and three U.S. Navy combatant ships.

USNS *William McLean* (T-AKE 12)
- Laid down on March 23, 2010, and launched on April 16, 2011.
- Placed in service on September 28, 2011.
- Served in 2014 as the primary combat logistics force ship supporting the Iwo Jima (LHD 7) Amphibious Ready Group/Marine Expeditionary Unit exercise. The exercise was run to prepare Navy and Marine personnel for maritime security operations in the Arabian Gulf and Mediterranean areas.
- Replenished the hospital ship [q.v.] USNS *Comfort* (T-AH 20) while en route to Puerto Rico to assist in humanitarian relief efforts there and in the U.S. Virgin

1. Combat Logistics and Fleet Support Ships

On December 4, 2017, USNS *William McLean* (T-AKE 12) is steaming alongside the aircraft carrier USS *Gerald R. Ford* (CVN 78) for an UNREP. The carrier, which had been commissioned five months earlier, was conducting test and evaluation operations in the Atlantic (U.S. Navy photograph).

Islands following Hurricane Irma in 2017. As of September 11, *William McLean* had pumped 620,000 gallons of diesel fuel, 40,000 gallons of jet fuel and delivered 40 pallets of supplies to Navy units providing relief support.
- Departed Norfolk, Virginia, on January 23, 2018, to begin a deployment to the U.S. Sixth Fleet's area of responsibility in the Mediterranean Sea.

Notes

1. The initial nomenclature for the AKE was "ammunition cargo ship" as defined by the November 2006 Secretary of the Navy's General Guidance for the Classification of Naval Vessels. In June 2016 the official nomenclature was changed to "dry cargo and ammunition ship." Note that "and" is spelled out in that most recent guidance and that the official Naval Vessel Register uses an ampersand ("&") and not a slash ("/") between "cargo" and "ammunition."
2. "Dry Cargo/Ammunition Ships—T-AKE." http://www.navy.mil/navydata/fact_display.asp?cid=4400&tid=500&ct=4.
3. Fitzgerald and Pigott, "High-End Warfare Requires Changes to the Combat Logistics Force."
4. Laid down January 30, 2006, launched December 6, 2006, and placed in service June 26, 2007.
5. Laid down December 11, 2006, launched October 27, 2007, and placed in service June 5, 2008.
6. Laid down May 29, 2007, launched April 6, 2008, and placed in service October 30, 2008.
7. Laid down April 14, 2008, launched March 8, 2009, and placed in service September 1, 2009.
8. Laid down September 29, 2008, launched August 16, 2009, and placed in service February 24, 2010.
9. Laid down March 13, 2009, launched February 27, 2010, and placed in service July 14, 2010.
10. Laid down August 24, 2009, launched September 11, 2010, and placed in service February 23, 2011.
11. Laid down October 26, 2010, launched November 12, 2011, and placed in service April 24, 2012.
12. Laid down May 9, 2011, launched May 5, 2012, and placed in service October 24, 2012.

Oilers / Fleet Replenishment Oilers (AO / T-AO)1

The fleet replenishment oiler USNS *Walter S. Diehl* (T-AO 193) is transferring fuel to the amphibious assault ship USS *Bonhomme Richard* (LHD 6) in the South China Sea on October 3, 2016 (U.S. Navy photograph).

The Navy's oilers (AOs) carry fuel oil and transfer it in underway replenishment (UNREP) operations to naval ships at sea. They also supply their "customers" with lubricants, fresh water and small amounts of dry cargo. In an UNREP, the receiving ship steams about 120–200 feet alongside the oiler and the AO transfers fuel to the customer in hoses extended from the oiler on heavy metal wires.

Navy Lieutenant Chester W. Nimitz, two other lieutenants and a chief boatswain's mate have been credited with devising the UNREP method used by oilers to refuel warships while underway.[2] Nimitz, who was serving as the executive officer of the Navy's second oiler—USS *Maumee* (AO 2)—in 1917, developed a procedure in which the oiler towed a destroyer alongside by employing a large towing hawser and breast lines, and then swinging out the oiler's booms to support the fuel hoses running between the oiler and the destroyer, thereby keeping the hoses out of the water. (Nimitz, of course, went on to become a five-star fleet admiral and Commander-in-Chief of Pacific Ocean Areas during World War II.)

During World War I the Navy acquired some two dozen merchant tankers for temporary service during the conflict. Genuine "short-timers" serving only for a relatively few months, they were placed in commission in 1917–1918 and decommissioned in 1918–1919. (See World War I Roster below for a listing of these ships.)

The first Navy ship to be formally designated as an oiler was USS *Kanawha*. She was commissioned on June 5, 1915, and classified as Fuel Ship No. 13. When the service insti-

USS *Maumee* (AO 2) is refueling a "four-stacker" destroyer (seen at right) in the North Atlantic in this 1917 photograph (U.S. Navy photograph).

tuted a new system of hull classification and ship identification on July 17, 1920, *Kanawha* was classified as an oiler and designated as AO 1. (She was decommissioned in December 1929 and laid up in reserve for five years, before being recommissioned in June 1934. USS *Kanawha* was sunk by Japanese aircraft at the entrance to Tulagi Harbor in the British Solomon Islands on April 8, 1943.)

Between the end of World War I in 1918 and the end of World War II in 1945, the Navy acquired some 100 AOs, five of which were lost during the latter conflict. At the start of the Korean War, there were 95 oilers on the Vessel Register. Fifteen years later, in mid–1965, the Navy had 40 AOs in active service, another 17 civilian-manned vessels operated by the Military Sea Transportation Service (MSTS), and some 50 retired oilers laid up in the National Defense Reserve Fleet (NDRF).

Today, there are just 15 active oilers (now termed fleet replenishment oilers and designated as T-AOs), all of which are crewed by civilians under the aegis of the Military Sealift Command (MSC). These ships—the Henry J. Kaiser (T-AO 187) class—were procured between Fiscal Year 1982 and FY 1989 and entered service between 1986 and 1996. Designated T-AO 187–T-AO 204, they were built by Avondale Shipyards of New Orleans, Louisiana, and have an expected service life of 35 years. Their cargo capacity includes 180,000 barrels of fuel, 25,000 gallons of lubrication, 105,000 gallons of fresh water, and 88,000 gallons of boiler feed water. (See Specifications below for additional characteristics.)

In Fiscal Year 2016 seven of the 15 T-AOs were based in the Atlantic Ocean and conducted operations in support of Commander, Task Force 80, U.S. Sixth Fleet in the Mediterranean Sea, U.S. Fifth Fleet in the Arabian Gulf and U.S. Seventh Fleet in the Pacific, while eight of the T-AOs were based in the Pacific Ocean to support surface units in the U.S. Third, Fifth, and Seventh Fleets and participate in multiple large-scale naval exercises.

Three of the original members of the class (T-AOs 190–T-AO 192) have been struck from the Naval Vessel Register. *Andrew J. Higgins* was transferred to Chile in 2010. *Benjamin Isherwood* and *Henry Eckford*, while not yet completely built, were transferred to MARAD in 1999 and 1998, respectively, and ultimately towed to Brownsville, Texas, for dismantling. T-AO 193 is scheduled to be taken out of service in Fiscal Year 2021, T-AO 195 will follow in FY 2022, and T-AO 197 is to be inactivated in FY 2023. All three vessels are to be scrapped.

The planned successor of the current Henry J. Kaiser-class oilers is the John Lewis (T-AO 205)-class, which is projected to include 20 ships. The first ship in the T-AO 205 program—*John Lewis*—was funded in Fiscal Year 2016 at a cost of $674.2 million and is scheduled to be delivered to the Navy in November 2020. The planned cost of the second ship—*Harvey Milk*—is $539.1 million, of which $73.1 million has already been appropriated. The Navy plans to procure the third ship—*Earl Warren*—in Fiscal Year 2019.

On June 30, 2016, the service awarded a fixed price incentive block buy contract to General Dynamics/National Steel and Shipbuilding Company (NASSCO) for construction of the first six T-AO 205s, and it wants to procure these and the subsequent 14 oilers at the rate of at least one ship per year. In the Navy Department President's Budget PB2019 shipbuilding plan covering the FY 2019-FY 2023 period, two T-AO 205s will be funded at $1.052 million in FY 2019, one ship in FY 2020 at $536 million, two ships in FY 2021 at $1.035 million, one ship in FY 2022 at $523 million, and two ships in FY 2023 at $1.103 million, for a total of eight ships funded at $4.249 million over the five-year period.

The design of the new T-AOs will be similar to the current T-AO 187s, and they will be built with existing technologies as opposed to adopting new technologies. Like the later Kaiser-class oilers, the T-AO 205s are to be double-hulled as a guard against possible oil spills.

Generally the name source for oilers has been rivers with Indian names. Among the recent exceptions to this practice are the Henry J. Kaiser-class T-AOs, named for industrialists, engineers and naval architects, and the John Lewis-class T-AOs, honoring notable civil rights figures.

World War I Oiler Roster[3]

The tanker USS *John M. Connelly* is wearing razzle dazzle camouflage on May 6, 1918, three days before her commissioning in Philadelphia (U.S. Navy photograph).

Amabala	Herbert L. Pratt	Sylvan Arrow
Broad Arrow	Hisko	Topila
Chestnut Hill	Houma	W. L. Steed
Chinampa	Hoven	Wieldrecht
Edward L. Doheny III	Hoxbar	William Isom
Frank H. Buck	J. M. Guffey	William Rockefeller
Gargoyle	John M. Connelly	Winifred
George G. Henry	Los Angeles	
Gold Shell	Standard Arrow	

World War II AO Roster

The Chicopee (AO 34)-class oiler USS *Housatonic* (AO 35), at left, is refueling the aircraft carrier USS *Ranger* (CV 4) in the Atlantic on July 17, 1942. *Ranger* is ferrying U.S. Army P-40 Warhawk fighters to Africa and also carrying Navy SB2U Vindicator dive bombers. Two years after the war, *Housatonic* was sold to her former owners, Standard Oil of New Jersey (U.S. Navy photograph).

In the roster listings below an asterisk following the ship's name indicates a Navy oiler that was later assigned to MSTS or MSC and redesignated as a T-AO with the same hull number.

AO 1	Kanawha [Z]	AO 50	Tallulah[11] [SS]
AO 2	Maumee [T]	AO 51	Ashtabula [SS/SX]
AO 3	Cuyama [SS]	AO 52	Cacapon [SS]
AO 4	Brazos [SS]	AO 53	Caliente [K/D]
AO 5	Neches [Z]	AO 54	Chikaskia [SC/SS]
AO 6	Pecos [Z]	AO 55	Elokomin [SS]
AO 7	Arethusa [SC]	AO 56	Aucilla [SS]
AO 8	Sara Thompson [SC]	AO 57	Marias*[12] [SS]
AO 9	Patoka[4] [SS]	AO 58	Manatee [SS]
AO 10	Alameda [SS]	AO 59	Mississinewa[13] [Z]
AO 11	Sapelo [SS]	AO 60	Nantahala [SS]
AO 12	Ramapo [SC]	AO 61	Severn [SS]
AO 13	Trinity [SC]	AO 62	Taluga*[14] [SS]
AO 14	Robert L. Barnes [SC]	AO 63	Chipola [SS]
AO 15	Kaweah [SS]	AO 64	Tolovana*[15] [SS]
AO 16	Laramie [SS]	AO 65	Pecos*[16] [SS]
AO 17	Mattole [SS]	AO 66	Atascosa [SC]
AO 18	Rapidan [SS]	AO 67	Cache[17] [SS]
AO 19	Salinas [SC]	AO 68	Chiwawa [SC]
AO 20	Sepulga [SS]	AO 69	Enoree* [SS]
AO 21	Tippecanoe [SS]	AO 70	Escalante [SC]
AO 22	Cimarron [SS]	AO 71	Neshanic [SC]
AO 23	Neosho[5] [Z]	AO 72	Niobrara [D/SS]
AO 24	Platte [SS]	AO 73	Millicoma*[18] [SC]
AO 25	Sabine [SS]	AO 74	Saranac[19] [SC]
AO 26	Salamonie [SS]	AO 75	Saugatuck[20] [SS]
AO 27	Kaskaskia [SS]	AO 76	Schuykill[21] [SS]
AO 28	Sangamon[6] [C/SC]	AO 77	Cassatot [SS]
AO 29	Santee[7] [C/SS]	AO 78	Chepachet[22] [SS]
AO 30	Chemung [SS]	AO 79	Cowanesque[23] [SS]
AO 31	Chenango[8] [C/SS]	AO 80	Escambia* [SS]
AO 32	Guadalupe [SS]	AO 81	Kennebago* [SS]
AO 33	Suwannee[9] [C/SC]	AO 82	Cahaba* [SS]
AO 34	Chicopee [K/D]	AO 83	Mascoma* [SC]
AO 35	Housatonic [K/D]	AO 84	Ocklawaha* [SS]
AO 36	Kennebec [SS]	AO 85	Pamanset* [SC]
AO 37	Merrimack [SS]	AO 86	Ponaganset [SS]
AO 38	Winooski [SC]	AO 87	Sebec* [T/SS]
AO 39	Kankakee [SS]	AO 88	Tomahawk* [SC]
AO 40	Lackawanna [SC]	AO 89	Pasig [D]
AO 41	Mattaponi* [SC]	AO 90	Shikellamy[24]
AO 42	Monongahela*[SC]	AO 91	Pasig[25] [SS]
AO 43	Tappahannock [SS]	AO 92	Ataban[26]
AO 44	Patuxent [SC]	AO 93	Soubarissen* [SS]
AO 45	Big Horn [SC]	AO 94	Anacostia* [SC/SS]
AO 46	Victoria[10] [SC]	AO 95	Caney [T/SS]
AO 47	Neches* [SS]	AO 96	Tamalpais* [T/SS]
AO 48	Neosho [SC]	AO 97	Allagash [SS]
AO 49	Suamico* [SS]	AO 98	Caloosahatchee [SS]

AO 99	Canisteo [SS]	AO 104	Contoocook [X]
AO 100	Cukawan [SS]	AO 105	Mispillion* [SS]
AO 101	Cohocton* [K/C/SS]	AO 106	Navasota* [SS]
AO 102	Concho [X]	AO 107	Passumpsic* [SC/SS]
AO 103	Conecuh [X]	AO 108	Pawcatuck* [SS]

Post-War AO / T-AO Roster

Seen in August 1975 operating with the U.S. Sixth Fleet in the western Mediterranean, USS *Truckee* (AO 147) had been commissioned as a Neosho-class oiler in November 1955. She was placed out of service with MSC in October 1991 and ultimately sold for scrap in July 2008 (U.S. Navy photograph).

AO 109	Waccamaw*[27] [SS]	T-AO 123	Mission San Francisco[32] [Z]
AO 110	Conecu[28] [SS]	T-AO 124	Mission San Gabriel [SC]
T-AO 111	Mission Buenaventura [SS]	T-AO 125	Mission San Jose [SS]
T-AO 112	Mission Capistrano[29] [SS]	T-AO 126	Mission San Juan[21] [C/SS]
T-AO 113	Mission Carmel [SC]	T-AO 127	Mission San Luis Obispo [SC]
T-AO 114	Mission De Pala[30] [C/SS]	T-AO 128	Mission San Luis Rey [SS]
T-AO 115	Mission Dolores [SC]	T-AO 129	Mission San Miguel [K]
T-AO 116	Mission Loreto [SS]	T-AO 130	Mission San Rafael [OS/D]
T-AO 117	Mission Los Angeles [SS]	T-AO 131	Mission Santa Barbara [SC]
T-AO 118	Mission Purisima [SS]	T-AO 132	Mission Santa Clara[33] [T]
T-AO 119	Mission San Antonio [SC]	T-AO 133	Mission Santa Cruz [SS]
T-AO 120	Mission San Carlos [SC]	T-AO 134	Mission Santa Ynez[34] [SS]
T-AO 121	Mission San Diego [SC]		
T-AO 122	Mission San Fernando[31] [C/SS]		

T-AO 135	*Mission Solano* [SC]	T-AO 161	*Lone Jack* [T/SS]
T-AO 136	*Mission Soledad* [SC]	T-AO 162	*Memphis* [T/SS]
T-AO 137	*Mission Santa Ana* [SS]	T-AO 163	*Parkersburg* [SC]
T-AO 138	*Cedar Creek* [SS]	T-AO 164	*Petrolite* [SS]
T-AO 139	*Muir Woods* [SS]	T-AO 165	*American Explorer*[39] [SS]
T-AO 140	*Pioneer Valley* [SS]	T-AO 168	*Sealift Pacific*[40] [SC]
T-AO 141	*Sappa Creek* [SS]	T-AO 169	*Sealift Arabian Sea*[41] [SC]
T-AO 142	*Shawnee Trail* [SS]	T-AO 170	*Sealift China Sea*[42] [SC]
AO 143	*Neosho** [SS]	T-AO 171	*Sealift Indian Ocean*[43] [SC]
AO 144	*Mississinewa** [SS]		
AO 145	*Hassayampa** [SS]	T-AO 172	*Sealift Atlantic*[44] [SC]
AO 146	*Kawishiwi** [SS]	T-AO 173	*Sealift Mediterranean*[45] [SC]
AO 147	*Truckee** [SS]		
AO 148	*Ponchatoula** [SS]	T-AO 174	*Sealift Caribbean*[46] [SC]
T-AO 149	*Maumee*[35] [SS]	T-AO 175	*Sealift Arctic*[47] [SC]
T-AO 150	*Potomac*[36] [K]	T-AO 176	*Sealift Antarctic*[48] [SC]
T-AO 151	*Shoshone*[37] [SS]	AO 177	*Cimarron* [SS]
T-AO 152	*Yukon*[38] [SS]	AO 178	*Monongahela* [SS]
T-AO 153	*Cumberland* [SS]	AO 179	*Merrimack* [SS]
T-AO 154	*Lynchburg* [SC]	AO 180	*Willamette* [SS]
T-AO 155	*Roanoke* [SC]	T-AO 181	*Potomac*[49] [SS]
T-AO 156	*Bull Run* [SC]	T-AO 182	*Columbia*[50] [SS]
T-AO 157	*Paoli* [SC]	T-AO 183	*Neches*[51] [K]
T-AO 158	*Abiqua* [K/D]	T-AO 184	*Hudson*[52] [K]
T-AO 159	*French Creek* [T/SS]	T-AO 185	*Susquehanna*[53] [K]
T-AO 160	*Logan's Fort* [T/SS]	AO 186	*Platte* [SS]

Current T-AO Roster

On November 26, 2017, the fleet replenishment oiler USNS *Big Horn* (T-AO 198) is performing an UNREP in the Atlantic Ocean with the dock landing ship USS *Oak Hill* (LSD 21) on her starboard side. Abeam to port (at top) is the amphibious transport dock USS *New York* (LPD 21) (U.S. Navy photograph).

1. Combat Logistics and Fleet Support Ships

T-AO 187	*Henry J. Kaiser* [A]	T-AO 200	*Guadalupe* [A]
T-AO 188	*Joshua Humphreys* [A]	T-AO 201	*Patuxent* [A]
T-AO 189	*John Lenthall* [A]	T-AO 202	*Yukon* [A]
T-AO 190	*Andrew J. Higgins* [A]	T-AO 203	*Laramie* [A]
T-AO 191	*Benjamin Isherwood*[54] [SS]	T-AO 204	*Rappahannock* [A]
T-AO 192	*Henry Eckford*[55] [SS]	T-AO 205	*John Lewis* [to be built]
T-AO 193	*Walter S. Diehl* [A]	T-AO 206	*Harvey Milk* [to be built]
T-AO 194	*John Ericsson* [A]	T-AO 207	*Earl Warren* [to be built]
T-AO 195	*Leroy Grumman*[56] [A]	T-AO 208	*Robert Kennedy* [to be built]
T-AO 196	*Kanawha* [A]	T-AO 209	*Lucy Stone* [to be built]
T-AO 197	*Pecos* [A]	T-AO 210	*Sojourner Truth* [to be built]
T-AO 198	*Big Horn* [A]		
T-AO 199	*Tippecanoe* [A]		

SELECTED SPECIFICATIONS

Cimarron class: AO 22–AO 37, AO 30 and AO 32 (Type T3-S2-A1)

Length: 553 feet (overall)
Beam: 75 feet
Draft: 32.3 feet
Displacement: 7,470 tons (light); 25,440 tons (full load)
Propulsion: geared steam turbines; 13,500 shp; 2 shafts
Speed: 18.3 knots
Personnel: 303
Capacity: 146,000 barrels

Mattaponi class: AO 41–AO 44 & AO 47 (Type: T2-A)

Length: 520 feet (overall)
Beam: 68 feet
Draft: 30.6 feet
Displacement: 6,809 tons (light); 22,325 tons (full load)
Propulsion: geared turbine; 12,500 shp; 1 shaft
Speed: 17.5 knots
Personnel: 242
Capacity: 135,000 barrels

Ashtabula class: AO 51–AO 64 & AO 97–AO 100 (Type: T3-S2-A3)

Note: AOs 51, 98 and 99, originally commissioned in 1943 and 1945, were lengthened ("jumboized") by the addition of a 91-foot section in the mid–1960s to increase their cargo capacity.
Length: 553 feet; 644 feet (jumboized)
Beam: 75 feet
Draft: 32.3 feet
Displacement: 7,470 tons (light); 23,235 tons (full load)
             16,500 tons (light); 36,500 tons (full load) (jumboized)
Propulsion: 2 turbines; 13,500 hp; 2 shafts
Speed: 18.3 knots
Personnel: 350–398
Capacity: 123,700 barrels
          145,000 barrels (jumboized)

Mispillion class: AO 105–AO 109 (Type: T3-S2-A3)

Note: Originally commissioned in 1945 and 1946 and lengthened ("jumboized") by 93 feet in the mid-1960s to increase cargo capacity and service life.
Length: 646 feet
Beam: 75 feet
Draft: 35.5 feet
Displacement: 11,000 tons (light); 34,750 tons (full load)
Propulsion: geared turbines; 13,500 shp; 2 shafts
Speed: 18 knots
Personnel: 304
Capacity: 150,000 barrels

Mission Buenaventura class: T-AO 111–T-AO 137 (Type: T2-SE-A2)

Length: 523.5 feet
Beam: 68 feet
Draft: 30.8 feet
Displacement: 5,730 tons (light); 22,360 tons (full load)
Propulsion: turbo-electric; 10,000 shp; 1 shaft
Speed: 16.5 knots
Capacity: 50 120,400 barrels of oil & 575,000 gallons of gasoline

Neosho class: AO 143–AO 148

Length: 655 feet
Beam: 86 feet
Draft: 35 feet
Displacement: 11,600 tons (light); 38,000–40,000 tons (full load)
Propulsion: steam turbines; 28,000 shp; 2 shafts
Speed: 20 knots
Personnel: Approximately 300 Navy or 105 civilians in T-AO 144
Capacity: Approximately 180,000 barrels

Sealift class: T-AO 168–T-AO 176

Length: 587 feet
Beam: 84 feet
Draft: 34.3 feet
Displacement: 32,000 tons (full load)
Propulsion: Pielstick turbo-charged diesels; 14,000 shp; 1 shaft
Speed: 16 knots
Personnel: 30 civilians
Capacity: 220,000 barrels

Henry J. Kaiser class: T-AO 187—T-AO 204

Length: 677.5 feet
Beam: 97.5 feet
Draft: 35 feet
Displacement: 9,500 tons (light); 40,700 tons (full load)
Propulsion: 2 Colt-Pielstick diesels; 32,000 bhp; 2 shafts
Speed: 20 knots
Personnel: 89 civilians & 6 Navy plus 29 others
Capacity: 180,000 barrels (T-AOs 201, 203 & 204: 159,000 barrels)

Selected Histories

USS *John M. Connelly*

The tanker SS *John M. Connelly* was built in 1918 and commissioned in the Navy on May 9, 1918. During World War I she escorted submarine chasers to the Azores, delivered fuel there and in Bermuda and Gibraltar; transported fuel oil and seaplanes to Devonport and Plymouth, England; carried trucks for a naval aviation unit in France; and delivered fuel in Rhode Island and Maine.

She was decommissioned after the war on January 18, 1919, and transferred to the U.S. Shipping Board. But her career was not then over, as she went on to operate in commercial service for a number of years (at one point renamed as SS *Point Breeze*). The former Navy tanker was dismantled in 1946.

USS *Neches* (AO 5)

USS *Neches*, the first Navy oiler lost in World War II, was sunk by a Japanese submarine on January 23, 1942 (U.S. Navy photograph).

A Maumee-class oiler, *Neches* was laid down on June 8, 1919, at the Boston Navy Yard and launched on June 2, 1920. She was originally classified as Fuel Ship No. 1 but was redesignated as AO 5 in July 1920 shortly before her commissioning three months later on October 25.

The 475-foot long ship was initially armed with four single 5-inch/51 guns and two single 3-inch antiaircraft guns. This armament was later increased with the addition of two single 3-inch mounts and four .50-caliber machine guns.

USS *Neches* had a complement of 136 officers and enlisted personnel, steamed at 14 knots, and between her commissioning and early 1922, operated out of Boston in support of the Atlantic Fleet. In March 1922 she departed the East Coast for her new homeport of San Diego, California. During the 1920s, she provided fuel to various warships based in San Diego.

In December 1941, the oiler got underway from California on a fuel transport run to Pearl Harbor, arriving there three days after the Japanese attack. The next month, *Neches* was tasked with delivering a cargo of 45,000 barrels of fuel oil, 8,700 barrels of diesel fuel, and 100,000 gallons of gasoline to the western Pacific. She left Pearl Harbor alone on January 22, 1942, with 17 officers, 1 warrant officer and 218 enlisted sailors (including 65 men who were riding her in transit to new duty stations).

The next day, between 0310 and 0330 (3:10–3:30 am) the oiler was hit by three torpedoes, two of which exploded and opened her to the sea. *Neches* gun crews fired at the surfaced Japanese submarine I-72 but were unable to sink it because the oiler slowly listed to starboard and was unable to bring her guns to bear.[57] An hour and a half after the attack began and as she steadily flooded, Commander William B. Fletcher, Jr., the commanding officer, ordered the ship abandoned. USS *Neches* sank seven minutes later, at 0437, with the loss of 57 lives. The survivors were rescued by a PBY Catalina seaplane and the destroyer USS *Jarvis* (DD 393) later that morning.

USS *Alameda* (AO 10)

- Built in 1919 by William Crump & Sons of Philadelphia.
- Commissioned in 1919 as *Alameda* (Fuel Ship No. 10) but reclassified as oiler AO 10 in July 1920.
- Decommissioned in March 1922 and struck in August 1922.
- Operated in the merchant marine as *Olean* (torpedoed by German submarine U-158 on March 1, 1942) and as *Sweep* (in 1943).
- Acquired and commissioned on July 12, 1944, as the unclassified miscellaneous vessel USS *Silver Cloud* (IX 143) for service as a mobile storage tanker.
- During World War II fueled nearly 200 ships in the Marshall and Admiralty Islands, and operated in the Philippines.
- Decommissioned and transferred to WSA on March 29, 1946, and struck on April 17 of that year.
- Sold for $14,160 and delivered on January 21, 1947, to Pinto Island Metals Company for dismantling.

USS *Robert L. Barnes* (AO 14)

- Tanker built in 1917 by McDougall-Duluth Shipbuilding Company in Duluth, Minnesota.

- Acquired June 29, 1918, and commissioned on October 19, 1918.
- Between 1920 and 1941 operated out of Cuba, New York, Norfolk and California before becoming station ship in Guam.
- Reclassified as cargo ship [q.v.] AK 11 in 1920, oiler AO 14 in 1921, and miscellaneous auxiliary AG 27 in July 1938.
- Captured at Guam on December 10, 1941, and used by the Japanese for the duration of the war.
- Struck on July 24, 1942, but recovered by U.S. forces in 1945.
- Later sold and renamed *Fortune* and *M.T.S. No. 2* in 1945–1949, and dismantled in 1950.

USS *Cimarron* (AO 22)

Serving in her third war, the oiler USS *Cimarron* (middle) is refueling the aircraft carrier USS *Hornet* (CVS 12) (top) and the destroyer USS *Nicholas* (DD 449) (bottom) off the coast of North Vietnam in 1966 (U.S. Navy photograph).

- Built by Sun Shipbuilding and Drydock Company in Chester, Pennsylvania.
- Laid down on April 18, 1938, launched on January 7, 1939, and commissioned on March 20, 1939.
- Transported oil between West Coast and Hawaii 13 times between July 1939 and August 1940.

- Operated along the U.S. East Coast in early 1941 and in the Caribbean and South Atlantic later that year.
- One of two oilers that supported the naval task force conducting the famous Doolittle raid on Japan in April 1942.
- Fueled ships participating in Battle of Midway in June 1942.
- Engaged in various refueling and transport operations in the Pacific for the remainder of World War II.
- Between July 1946 and June 1950 ferried oil from Persian Gulf to naval bases in the Mariana and Marshall islands.
- Fueled naval task forces in the waters off Korea and Okinawa during the Korean War.
- Supported U.S. Seventh Fleet warships in various deployments in the 1950s.
- As of 1963 had the longest continuous commissioned service of any active ship in the U.S. Navy.
- Participated in the Vietnam War between May 1965 and September 1967.
- Decommissioned on October 1, 1968, and struck nine days later.
- Transferred to MARAD on September 15, 1969 and sold for scrapping to Levin Metals Corporation of San Jose, California.
- Earned ten battle stars for World War II service, seven battle stars for Korean War service, and the Armed Forces Expeditionary Medal and the Vietnam Service Medal with four campaign stars for her Vietnam War service.

USS *Big Horn* (AO 45)

The tanker SS *Gulf Dawn* was built in 1936 by the Sun Shipbuilding and Drydock Corporation in Chester, Pennsylvania, and was owned by the Gulf Oil Corporation. The Navy acquired her on March 31, 1942, and three days later renamed her *Big Horn* and designated her as AO 45. The new Navy oiler was placed in commission on April 15, 1942, to serve in an unusual role.

Between March and July 1942 *Big Horn* was converted into a Q-ship, i.e., disguised as an innocent merchant vessel for the purpose of luring a submarine to the surface and attacking the sub with her hidden guns. Accordingly, for her Q-ship mission *Big Horn* was outfitted with five 4-inch/50 guns, two .50-caliber machine guns, and for close up and personal warfare, five sawed-off shotguns and five "Tommy" guns. The ship was manned by 13 officers and 157 enlisted personnel (later increased to 15 officers and 224 enlisted).

During the second-half of 1942, *Big Horn* sailed in two convoys in the Caribbean but failed to attract the attention of any German U-boats. In November and December she received a hedgehog projector and direction-finding equipment to enhance her ASW capabilities.

On May 3, 1943, the oiler was steaming with Mediterranean-bound convoy UGS-7A when she spotted a periscope and delivered two hedgehog attacks and a one depth charge run. Although there were some indications from underwater explosions and an oil patch that the German submarine had been at least damaged, post-war analysis determined that no U-boats had been lost at that time and place. On August 8, 1943, *Big Horn* attacked a suspected U-boat near the Azores but again, there was no conclusive evidence of a kill.

In 1944 the oiler was tasked with weather patrol duty in the North Atlantic and manned by a Coast Guard crew. She was formally transferred to that service on January 10 1944, redesignated as WAO 124, and operated out of Boston and Halifax.

Big Horn was returned to the Navy on February 1, 1945, but reclassified two days later not as an AO but as the unclassified miscellaneous ship IX 207. The change in classification was made because she was to be converted into an oil shuttle and storage vessel and sent to the western Pacific for the duration of the war. From May to July she made four voyages between Ulithi and the Philippines delivering about 7,900 tons of oil to recipient AOs on each trip.

In February 1946 she transferred her final load of oil to USS *Beagle* (IX 112) and left the Far East for home on February 25. The former Q-ship was decommissioned on May 6, 1946, and her name struck on July 3. *Big Horn* was sold on June 27, 1947, to Sabine Transportation Company for merchant service and went on to steam for four different commercial owners under four different names before meeting the scrapper's torch in 1960.

USS *Ashtabula* (AO 51)

The veteran oiler USS *Ashtabula* is operating off the coast of Oahu, Hawaii, on May 2, 1978 (U.S. Navy photograph).

Laid down on October 1, 1942, as a Cimarron-class oiler, *Ashtabula* was launched on May 22, 1943, at Bethlehem Steel's Sparrows Point shipyard in Maryland. She was acquired and commissioned as AO 51 on August 7, 1943.

In the first month of her naval service, USS *Ashtabula* operated in the South Pacific as a unit of Service Squadron 8. During the first-half of 1944 she support fast carrier task forces in the Marshall Islands and the Marianas. Later that year the oiler participated in the successful effort to liberate the Philippines, and was hit by a Japanese air-dropped torpedo on October 23. Despite incurring a 16-degree list to port, *Ashtabula* continued operations but had to return to the United Sates in December for repairs.

For most of 1945, the oiler operated out of Eniwetok and Ulithi fueling warships in the U.S. Fifth Fleet. After the Japanese surrender, AO 51 steamed between Korea, Japan and China conducting UNREP for deployed Navy ships.

Unlike many of the Navy's auxiliaries, *Ashtabula* was not deactivated after World War II but continued on with her job of transporting and delivering her cargoes of aviation gas and fuel oil. As a result, she participated in the Korean War in 1950–1952, and for the following 10 years routinely deployed to the western Pacific from her homeport of Long Beach, California.

On August 2, 1964, *Ashtabula* was in the Gulf of Tonkin and refueled the destroyers USS *Maddox* (DD 731) and USS *Turner Joy* (DD 951) shortly after the North Vietnamese attack on the former. Over the next eight years, AO 51 continued to serve in the waters off Vietnam during her WestPac deployments, for which she earned the Vietnam Service Medal with eight campaign stars.

In 1968, a new 400-foot midsection was inserted between the bow and stern to replace the old 310-foot midsection. This "jumboization" increased the ship's liquid cargo capacity by more than a third.

Ashtabula operated in the Indian Ocean late in 1973 after which she provided services to ships in the western Pacific and Pearl Harbor areas periodically up until 1982. The nearly 40-year-old oiler deployed on her last cruise to the Far East on April 30, 1982, and returned to Pearl Harbor on August 5 of that year to be deactivated. She was decommissioned on September 30, 1982, and transferred to the NDRF in Suisun Bay, California. Although sold for scrapping on October 25, 1995, *Ashtabula* was not dismantled but instead five years later was expended as a target on October 15, 2000.

Besides the Vietnam Service Medal, USS *Ashtabula* earned five battle stars for her World War II service and seven battle stars for her Korean War service.

USS *Conecuh* (AO 110)

- Built as *Dithmarschen* in 1938 for the German Navy as a combination oil and supply tender for U-boats.
- Allocated to the United States in January 1946 as a war prize and placed in service on May 2, 1946, as the unclassified miscellaneous vessel IX 301.
- *Dithmarschen* used to evaluate concept of "one-stop" oil and supply replenishment.
- Renamed *Conecuh* and reclassified as a fleet oiler (AO 110) on October 1, 1946; lack of funds for conversion caused her to be taken out of service on October 24.
- Reclassified as replenishment oiler [q.v.] AOR 110 on September 4, 1952, and commissioned on February 16. 1953.
- Deployed to the Mediterranean in the spring of 1954 and refueled ships in the Atlantic and Caribbean in 1954 and 1955. Her performance validated the concept

Seen here in the mid-1950s, USS *Conecuh* began her career in Hitler's Navy in 1938 and served in the U.S. Navy for 10 years after World War II (U.S. Navy photograph).

of combination oiler/replenishment ships and led to the development of the fast combat support ship (AOE) (see Fast Combat Support Ship section below).
- Decommissioned on April 3, 1956, and struck on June 1, 1960.
- Sold for $136,688 to Southeastern Rail & Steel Company on November 23, 1960, to be dismantled.

USNS *Henry J. Kaiser* (T-AO 187)

- Built in 1984–1985 by Avondale Shipyard, Inc., in New Orleans, Louisiana.
- Laid down on August 22, 1984, and launched on October 5, 1985.
- Entered service with MSC on December 19, 1986.
- In March 1997 participated in Exercise Tandem Thrust 97, a joint U.S. and Australian military exercise involving more than 28,170 troops, 252 aircraft and 43 ships. MSC reported that T-AO 187 saved the Navy more than $1.5 million in fuel and operational costs resulting from her refueling ships at sea and eliminating their need to return to port and purchase fuel in Australia.
- In 2009 provided underway replenishment training for U.S. Third Fleet (West Coast) Navy carrier strike groups—including USS *Nimitz* (CVN 68) and USS *Ronald Reagan* (CVN 76)–and amphibious ready groups—including amphibious assault ships USS *Boxer* (LHD 4) and USS *Bonhomme Richard* (LHD 6)—to prepare them for deployment around the world.

On August 9, 2017, the fleet replenishment oiler USNS *Henry J. Kaiser* (T-AO 187) is underway in the Pacific preparing to refuel the guided missile cruiser USS *Bunker Hill* (CG 52) (U.S. Navy photograph).

- In 2010 continued to assist in pre-deployment preparations for Third Fleet ships homeported in San Diego.
- In June–August 2012 supported Exercise Rim of the Pacific (RIMPAC) 2012 near Hawaii by delivering fuel to participating ships. On July 17–18 provided 900,000 gallons of a 50–50 blend of advanced biofuels and a traditional petroleum-based fuel to the USS *Nimitz* (CVN 68) carrier strike group, including the destroyers USS *Chung-Hoon* (DDG 93) and USS *Chaffee* (DDG 90) and missile cruiser USS *Princeton* (CG 59), as well as *Nimitz* herself. Together with USNS *Yukon* (T-AO 202) and USNS *Matthew Perry* (T-AKE 9), delivered more than 9.8 million gallons of diesel fuel, more than 1.8 million gallons of aviation fuel and nearly 2,000 pallets of food and supplies during the exercise.
- Took part in Exercise Fortune Guard 2014 in August 2014; conducted boarding at sea training with Japanese, Korean Navy and Coast Guard, and U.S. Coast Guard vessels and teams.
- BAE Systems Ship Repair San Francisco Inc. contracted in September 2014 to provide a regular 55-day overhaul and dry-docking for the ship. The $9.5 million contract provided for *Henry J. Kaiser* to have her port main engine overhauled, underwater hull cleaned and painted, preservation of her cargo tank, and replacement of the rudder bearing.
- In August 2015 participated in a three-week Composite Unit Training Exercise

1. Combat Logistics and Fleet Support Ships

(COMPTUEX) off California by providing logistics support to the aircraft carrier USS *John C. Stennis* (CVN 74) and the nine warships comprising her battle group. (COMPTUEX is a required exercise for each carrier battle group prior to a six-month deployment.) The more than 4 million gallons of diesel fuel, nearly 4.5 million gallons of jet fuel and 729 pallets of food and supplies delivered by T-AO 187 and T-AO 202 during UNREP evolutions enabled the strike group to stay on station without returning to port for fuel and supplies.

Notes

1. The longtime nomenclature for oilers was changed to "fleet replenishment oiler" (T-AO) in the Secretary of the Navy's General Guidance for the Classification of Naval Vessels promulgated in June 2016.
2. Marvin O. Miller, "Standby for Shotline," 76; *U.S. Navy Oilers and Tankers*, 3–4.
3. This listing was derived from information compiled by Stephen S. Roberts and made available on his excellent ShipScribe Web site (http://shipscribe.com/usnaux/wwl/w1ao.htm).
4. Originally an oiler built at a cost of $2.122 million and commissioned in October 1919, designated as AO 9 in 1920, fitted with mooring mast and assigned as tender to rigid airship *Shenandoah* and later operated with airships *Los Angeles* and *Akron* in 1924–1933, decommissioned 1933–1939, reclassified as seaplane tender [q.v.] AV 6 in October 1939 and reclassified back to AO 9 in June 1940, converted to mine craft tender and redesignated as miscellaneous auxiliary [q.v.] AG 125 in August 1944, decommissioned in July 1946, and sold in January 1946 for scrapping.
5. Commissioned in August 1939 and heavily damaged during Japanese air attack in the Coral Sea on May 7, 1944, and expended by gunfire from destroyer USS *Henley* (DD 391) four days later.
6. Originally tanker *Esso Trenton* acquired in October 1940 and designated as AO 28, converted to an aircraft carrier in 1942 and redesignated sequentially as AVG 26, ACV 26 and CVE 26.
7. Originally tanker *Seakay* acquired in October 1940 and designated as AO 29, converted to aircraft carrier in 1942 and redesignated sequentially as ACV 29, CVE 29 and CVHE 29.
8. AO 31 was originally tanker *Esso New Orleans* acquired in May 1941, converted to aircraft carrier in 1942 and redesignated sequentially as AVG 28, ACV 28, CVE 28 and CVHE 28; AO 33 was originally tanker *Markay* acquired in June 1941, converted to aircraft carrier in 1942 and redesignated sequentially as AVG 27, CVE 27 and CVHE 27.
9. *Ibid.*
10. Built in 1917 as *George G. Henry*, acquired by Navy and commissioned as USS *George G. Henry* in August 1918, decommissioned and struck in May 1919, reacquired and commissioned as USS *George G. Henry* (AO 46) in April 1942, renamed USS *Victoria* (AO 46) that same month, decommissioned in December 1945, struck in January 1946, and returned to owner in March 1946.
11. Commissioned in September 1942, decommissioned in April 1946, placed in service with MSTS in October 1949 as T-AO 50, and later reclassified as T-AOT 50, placed out of service in May 1975, and sold for scrapping in November 1986.
12. Reclassified as T-AO 57 in October 1973.
13. Sunk at Ulithi on November 20, 1944, by Japanese manned torpedo.
14. Reclassified as T-AO 62 in 1972.
15. Reclassified as T-AO 64 in August 1949.
16. Reclassified as T-AO 65 in July 1950.
17. Later reclassified as a transport oiler and redesignated as T-AOT with the same hull number. (See Transport Oiler [AOT] section in Chapter 2 for additional information.)
18. *Ibid.*
19. Converted to power barge in 1946, later reclassified as YFP 9, struck in March 1956 and sold in December 1957.
20. Later reclassified as a transport oiler and redesignated as T-AOT with the same hull number. (See Transport Oiler [AOT] section in Chapter 2 for additional information.)
21. *Ibid.*
22. *Ibid.*
23. *Ibid.*
24. Reclassified as AOG 67 in July 1943.
25. *Pasig* and *Ataban* reclassified as distilling ships [q.v.] AW 3 and AW 4, respectively, in December 1944.
26. *Ibid.*
27. Later reclassified as a transport oiler and redesignated as T-AOT with the same hull number. (See Transport Oiler [AOT] section in Chapter 2 for additional information.)
28. See Selected Histories for details.
29. Reclassified as miscellaneous auxiliary AG 162 in July 1960 and placed in service as T-AG 162, struck in October 1971, and sold for scrapping in July 1972.
30. Converted to missile range instrumentation ship (AGM) in the 1960s; T-AO 114 reclassified as T-AGM 20, T-AO 122 reclassified as T-AGM 19, and T-AO 126 reclassified as T-AGM 21. (See AGM section in Chapter 2 for details.)
31. *Ibid.*

32. Collided with freighter SS *Elna II* on March 7, 1957, on the Delaware River. Bow section sunk. Struck on March 20, 1957, and stern section sold for scrap in September 1957.
34. Later reclassified as a transport oiler and redesignated as T-AOT with the same hull number. (See Transport Oiler [AOT] section in Chapter 2 for additional information.)
35. *Ibid.*
36. See AOT section in Chapter 2 for details.
37. Later reclassified as a transport oiler and redesignated as T-AOT with the same hull number. (See Transport Oiler [AOT] section in Chapter 2 for additional information.)
38. *Ibid.*
39. *Ibid.*
40. *Ibid.*
41. *Ibid.*
42. *Ibid.*
43. *Ibid.*
44. *Ibid.*
45. *Ibid.*
46. *Ibid.*
47. *Ibid.*
48. *Ibid.*
49. *Ibid.*
50. *Ibid.*
51. *Ibid.*
52. *Ibid.*
53. *Ibid.*
54. Original contract awarded to Pennsylvania Shipbuilding was cancelled in August 1989 for default on construction. The unfinished ships were then transferred to American Shipbuilding in Tampa, Florida, for completion but were not finished there either and their construction cancelled on August 15, 1993, with T-AO 191 95.3 percent complete and T-AO 192 84 percent complete. Laid up in NDRF and transferred to MARAD in February 1999 and February 1998, respectively. Ultimately, both vessels were towed to shipbreakers in Brownsville, Texas, to be dismantled.
55. *Ibid.*
56. Deployed to the Mediterranean Sea from September 2017 to February 2018. During the deployment, performed more than 30 UNREPs and provided 3.7 million gallons of fuel and 1,019 pallets of materials and provisions to U.S., Canadian, Italian, Turkish, German and U.K. customer ships
57. I-72 was redesignated as I-172 in May 1942.

Fast Combat Support Ships (AOE / T-AOE)

The fast combat support ship (AOE) combines in one hull the separate capabilities of the ammunition ship [q.v.] (AE), oiler [q.v.] (AO) and cargo ship [q.v.] (AK). Able to accompany and keep pace with fast moving carrier strike groups, the AOE supplies the group's warships with fuel, ammunition and stores in a single underway replenishment (UNREP) rather than in three separate transfers from three different auxiliary ships. Similarly, the one-stop-shopping service provided by the AOE reduces the risks and vulnerabilities of "customer" ships by eliminating the need for multiple replenishments to acquire the same materials. Forward-deployed fast combat support ships, in turn, are supplied by one-product auxiliary ships that shuttle between shore-based depots and the AOEs at sea, thereby allowing the AOE to remain constantly with the deployed strike group.

In recent years, the Navy has employed its Henry J. Kaiser (T-AO 187)-class replenishment oilers [q.v.] and Lewis and Clark (T-AKE 1)-class dry cargo and ammunition ships much like the AOEs, i.e., as station ships attached to the strike group to supply its ships directly rather than as shuttle ships fetching cargo from shore and distributing it to the AOE for further delivery to the ultimate customers. Some of this shift in practice is because the Navy now has only two active AOEs, whereas it once operated twice as many.

1. Combat Logistics and Fleet Support Ships 61

The fast combat support ship USNS *Arctic* (T-AOE 8) (center) is replenishing the aircraft carrier USS *Harry S. Truman* (CVN 75) (left) and the guided missile cruiser USS *Monterey* (CG 61) (right) in the North Persian Gulf on February 26, 2005 (U.S. Navy photograph).

The origin of the fast combat support ship is traceable to World War II when the Navy's supply chain was increasingly stretched to provide logistical support to Pacific Fleet warships operating ever closer to Japan. After the war, the Navy began to consider the need for a one-stop replenishment ship to enhance its underway replenishment capabilities. In December 1950, the service approved the conversion of a former German tanker into combination fleet oiler-replenishment ship which was commissioned as USS *Conecuh* (AOR 110) in 1953[1] The following year, the Bureau of Ships was tasked with designing a new 20-knot replenishment-oiler but construction of the resulting design was not funded by Congress. In June 1958 the Chief of Naval Operations approved the design of a larger and faster "logistics support vessel," which was authorized by Congress in the Fiscal Year 1961 Navy budget submission. On August 8, 1960, the Bureau of Ships ordered this new ship from the Puget Sound Naval Shipyard and construction began on March 1 of the following year. The keel was laid down on June 30, 1961, and the ship was launched and christened on September 14, 1963. Thus, the Navy's first fast combat support ship, USS *Sacramento* (AOE 1), was commissioned on March 14, 1964 (see her history below). She had cost $66 million.

By at least one measure that 792-foot long ship could be considered as the "battleship" of auxiliary vessels, in that she was very large and propelled by two of the four steam turbines originally built for the never completed Iowa-class battleship *Kentucky* (BB 66). *Sacramento* was armed with four 3-inch/50 twin gun mounts, and she had a hangar for three UH-46A Sea Knight helicopters used in vertical replenishment. AOE 1 carried 177,000 barrels (more than 5 million gallons) of petroleum products (Navy standard fuel oil, JP-5 aviation fuel and aviation gas), 1,600 tons of ammunition, 250 tons of dry stores and 250 tons of refrigerated stores. She had nine replenishment stations to port and six to starboard, and by pumping simultaneously to port and starboard, the ship could deliver more than 1.5 million gallons an hour.

As the lead ship of the AOE 1 class, *Sacramento* was joined over the next six years by three other fast combat support ships (AOE 2–AOE 4) between April 1967 and March 1970. A planned fifth ship (AOE 5) was cancelled in November 1968. All four sister ships were decommissioned between October 2004 and September 2005, and have since been dismantled (see histories below).

They were succeeded by the four ships of the Supply (AOE 6) class, which were commissioned between February 1994 and March 1998. Congress appropriated funds for the lead ship in 1987. USS *Supply* was commissioned as a Navy-manned ship on February 25, 1994, but was decommissioned on July 13, 2001, and transferred to the Military Sealift Command (MSC). She was then placed in service as a United States Naval Ship (USNS), redesignated as T-AOE 6, and crewed by civilian civil service mariners. Her sister ship USS *Arctic* (AOE 8) was similarly transferred to the MSC and redesignated in June 2002, followed by USS *Rainier* (AOE 7) in August 2003 and USS *Bridge* (AOE 10) in June 2004. Construction of the planned AOE 9 was cancelled.

The Supply-class vessels are somewhat smaller than their AOE 1 predecessors and have different propulsion plants (gas turbines rather than steam turbines). Built with one less cargo hold than the AOE 1-class, their cargo capacity is nevertheless comparable to the Sacramento class and in some cases, greater. The AOE 6 ships can carry 2,150 tons of ammunition, 250 tons of refrigerated stores, 500 tons of dry stores, and 177,000 barrels of fuel. The Navy armament they carried at time of transfer to MSC has been removed. Two CH-46E Sea Knight or two MH-60S Seahawk helicopters are normally embarked for use in vertical replenishments.

Two of the Supply-class fast combat support ships (T-AOE 7 and T-AOE 10) have been laid up in reserve in Bremerton, Washington. As there are no current plans to build additional T-AOE-type ships, and given the projected service life of these vessels, the Navy will have no fast combat support ships serving the fleet by the decade of the 2030s.

The AOE 1-class ships were named for U.S. cities and the AOE 6-class vessels were assigned the names of earlier supply-type ships.

AOE / T-AOE Roster

AOE 1	*Sacramento* [SS]	T-AOE 6	*Supply* [A]
AOE 2	*Camden* [SS]	T-AOE 7	*Rainier*[3] [L]
AOE 3	*Seattle* [SS]	T-AOE 8	*Arctic* [A]
AOE 4	*Detroit* [SS]	T-AOE 9	"*Conecuh*"[4] [X]
AOE 5[2] [X]		T-AOE 10	*Bridge*[5] [L]

Specifications

Sacramento class: AOE 1–AOE 4

Length: 792.75 feet
Beam: 107 feet
Draft: 39.3 feet
Displacement: 19,200 tons (light); 53,600 tons (full load)
Propulsion: twin steam turbines from *Kentucky* (BB 66); 100,000 hp; 2 shafts
Speed: 26 knots (10,000 miles at 17 knots)
Personnel: 33 Navy officers & 567 enlisted personnel

Supply class: T-AOE 6–T-AOE 10

Length: 754 feet (overall)
Beam: 107 feet
Draft: 39 feet
Displacement: 19,700 tons (light); 48,800 tons (full load)
Propulsion: 4 General Electric LM2500 gas turbines; 105,000 shp; 2 shafts
Speed: 25 knots
Personnel: 160 civilians & 29 Navy

Histories

USS *Sacramento* (AOE 1)

On Independence Day 1969, USS *Sacramento* is steaming in Vietnam's Gulf of Tonkin (U.S. Navy photograph).

The first combat support ship was built by the Puget Sound Naval Shipyard in Bremerton, Washington. Her keel was laid on June 30, 1961, and she was launched two years later on September 14, 1963. USS *Sacramento* was commissioned on March 14, 1964, with Seattle, Washington, as her designated homeport (changed to Bremerton on September 2, 1971).

Her propulsion plant included two of the four steam turbines that had been intended for the Iowa-class battleship *Kentucky* (BB 66), the construction of which was halted on February 17, 1947, when she was 72.1 percent completed.

From April 7 to October 9, 1964, USS *Sacramento* engaged in builder's and familiarization trials, underway training, and replenishment-at-sea (RAS) trials and a post-shakedown yard availability. She departed Long Beach, California, for her first western Pacific (WestPac) deployment on November 28, 1964. During that deployment in the South China Sea, the ship serviced 294 customers, transferred 35 million gallons of fuel, 1,191 short tons of provisions and 670 tons of ammunition over a four-month stretch. On that first deployment, AOE 1 steamed over 39,000 miles, with visits to two ports in Japan, and Hong Kong and Pearl Harbor. After another yard availability in Bremerton during the summer, *Sacramento* left for her second WestPac deployment on October 14, 1965.

Assigned to Task Force 73, which was the U.S. Seventh Fleet's replenishment and mobile logistics support force, AOE 1 steamed back and forth between Subic Bay in the Philippines (to load supplies over five days) and Yankee Station off Vietnam (to deliver her cargoes over an 18-day span to Seventh Fleet aircraft carriers and other combatants). After nine months of operating in TF 73, *Sacramento* returned to Seattle on July 17, 1966.

She wasn't there long. She started a third six-month WestPac deployment on November 25, 1966, during which she replenished some 570 ships, transferred more than 38 million gallons of fuel oil, 27 million gallons of jet fuel, 900,000 gallons of aviation gasoline, 14,000 short tons of ammunition, and 2,000 short tons of provisions and freight. She also delivered 250,000 gallons of fresh water and transported 930 men for transfer to other ships. This cruise was followed by a fourth beginning January 6, 1968 (during which she replenished 351 ships). With time out for three months of yard work in 1969, a restricted availability in 1970, an overhaul in December 1971–June 1972, USS *Sacramento* deployed to WestPac for the fifth time in February 1969 (accomplishing 471 replenishments), a sixth time in February 1970, a seventh time in March 1971, an eighth time in August 1971, and a ninth time in February 1974.

She also operated off Korea in January–March 1968 and in April 1968, off Iran and in the Indian Ocean April to July 1980, off Libya April to June 1986, participated in the Gulf War January to March 1991, steamed off Liberia in December 1992 and in the Indian Ocean again October 1997 to January 1998 and August to September 1999.

These multi-month operations in distant seas came to an end on October 1, 2004, when *Sacramento* was decommissioned in the shipyard of her birth and her name struck from the Naval Vessel Register (NVR). She was inactivated and laid up in the Naval Inactive Ship Maintenance Facility in Bremerton, slated to be eventually expended as a target in a fleet training exercise. However, that outcome did not come to pass. Instead, ESCO Marine Inc. of Brownsville, Texas, was awarded a contract on April 13, 2007, to dismantle the ship, and *Sacramento* was "recycled" (turned into scrap metal and disposable materials) by July 11, 2008.

USS *Sacramento* earned the Armed Forces Expeditionary Medal and the Vietnam Service Medal with 13 campaign stars for her service during the Vietnam War.

USS *Camden* (AOE 2)

Having just completed a vertical replenishment, USS *Camden* is standing off from the aircraft carrier USS *Abraham Lincoln* (CVN 72) in the Philippine Sea on February 17, 2005 (U.S. Navy photograph).

- Built by the New York Shipbuilding Corporation in Camden, New Jersey.
- Laid down on February 17, 1961, and launched on May 29, 1965.
- Fitted with two steam turbines from incomplete battleship *Kentucky*.
- Commissioned into the Navy on April 1, 1967.
- Operated off Vietnam July 1968 to February 1969, September 1969 to March 1970, September 1970 to March 1971, and February to August 1972.
- Operated off Korea in 1970, and in the Indian Ocean April to June 1979, December 1980 to April 1981, July to November 1998, and September 2000 to January 2001.
- Operated in the Persian Gulf in June and July 1987, off Libya in April and May 1989, and off Liberia in May and June 1994.
- Participated in the Gulf War (Operation Desert Storm) January to July 1991 and in the Iraq War (Operation Iraqi Freedom) in 2003.
- Got underway on her final deployment on January 18, 2005, to support various units of the U.S. Fifth Fleet and coalition forces operating in the Gulf region, including the aircraft carrier USS *Carl Vinson* (CVN 70) Strike Group 3, Destroyer Squadron 31, the guided missile cruiser USS *Antietam* (CG 54), and the guided missile destroyers USS *O'Kane* (DDG 77) and USS *Mustin* (DDG 89).

- Decommissioned and struck on September 29, 2005.
- Sold on April 13, 2007, to ESCO Marine Inc. for dismantling, which was completed on May 13, 2008.
- USS *Camden* earned seven campaign stars for her service during the Vietnam War.

USS *Seattle* (AOE 3)

USS *Seattle* is replenishing the aircraft carrier USS *America* (CVA 66) in the Atlantic on January 25, 1970. Note the AOE's CH-46 on the helicopter deck and the fenders rigged along her port side (U.S. Navy photograph).

The third Sacramento-class AOE was laid down at the Puget Sound Naval Shipyard on October 1, 1965, and launched on March 2, 1968. USS *Seattle* was commissioned a year later on April 5th to be homeported in Norfolk, Virginia.

After arriving in Norfolk on November 22, 1969, *Seattle* spent the first-half of 1970 undergoing shakedown training and participating in various exercises. She deployed east to the U.S. Sixth Fleet on August 27 and served as the primary logistics ship for the attack carrier USS *Saratoga* (CVA 60) and her escorts in the eastern Mediterranean. AOE 3 later operated off Greece, Sicily and Spain, before returning home on March 1, 1971. That summer she worked in the Caribbean before leaving Virginia on December 1st for her second Mediterranean deployment. After seven months with the Sixth Fleet, *Seattle* arrived back in Norfolk on June 29, 1972. Her stay in U.S. waters was short-lived, however, because she had to again steam to the Mediterranean four months later on an unscheduled deployment. Happily, she was back home in Norfolk on December 19, just in time for Christmas.

In the first-half of 1973, USS *Seattle* operated out of Norfolk and then in June again voyaged out to the Med, remaining with the Sixth Fleet until late November. Back in Norfolk on December 1, 1973, the ship spent the first months of 1974 in Virginia and off the U.S. East Coast.

Over the years. USS *Seattle* was often far from her home port. For example, in August to October 1981 she was off Iran and in the Indian Ocean; in September–November 1982, June 1984, and January–April 1986 off Lebanon; and in November 1997–March 1998, and October 1999–March 2000 in the Indian Ocean. She also took part in the Gulf War between September 1990 and March 1991.

In August 2004, while operating as part of the aircraft carrier USS *John F. Kennedy* (CV 67) Strike Group, the AOE rescued the 12-man crew of the sinking cargo ship *Edha II* in the North Arabian Gulf.

USS *Seattle* was decommissioned and struck on March 15, 2005, and like her two predecessors, sold to ESCO Marine Inc. for dismantling. The scrapping contract was awarded in September 2005, ESCO took possession of the ship on February 9, 2006, and by January 26, 2007, she had been broken up.

USS *Detroit* (AOE 4)

Riding high in the water without a load of cargo, USS *Detroit* is at the Puget Sound Naval Shipyard on July 31, 1970, four months after her commissioning (U.S. Navy photograph).

The last AOE 1-class fast combat support ship was built, as was the first, at the Puget Sound Naval Shipyard. USS *Detroit* was laid down on November 29, 1966, launched on June 21, 1969, and commissioned on March 28, 1970. She was initially homeported in Newport, Rhode Island, but was shifted to Norfolk, Virginia, in January 1974, and after that to Naval Weapons Station, Earle, in New Jersey in October 1989.

For almost all of her career, USS *Detroit* was repeatedly and often deployed to the Mediterranean and Persian Gulf. She made at least 16 such deployments: in 1971, 1973, 1974, 1975 (during which she performed more than 200 replenishments), 1978 (232 replenishments), 1979, 1980, 1981, 1983–1984 (301 replenishments), 1986, 1990, 1992, 1994, 1996, 1998–1999, and 2003–2004.

On *Detroit*'s 11th Mediterranean deployment, she was immediately sent to the Red Sea following Iraq's August 1990 invasion of Kuwait. Consequently, when Operation Desert Storm kicked off on January 17, 1991, she was one of two AOEs on station and available to support naval units participating in the war.

On her 14th Mediterranean deployment, *Detroit* supported the USS *Theodore Roosevelt* (CVN 71) battle group and operated in the Adriatic Sea, and also supported U.S. Fifth Fleet participation in Operation Southern Watch.

Of course, throughout her service, USS *Detroit* was periodically overhauled and underwent shipyard maintenance and upkeep. In between her voyages to Europe and Africa, for example, she was in the yard in July 1976–July 1977, January 1982–January 1983, July 1993–January 1994, July–November 1997, and November 1999–February 2000.

USS *Detroit* was decommissioned and her name struck from the NVR on February 17, 2005, and she was then laid up at the Naval Inactive Ship Maintenance Facility in Philadelphia, Pennsylvania. Seven months later, ESCO Marine, Inc., was awarded a contract to dismantle the ship. She was transferred to ESCO on October 17, 2005, towed to Brownsville, Texas, and broken up by November 3, 2006. Reportedly, the scrapped materials were shipped to Mexico.

USNS *Supply* (T-AOE 6)

- The lead ship of the AOE 6 class (and the fourth naval vessel of her name) was laid down on February 24, 1989, by National Steel & Shipbuilding Company at San Diego, California.
- Launched on October 6, 1990, and commissioned as USS *Supply* (AOE 6) on February 26, 1994.
- Operated in the Indian Ocean during October and November 1998, and July to September 2000.
- Decommissioned and placed in service with MSC as USNS *Supply* (T-AOE 6) on July 13, 2001. Entered shipyard thereafter for post-transfer work.
- In June 2002 deployed for service with the U.S. Fifth and Sixth Fleets—for the first time with a civilian crew.
- In 2004 deployed to the Mediterranean and then to the Persian Gulf for five months to support Fifth Fleet operations.
- Following Hurricane Katrina in August 2005, *Supply* refueled aircraft carrier USS *Harry S. Truman* (CVN 75) with 1.3 million gallons of jet fuel, so the carrier could support Navy and Army helicopters flying relief missions for victims of the catastrophic storm.

1. Combat Logistics and Fleet Support Ships

Caught by the camera's fisheye lens on November 27, 2006, USNS *Supply* is conducting an UNREP in the Arabian Sea with the unseen amphibious assault ship USS *Saipan* (LHA 2) off her port side and the barely visible guided missile destroyer USS B*enfold* (DDG 65) on her starboard side (U.S. Navy photograph).

- Deployed to the Mediterranean Sea and Persian Gulf in 2006–2007 as part of the USS *Enterprise* (CVN 65) Carrier Strike Group. Took part in 144 UNREPs and delivered more than 28 million gallons of fuel and 6,254 tons of cargo and supplies. Deployed again to those waters in 2008 and 2009.
- During the period 2010–2015 supported the U.S. Second, Fifth and Sixth Fleets at various times while operating in the Atlantic Ocean, the Mediterranean Sea, the Indian Ocean and the Arabian Gulf.
- Completed a major overhaul in 2015–2016, including complete replacement and modernization of the ship's machinery control system.
- In 2016 supported work-up exercises in preparation for a deployment to the Fifth Fleet in the Middle East.
- Current homeport is Naval Weapons Station, Earle, in New Jersey.

USNS *Rainier* (T-AOE 7)

- Laid down at National Steel and Shipbuilding in San Diego on May 31, 1990.
- Name changed during construction from *Paul Hamilton* to *Rainier*.
- Launched on September 28, 1991 and commissioned as USS *Rainier* (AOE 7) on January 21, 1995.

USNS *Rainier* is underway in the western Pacific on December 31, 2004, while operating with Carrier Strike Group 9 (U.S. Navy photograph).

- Decommissioned on August 29, 2003, and placed in service with MSC as USNS *Rainier* (T-AOE 7).
- Participated in Pacific Fleet exercises Northern Edge and RIMPAC in 2004 while serving as combat logistics ship for the aircraft carrier USS *John C. Stennis* (CVN 74) Carrier Strike Group.
- Provided support to various U.S. ships engaged in Operation Unified Assistance following a December 26, 2004, magnitude 9.0 earthquake and tsunami off the west coast of Sumatra in Indonesia. *Rainier* delivered fuel and various materials to 32 ships in the first 20 days of January 2005.
- During the five-month deployment to WestPac in 2004 the T-AOE provided more than 49 million gallons of fuel to the strike group and transferred more than 10 million pounds of food, ammunition, mail and various dry cargo to resupply other ships.
- In Fiscal Year 2005, conducted back-to-back deployments with the USS *John C. Stennis* (CVN 74) and USS *Abraham Lincoln* (CVN 72) Strike Groups, and also participated in an exercise with the Mexican navy.
- During the 2006–2008 period *Rainier* operated off southern California prior to deploying to the U.S. Seventh and Fifth Fleets.
- In 2009 she supported operations of the U.S. Third Fleet in the eastern Pacific and deployed to the Fifth and Seventh Fleets.
- During the 2010–2014 period she worked with the Third, Fourth and Seventh Fleets in the Pacific Ocean.

- In 2015 and 2016 operated with the Third and Seventh Fleets in the Pacific.
- Taken out of service on September 30, 2016 and laid up at the Naval Inactive Ship Maintenance Facility in Bremerton, Washington.

USNS *Arctic* (T-AOE 8)

On July 15, 2015, USNS *Arctic* is in the Arabian Gulf conducting a replenishment at sea with the aircraft carrier USS *Theodore Roosevelt* (CVN 71). A helicopter is delivering some cargo to the carrier (U.S. Navy photograph).

- Built by National Steel & Shipbuilding Company in San Diego, California.
- Laid down on December 2, 1991, and launched on October 30, 1993.
- Commissioned as USS *Arctic* (AOE 8) on September 16, 1995.
- Deployed to Indian Ocean in August–September 1997, July–September 1999 and July–September 2001.
- In September 2001: rescued nine Iranian crewmen in adrift fishing boat and with destroyer USS *Nicholson* (DD 982) towed Iraqi oil smuggler *Al Hassan* hundreds of miles to holding area; on the 8th, rescued distressed Iraqi merchant ship *Muhammad One*; on the 11th, refueled aircraft carrier USS *Enterprise* (CVN 65) and steamed to the northern Arabian Sea following the 9/11 terrorist attacks in the United States.
- On October 7, 2001, replenished *Enterprise*'s fuel supply, enabling the carrier to launch air strikes against terrorist and Taliban targets in Afghanistan.
- Decommissioned on June 14, 2002, and transferred to MSC as USNS *Arctic* (T-AOE 8).

- In February 2003, deployed to the U.S. Fifth and Sixth Fleets for the first time with a crew of civilian mariners.
- Operated primarily in the western Atlantic for most of 2004.
- Deployed with the USS *Harry S. Truman* (CVN 75) Carrier Strike Group to the Persian Gulf in October 2004 and performed 118 UNREPs between then and March 2005.
- Served in the Mediterranean Sea and Persian Gulf in the first half of 2005 and later assisted in humanitarian and disaster relief operations in the Gulf of Mexico following Hurricane Katrina in August.
- In Fiscal Years 2006–2008 operated in the Mediterranean Sea and Persian Gulf.
- While replenishing the aircraft carrier USS *Harry S. Truman* (CVN 75) on December 23, 2007, *Arctic* rescued seven mariners from a drifting raft.
- Supported U.S. Second Fleet vessels in the Atlantic Ocean during 2009–2011.
- During the period 2014–2016 T-AOE 8 supported Task Force 80 in the Atlantic.
- Late in 2016, *Arctic* supported the USS *Dwight D. Eisenhower* (CVN 69) Carrier Strike Group participating in Operation Inherent Resolve in the Fifth Fleet area of operations (Arabian Gulf).
- On March 23, 2017, performed underway replenishments in the western Atlantic with cruisers USS *San Jacinto* (CG 56) and USS *Monterey* (CG 61), destroyer USS *Bainbridge* (DDG 96) and amphibious transport dock USS *Arlington* (LPD 24), and on that same day, performed three training System Qualification Trials for feet replenishment oiler [q.v.] USNS *Laramie* (T-AO 203). In under 24 hours, *Arctic* delivered 677,000 gallons of fuel to the warships.
- Current Homeport is Naval Weapons Station, Earle, in New Jersey.

USNS *Bridge* (T-AOE 10)

The last of the Supply-class AOEs was built, like the others, by National Steel and Shipbuilding Company. Laid down on August 2, 1994, and launched on August 24, 1996, USS *Bridge* (AOE 10) was commissioned on August 5, 1998.

Also like her sister ships, *Bridge* was always on the go. She operated in the western Pacific, Indian Ocean and Arabian Gulf during the first half of 2000, and supported Operation Enduring Freedom in WestPac, the Indian Ocean, Arabian Sea and off the Horn of Africa between November 2001 and May 2002. Among her many customers were the aircraft carriers USS *John C. Stennis* (CVN 74) and USS *John F. Kennedy* (CV 67), and the amphibious assault ships USS *Bataan* (LHD 5), USS *Bonhomme Richard* (LHD 6) and USS *Peleliu* (LHA 5), along with their escorts as well as allied vessels from Australia, Canada, France, Italy, Japan and Spain.

AOE 10 got underway on her last voyage as a commissioned U.S. Navy vessel on February 24, 2004. She spent the next four days completing a Ship's Material Assessment and Readiness Test (the MSC version of the Navy's Board of Inspection and Survey) and offloading all of her ammunition at the Naval Magazine Indian Island in Washington State. Those evolutions were required before the ship could be turned over to the Military Sealift Command. USS *Bridge* was decommissioned, and transferred to MSC as USNS *Bridge* (T-AOE 10) on June 24, 2004. Her Navy complement of 544 officers and enlisted

1. Combat Logistics and Fleet Support Ships

USNS *Bridge* is replenishing the aircraft carrier USS *Nimitz* (CVN 68) on December 9, 2006. The carrier is in the eastern Pacific off the coast of California conducting a training exercise (U.S. Navy photograph).

sailors was replaced by a civilian crew of 160 civil service mariners and a small contingent of 28 Navy personnel. (An additional group of some 50 Navy personnel would augment the crew when necessary to support helicopter operations.) Following the transfer, the ship spent the remainder of the year in a shipyard to be modified for operation by her civilian crew.

During the period 2005–2009, *Bridge* supported the U.S. Third Fleet and conducted operations in the southern California operating area prior to deploying to the U.S. Seventh and Fifth Fleets in the Pacific Ocean, Indian Ocean and Arabian Gulf in Fiscal Year 2009. She continued in that role right through Fiscal Year 2013. In just one snapshot of her service at that time, *Bridge* operated with the aircraft carrier USS *Nimitz* (CVN 68) on August 14, 2009, and on that day transferred more than 1 million gallons of aviation fuel and 42 tons of ammunition to the carrier.

Following the March 11, 2011, earthquake and tsunami off the Tohoku region of Honshu, Japan, *Bridge* was diverted from a cruise to South Korea and sent instead to the stricken area, arriving there on March 13. The ship's embarked MH-60S Seahawk helicopters then delivered more than 30,000 pounds of relief supplies ashore. During Operation Tomodachi ("Friend"), she replenished multiple ships, with, at times, two vessels concurrently alongside both her starboard and port sides and another two in tow.

USNS *Bridge* spent 2014 in reduced operating status and was taken out of service on September 30, 2014. She was then inactivated and laid up in the Naval Inactive Ship Maintenance Facility in Bremerton, Washington.

Notes

1. See *Conecuh* (AO 110) history in oiler section above.
2. Planned for the Fiscal Year 1968 shipbuilding program but cancelled on November 4, 1968.
3. Inactivated on September 30, 2016, and laid up in Bremerton, Washington.
4. Authorized in Fiscal Year 1992 to be named *Conecuh* but construction deferred. Vessel instead was reauthorized in Fiscal Year 1993 and built as *Bridge* (AOE 10).
5. Inactivated on September 30, 2014, and laid up in Bremerton.

Salvage Ships / Rescue and Salvage Ships (ARS / T-ARS)[1]

The salvage ship USS *Deliver* (ARS 23), a veteran of World War II, the Korean War and the Vietnam War, is underway off Oahu, Hawaii, on October 18, 1978 (U.S. Navy photograph).

Naval salvage ships extract grounded or beached vessels from their predicament, lift heavy loads from the ocean depths, tow vessels, and serve as platforms for manned diving operations. When operating in a rescue role, they can deliver foam or sea water to fight fires aboard other vessels, or employ various pieces of equipment to provide electrical power, patch holes, and pump out water in disabled vessels.

The Navy's earliest salvage ships were acquired during World War I when some ten civilian merchant vessels were brought into temporary naval service and commissioned between September 1917 and August 1919 (see Roster below). All ten were decommissioned in 1919.

The first ships to be formally designated as salvage vessels were seven former World War I minesweepers, first commissioned in 1919 and later reclassified as salvage ships (ARS) of the Viking class between June 1941 and September 1942 for service in World War II. (They retained their "Bird" minesweeper names after their reclassification.)

By the end of the war, the Navy had 49 salvage vessels listed on the Vessel Register, excluding two that were lost during the conflict and including six that had been intended for the Royal Navy but were retained for U.S. service (see BARS Roster listing below). Additionally, ARS 44–ARS 49 had been cancelled in 1945. Most of the ARS ships were discarded after World War II, either sold to civilian purchasers or more often, to ship breakers for scrapping. Seven were transferred to other navies (ARS 23 and ARS 24 to South Korea, ARS 7 and ARS 43 to Taiwan, ARS 3 to Venezuela, ARS 17 to Denmark, and ARS 25 to Turkey). Despite this wholesale housecleaning, the Navy still had 13 ARS vessels in active service during the Vietnam War era, with one other laid up in the NDRF and five others sent to other organizations.

At the beginning of the 1980s, there were only six active salvage ships left in the fleet, with another two assigned to the Naval Reserve Force and one laid up in mothballs. In the mid-1980s, the Navy acquired four new Safeguard (ARS 50)-class salvage ships and this quartet eventually replaced the surviving members of the Escape (ARS 6) class and Bolster (ARS 38) class. Although the Safeguard-class vessels began their service in 1985–1986 as commissioned ships (designated as ARS 50–ARS 53) manned by Navy personnel, they were transferred to the Military Sealift Command in 2006–2007, redesignated as T-ARS 50–T-ARS 53, and operated by civilian crews. Two of the four—USNS *Safeguard* and USNS *Grapple*—were inactivated in 2016, leaving the Navy today with only USNS *Grasp* and USNS *Salvor* in active service.

Aside from the former minesweepers, salvage ships have been given names evocative of diving and salvage activities.

World War I Salvage Vessel Roster

Biesbosch
Chesapeake
Favorite
I. J. Merritt

Manna Hata
Relief
Rescue
Resolute

San Juan
Tasco

BARS Roster

The following vessels were built in the United States originally intended for service in the Royal Navy and assigned the U.S. designation of BARS. Six of these ships, however, actually served with the U.S. Navy and are noted in the listing below with their USN ARS hull number in parentheses.

BARS 1	*Caledonian Salvor*	BARS 5	*American Salvor*
BARS 2	*Cambrian Salvor*	BARS 6	*Boston Salvor*
BARS 3	*Atlantic Salvor* (ARS 33)	BARS 7	*Plymouth Salvor* (ARS 35)
BARS 4	*Pacific Salvor* (ARS 34)	BARS 8	*York Salvor* (ARS 36)

BARS 9	Lincoln Salvor	BARS 11	Quebec Salvor (ARS 28)
BARS 10	Southampton Salvor	BARS 12	Queen Salvor (ARS 29)

ARS Roster

ARS 1	Viking[2] [SS]	ARS 26	Seize[11] [SX]
ARS 2	Crusader[3] [S]	ARS 27	Snatch[12] [C/SS]
ARS 3	Discoverer[4] [T]	ARS 28	Valve[13] [SC]
ARS 4	Redwing[5] [Z]	ARS 29	Vent[14] [SC]
ARS 5	Diver [SC]	ARS 30	Accelerate [SC]
ARS 6	Escape [SS]	ARS 31	Harjurand [SC]
ARS 7	Grapple [T]	ARS 32	Brant[15] [D]
ARS 8	Preserver [SS]	ARS 33	Clamp[16] [SS/X]
ARS 9	Shackle [S]	ARS 34	Gear[17] [SS]
ARS 10	Assistance[6]	ARS 35	Weight[18] [SC]
ARS 11	Warbler[7] [S]	ARS 36	Swivel[19] [SS]
ARS 12	Willett[8] [SS]	ARS 37	Tackle[20] [C/K]
ARS 13	Anchor [SC]	ARS 38	Bolster [SS]
ARS 14	Protector [SC]	ARS 39	Conserver [SX]
ARS 15	Extractor [Z]	ARS 40	Hoist [SS]
ARS 16	Extricate[9] [Z]	ARS 41	Opportune [SS]
ARS 17	Restorer [T]	ARS 42	Reclaimer [SS]
ARS 18	Rescuer [Z]	ARS 43	Recovery [T]
ARS 19	Cable [SX]	ARS 44	Retriever [X]
ARS 20	Chain[10] [C/SS]	ARS 45	Skillful [X]
ARS 21	Curb [Z]	ARS 46	Support [X]
ARS 22	Current [SS]	ARS 47	Toiler [X]
ARS 23	Deliver [T]	ARS 48	Urgent [X]
ARS 24	Grasp [T]	ARS 49	Willing [X]
ARS 25	Safeguard [T]		

Current T-ARS Roster

T-ARS 50	Safeguard [L]	T-ARS 52	Salvor [A]
T-ARS 51	Grasp [A]	T-ARS 53	Grapple [L]

SELECTED SPECIFICATIONS

Viking class: ARS1–ARS 3, ARS 11, ARS 12 & ARS 32

Length: 188 feet
Beam: 36.5 feet
Draft: 14 feet
Displacement: 1,350 tons (full load)
Propulsion: triple expansion engine; 1,400 shp, 1 shaft
Speed: 12.4 knots
Personnel: 72

Diver class: ARS 5–ARS 9, ARS 19–ARS 27, ARS 32–ARS 34 & ARS 38–ARS 49

Length: 213.5 feet
Beam: 39 feet
Draft: 15 feet

Displacement: 1,950 tons (full load)
Propulsion: 4 diesel-electric engines; 3,000 shp; 2 shafts
Speed: 13 knots (maximum)
Personnel: 120

Anchor class: ARS 13–ARS 17, ARS 28–ARS 29 & ARS 35–ARS 36

Length: 183 feet
Beam: 36 feet
Draft: 13 feet
Displacement: 1,425 tons (full load)
Propulsion: four diesel-electric engines; 1,200 shp; 2 shafts
Speed: 12 knots
Personnel: 65

Safeguard class: T-ARS 50—T-ARS 53

Length: 255 feet
Beam: 50 feet
Draft: 16.6 feet
Displacement: 3,336 tons
Propulsion: 4 Caterpillar 399 diesel engines; 4,200 bhp; 2 shafts
Speed: 14 knots
Personnel: 26 civilians and 4 Navy (with a maximum of 48 additional)

SELECTED HISTORIES

USS *Manna Hata* (SP-3396)

USS *Manna Hata* is in the New York Navy Yard on April 2, 1919, shortly after her commissioning (U.S. Navy photograph).

Built in 1900 by Harlan & Hollingsworth of Wilmington, Delaware, SS *Manna Hata* was owned by the New York & Baltimore Transportation Company. She was acquired by the Navy on September 7, 1918, and converted into a salvage ship. USS *Manna Hata* was commissioned on March 22, 1919.

A month after her commissioning, the ship joined the First Salvage Division in Europe. In August 1919 she participated in the mine clearing operation in the North Sea, generally ferrying sweeping equipment and materials from Best, France, and Liverpool, England, out to Kirkwall in the Orkney Islands, locus of the minesweeping effort.

Manna Hata was decommissioned on October 25, 1919, after just seven months of service and sold to Maritime Salvors, Ltd., in London. The new owner renamed the vessel *Reliant*. Sold for a second time in 1925 to a purchaser in the United States, SS *Reliant* sank 400 miles off Iceland on May 29, 1925, as she was in transit from England to New York.

USS *Viking* (ARS 1)

USS *Viking* (ARS 1) was the first naval vessel formally classified as a salvage ship. Seen here off San Diego, California, on November 2, 1951, she was being operated by the Merritt, Chapman and Scott salvage firm under a Navy contract (U.S. Navy photograph).

The Navy's first designated salvage ship began life as a World War I minesweeper and later operated as an oceanographic survey ship by the U.S. Coast and Geodetic Survey (USC&GS) decades before she actually became a salvage ship in World War II.

Built by the New Jersey Drydock and Transportation Company in Elizabethport, New Jersey, the minesweeper *Flamingo* was laid down on October 18, 1917, and launched on August 24, 1918. USS *Flamingo* was commissioned on February 12, 1919, and designated as Minesweeper No. 32.

She left the United States on May 18, 1919, on a deployment to Kirkwall, Scotland, for duty with the U.S. Minesweeping Detachment in the North Sea. After arriving on site on June 5, *Flamingo* began three months of mine clearing operations. She also occasionally doubled as a tug boat and transport vessel.

On July 16, 1919, a mine exploded under her stern, requiring a few weeks of dry docking and repairs in Invergordon, Scotland. She completed her North Sea minesweeping duties on October 1, 1919, and after several stops in Europe, returned to the United States on November 20, 1919.

Flamingo underwent an overhaul in Portsmouth, New Hampshire, in the winter of 1919–1920, and was assigned to the Atlantic Fleet's 1st Division of the 2nd Mine Squadron on July 1, 1920. Seventeen days later she was formally classified as AM 32 in the Navy's new ship classification system. During the summer and autumn of 1920, AM 32 operated with the 2nd Mine Squadron but was laid up in reserve in the Portsmouth Navy Yard on November 18, 1920.

On March 25, 1922, the Navy was ordered to transfer *Flamingo* to the U.S. Commerce Department. Thus, she was decommissioned on May 5, 1922, and handed over to the USC&GS in Portsmouth on January 23, 1923. She was renamed *Guide* by her new operators, and converted and fitted out as a survey ship. Sent to a new homeport of San Diego, California, *Guide* transited the Panama Canal on December 8, 1923, collecting oceanographic data while en route. She spent the next 17 years surveying off the West Coast of the United States.

In the months leading up to the U.S. entry into World War II, the former minesweeper was called back to naval service. On June 27, 1941, *Guide* was transferred from the Coast & Geodetic Survey to the Navy to be converted into a salvage ship. The San Diego Marine Construction Company began the conversion work on July 25. On August 5 the Navy renamed the ship *Viking* and designated her as ARS 1. She was placed in service (not formally commissioned) on January 3, 1942, and determined to be ready for her new role on February 12.

The Navy's Bureau of Ships contracted with the salvage firm of Merritt, Chapman and Scott to operate *Viking* and perform salvage and rescue work in the 11th Naval District (southern California). She generally spent the World War II and immediate post-war years operating out of San Diego and San Pedro, California, performing salvage operations in the eastern Pacific. For example, in early July 1942, *Viking* towed two patrol craft—YP 267 and YP 269—back to port after their grounding. On New Year's Eve of 1944, she and the fleet tug [q.v.] USS *Tenino* (ATF 115) and salvage ship *Seize* (ARS 26) helped to free the grounded LST 563 on Clipperton Island off the Pacific coast of Central America. In December 1949, *Viking* assisted the grounded steamer SS *Aristocratus* off Santa Rosa Island, California.

After being relieved by USS *Gear* (ARS 34) as the 11th Naval District salvage vessel, *Viking* was returned to the Navy by her civilian operators, "placed out of service and decommissioned," and authorized for disposal on March 17, 1953. Her name was struck from the Vessel Register on April 19 of that year and she was sold on July 22, 1953, to Nathan Cohen and Sons, Inc., of Los Angeles, California. *Viking* was subsequently broken up and scrapped.

USS *Grapple* (ARS 7)

USS *Grapple* was one of the first purpose-built salvage ships with service in three wars: World War II, Korea and Vietnam. The Diver-class vessel was launched on December 31, 1942, by Basalt Rock Company, Inc., in Napa, California, and commissioned a year later on December 16.

Operating with the U.S. Pacific Fleet, *Grapple* was attacked by Japanese dive bombers on June 15, 1944; pulled stranded landing craft off the beach and repaired damaged ships during the July 1945 amphibious assault at Guam; assisted the mine-damaged destroyer USS *Wadleigh* (DD 689) at Peleliu in September; salvaged the abandoned Liberty ship SS *William Sharon* in the Mindanao Gulf in December 1944; and fought fires aboard the aircraft carrier USS *Randolph* (CV 15), which had been struck by kamikazes at Ulithi on March 11, 1945. *Grapple* returned home on May 15, 1945, and was decommissioned on August 30, 1945, and laid up in the San Diego group of the Pacific Reserve Fleet.

After North Korea attacked South Korea in June 1950, *Grapple* was taken out of mothballs and recommissioned on December 26, 1951. By mid–May 1952 she was off the Korean coast. Anchored near Wonsan on August 12, *Grapple* was hit just below the water line by an unexploded shell fired by shore batteries. Her expert damage control personnel removed the projectile and patched up the six- by 15-foot hole. Three days later she was hit again, this time in error by friendly fire from the minesweeper USS *Chief* (AM 315), which killed two and wounded 11 men of her ship's company.

Following the Korean conflict and an overhaul in Seattle, *Grapple* performed a variety of duties in the Pacific in the mid–1950s, carried supplies up to the Arctic Circle, and trained Korean and Taiwanese divers in salvage techniques. In April 1954 she helped to widen the harbor entrance of Johnston Island by blasting the coral reef, assisted Hilo, Hawaii, after a damaging tidal wave in May 1960, and helped free the grounded destroyer USS *Frank Knox* (DDR 742) off a reef in the South China Sea in August 1964.

Grapple served during the Vietnam War between December 1968 and March 1971. She was struck on December 1, 1977, and sold that same day to Taiwan. That navy renamed her ROCS *Ta Hu* (ARS 552), and at last report, she remains active in that service today.

Grapple earned one battle star for her World War II service and one for Korean War service.

USS *Extricate* (ARS 16)

- Anchor-class salvage ship built by Snow Shipyards, Inc.
- Launched on September 12, 1942, and commissioned on July 27, 1943.
- Served as firefighting ship at Naples, Italy, in October-November 1943; saved the burning SS *Iredell* which was carrying a cargo of aviation gas.
- Raised two ships, beached a third, and extracted three grounded barges off the beach at Bari, Italy.
- Redeployed to the Pacific Theater in 1945.
- During a typhoon at Okinawa on October 9, 1945, *Extricate* was beached and flooded, and then abandoned.

1. Combat Logistics and Fleet Support Ships

- Decommissioned on December 5, 1945, and intentionally destroyed by explosives on March 4, 1946.
- *Extricate* earned two battle stars for her World War II service.

USS *Hoist* (ARS 40)

- Bolster-class salvage ship built by Basalt Rock Company, Inc., of Napa, California.
- Launched March 31, 1945, and commissioned on July 21, 1945.
- Conducted salvage and repair operations in Okinawa and Japan between October 1945 and March 1946.
- Trained students at a naval salvage training facility in Bayonne, New Jersey, in early 1947.
- Performed salvage operations along the U.S. East Coast and Gulf of Mexico between March 1947 and December 1948.
- Repaired an underwater pipe line in the Azores early in 1949.
- Assisted the coastal surveying ship [q.v.] USS *Simon Newcomb* (AGSC 14) aground in Mother Burns Cove in Labrador in August 1949.
- Continued salvage and repair duties, as well as towing operations, in North Atlantic, Caribbean and off Florida through 1964.
- Between May 29 and August 25, 1964, operated with the bathyscaphe *Trieste II* at the site of the lost nuclear attack submarine USS *Thresher* (SSN 593).
- In a two-day operation along with the fleet tug [q.v.] USS *Seneca* (ATF 92) and salvage lifting vessel [q.v.] *Windlass* (ARSD 1), *Hoist* freed grounded stores ship [q.v.] USNS *Blue Jacket* (T-AF 51) which had run aground on March 2, 1965.
- In a three-week operation along with USS *Recovery* (ARS 43), salvaged the sunken medium auxiliary repair dock [q.v.] *Alamogordo* (ARDM 2) in November 1965.
- In February–April 1966 participated in the successful recovery of a lost H-bomb at Palomares, Spain. The unarmed bomb was dropped from an Air Force B-52 Stratofortress bomber which had collided with a KC-135 Stratotanker aircraft.
- Decommissioned and struck on September 30, 1994.
- Transferred to MARAD on November 29, 2001 and laid up in the James River Group of the NDRF.
- Sold initially for $61,000 on July 17, 2007 to North American Ship Recycling to be dismantled. The scrapping contract was re-issued on November 30, 2007, to Bay Bridge Enterprises of Chesapeake, Virginia, for $95,000. *Hoist* was towed from Baltimore to Chesapeake the next day to be cut up.

USNS *Safeguard* (T-ARS 50)

- Safeguard-class salvage ship built by Peterson Builders, Inc., in Sturgeon Bay, Wisconsin.
- Laid down on November 8, 1982, and launched on November 12, 1983.
- Commissioned as USS *Safeguard* (ARS 50) on August 17, 1985.
- Decommissioned in Sasebo, Japan, on September 26, 2007, and placed in service with MSC as USNS *Safeguard* (T-ARS 50).
- In early February 2008 launched six surface-to-air drone missiles as targets for Marine Corps F/A-18 Hornet aircraft about 100 miles off Okinawa.

- In early March 2008 *Safeguard* located the wreckage of a Navy EA-6B Prowler aircraft in more than 8,000 feet of water off the northeastern coast of Guam. The aircraft's crew had ejected safely prior to the crash.
- Ship's divers conducted bilateral dive exercises with Indian and Bangladeshi navies in October and November 2008.
- Raised the partially submerged Filipino patrol boat BRP *Tomas Batilo* (PG-110) in May 2009. The boat had sunk during a 2003 typhoon.
- Between August 27 and September 12, 2009, underwent minor repairs at the Saigon Marin Shipyard in Ho Chi Minh City, Vietnam—the first MSC ship to have used a Vietnamese shipyard since the Vietnam War.
- In November 2009 continued clearing the Saipan Channel of massive rocks and dead coral formations. The ship had previously performed that job in February 2008 and January 2009, having removed, crushed or degraded 29 obstructions from the channel (the largest of which weighed more than 100,000 pounds).
- Joined with 18 navies in an international submarine search and rescue exercise held in the South China Sea in August 2010. *Safeguard* served as the Navy's primary surface support ship, which was conducted some 180 miles off Malaysia's eastern coast.
- Participated in Cooperation Afloat Readiness and Training (CARAT) 2010, a five-month bilateral training exercise from May to October 2010 involving the navies of Brunei, Thailand, Indonesia, Malaysia, Philippines, Singapore, Cambodia and Bangladesh.
- Served in Operation Tomadachi ("Friend") between March and May 2011 to provide humanitarian relief to victims of magnitude 9.0 earthquake and tsunami off the Tohokuo region of Honshu, Japan.
- Visited Da Nang, Vietnam, in July 2011.
- Participated in CARAT 2012 in a week-long bilateral training exercise with the Bangladeshi navy in September, 2012.
- As part of Task Group 73.1 in June 2013 took part in Exercise CARAT 2013 involving nine Southeast Asia nations.
- Collaborated on a survey of the wreckage of the lost heavy cruiser USS *Houston* (CA 30) in June 2014. The cruiser had been torpedoed and sunk during the Battle of Sunda Strait on March 1, 1942. *Safeguard* divers were assisted by Indonesian naval personnel as part of CARAT 2014.
- Taken out of service and inactivated on October 1, 2016.
- Currently laid up at the Naval Inactive Ship Maintenance Facility in Pearl Harbor, Hawaii.

USNS *Grasp* (T-ARS 51)

- Safeguard-class salvage ship built by Peterson Builders, Inc., in Sturgeon Bay, Wisconsin.
- Laid down on March 30, 1983, and launched on May 2, 1985.
- Commissioned as USS *Grasp* (ARS 51) on December 14, 1985.
- Assisted in the tow of the battleship USS *Wisconsin* (BB 64) to Ingalls Shipbuilding in Pascagoula, Mississippi.

- Between April and October 1987 deployed with the U.S. Sixth Fleet in the Mediterranean Sea.
- In March-April 1988 performed salvage and recovery of a crashed U.S. Air Force F-16 Fighting Falcon fighter aircraft near Fort Myers, Florida.
- Along with the fleet tug [q.v.] USNS *Mohawk* (T-ATF 170) in January and February 1989, *Grasp* refloated the destroyer USS *Spruance* (DD 963) grounded east of St. Andros Island in the Bahamas and towed her to Pascagoula.
- Between April and October 1989 deployed to the Mediterranean for the second time and conducted mine clearing exercises, port visits and contingency operations off Lebanon.
- Located and salvaged the wreckage of an SH-2E Seasprite helicopter in May 1990. The aircraft had crashed off Mayport, Florida.
- Later that month and into July located and salvaged the wreckage of an S-3B Viking antisubmarine aircraft sunk in 10,430 feet of water off the Virginia Capes. *Grasp* employed the Orion deep ocean search system and the CURV III remote operating vehicle in the mission.
- Between August 1991 and February 1992 deployed to the Sixth Fleet for the third time.
- Performed various tows and salvages between May 1992 and November 1993.
- Deployed to the Mediterranean for the fourth time between February and August 1994.
- Participated in Operation Uphold Democracy in Haiti in September 1994.
- Made her fifth Mediterranean deployment between February and July 1996.
- Assisted in salvaging the wreckage, including the flight data recorders, of lost TWA flight 800—a Boeing 747-100—off Long Island, New York, in July and August 1996.
- In March 1997 recovered a lost HH-60 Seahawk helicopter at a depth of 350 feet off Cape Hatteras.
- Performed various towing and recovery operations between May and September 1997.
- Between January and July 1998 operated in the Mediterranean and conducted diving-related exercises with various navies.
- Simultaneously towed two decommissioned submarines—*Phoenix* (SSN 702) and *Baltimore* (SSN 704) in April 1999 from Boston to and through the Panama Canal.
- In June 1999 assisted in site surveys of the lost Civil War warship USS *Monitor*.
- Conducted search and recovery operations near Martha's Vineyard, Massachusetts, in July 1999 for the crashed Piper 32 aircraft flown by John F. Kennedy, Jr.
- Following an overhaul early in 2000, deployed to the Sixth Fleet between March and September 2000.
- Performed a number of tows and three aircraft search and recovery operations between March 2001 and June 2002.
- Supported Operation Iraqi Freedom during an eighth Mediterranean deployment between October 2002 and May 2003.
- Underwent a shipyard overhaul in Norfolk, Virginia, in June–October 2003.

- Decommissioned on January 19, 2006, and placed in service with MSC as USNS *Grasp* (T-ARS 51).
- In March 2008 recovered two Air Force F-15C Eagle fighters from a depth of about 180 feet 50 miles off Florida in the Gulf of Mexico.
- Completed a three-month, seven-nation international outreach and maritime security mission in the Caribbean Sea in the summer of 2008.
- In December 2008 towed the Navy's nuclear-powered deep submergence submarine NR-1 on her last voyage.
- As part of Task Force 42, supported Operation Unified Response between January and March 2010 to provide recovery assistance to Haiti following a devastating magnitude 7.0 earthquake on January 12.
- Performed a survey mission with the oceanographic survey ship [q.v.] USNS *Henson* (T-AGS 63) in the summer of 2011 to locate the wreckage of John Paul Jones's *Bonhomme Richard*, lost in battle in the North Sea on September 25, 1779.
- During a Sixth Fleet deployment in 2012, *Grasp* participated in Exercise Sea Breeze in the Black Sea with the Ukrainian Navy.
- Salvaged a downed Air Force F-16C Fighting Falcon aircraft off the coast of Virginia in August 2013.
- Conducted dive training with Mobile Diving and Salvage Unit 2 in 185 feet of water off Key West, Florida, in January 2015.
- Completed a four-month deployment to the Sixth Fleet in the Mediterranean in November 2017.
- Currently assigned to the MSC Service Support (PM4) force and homeported in Little Creek, Virginia.

USNS *Salvor* (T-ARS 52)

On April 11, 2010, USNS *Salvor* (T-ARS 52) is assisting in the search, recovery and salvage of a sunken South Korean patrol vessel (U.S. Navy photograph).

1. Combat Logistics and Fleet Support Ships 85

- Safeguard-class salvage ship built by Peterson Builders, Inc., in Sturgeon Bay, Wisconsin.
- Laid down on September 16, 1983, and launched on December 8, 1984.
- Commissioned as USS *Salvor* (ARS 52) on November 15, 1986.
- Deployed to the western Pacific during September–December 1987, January–July 1991, August–December 1996, and March–September 1998.
- Deployed to South Pacific June–August 1989.
- Deployed to and operated in the eastern Pacific during March–May 1992, September-October 1992, January–March 1994, April 1999, June-July 1995, March 1999–January 2000, and March–August 2000.
- Provided rescue or aided ships at sea in seven incidents between 1987 and 2001.
- Performed 23 towing operations between November 1987 and January 2003.
- Between January 13 and February 26, 2003, recovered nearly two million gallons of fuel oil from the wreck of the oiler [q.v.] USS *Mississinewa* (AO 59) sunk by a Japanese torpedo at Ulithi on November 20, 1944.
- During Exercise CARAT 2006 drivers from *Salvor* identified the wreckage of the lost submarine USS *Lagarto* (SS 371), sunk in battle on May 3, 1945, in the Gulf of Siam off Thailand. The salvage ship returned home to Pearl Harbor on October 2, 2006, after a five-month deployment to Southeast Asia in support of the exercise.
- Decommissioned and placed in service with MSC as USNS *Salvor* (T-ARS 52) on January 12, 2007.
- Conducted towing operations during Exercise RIMPAC 2008.
- Successfully freed the grounded guided missile cruiser USS *Port Royal* (CG 73) on February 9, 2009, three days after she had grounded on a rock and sand shoal off Honolulu, Hawaii.
- Assisted the South Korean Navy in the search, recovery and salvage of the patrol vessel ROKS *Cheonan* (PCC-772) in March and April 2010.
- During RIMPAC 2012 *Salvor* delivered three inactivated MSC ships—combat stores ships [q.v.] *Niagara Falls* (T-AFS 3) and *Concord* (T-AFS 5), and ammunition ship [q.v.] *Kilauea* (T-AE 26)—to be expended as SINKEX targets off Hawaii in July 2012. She also towed the former command ship [q.v.] USS *Coronado* (AGF 11) from Pearl Harbor to Guam in August for use as a target during Exercise Valiant Shield 2012.
- In November and December 2012 searched for long-missing World War II U.S. aircraft from in the waters off Papua New Guinea.
- Towed the former frigate USS *Thatch* (FFG 43) and Canadian Navy oiler HMCS *Protecteur* (AOR 509) in the spring of 2014.
- Conducted recovery tests of the NASA Orion spacecraft crew module in September and December 2014.
- In September 2017 recovered sunken wreckage of a Marine Corps MV-22B Osprey aircraft from a depth of 165 feet off Queensland, Australia.
- Visited Cam Ranh International Port in Vietnam and practiced various evolutions and procedures with Vietnamese naval personnel in July 2017.
- Served as the platform for the February 2018 recovery of a World War II pilot's

remains near Ngerekebesang Island, Republic of Palau. His aircraft had been shot down in 1944.
- Currently assigned to the MSC Service Support (PM4) force and homeported in Pearl Harbor, Hawaii.

USNS *Grapple* (T-ARS 53)

Seen anchored on June 7, 2012, USNS *Grapple* (T-ARS 53) is nearing the end of a four-month deployment to the U.S. Southern Command during which she participated in exercises with five Latin American nations (U.S. Navy photograph).

- Safeguard-class salvage ship built by Peterson Builders, Inc., in Sturgeon Bay, Wisconsin.
- Laid down on April 25, 1984, and launched on December 8, 1984.
- Commissioned as USS *Grapple* (ARS 53) on November 15, 1986.
- Deployed to the Mediterranean Sea February–August 1990, August 1991–February 1992, March–September 2000, and October 2002–May 2003.
- Deployed to the Mediterranean and Red Seas September 1987–March 1988 and February–August 1994.
- Deployed to the Mediterranean and Black Seas February–July 1996 and January–July 1998.
- Deployed to the Mediterranean and Adriatic Seas April–October 2005.
- Operated in the North Atlantic between August and November 1988.
- In 1988 and 1989 towed several decommissioned submarines and guided missile destroyers.

1. Combat Logistics and Fleet Support Ships 87

- Decommissioned and placed in service with MSC as USNS *Grapple* (T-ARS 53) on July 13, 2006.
- In April 2008 towed the decommissioned nuclear submarine USS *Hyman G. Rickover* (SSN 709) from Kittery, Maine, to and through the Panama Canal, where the fleet ocean tug [q.v.] USNS *Sioux* (T-ATF 171) assumed the tow.
- On July 9, 2009, retrieved three pieces weighing 25 tons of a NASA rocket from the bottom of the Atlantic off Virginia. The rocket had been launched to test the Max Launch Abort System (MLAS), which enables an emergency escape from a spacecraft during the first minutes after liftoff.
- Assisted Lebanese armed forces personnel in January 2010 performing recovery operations for Ethiopian Airlines Flight 409—a Boeing 737—that crashed off the coast of Lebanon on January 25.
- In March 2010 recovered the wreckage of a Marine Corps F/A-18 Hornet fighter from 100 feet under the Atlantic 30 miles east of Beaufort, South Carolina.
- In August 2010 removed seven sunken Albanian Coast Guard patrol boats from pier side in Saranda, Albania.
- Completed a five-month deployment to the U.S. Sixth Fleet area of responsibility in September 2010.
- Between November 2012 and January 2013 conducted training operations with various allied and partner nations in the U.S. Africa Command area of responsibility.
- Searched offshore of Longue-Pointe-de-Mingan, Quebec, in July 2012 for the remains of five Americans lost when their Navy PBY-5A Catalina patrol aircraft crashed in November 1942.
- In February 2013 recovered the wreckage of a lost Air Force F-16 Fighting Falcon fighter that crashed in the Adriatic Sea off the coast of Italy.
- Deployed to Africa in February 2016.
- Taken out of service on October 1, 2016, and laid up at the Naval Inactive Ship Maintenance facility in Philadelphia, Pennsylvania.

Notes

1. "Salvage ship" is the current nomenclature of the ARS hull classification as listed in the Secretary of the Navy's General Guidance for the Classification of Naval Vessels and Battle Force Counting Procedures (SECNAV Instruction 5030.8C) of June 14, 2016. The Military Sealift Command refers to these vessels as "rescue and salvage ships."
2. Originally minesweeper *Flamingo* (AM 32). See *Viking* Selected History for details.
3. Originally minesweeper *Osprey* (AM 29).
4. Originally minesweeper *Auk* (AM 38).
5. Commissioned as USS *Redwing* (Minesweeper No. 48) in October 1919, designated as AM 48 in July 1920, decommissioned in April 1922, transferred to USCG in May 1924, commissioned as USCG *Redwing* (WAT 48) in October 1924, returned to Navy in August 1941 and converted to salvage ship, recommissioned as USS *Redwing* (ARS 4) in October 1941, lost off Bizerte, Tunisia, from a mine explosion on June 29, 1943, and struck on August 19, 1943.
6. Not acquired by Navy.
7. Originally minesweeper AM 53 AM 54, respectively.
8. *Ibid.*
9. Lost in a typhoon in 1945. See USS *Extricate* (ARS 16) Selected History for details.
10. Reclassified as an oceanographic research ship [q.v.] in April 1967 and assigned to MSTS as USNS *Chain* (T-AGOR 17).
11. Transferred to USCG in June 1946 and commissioned as USCGC *Yocona* (WAT 168), struck in November 1946, reclassified as medium endurance cutter (WMEC 168) in 1965, decommissioned in May 1968 and returned to USN, and was expended as a target on June 20, 2006.
12. Reclassified as oceanographic research ship (T-AGOR 17) in 1967.
13. Authorized as *Quebec Salvor* (BARS 11) but commissioned as ARS 28 in February 1944.

14. Authorized as *Queen Salvor* (BARS 12) but commissioned as ARS 29 in April 1944.
15. Originally minesweeper AM 24 and fleet tug [q.v.] AT 132, and reclassified as ARS 32 in September 1942.
16. Was to have been *Atlantic Salvor* (BARS 3) but commissioned as ARS 33 in August 1943.
17. Was to have been *Pacific Salvor* (BARS 4) but commissioned as ARS 34 in September 1943.
18. Was to have been *Plymouth Salvor* (BARS 7) but commissioned as ARS 35 in August 1943.
19. Was to have been *York Salvor* (BARS 8) but commissioned as ARS 36 in October 1943.
20. Reclassified as salvage craft tender [q.v.] ARST 4 and unclassified miscellaneous vessel IX 217 in February 1945.

Submarine Tenders (AS)

Photographed in Baltimore on June 30, 1941, a month after her conversion to a submarine tender and commissioning, USS *Antaeus* (AS 21) is wearing three-tone camouflage. She was converted again in 1944 to a hospital ship and renamed USS *Rescue* (AH 18) in January 1945 (U.S. Navy photograph).

Submarine tenders (AS) provide maintenance and other support to the Navy's nuclear-powered attack (SSN) and ballistic missile (SSBN) submarines. The tenders' onboard facilities include pattern shops, foundries and machine shops; store rooms for a vast array of spare parts, supplies and provisions; weapons storage, and an operating room, dental clinic and hospital ward.

With the arrival of the first U.S. submarines, the Navy initially acquired a variety of vessels to support them, including a yacht, steam sloop-of-war, yard tug, monitor, bark, and U.S. Army transport (see Early Submarine Tenders listed below). The first purpose-built submarine tenders were commissioned shortly before the U.S. entry into World War I, and by the end of the 1930s, there were six such vessels in commission and one other under construction.

During World War II an ever expanding and forward deployed U.S. submarine force required additional surface vessels for support, and by war's end some 30 ships had been classified as submarine tenders. While AS 1 through AS 3 had been built specifically as submarine tenders, several of the others that followed were converted from other ship types. For example, AS 10 was a converted transport, AS 13 and AS 14 were Maritime Commission C3 cargo ship types, AS 10 was a C1-B type, and AS 23 to AS 26 were C3-S-A2 types. (AS 27 and AS 28 were initially classified as submarine tenders but were quickly reclassified as destroyer tenders [q.v.] (AD) and never completed.)

Although USS *Proteus* (AS 19) was commissioned in January 1944, she can be considered as the first "modern" submarine tender as she had been rebuilt in 1959–1960 to service the Navy's new Polaris-armed ballistic missile submarines (SSBNs). (See Selected History below.)

In the years immediately following the Korean War, the Navy listed 14 submarine tenders on the Vessel Register. Of these, seven were Fulton (AS 11)-class sub tenders in active service and another seven were laid up in the NDRF.

Commissioned in 1962 and 1963, the Hunley-class tenders (AS 31 and AS 32) were the first ships built for the purpose of supporting SSBNs. They were followed by the L.Y. Spear class (AS 36 and AS 37), commissioned in 1970 and 1971 as the first tenders designed to support SSNs.

Today there are only two active submarine tenders—members of the Emory S. Land class (AS 39 to AS 41)—and they are assigned to the Military Sealift Command (MSC) Service Support (PM4) force. Even though they are commissioned Navy ships commanded by a Navy officer, these tenders are operated by a combination of Navy and civilian MSC personnel—what MSC calls a "hybrid" crew. This unusual hybrid manning arrangement began in 2008 with AS 39 and was followed two years later by AS 40.[1]

USS *Emory S. Land* (AS 39) was previously based at La Maddalena in Sardinia supporting U.S. Sixth Fleet subs in the Mediterranean and later at Diego Garcia in the Indian Ocean. Now she is homeported in Guam, as is her sister ship, USS *Frank Cable* (AS 40). Typically one of the two tenders works at the island while the other is at sea providing services to deployed submarines and Navy surface vessels. Although now more than 30 years old, both tenders are expected to remain in service until about 2030. The third member of the class, USS *McKee* (AS 41), was decommissioned in October 1999 and struck in April 2006.

Submarine tenders generally been named for mythological figures, submarine pioneers and builders.

Early Submarine Tenders

Ajax[2]
Cheyenne[3]
Hist[4]
Mohican[5]

Nina[6]
Severn[7]
Tonopah[8]
Yosemite[9]

AS Roster

AS 1	Fulton[10] [SS]	AS 22	Euryale [SS]
AS 2	Bushnell[11] [SS]	AS 23	Aegir [SS]
AS 3	Holland[12] [SS]	AS 24	Anthedon [T]
AS 4	Alert [SS]	AS 25	Apollo [SS]
AS 5	Beaver[13] [SS]	AS 26	Clytie [SS]
AS 6	Camden[14] [S]	AS 27	Canopus[19] [C/X]
AS 7	Rainbow [SS]	AS 28	New England[20] [C/X]
AS 8	Savannah [SC]	AS 29	[X]
AS 9	Canopus[15] [Z]	AS 30	[X]
AS 10	Argonne[16] [SS]	AS 31	Hunley [SS]
AS 11	Fulton [SS]	AS 32	Holland [SS]
AS 12	Sperry [SS]	AS 33	Simon Lake[21] [L]
AS 13	Griffin [SS]	AS 34	Canopus [SS]
AS 14	Pelias [SS]	AS 35	[X][22]
AS 15	Bushnell [SX]	AS 36	L. Y. Spear [SS]
AS 16	Howard W. Gilmore [SS]	AS 37	Dixon [SX]
AS 17	Nereus [SS]	AS 38	[X][23]
AS 18	Orion [SS]	AS 39	Emory S. Land [A]
AS 19	Proteus [SS]	AS 40	Frank Cable [A]
AS 20	Otus[17] [SS]	AS 41	McKee[24] [K/L]
AS 21	Antaeus[18] [SS]		

SELECTED SPECIFICATIONS

Fulton class: AS 11–AS 12 & AS 15–AS 19

Length: 530.5 feet
Beam: 73 feet
Draft: 25.5 feet
Displacement: 17,200 tons (full load)
Propulsion: General Motors diesel electric; 11,520 shp; 2 shafts
Speed: 18.5 knots (maximum)
Personnel: 1,300

Aegir class: AS 23–AS 26

Length: 492 feet
Beam: 69.5 feet
Draft: 27 feet
Displacement: 16,500 tons (full load)
Propulsion: Westinghouse geared turbine; 8,500 shp; 1 shaft
Speed: 18.4 knots
Personnel: 1,460

Hunley class: AS 31 & AS 32

Length: 599 feet
Beam: 90.4 feet
Draft: 24.3 feet
Displacement: 18,300 tons (full load)
Propulsion: Diesel electric; 15,000 bhp; 1 shaft
Speed: 19 knots
Personnel: 1,081

Simon Lake class: AS 33–AS 35
Length: 643.75 feet
Beam: 85 feet
Draft: 28.5 feet
Displacement: 19,934 tons (full load)
Propulsion: steam turbine; 20,000 shp; 1 shaft
Speed: 18 knots
Personnel: 1,420

L.Y. Spear class: AS 36–AS 38
Length: 645.6 feet
Beam: 85 feet
Draft: 25.5 feet
Displacement: 22,650 tons (full load)
Propulsion: Steam turbine; 20,000 shp; 1 shaft
Speed: 18 knots
Personnel: 1,112

Emory S. Land class: AS 39–AS 41
Length: 644 feet
Beam: 85 feet
Draft: 26 feet
Displacement: 23,000 tons
Propulsion: Geared turbines; 20,000 shp; 1 shaft
Speed: 20 knots
Personnel: 157 civilians & 292 Navy

SELECTED HISTORIES

USS *Fulton* (AS 1)

USS *Fulton* served as a submarine tender for 16 years before becoming a gunboat (PG 49) in 1930 (U.S. Navy photograph).

Congress authorized the construction of Submarine Tender No. 1, initially named *Niagara*, on March 4, 1911. New England Ship and Engine Company of Groton, Connecticut, was the sole bidder on the contract, with the Fore River Shipbuilding Corporation of Quincy, Massachusetts, as the actual builder.[25] The vessel's name was changed to *Fulton* on February 10, 1913, and her keel was laid down on October 2 of that year. She was launched on June 6, 1914, but not delivered until December 2. USS *Fulton* was commissioned on December 7, 1914.

Her first jobs early in 1915 were supporting submarines in Virginia, South Carolina, New York and Rhode Island. Following an overhaul, she was based in New London, Connecticut, and tended subs along the East Coast between Massachusetts and as far south as Panama. In 1923 *Fulton* (now designated as AS 1) was sent to the submarine base in Coco Solo in the Canal Zone, and while deployed there as a tender, also undertook a surveying mission along the north coast of Panama for the Hydrographic Office. She left Panama on July 1, 1925, and headed for Philadelphia, where she was decommissioned on October 5, 1925, and laid up.

Fulton remained inactive for five years and was brought back into service and recommissioned on September 2, 1930. However, her new role was not to tend submarines but rather to serve as a gunboat and surveying ship. Accordingly, she was redesignated as PG 49 on September 29, reconditioned during the winter, and sent to the Canal Zone to conduct surveys into the summer of 1932. At that point, the Navy then dispatched *Fulton* to Hong Kong for duty with the Asiatic Fleet. After arriving on station November 3, 1932, and over the next 16 months, she patrolled the South China coast and performed surveys in the Philippines.

On March 14, 1934, an engine room fire badly damaged the ship while she was underway out of Hong Kong. She was towed by the oiler [q.v.] USS *Pecos* (AO 6) to Cavite in the Philippines, where *Fulton* was decommissioned on May 12, 1934. As the damage was so extensive, the Navy directed on May 8, 1935, that the former submarine tender be sold off. Her name was struck ten days later and she was purchased on June 6, 1935, by Lavoniera Filipino in Cavite for $2,550.50.

USS *Canopus* (AS 9)

Naval historian Robert J. Cressman called USS *Canopus* the "sub tender with the spirit of a battleship."[26] That is a fitting description for an auxiliary ship that fought as hard as she could against a much more powerful adversary.

Built as the merchant ship *Santa Leonora* in 1919 by New York Shipbuilding Company of Camden, New Jersey, *Canopus* was acquired from the U.S. Shipping Board on November 22, 1921. She was converted to a submarine tender at the Boston Navy Yard and commissioned as AS 9 on January 24, 1922.

Her initial duties included serving as tender for Submarine Division 9 at San Pedro, California, until July 1923, and for Submarine Division 17 at Pearl Harbor until September 1924. Between 1924 and 1931, *Canopus* operated in the Philippines and China and served as tender and flagship for the Asiatic Fleet's submarine divisions, and later as tender for Submarine Division 10 and Submarine Squadron 5.

War came to *Canopus* after midnight on December 7, 1941, when she was anchored at Cavite Navy Yard in the Philippines as tender for the 17 boats of Submarine Division 20. Following the Japanese attack, her crew worked tirelessly to repair ships damaged in bombing raids and to continue servicing her brood of submarines. In addition, the ten-

1. Combat Logistics and Fleet Support Ships 93

On October 29, 1924, the submarine tender USS *Canopus* (AS 9) is moored in Apra Harbor, Guam, with six S-class diesel submarines nested on her port side. The boats belong to Submarine Division 17 and include: USS S-36 (SS 141), USS S-37 (SS 142), USS S-38 (SS 143), USS S-39 (SS 144), USS S-40 (SS 145), and USS S-41 (SS 146) (U.S. Navy photograph).

der's crew rigged camouflage netting and painted her to blend in with the yard's docks, and moved her three times to keep her out of the crosshairs of Japanese bombers. Moved again to Mariveles Bay on the Bataan Peninsula, *Canopus* was hit by a bomb on December 29 and struck for a second time on January 5, 1942. Those two hits resulted in substantial damage to the ship and wounded 13 sailors. With no submarines to support any longer—the boats had left for the Netherlands East Indies and Australia—*Canopus* still carried on by repairing U.S. Army vessels and Filipino motor torpedo boats, and fixing land-based Army vehicles, weapons and equipment. She also employed her own motorboats and launches as miniature gunboats to attack Japanese forces advancing on the peninsula.

By early April the enemy could no longer be held off and so U.S. forces evacuated to Corregidor, an island in Manila Bay. To prevent *Canopus* from falling into Japanese hands, she was backed out of Lilimbon Cove on April 10, 1932, and scuttled in 80 feet of water in a position to partially block the cove. Her fight was over, even as surviving members of her crew continued to battle the Japanese until they were either killed or captured on May 6, 1942.

USS *Canopus* earned one battle star for her service in World War II.

USS *Proteus* (AS 19)

Although she was commissioned during World War II, USS *Proteus* played a key supporting role two decades later in the deployment of the Navy's strategic fleet ballistic missile system.

Built as a Fulton-class submarine tender by the Moore Shipbuilding and Dry Dock

The submarine tender USS *Proteus* is moored at Midway Island in May 1944, with three fleet submarines—[from left to right] USS *Bang* (SS 385), USS *Pintado* (SS 387) and USS *Pilotfish* (SS 386)—nested on her port side (U.S. Navy photograph).

Company of Oakland, California, *Proteus* was laid down on September 15, 1941. She was launched on November 12, 1942, and commissioned as AS 19 on January 31, 1944.

During the Pacific war she operated at Midway and Guam, and performed 55 voyage repairs and 38 refits for her submarine customers. Following the Japanese surrender in August 1945, *Proteus* supported Submarine Squadron 20 in Sagami Bay in Honshu as squadron personnel demilitarized Japanese submarines, human torpedoes, and torpedo-carrying vessels.

USS *Proteus* was decommissioned on September 26, 1947, but placed "in service" deactivating surplus U.S. submarines in New London, Connecticut. On January 15, 1959, her career was significantly extended when she entered the Charleston Naval Shipyard to be converted into the Navy's first tender for the new Polaris missile-carrying submarines of the George Washington (SSBN 598) class.

The conversion entailed cutting the ship in half and inserting a 44-foot section amidships, thereby increasing her length to 573 feet and her displacement by 3,000 tons to 19,700 tons (full load). The new hull section contained the Polaris missile magazine, and all of the shops, components and equipment associated with the missile. The added section also contained spaces for maintaining and repairing an SSBN's nuclear propulsion plant. To service the missile tubes of an SSBN customer, *Proteus* was fitted with a large crane with outriggers on each side of the ship. In another facilitator of her new role, the tender's storage space was enhanced to enable her to carry approximately 80,000 line items in her storerooms, compared to the 25,000 items usually held by tenders supporting diesel submarines.

With the conversion completed after six months, *Proteus* was recommissioned on July 8, 1960. She performed her first full-scale refit of an SSBN (USS *George Washington*) in January-February 1961, after which she deployed to Holy Loch, Scotland, to support USS *Patrick Henry* (SSBN 599). After two years in Scotland, *Proteus* was relieved by the new sub tender USS *Hunley* (AS 31) [see below] in March 1963 after she had performed 38 refits and was herself in need of a six-month overhaul in Charleston.

During her second stay in Charleston, *Proteus* was modified to be able to service "boomers" of the Lafayette (SSBN 616) class, which were commissioned in 1963 and 1964, and the new Polaris A-2 missiles they carried. The tender's machinery was overhauled, new navigation equipment was installed, new storerooms were added and additional berthing was created to house the expanded crew needed to man a fully deployed tender.

Upon completion of the overhaul, *Proteus* returned to Holy Loch in January 1964 to support the SSBNs of Submarine Squadron 14 and, shortly thereafter, shifted to Rota, Spain, on February 24 to establish the second overseas replenishment site for the Navy's boomers. She was relieved there at the end of March 1964 by the newly arrived sub tender USS *Holland* (AS 32), and then returned to Holy Loch. She performed five SSBN upkeeps in Scotland, after which she departed Holy Loch for Charleston in mid-June.

During a 90-day yard availability that summer, *Proteus* was readied for her next deployment—to Guam to establish the third overseas replenishment site for SSBNs and to support the new James Madison (SSBN 627)–class ballistic missile submarines and their A-3 version of the Polaris missile. The tender left Charleston on October 16, 1964, and after a stop in Hawaii to embark the Submarine Squadron 15 commander and staff, arrived in Apra Harbor, Guam, on November 29, 1964. There she remained more or less continuously into and through the 1970s. She underwent an overhaul at the Long Beach Naval Shipyard between 1978 and 1980.

In the 1980s, the tender split her time in Guam with two deployments to Diego Garcia in the Indian Ocean. She also provided general repairs and support for surface ships, as well as submarines, during her service in the Asia-Pacific area.

USS *Proteus* was decommissioned and struck on September 30, 1992. The former submarine tender was placed "in service, in reserve" and redesignated as the unclassified miscellaneous vessel IX 518 on February 1, 1994. Minus a name, she was assigned to the Bremerton Naval Shipyard in Washington for service as a barracks ship to house crews of ships undergoing conversion and modernization. That pedestrian duty ended on September 24, 1999, when the former *Proteus* was transferred to MARAD custody. IX 518 was struck on March 13, 2001, and removed from the NDRF on June 7, 2007, because she had been sold for $1,431,500 to ESCO Marine to be scrapped. The old tender was towed to Brownsville, Texas, where she arrived on July 1, 2007, and was completely dismantled by March 6, 2008.

USS *Hunley* (AS 31)

- Built by Newport News Shipbuilding and Dry Dock Company of Newport News, Virginia.
- Laid down on November 28, 1960, and launched September 28, 1961.

The first ship designed and constructed to service the Navy's ballistic missile submarines, USS *Hunley* (AS 31) is underway in the western Atlantic Ocean on December 14, 1962 (U.S. Navy photograph).

- Commissioned as USS *Hunley* (AS 31) on June 16, 1962.
- Conducted shakedown training and underwent post-shakedown alterations in late 1962.
- Deployed to Holy Loch, Scotland, on December 29, 1962, arrived there on January 9, 1963, and relieved USS *Proteus* (AS 19) as tender to Submarine Squadron 14 on March 15, 1963.
- Departed Holy Loch on April 12, 1964, for modifications to enable her to support the new A-3 version of the Polaris missile carried by SSBNs. She returned to Scotland on June 15, 1964.
- In December 1965 performed her 100th refit of a ballistic missile submarine (USS *Thomas A. Edison* [SSBN 610]).
- Returned to the United States in late 1966, and in 1967 operated out of Charleston, South Carolina.
- Deployed to Guam on December 26, 1967, and relieved USS *Proteus* there between January and June 1968.
- Returned to Charleston in July 1968.
- Relieved *Proteus* in Guam in 1971. That year her machinery repair personnel marked 4,500 hours of repair work on vessels of the U.S. Pacific Fleet.

- Underwent an overhaul at the Bremerton Naval Shipyard in 1973, following which the tender returned to Charleston to support the Atlantic Fleet submarine force.
- Decommissioned on September 15, 1994, and struck on May 30, 1995.
- Transferred to MARAD on May 1, 1999.
- MARAD assumed custody on October 12, 1995 and the former *Hunley* was laid up in the James River group of NDRF.
- Sold for $150,000 on January 5, 2007, to Southern Scrap Materials Company of New Orleans, Louisiana, to be broken up, and departed the Reserve Fleet on March 7.

USS *Emory S. Land* (AS 39)

On February 18, 2004, USS *Emory S. Land* (AS 39) is being assisted by tugboats in Gaeta, Italy, as she is maneuvering to come alongside the command ship USS *La Salle* (AGF 3) (U.S. Navy photograph).

- Built by Lockheed Shipbuilding and Construction Company of Seattle, Washington.
- Laid down on March 2, 1976, and launched on May 4, 1977.
- Commissioned as USS *Emory S. Land* (AS 39) on July 7, 1979.
- Initially served as flagship of Submarine Squadron 8 in Norfolk, Virginia.
- Deployed to the Pacific Fleet in September 1980 to support units of the Indian Ocean Battle Group.

- Participated in the July 1986 International Naval Review and Statue of Liberty rededication ceremonies in New York City.
- Deployed for six months in 1988 and supported surface ships of Joint Task Force Middle East and two carrier battle groups.
- Stationed at the Naval Support Activity in La Maddalena, Italy, as the only permanently assigned Submarine Group 8 vessel from June 1999 to September 2007.
- The Navy's Military Sea Command (MSC) assumed responsibility for the sub tender in February 2008. Over the next two years, she transitioned from an all–Navy crew of 1,005 personnel to a hybrid crew planned to consist of 160 civil service mariners and 292 uniformed Navy personnel.[27]
- Following a two-year shipyard availability and completion of the hybrid crew transition, *Emory S. Land* departed her former homeport of Bremerton, Washington, on a two-month voyage to a new homeport of Diego Garcia in the Indian Ocean.
- Visited Goa, India, in April 2011, and provided support services there to the fast attack submarine USS *La Jolla* (SSN 701). Visited Sepangar, Malaysia, in October 2011 and tended the fast attack submarine USS *Columbia* (SSN 771).
- Arrived in Guam on November 21, 2011, as the site's main submarine repair facility, and relieved the submarine tender USS *Frank Cable* (AS 40) which was to head to Portland, Oregon, for an overhaul and dry-docking.
- In 2016 the ship's homeport was shifted from Diego Garcia to Guam.
- Deployed to the Indo-Pacific region early in 2018, with a visit to Sasebo, Japan, in April.

USS *Frank Cable* (AS 40)

With her sailors manning the rails, the submarine tender USS *Frank Cable* (AS 40) arrives back in Guam on January 23, 2018, following operations in the eastern Pacific and a maintenance availability in Portland, Oregon (U.S. Navy photograph).

1. Combat Logistics and Fleet Support Ships

- Built as an Emory S. Land–class submarine tender by Lockheed Shipbuilding and Construction Company of Seattle, Washington.
- Laid down on March 2, 1976, and launched on January 14, 1978.
- Commissioned as USS *Frank Cable* (AS 40) on July 7, 1979.
- Transferred to MSC on February 1, 2010. Her complement at the time was 599 Navy personnel and additional 764 uniformed members of the ship's embarked repair department. The tender's hybrid crew was to consist of 157 civilian mariners and 206 uniformed Navy personnel.[27]
- The ship's mission is to conduct maintenance and support of submarines and surface vessels deployed in the U.S. Seventh Fleet (western Pacific) area of responsibility.
- Arrived in Subic Bay in the Philippines in July 2011 for hull repair work and to support a Los Angeles (SSN 688)-class submarine.
- South Korean sailors visited the ship in Guam in November 2011.
- Visited Pearl Harbor in January 2012 while en route to Portland, Oregon, for a regular overhaul and dry-docking.
- Arrived in Yokosuka, Japan, on October 15, 2013, for a five-day port visit. She had previously visited Yokosuka in 2008.
- On April 3, 2014, completed an UNREP with the dry cargo and ammunition ship [q.v.] USNS *Cesar Chavez* (T-AKE 14). The T-AKE transferred 280,000 gallons of F76 fuel to the tender, whose last underway replenishment was in 2004.
- Departed Guam on June 6, 2016, on a five-month deployment to the Indo-Asia-Pacific region and U.S. Central Command area of operations in support of units of the U.S. Fifth and Seventh Fleets. She returned to Guam on November 8, 2016.
- Departed Guam on March 7, 2017, en route to the U.S. Third Fleet area of operations. Two weeks later, on March 21, 2017, she refueled from fleet oiler [q.v.] USNS *Guadalupe* (T-AO 200) and received 120,000 gallons from the oiler.
- Completed an eight-month dry-dock availability at Vigor Industrial shipyard in Portland, Oregon, in 2017. She received $56 million in upgrades and improvements, including repair and shafting of the main reduction gear, replacement of a collection holding tank, renewal of hull steel, and repairs to various pieces of equipment.
- *Frank Cable* returned to Guam on January 23, 2018.

Notes

1. Other Navy auxiliary ship types which have been transferred to the MSC—such as salvage ships, fleet replenishment oilers and combat support ships—are commanded by a civil service mariner and operated by an all-civilian crew.

2. Former screw steamer *Scindia* acquired and commissioned in May 1898 for service as a collier, renamed *Ajax* in 1901, carried submarines B-2 and B-3 from U.S. to Philippines in 1913, served as receiving ship, submarine tender and aircraft tender, redesignated as miscellaneous auxiliary AG 15 in July 1924, decommissioned and struck in July 1925, and sold the next month.

3. Commissioned as monitor *Wyoming* in December 1902, renamed *Cheyenne* in January 1909, converted to submarine tender in 1913 and served as such on East and West Coasts, designated as monitor BM 10 in July 1920 and as unclassified miscellaneous vessel IX 4 in July 1921, decommissioned in June 1926, struck in January 1937, and sold in April 1939.

4. Built in 1895 as the yacht *Thespia*, acquired in April 1898 and commissioned as USS *Hist* in May 1898, decommissioned in February 1899, recommissioned in July 1902, assigned as a submarine tender in June 1903, decommissioned in May 1907 and again in July 1911, struck in July 1911 and sold in November 1911.

5. Built by the Navy, commissioned in May 1885, served as a school ship and then as station ship 1898–1905,

served as tender for Asiatic Fleet submarines in the Philippines beginning December 1909 and at least until 1913, decommissioned in October 1921, and sold for scrapping in March 1922.

6. Built in 1864–1865, initially served as yard tug, later converted to torpedo boat and commissioned as USS *Nina* in March 1870, converted to a submarine tender in 1906, lost at Fenwick Island Shoals off Delaware on February 6, 1910, and struck in March 1910.

7. Built in 1898–1899, commissioned as USS *Chesapeake* in April 1900 for duty as station and school ship at Annapolis, renamed USS *Severn* in June 1905, converted to submarine tender in May 1910, served in Panama Canal Zone, decommissioned in October 1916 and sold that December.

8. Commissioned in March 1903 as monitor *Nevada*, renamed *Tonopah* in March 1909, served as submarine tender along the East Coast and then in Bermuda and the Azores until December 1919, decommissioned in July 1920 and sold in January 1926.

9. Originally SS *Clearwater* and Army transport *Ingalls*, transferred to Navy in December 1910, commissioned in November 1911, decommissioned in January 1912, and sold.

10. See Selected History.

11. Commissioned in November 1915, tended submarines deployed in Ireland during World War I, served in the Pacific in the 1930s, redesignated as miscellaneous auxiliary AG 32 in July 1940 and renamed *Sumner* in August 1940, reclassified as surveying ship [q.v.] AGS 5 in December 1943, decommissioned in September 1946, and sold for scrapping in January 1948.

12 Commissioned in June 1926, reclassified as internal combustion engine repair ship [q.v.] ARG 18 in August 1945, decommissioned in March 1947, struck in June 1952, and sold for scrapping in October 1953.

13. Acquired in July 1917 as ID-2302, converted to submarine tender and commissioned in October 1918, designated as AS 5 in July 1950, reclassified as ARG 19 in June 1945, decommissioned in July 1946, and sold for scrapping in August 1950.

14. Seized by U.S. in 1917 and commissioned as cargo ship (ID-3143), decommissioned in May 1918, converted to submarine tender and recommissioned in February 1919, designated as AS 6 and supported R-class submarines, decommissioned in May 1931, redesignated as unclassified miscellaneous vessel IX 42 in September 1940, and served as barracks ship in New York until sold in October 1946.

15. See Selected History.

16. Commissioned in November 1921, classified as transport [q.v.] AP 4 in November 1921, converted to submarine tender and designated as AS 10 in July 1924, supported submarines in both the Atlantic and Pacific in the 1920s and 1930s, reclassified as AG 31 in July 1940, decommissioned in July 1946, struck in August 1946 and sold for scrapping in August 1950.

17. Acquired in December 1940 and converted to submarine tender, commissioned in March 1941, reclassified as ARG 20 in June 1945, decommissioned in August 1946, struck in September 1946, and sold for scrapping in November 1970.

18. Acquired in April 1941 and commissioned as AS 21 in May 1941, redesignated as AG 67 in September 1942, converted to hospital ship [q.v.] and renamed USS *Rescue* (AH 18) in January 1945, decommissioned in June 1946, and struck in August 1946.

19. Reclassified as destroyer tender [q.v.] AD 33 in September 1944 and cancelled in August 1945.

20. Ordered as AS 28 but reclassified as AD 32 in August 1944, and cancelled in August 1945.

21. Commissioned in November 1964, decommissioned in July 1999, laid up in Philadelphia in September 1999, struck in April 2006, laid up Portsmouth, Virginia, in 2008, and laid up in the James River group of NDRF in December 2015, and currently listed as available for disposal.

22. Cancelled in 1964.

23. Cancelled in 1969.

24. Commissioned on August 15, 1981, decommissioned on October 1, 1999, struck on April 25, 2006, currently laid up at the Norfolk Naval Shipyard in Portsmouth Virginia, with final disposition pending.

25. The DANFS history of the vessel indicates that *Fulton* was launched by the New London Ship and Engine Company.

26. Cressman, "Sub Tender with the Spirit of a Battleship," *Naval History*, December 2014, 14.

27. A Navy fact sheet updated in 2017 puts the tenders' complement at 157 civilians and 292 "military."

Fleet Tugs / Fleet Ocean Tugs (ATF)

The Navy's fleet ocean tugs perform a variety of tasks—everything from towing ships, barges and gunnery exercise targets to serving as salvage and diving work platforms, conducting search and rescue missions, recovering downed aircraft and ships, helping to clean up oil spills, and fighting fires.

Today the Navy's Military Sealift Command (MSC) operates three fleet ocean tugs (T-ATFs) of the Powhatan (T-ATF 166) class. They carry a 10-ton capacity crane and a

1. Combat Logistics and Fleet Support Ships

Commissioned in December 1943, USS *Alsea* (ATF 97) is seen here on July 26, 1954, operating with the Atlantic Fleet. She was decommissioned a year later and eventually sold to a Panamanian business in 1976 (U.S. Navy photograph).

bollard pull of at least 87 tons. The tugs are equipped with two fire pumps capable of supplying up to 2,200 gallons of foam per minute. Their after decks are fitted with a grid enabling them to bolt down various types of portable equipment.

The first ATFs were commissioned in the early 1940s as ocean-going tugs of the Navajo (AT 64) class and designated as ATs (see Chapter 3).[1] On May 15, 1944, AT 66–AT 155 were reclassified as fleet tugs and redesignated as ATF 66–ATF 155, respectively. Sixty-five ATFs were in service or being completed by the end of 1944 (three ATs had been lost in 1942–1943 before the reclassification: AT 65, AT 66 and AT 89). The final World War II roster of fleet ocean tugs reached hull number ATF 165 by the time of the August 1945 Japanese surrender.

In 1973 and 1974, four of the ATFs were assigned to the MSC. They were then redesignated as T-ATF 76, T-ATF 85, T-ATF 149 and T-ATF 158, and manned by civilians with six Navy communications personnel occasionally on board. The last all–Navy-manned ship, USS *Shakori* (ATF 162), was decommissioned in February 1980 and transferred to Taiwan.

During the post-war years, 39 of the ATFs were either leased, sold or transferred to foreign navies. Taiwan received the most (eight), with Argentina, Colombia, Mexico and Venezuela each acquiring four. Brazil, Chile, Dominican Republic, Ecuador, Italy, Indonesia, Pakistan, Peru and Turkey were other recipients. A few of the Navy tugs went on to serve with the U.S. Coast Guard but the other veteran ATFs were either sold for scrap or expended as targets.

The most recent ATFs are the seven MSC-operated ships of the Powhatan class

(T-ATF 166—T-ATF 172), which were placed in service between January 1979 and July 1981. Of these, only three—*Catawba*, *Sioux* and *Apache*—are still active, and the Navy plans to remove them from service in 2021 to be dismantled. The Navy's current shipbuilding plan for the Fiscal Year 2019–2023 period includes no new ATF construction so as matters now stand, the three T-ATFs will be the Navy's last fleet ocean tugs.

Fleet ocean tugs carry Indian names.

ATF / T-ATF Roster

ATF 66	*Cherokee* [SX]	ATF 108	*Pakana* [SX]
ATF 67	*Apache* [T]	ATF 109	*Potawatomi* [T]
ATF 68	*Arapaho* [T]	ATF 110	*Quapaw* [SS]
ATF 69	*Chippewa*[2] [Z]	ATF 111	*Sarsi*[8] [Z]
ATF 70	*Choctaw* [T]	ATF 112	*Serrano*[9] [SS]
ATF 71	*Hopi* [T]	ATF 113	*Takelma* [T]
ATF 72	*Kiowa* [T]	ATF 114	*Tawakoni* [T]
ATF 73	*Menominee* [T]	ATF 115	*Tenino*[10] [SX]
ATF 74	*Pawnee* [SS]	ATF 116	*Tolowa* [T]
ATF 75	*Sioux* [T]	ATF 117	*Wateree*[11] [K]
ATF 76	*Ute*[3] [SX]	ATF 118	*Wenatchee* [T]
ATF 81	*Bannock* [T]	ATF 148	*Achomawi* [T]
ATF 82	*Carib* [T]	ATF 149	*Atakapa*[12] [SX]
ATF 83	*Chickasaw* [T]	ATF 150	*Avoyel*[13] [T]
ATF 84	*Cree* [SX]	ATF 151	*Chawasha*[14] [SX]
ATF 85	*Lipan*[4] [SX]	ATF 152	*Cahuilla* [T]
ATF 86	*Mataco* [SS/Z]	ATF 153	*Chilula*[15] [T/SX]
ATF 87	*Moreno*[5] [K]	ATF 154	*Chimariko* [SX]
ATF 88	*Narragansett* [T]	ATF 155	*Cusabo* [T]
ATF 90	*Pinto* [T]	ATF 156	*Luiseno* [T]
ATF 91	*Seneca* [SX]	ATF 157	*Nipmuc* [T]
ATF 92	*Tawasa* [Z]	ATF 158	*Mosopelea* [SX]
ATF 93	*Tekesta* [T]	ATF 159	*Paiute* [SC]
ATF 94	*Yuma* [T]	ATF 160	*Papago*[16] [L/SS]
ATF 95	*Zuni*[6] [T]	ATF 161	*Salinan* [T]
ATF 96	*Abnaki*[7] [T]	ATF 162	*Shakori* [T]
ATF 97	*Alsea* [SC]	ATF 163	*Utina* [T]
ATF 98	*Arikara* [T]	ATF 164	*Yurok*[17] [T]
ATF 100	*Chowanoc* [T]	ATF 165	*Yustaga*[18] [T]
ATF 101	*Cocopa* [T]	T-ATF 166	*Powhatan* [T]
ATF 102	*Hidatsa* [T]	T-ATF 167	*Narragansett*[19] [K]
ATF 103	*Hitchiti* [T]	T-ATF 168	*Catawba*[20] [A]
ATF 104	*Jicarilla* [T]	T-ATF 169	*Navajo*[21] [L]
ATF 105	*Moctobi* [SC]	T-ATF 170	*Mohawk*[22] [L]
ATF 106	*Molala* [T]	T-ATF 171	*Sioux*[23] [A]
ATF 107	*Munsee* [SC]	T-ATF 172	*Apache*[24] [A]

Selected Specifications

Navaho (Cherokee) class: ATF 66–ATF 76 & ATF 81–ATF 118

Length: 205 feet (overall)
Beam: 38.5 feet
Draft: 15.3 feet
Displacement: 1,674 tons (full load)

Propulsion: Diesel-electric; 3,000 shp; 1 shaft
Speed: 16.5 knots
Personnel: 85

Achomawi class: ATF 148–ATF 165
Virtually identical to Navajo-class

Powhatan class: T-ATF 166–T-ATF 172
Length: 240 feet (overall)
Beam: 42 feet
Draft: 15.1 feet
Displacement: 2.296 tons (full load)
Propulsion: Diesel-electric (GM 20–645F7B diesels); 4,500 shp; 2 shafts
Speed: 15 knots
Personnel: 18 civilian & 4 Navy

Selected Histories

USS Lipan (ATF 85)

USS *Lipan* is underway in San Francisco Bay on May 2, 1943, three days after she was commissioned (U.S. Navy photograph).

- Built as a Navajo-class oceangoing tug by United Engineering Company of San Francisco, California.
- Laid down on May 30, 1942, and launched on September 17, 1942.
- Commissioned as USS *Lipan* (AT 85) on April 29, 1943.
- Operated in the Southwest Pacific in 1943, primarily at Espiritu Santo and Guadalcanal.

- Reclassified as fleet tug ATF 85 on April 13, 1944.
- Supported the invasions of Saipan and Guam in July 1944.
- With USS *Arapaho* (ATF 68), towed disabled light cruiser USS *Houston* (CL 81) to Manus Island in December 1944.
- Following an overhaul in San Francisco, *Lipan* performed salvage and firefighting duties during the Okinawa campaign early in 1945.
- During the late 1940s, *Lipan* operated off the U.S. West Coast and in the western Pacific towing barges, landing craft, disabled submarines, dry docks and target sleds.
- Performed various towing and salvage assignments during the amphibious assault at Inchon during the Korean War.
- Based at Pearl Harbor from 1954 to 1969.
- Participated in Vietnam War between 1966 and 1968.
- Decommissioned in 1972 and assigned to MSC as USNS *Lipan* (T-ATF 85).
- Placed out of service in 1980 and lent to USCG.
- Commissioned in Coast Guard as medium endurance cutter USCGC *Lipan* (WMEC 85) on September 30, 1980.
- Decommissioned by USCG on March 31, 1988, and returned to USN.
- Struck on January 23, 1989.
- Expended as a target on January 22, 1990.
- Earned two battle stars for World War II service, four battle stars for Korean War service, and three campaign stars for Vietnam War service.

USS *Abnaki* (ATF 96)

In December 1967 USS *Abnaki* (ATF 96) is keeping a close eye on the Soviet electronics intelligence trawler (AGI) *Gidrofon* (left) in the South China Sea (U.S. Navy photograph).

1. Combat Logistics and Fleet Support Ships

- Built as an Abnaki-class oceangoing tug by Charleston Shipbuilding & Dry Dock Company of Charleston, South Carolina.
- Laid down on November 28, 1942 and launched on April 22, 1943.
- Commissioned as USS *Abnaki* (AT 96) on November 15, 1943.
- Operated off the U.S. East Coast until spring 1944.
- Towed the captured German submarine U-505 to Bermuda in June 1944.
- Performed various tows in the Atlantic in 1944 and early 1945.
- Transferred to the U.S. Pacific Fleet in May 1945 and operated in the Marshall Islands from July to August 1945.
- Served with the occupation forces in Japan from late 1945 to early 1946.
- Operated in China from July to October 1946.
- Caught in a November 1946 typhoon while towing the floating dry dock ARD 31, *Abnaki* was rammed by the dry dock and damaged. After arriving in Guam on November 26, she was docked in ARD 31 for temporary repairs.
- Returned to U.S. in April 1947 and operated off the West Coast until October 28, when she left for Pearl Harbor.
- Served in Hawaii, Japan, and China in 1947–1948.
- Operated off Alaska in early 1949.
- Deployed to WestPac in the summer of 1949.
- During the Korean War served in Japanese and Korean waters.
- In mid-1952 performed towing, escort, patrol and research duties in Midway, San Diego, Long Beach, Guam, Saipan, and the Philippines.
- Between 1953 and 1960, operated off U.S. West Coast, in the Central Pacific, and Hawaii, and in the western Pacific and Southeast Asia, and underwent various overhauls.
- Towed the light cruiser USS *Springfield* (CL 66) from San Francisco to the Panama Canal in March 1957.
- Served in Vietnam as a tender for a squadron of mine craft in March 1965.
- Operated in the South China Sea during the Vietnam War (1965–1972 inclusively), and performed various towing and salvage operations.
- For the remainder of her career, *Abnaki* made frequent voyages to the western Pacific, conducted operations out of Pearl Harbor, Subic Bay and Guam, as well as off the West Coast.
- Sold to Mexico on September 1, 1978.
- Decommissioned, struck and transferred to Mexico on September 30, 1978. Subsequently renamed ARM *Yaqui* (A-18), ARM *A.H. Ehecati* (A-53) and then ARM *Yaqui* (ARE-02).
- USS *Abnaki* earned three battle stars for her service during the Korean War and the Armed Forces Expeditionary Medal and Vietnam Service Medal with six campaign stars for her Vietnam War service.

USNS *Powhatan* (T-ATF 166)

- Built in 1978–1979 by Marinette Marine Corporation of Marinette, Wisconsin.
- Laid down on June 6, 1978, and launched on June 24, 1978.
- Placed in service with MSC on June 15, 1979 as USNS *Powhatan* (T-ATF 166).

The lead ship of the Powhatan class of fleet ocean tugs is underway in 1979, her first year of service (U.S. Navy photograph).

- Served in the Indian Ocean December 1995 to February 1996.
- Taken out of service on February 10, 1999, and leased on February 26, 1999 to Donjon Marine Company, Inc., of Hillside, New Jersey, for five years.
- Wheelhouse reconfigured for civilian use.
- Struck on February 25, 2008.
- Sold to Turkey in 2008 and renamed TCG *Inebolu* (A-590); still in Turkish service.

USNS *Catawba* (T-ATF 168)

- Built in 1979 as a Powhatan-class fleet ocean tug by Marinette Marine Corporation of Marinette, Wisconsin.
- Laid down on December 14, 1977, and launched on September 22, 1979.
- Placed in service with MSC on May 23, 1980, as USNS *Catawba* (T-ATF 168).
- In June 1999 assisted the sinking mine countermeasures ship USS *Dextrous* (MCM 13) and safely escorted her back to port in Bahrain.
- In October 2000 towed the guided missile destroyer USS *Cole* (DDG 67) after she was damaged in a terrorist attack in Aden, Yemen.
- In February and March 2003 deployed to the northern Persian Gulf during Operation Iraqi Freedom in 2003.
- Assisted in the March 2003 recovery of bodies of crew of two Royal Navy Sea King ASaC.7 helicopters from the aircraft carrier HMS *Ark Royal*. The aircraft had collided on March 22.
- In May 2003 recovered the wreckage of a downed helicopter in the Persian Gulf.

The fleet ocean tug USNS *Catawba* is operating in the Arabian Gulf on June 18, 2003 (U.S. Navy photograph).

- In May 2008 participated in Exercise Goalkeeper III in the Persian Gulf, which included participants from Bahrain, New Zealand, the United Kingdom and other regional countries.
- In 2009 assisted the Ukrainian motor vessel *Faina* following her release by Somali pirates.
- In 2015 served as a U.S. Fifth Fleet emergency towing asset and provided salvage support for the July 2015 recovery of an F/A-18F Super Hornet aircraft. She also supported numerous mine countermeasure and dive training events, including support of autonomous underwater vehicle (AUV) missions, and large-scale oil-spill containment and recovery training.
- Currently assigned to duty in the Pacific Ocean and in the Middle East.
- Scheduled to be taken out of service in 2021 and dismantled.

USNS *Navajo* (T-ATF 169)

- Built in 1977–1979 as a Powhatan-class fleet ocean tug by Marinette Marine Corporation of Marinette, Wisconsin.
- Laid down on December 14, 1977, and launched on December 20, 1979.
- Placed in service with MSC on June 13, 1980, as USNS *Navajo* (T-ATF 169).
- Decommissioned and struck on October 1, 2010.

USNS *Navajo* is underway in 1980, her first year of service with the Military Sea Command (U.S. Navy photograph).

• Currently laid up at the Naval Inactive Ship Maintenance Facility in Pearl Harbor with "final disposition pending."

USNS *Sioux* (T-ATF 171)

On March 6, 2014, the fleet ocean tug USNS *Sioux* (T-ATF 171) is towing HMCS *Protecteur* (AOR 509), an auxiliary oil replenishment ship of the Royal Canadian Navy, into Pearl Harbor, Hawaii. The Canadian ship had lost power following a February 27 engine room fire when she was more than 300 miles from Hawaii (U.S. Navy photograph).

- Built in 1979–1980 as a Powhatan-class fleet ocean tug by Marinette Marine Corporation of Marinette, Wisconsin.
- Laid down on March 22, 1979, and launched on October 30, 1980.
- Placed in service with MSC on May 12, 1981, as USNS *Sioux* (T-ATF 171).
- Participated in the Persian Gulf War (Operation Desert Storm) between May and November 1991.
- Served as a platform in February 2012 for SALVEX diver training for U.S. and Indian divers off the coast of Hawaii.
- During March 2–6, 2014, towed the disabled Canadian oiler HMCS *Protecteur* (AOR 509)—a vessel nearly three times her size—approximately 300 miles to Hawaii.
- In 2015 provided towing services for decommissioned nuclear attack submarine USS *Miami* (SSN 755) from Portsmouth, New Hampshire, to Bremerton, Washington.
- Currently homeported in San Diego, California.
- Scheduled to be taken out of service in 2021 and dismantled.

USNS *Apache* (T-ATF 172)

The fleet ocean tug USNS *Apache* (T-ATF 172) getting underway from her homeport in Little Creek, Virginia, on August 5, 2016, to participate in the National Transportation Safety Board on-site investigation of the sinking of the cargo ship *El Faro* (U.S. Navy photograph).

- Built in 1979–1981 as a Powhatan-class fleet ocean tug by Marinette Marine Corporation of Marinette, Wisconsin.
- Laid down on March 22, 1979, and launched on March 22, 1981.
- Placed in service with MSC on July 30, 1981 as USNS *Apache* (T-ATF 172).
- Towed the decommissioned destroyer USS *Barry* (DD 933) on November 18, 1983, to her mooring in the Washington Navy Yard, where she was to serve as a display ship until 2015.
- Served in Liberia between September 1993 and February 1994, Haiti in September 1994, and in the Indian Ocean in January and February 1996.
- On November 25, 2001, rescued four people from the floundering sailing yacht *Bossa Nova II* 1,400 miles southwest of the Azores.
- Rescued seven fisherman from the waters off the coast on Monrovia, Liberia, on August 14, 2006.
- In August 2011 served as the base of operations and diving platform for archaeologists searching for the remains of three Americans killed in the October 1942 crash of a Sikorsky V-44 flying boat in the Bay of Exploits in Newfoundland, Canada.
- Participated in the 2016 NTSB on-site investigation of the loss of the cargo ship *El Faro* off the Bahamas, and recovered the vessel's data recorder.
- Currently homeported in Little Creek, Virginia.
- Scheduled to be taken out of service in 2021 and dismantled.

Notes

1. These tugs are generally known as the Cherokee (ATF 66) class as *Navajo* herself was lost in 1943 after being torpedoed by the Japanese submarine I-39. The next vessel on the list, USS *Seminole* (AT 65), was sunk by Japanese destroyers in 1942.

2. Decommissioned in February 1947, struck in September 1961, transferred in January 1989 to an explosives disposal unit in Panama City, Florida, for use in tests, and sunk on February 8, 1990, for use as an artificial reef off Destin, Florida.

3. Served in World War II, Korea and Vietnam, decommissioned in August 1974, transferred to MSTS and placed in service as USNS *Ute* (T-ATF 76), transferred to USCG and commissioned as medium endurance cutter USCGC *Ute* (WMEC 76) in September 1980, later returned to USN, struck in January 1989, and expended as a target on August 4, 1991.

4. See Selected History.

5. Decommissioned in August 1946, laid up in NDRF in Orange, Texas, struck in September 1961, and withdrawn from NDRF on December 15, 1986.

6. Decommissioned and transferred to USCG in June 1946, struck in July 1946, commissioned in USCG as USCGC *Tamaroa* (WAT 166) in 1946, redesignated as WATF 166 in 1956, reclassified as medium endurance cutter WMEC 166 in 1966, decommissioned by USCG in February 1994, acquired by Zuni Maritime Foundation in Portsmouth, Virginia, and sunk as an artificial reef off New Jersey and Delaware on May 10, 2017.

7. See Selected History.

8. War loss from an August 27, 1952, mine explosion off the Korean coast.

9. Decommissioned in May 1950 and laid up in NDRF, reactivated and converted to a surveying ship [q.v.] in 1960, recommissioned as AGS 24 in June 1960, decommissioned and struck in January 1970, and sold for scrapping in November 1971.

10. Decommissioned in May 1947 and laid up in NDRF, withdrawn from NDRF on August 18, 1986, for use as a missile target.

11. Grounded during a typhoon at Okinawa in October 1945 and struck in November 1946.

12. Decommissioned in November 1946, laid up in NDRF, recommissioned in August 1951, decommissioned in July 1974 and placed in service with MSC as USNS *Atakapa* (T-ATF 149), taken out of service in 1981 and laid up at the NISMF in Portsmouth, Virginia, struck in February 1992, transferred to MARAD for layup in NDRF's James River Group, and expended as a target on August 25, 2000.

13. Decommissioned in January 1947, lent to USCG in July 1956 and commissioned as USCGC *Avoyel* (WAT 150) in October 1956, reclassified as WMEC 150 in 1966, struck from NVR in June 1969, decommissioned by USCG in September 1969 and sold for commercial service.

14. Decommissioned in September 1946 and laid up in NDRF, withdrawn from NDRF in August 1978 for use as a target.
15. Decommissioned in February 1947, lent to USCG in July 1956 and commissioned as USCGC *Chilula* (WAT 153) in October 1956, redesignated as WATF 153 in 1956 and as WMEC 153 in May 1966, decommissioned in June 1991, returned to USN, and expended as a target in 1997.
16. Laid up at NISMF in Philadelphia as of June 2010 but not listed by NAVSEA in September 2017 as berthed at that facility. Unofficially reported as dismantled in Portsmouth, Virginia, in October 2002.
17. Laid down as *Yurok* (AT 164) but reclassified as submarine rescue ship ASR 19 in November 1945, launched in December 1945 as *Bluebird* and commissioned as *Bluebird* (ASR 19) in May 1946, and decommissioned and transferred to Turkey in August 1950.
18. Laid down as *Yustaga* (ATF 165) but redesignated as ASR 20 in November 1945, renamed *Skylark* in December 1945, launched in March 1946 and laid up prior to commissioning, later commissioned as *Skylark* (ASR 20) in March 1951, and decommissioned and sold to Brazil in June 1993.
19. Placed out of service in February 1999, inactivated in September 1999, struck in June 2002, transferred to Naval Air Systems Command in August 2002 for use in towing and as a service vessel, reclassified as a "combatant craft or boat" in February 2009, and at last report is leased by NAVSEA to Donjon Marine Company, Inc. In March 2017 NAVSEA sought a contractor to perform an overhaul, including dry-docking, for the vessel.
20. To be taken out of service in 2021 and dismantled.
21. See Selected History.
22. Struck on August 31, 2015, and laid up at NISMF in Philadelphia with "final disposition pending."
23. To be taken out of service in 2021 and dismantled.
24. *Ibid.*

SALVAGE TUGS / SALVAGE AND RESCUE SHIPS / TOWING, SALVAGE AND RESCUE SHIPS

(ATS / T-ATS[X])[1]

In 1971–1972 the Navy acquired three British-built ocean-going salvage tugs. They were classified as salvage and rescue ships and designated as ATS 1–ATS 3 when commissioned. The trio was in active service until March 1996, when they were decommissioned and transferred: ATS 1 went to the U.S. Coast Guard, and ATS 2 and ATS 3 to South Korea.

A fourth ATS had been authorized in Fiscal Year 1972 and fifth vessel in Fiscal Year 1973. However, the construction of ATS 4 and ATS 5 was deferred in 1973 and the Navy decided against procuring additional vessels of the ATS 1 class because of difficulty in maintaining them (owing to their foreign-made components) and their overall high cost. As an alternative, the Navy instead procured seven fleet ocean tugs [q.v.] of the Powhatan (T-ATF 166) class.

Although there are today no ATS ships in the fleet, the Navy still carries the hull type on its formal listing of fleet support naval vessel classifications.[2] However, the current ATS nomenclature is "towing, salvage, and rescue ship" which is referred to in Navy planning documents with the interim designation as T-ATS(X). The Navy has said that the service intends to fund the acquisition of six of these new vessels in the Fiscal Year 2019–2023 period: one in Fiscal Year 2019, two in Fiscal Year 2020, and one each in Fiscal Years 2021–2023, at a projected total cost of $459 million.[3] Under this plan the first T-AFS(X) would be delivered sometime in 2020.

The new class of T-ATS(X) vessels is intended to be a common hull replacement for both the Safeguard (T-ARS 50)-class salvage and rescue ships [q.v.] and Powhatan (T-ATF 166)-class fleet ocean tugs. As such, their primary missions will include submarine rescue operations, emergency towing, diving operations, surface salvage and underwater

The lead ship of the Navy's salvage and rescue vessels, USS *Edenton* (ATS 1) is underway with the wind off her port side (U.S. Navy photograph).

salvage. In addition, the T-ATS(X) would also support special operations forces, remove environmental hazards and support undersea warfare operations. The ship would be similar to current offshore or platform supply vessels used by the oil and gas industry, with a minimum bollard pull of 130 short tons (capable of towing an aircraft carrier) and an unobstructed deck space of at least 5,000 square feet.

In July 2016 the Naval Sea Systems Command (NAVSEA) issued Phase 1 T-ATS(X) design study contracts, valued at about $200,000 each, to four shipyards: Bollinger Shipyards Lockport, Eastern Shipbuilding Group, Inc., Fincantieri Marine Group, and VT Halter Marine. Phase 2 would involve detailed design and construction. In March 2017 NAVSEA stated that it required the new ATS builder to have the design capabilities, production facilities and internal management to be able to design, construct and house up to five T-ATS vessels at various stages of production simultaneously, and that the builder must either own or have access to a certified dry dock prior to the contract award.

In the event, none of the four Phase 1 contractors were selected to build the new T-ATS ships. On March 16, 2018, NAVSEA announced that Gulf Island Shipyards of Houma, Louisiana, had been awarded a $63,560,942 firm-fixed-price contract for the detail design and construction of the new towing, salvage and rescue ships. The contract includes an option for seven additional vessels, which, if exercised, would increase the cumulative value of the contract to $522,701,092. Almost all of the work (92 percent) will be performed in Houma, with 5 percent to be performed in Hampton, Virginia, 2 percent in Stord, Norway, and 1 percent in New Orleans, Louisiana. The builder is expected to complete the first T-ATS(X) by September 2020.

The three transferred salvage and rescue ships carried the names of communities in the southeastern United States.

ATS Roster

ATS 1	*Edenton* [T]
ATS 2	*Beaufort* [T]
ATS 3	*Brunswick* [T]

SPECIFICATIONS

Edenton class: ATS 1–ATS 3

Length: 282.16 feet
Beam: 50 feet
Draft: 15.16 feet
Displacement: 3,117 tons (full load)
Propulsion: Paxman diesels; 6,000 shp; 2 shafts
Speed: 16 knots
Personnel: 96–102

HISTORIES

USS *Edenton* (ATS 1)

Prominent in this view of USS *Edenton* (ATS 1) is the 10-ton-capacity crane on her forecastle (U.S. Navy photograph).

- Built as Edenton-class salvage and rescue ship in 1967–1968 by Brooke Marine Ltd. of Lowestoft, England.
- Laid down on March 28, 1967, and launched May 15, 1968.
- Commissioned as USS *Edenton* (ATS 1) on January 23, 1971.
- Assigned to U.S. Atlantic Fleet.
- Deployed to the Mediterranean November 1975–April 1976, August 1978–February 1979, January–July 1981, July 1982–January 1983, November 1985–June 1986, September 1988–March 1989, and April–October 1993.
- Crossed the Equator in October 1994.
- Decommissioned on March 29, 1996.
- Transferred to U.S. Coast Guard on November 18, 1997.
- Struck from NVR on December 29, 1997.
- Commissioned by USCG as medium endurance cutter USCGC *Alex Haley* (WMEC 39) on July 10, 1999.
- Currently homeported in Kodiak, Alaska.

USS *Beaufort* (ATS 2)

USS *Beaufort* (ATS 2) is underway in the Persian Gulf in 1991 during mine-clearing operations following Operation Desert Storm (National Archives).

- Built as Edenton-class salvage and rescue ship by Brooke Marine Ltd. of Lowestoft, England.
- Laid down on February 19, 1968, and launched on December 20, 1968.
- Delivered January 5, 1972.

- Commissioned as USS *Beaufort* (ATS 2) on January 22, 1972, for duty with the U.S. Pacific Fleet.
- Initially assigned to Service Squadron 5 in Pearl Harbor, Hawaii, beginning in May 1972.
- Towed the former miscellaneous auxiliary [q.v.] USS *Observation Island* (AG 154) from Hawaii to San Francisco in October–November 1972.
- Deployed to WestPac between May and November 1973, and generally operated out of Subic Bay in the Philippines.
- Supported Operation End Sweep in Haiphong Harbor, North Vietnam, in July 1973.
- Assisted in refloating grounded cargo ship [q.v.] USNS *Jack J. Pendleton* (T-AK 276) in September 1973.
- Following a January to May 1974 yard availability, departed Hawaii for U.S. West Coast beginning in August 1974.
- Returned to Pearl Harbor in November 1974.
- Deployed to WestPac in September 1975, with operations out of Japan, Korea, Taiwan and the Philippines.
- Returned to Pearl Harbor in March 1976 and was overhauled in 1976–1977.
- Deployed to WestPac in November 1977 and performed various tows and salvage training exercises in the Far East until returning to Hawaii in May 1978.
- Operated out of Pearl Harbor between June 1978 and April 1979.
- Deployed to WestPac between April and October 1979.
- Visited U.S. West Coast in September 1979.
- Deployed to WestPac on September 20 and operated with the U.S. Seventh Fleet until April 1980.
- Resumed operations in Hawaii in June 1980.
- Decommissioned on March 8, 1996.
- Transferred to South Korea on August 29, 1996.
- Struck on December 12, 1996.
- Commissioned in the South Korean Navy as ROKS *Pyeongtaek* (ATS-27) and then decommissioned on January 4, 2017.

USS *Brunswick* (ATS 3)

- Built as Edenton-class salvage and rescue ship by Brooke Marine Ltd. of Lowestoft, England.
- Laid down on June 5, 1968, and launched on October 14, 1969.
- Delivered November 21, 1972.
- Commissioned as USS *Brunswick* (ATS 3) on December 9, 1972.
- Arrived at Pearl Harbor, Hawaii, on May 31, 1973, to begin duty with the U.S. Pacific Fleet.
- Deployed to WestPac between June and December 1974. During the deployment she conducted salvage training and target towing.
- Recovered a downed helicopter near Maui in January 1975.
- Monitored Soviet vessels, performed local tows and conducted diving drills in 1975 and early 1976.
- Deployed to the U.S. Seventh Fleet in WestPac between April and September 1976.

With her crew manning the rails, USS *Brunswick* (ATS 3) is approaching Majuro Atoll in the Marshall Islands (National Archives).

- Visited the U.S. West Coast in 1976 and towed the former aircraft carrier USS *Oriskany* (CV 34) from San Francisco to Bremerton, Washington, in October.
- During the first quarter of 1977 operated off Pearl Harbor before returning to the U.S. in in April.
- Towed the former destroyer tender [q.v.] USS *Isle Royal* (AD 29) from San Francisco to Pearl Harbor in May 1977.
- Salvaged a wrecked Navy EC-130Q Hercules aircraft near Wake Island in August 1977.
- Deployed to WestPac in November 1977 and returned to Pearl Harbor in May 1978. During the deployment, *Brunswick* towed the disabled frigate USS *Davidson* (FF 1045) in February 1978 and embarked 29 Vietnamese refugees rescued at sea by the frigate USS *Downes* (FF 1010) and transported them to the Philippines in April.
- Returned to Pearl Harbor on May 24, 1978 and conducted local operations and training over the next 12 months.
- Deployed to WestPac in June 1980 and operated in the Far East until her return to Pearl Harbor in December 1980.
- Performed local operations and underwent a two-month yard availability during the first nine months of 1981.

1. Combat Logistics and Fleet Support Ships

- Visited the U.S. West Coast in October 1981.
- Decommissioned on March 8, 1996.
- Transferred to South Korea on August 29, 1996.
- Struck from the NVR on December 12, 1996.
- Commissioned in South Korean Navy as ROKS *Gwangyang* (ATS-28).
- Dismantled in Busan, South Korea, in October 2016.

Notes

1. The initial classification of these vessels was salvage tug (ATS) but the ATS nomenclature was changed to salvage and rescue ship on February 16, 1971.
2. General Guidance for the Classification of Naval Vessels and Battle Force Counting Procedures (SECNAV Instruction 5030.8C), June 14, 2016.
3. Report to Congress on the Annual Long-Range Plan for Construction of Naval Vessels for Fiscal Year 2019, Office of the Chief of Naval Operations, February 2018.

Expeditionary Fast Transports (T-EPF)

On April 22, 2016, the expeditionary fast transports USNS *Trenton* (T-EPF 5) (left) and USNS *Brunswick* (T-EPF 6) (right) are moored at the Joint Expeditionary Base Little Creek–Fort Story, in Virginia. *Brunswick* had been in service only three months at the time (U.S. Navy photograph).

On November 13, 2008, the Navy awarded Austral USA of Mobile, Alabama, a $185.4 million fixed-price incentive fee contract modification for the detail design and construction of a Joint High Speed Vessel (JHSV). The JHSV was conceived as a catamaran capable of transporting troops and vehicles within a theater of operations at speeds in the 35 to 40 knot range. The 2008 contract modification included an option for the construction of as many as nine additional JHSVs, and that option was later exercised.

In early JHSV planning, the U.S. Army and the Navy were each to acquire five vessels—hence the "Joint" in the vessel's nomenclature. However, in December 2010 discussions between the two services, the Army decided that it would transfer its five JHSVs to the Navy for operation and for support of Army activities in forward areas. In September 2015, the Navy reclassified the joint high speed vessels as expeditionary fast transports and redesignated them as T-EPFs. On September 15, 2016, the Navy awarded Austral a $249 million contract for the design and construction of two additional T-EPFs, thereby extending Austral's total EPF build to 12 vessels valued at $1.9 billion. The first nine ships have already been delivered and the current construction schedule now runs into 2022.

The expeditionary fast transport is a shallow-draft commercially-based catamaran built of aluminum to provide combatant commanders with high-speed sealift mobility along with a cargo-handling capability. It bridges the gap between high-speed/low-capacity airlift and low-speed/high-capacity sealift. As the Navy so clearly puts it, EPFs "transport personnel, equipment and supplies over operational distances with access to littoral offload points including austere, minor and degraded ports in support of the Global War on Terrorism (GWOT)/Theater Security Coordination Program (TSCP), Intra-theater Operational/Littoral Maneuver and Sustainment and Seabasing. EPFs enable the rapid projection, agile maneuver and sustainment of modular, tailored forces in response to a wide range of military and civilian contingencies" such as humanitarian assistance, disaster relief and the evacuation of non-combatants.[1] The Navy is considering other missions for the expeditionary fast transports, including acting as a command ship for operations and engagements with regional nations.

These ships are designed to carry 600 short tons of military cargo over 1,200 nautical miles at an average cruising speed of 35 knots in Sea State 3 (waves of 4–8 feet). With a draft of 13 feet, the EPF can enter shallow draft ports and waterways, and when mated to a roll-on/roll-off facility, it can on- or offload a combat-loaded M1A2 Abrams tank. In addition, the ship has a flight deck for helicopter operations and an offload ramp to allow vehicles to quickly drive off the ship.

EPFs are crewed and operated by 26–28 civilian mariners of the Military Sealift Command (MSC) and can carry 312 embarked troops in airliner-type seating with berthing for an additional 104 people.

In recent months, T-EPF 1, T-EPF 5, T-EPF 7 and T-EPF 8 have operated in the Atlantic and/or Mediterranean areas; while T-EPF 3, T-EPF 4, and T-EPF 6 have been deployed to the western Pacific, and T-EPF 2 has worked in the Arabian Gulf. T-EPF 9 is scheduled to be employed in the Pacific, and the Navy is planning to use T-EPF 10 in the Atlantic and T-EPF 11 in the central and western Pacific after they are delivered.

The ships have various name sources. For example, the first expeditionary fast transport (JHSV 1) was named for a force that leads an attack (probably because it was originally slated for Army service). The second JHSV was originally named *Vigilant* but because there already was a USCG medium endurance cutter (WMEC 617) with the same name, she was renamed on November 6, 2011, by Navy Secretary Ray Mabus as *Choctaw County*, his place of birth.[2] Later EPFs were named for U.S. cities, with the exception of T-EPF 11 which is named for a U.S. territory.

T-EPF Roster

In the listing below, T-EPF 1–T-EPF 7 were originally designated T-JHSV 1–T-JHSV 7, respectively, before being reclassified as expeditionary fast transports in September 2015.

USNS *Millinocket* (T-EPF 3) is lowering her cargo ramp onto a pier in Puerto Princesa, Philippines, on October 1, 2016. The ship is about to embark troops and equipment of the Philippine armed forces who will be participating with U.S. troops in the PHIBLEX 33 amphibious landing exercise (U.S. Navy photograph).

T-EPF 1	*Spearhead*[3] [A]	T-EPF 7	*Carson City*[9] [A]
T-EPF 2	*Choctaw County*[4] [A]	T-EPF 8	*Yuma*[10] [A]
T-EPF 3	*Millinocket*[5] [A]	T-EPF 9	*City of Bismarck*[11] [A]
T-EPF 4	*Fall River*[6] [A]	T-EPF 10	*Burlington*[12] [B]
T-EPF 5	*Trenton*[7] [A]	T-EPF 11	*Puerto Rico*[13] [B]
T-EPF 6	*Brunswick*[8] [A]	T-EPF 12	*Newport*[14] [B]

Specifications

Length: 338 feet
Beam: 93.5 feet
Draft: 13 feet
Displacement: 2,400 tons (full load)
Propulsion: 4 MTU 20V8000 M71L diesel engines; 48,800 bhp; 4 Wartsila WLD 1400 SR waterjets
Speed: 35–40 knots
Personnel: 28 MSC civilians & more than 300 troops

Selected Histories

USNS *Spearhead* (T-EPF 1)

USNS *Spearhead* was laid down by Austral USA on July 22, 2010, and launched in Mobile, Alabama, on September 17, 2011. After successfully completing acceptance trials

A U.S. Army UH-60 Black Hawk helicopter has just taken off from USNS *Spearhead* (T-EPF 1) in the Gulf of Panama on September 25, 2016, as the ship participates in UNITAS 2016, an annual multinational regional exercise (U.S. Navy photograph).

on August 16, 2012, she was placed in service with MSC as T-JHSV 1 on December 5, 2012.

Following her delivery and acceptance by the Navy, *Spearhead* proceeded to her new homeport in Little Creek, Virginia, in February 2013. She left there on January 16, 2014, on her first deployment out to the U.S. Sixth Fleet in the Mediterranean. The joint high speed vessel arrived in Souda Bay, Greece, on February 24, 2014. Early the next month, she participated with 12 European and West African nations in Exercise Saharan Express in the waters off West Africa. In mid–April *Spearhead* was in the Gulf of Guinea participating in Exercise Obangame Express, after which she departed for home on May 2, 2014.

T-JHSV 1 deployed back across the Atlantic very early in 2015, paying a port visit to Rota, Spain, on January 6. Two months later she took part in Exercise Obangame 2015 with an embarked detachment of U.S., Spanish and British Marines. On April 23, 2015, the ship visited Libreville, Gabon, two days later members of a Moroccan Navy boarding team trained on board her, and on April 26–27, she called at Dakar, Senegal. Between June and October, *Spearhead* operated in the U.S. Southern Command area of responsibility (AOR). During that deployment, she visited Cuba, Honduras, Belize, Guatemala and Colombia before arriving in Mayport, Florida, on October 9. The ship was reclassified as an expeditionary fast transport and redesignated as T-EPF 1 on September 3, 2015.

Spearhead's crew trained in late December 2015 for the upcoming 2016 deployment—her third—to the Sixth Fleet area of responsibility. During that voyage they would be working with personnel from six African partner nations on maritime law enforcement as part of an African Partnership Station (APS) mission. T-EPF 1 departed her homeport on December 29, 2015, and returned to Little Creek on May 5, 2016. While overseas, she had operated in the Gulf of Guinea, and made port calls in Cameroon, Gabon, Ghana, Senegal and Spain.

Spearhead visited Key West, Florida, on July 3–4, 2017, en route to a deployment to the Southern Command. Two weeks later she was in Gulfport, Mississippi, to embark nearly 800,000 pounds of cargo, including construction equipment and medical supplies, for use on the deployment to Central and South America. As part of her participation in Southern Partnership Station 2017, *Spearhead* supported disaster relief efforts in the Caribbean following Hurricanes Irma and Maria in September 2017. She arrived in St. Martin on September 16 to assist the U.S. Agency for International Development (USAID), and the ship offloaded 1,000 meals and 81,000 bottles of water at the island. On September 29, she picked up equipment and USAID and military personnel at Philipsburg, Saint Maarten, and transported them to Martinique, for disaster relief and assistance following the devastating Hurricane Maria that followed in the wake of Irma. Also in 2017 she performed detection and maneuvering patrols in the Southern Command AOR, and provided an additional anti-drug trafficking capability to Joint Interagency Task Force South and the U.S. Coast Guard.

Spearhead departed Little Creek on February 27, 2018, for a three-month Continuing Promise 2018 training mission, her second, during which the ship transported personnel who provided medical, environmental, veterinary and humanitarian assistance in Honduras, Guatemala and Colombia.

Spearhead is currently homeported at Joint Expeditionary Base Little Creek-Fort Story, Virginia, and periodically deploys on operations in Central and South America, and western Africa.

USNS *Fall River* (T-EPF 4)

USNS *Fall River* (T-EPF 4) is underway on acceptance trials in the Gulf of Mexico on July 25, 2014 (U.S. Navy photograph).

- Laid down on May 20, 2013, and christened on January 11, 2014.
- Completed acceptance trials on July 25, 2014.
- Delivered as T-JHSV 4 to MSC on September 16, 2014.
- Reclassified as expeditionary fast transport and reclassified as T-EPF 4 in September 2015.
- Departed Singapore on March 4, 2017, to serve as the command platform for the Pacific Partnership 2017 multilateral disaster response preparedness mission in the Indo-Asia-Pacific region. The mission involved stops in Sri Lanka, Malaysia and Vietnam, and was completed in May 2017.
- Visited Yangon, Myanmar, March 23–25, 2017—the first U.S. Navy ship to make an official call to Myanmar since the World War II era.
- *Fall River* was replaced in March 2018 by USNS *Brunswick* (T-EPF 6) as the secondary mission platform for the Pacific Partnership 2018 mission because additional maintenance and repairs would have prevented her participation.

Notes

1. "Expeditionary Fast Transport (EPF)," U.S. Navy Fact File, January 12, 2018.
2. This name selection is further evidence of the inconsistency and irregularity that has distorted long-standing Navy protocols for naming and classifying its ships. Until recently a name like "Choctaw County" would have been given to a tank landing ship (LST) and the "E" prefix in the EPF hull classification symbol would have indicated a vessel in experimental use, e.g., the test ship and former destroyer *Paul F. Foster* (EDD 964).
3. See Histories for additional information.
4. Laid down on November 8, 2011, christened on September 15, 2012, launched on October 1, 2012, placed in service as joint high speed vessel T-JHSV 2 on June 6, 2013, reclassified as expeditionary fast transport and redesignated as T-EPF 2 in September 2015. Provided logistical support in the Arabian Gulf in 2017.
5. Laid down on May 3, 2012, christened on April 20, 2013, delivered to MSC as T-JHSV 3 on March 25, 2014, reclassified as expeditionary fast transport and redesignated as T-EPF 3 in September 2015. Participated in the Pacific Partnership 2015 exercise in the western Pacific. While assigned to Destroyer Squadron 7 in 2018, paid the Navy's first visit to Makassar, Indonesia, on May 4. On June 11, 2018, arrived in Manila, the Philippines, completing a U.S. Seventh Fleet theater security cooperation patrol.
6. See Histories for additional information.
7. Laid down on March 10, 2014, launched on September 30, 2014, christened on January 10, 2015, and placed in service with MSC as T-JHSV 5 on April 13, 2015, and reclassified as expeditionary fast transport and redesignated as T-EPF 5 in September 2015. Supported maritime security operations in the Mediterranean Sea and Atlantic during 2017. Early in 2018 *Trenton* personnel participated in humanitarian relief and cleanup efforts following deadly floods in Mandra, Greece. Rescued 41 mariners in the Mediterranean Sea on June 12, 2018, and transferred them to the Italian Coast Guard five days later.
8. Laid down on December 2, 2014, christened on May 9, 2015, launched on May 19, 2015, and placed in service with MSC as T-EPF 6 on January 14, 2016. Visited Kuching, Malaysia, in January 2018 and participated in mission Pacific Partnership 2018 beginning in March and concluding in Pattaya, Thailand, on May 24.
9. Laid down on July 31, 2015, completed acceptance trials on May 25–26, 2016, delivered to MSC as T-EPF 7 on June 24, 2016, conducted mock final contract trials in January 2017, and supported maritime security operations in the Mediterranean Sea and Atlantic Ocean during 2017. Participated in exercise BALTOPS 2018 in June 2018.
10. Laid down on March 29, 2016, christened in August 2016, launched on September 17, 2016, completed acceptance trials on January 26, 2017, accepted by the Navy on April 21, 2017, and placed in service with MSC on April 24, 2017.
11. Laid down on January 18, 2017, christened on May 13, 2017, launched on June 8, 2017, completed builder's trials in September 2017 and acceptance trials on October 20, 2017, and delivered to MSC on December 19, 2017. In May 2018 hosted 2,550 visitors in New York City during Fleet Week New York 2018.
12. Laid down on September 26, 2017, christened on February 24, 2018, and launched on March 1, 2018.
13. First aluminum cut on January 18, 2017.
14. Named on February 13, 2018.

Expeditionary Sea Bases (T-ESB) / Expeditionary Transfer Docks (T-ESD)

The expeditionary transfer dock USNS *Montford Point* (T-ESD 1) in the foreground is performing a "skin-to-skin" maneuver with the cargo ship USNS *GYSGT Fred W. Stockham* (T-AK 3017) at sea off Pohang, South Korea, on March 13, 2016. In this maneuver, *Montford Point* is serving as a mobile transfer platform or floating pier to receive offloaded equipment and materials from the cargo ship (U.S. Navy photograph).

Beginning in 2005 the Navy conducted various exercises to test and evaluate its ability to transfer vehicles and equipment between cargo ships and a self-propelled floating dock or mobile landing platform (MLP). In this concept, the MLP functions as intermediate transfer point between large cargo ships and smaller vessels such as air cushion landing craft (LCAC) which ferry the transferred cargo ashore. This process thereby eliminates the need for the original cargo ship to transport its load all the way into port for conventional offloading at a pier and would be most useful in areas lacking adequate shore-based cargo-handling facilities and equipment.

In 2010 the Navy employed the commercial semi-submersible heavy lift ship MV *Mighty Servant 3* as a surrogate or stand-in MLP in exercises to assess this concept. In one such exercise, *Mighty Servant 3* successfully transferred personnel along with wheeled and tracked vehicles to the vehicle cargo ship [q.v.] USNS *Soderman* (T-AKR 317) using a new "motion compensating vehicle transfer ramp" specially designed for this purpose. The exercise proved that the MLP could transfer cargo in high sea state three and low sea state four conditions.

Accordingly, the Navy engaged General Dynamics/National Steel and Shipbuilding Company (NASSCO) to undertake a MLP design and production study. After evaluating NASSCO's design and production capabilities, on May 27, 2011, the Navy awarded a fixed-price incentive fee contract to the builder for construction of the first two MLPs. They were laid down in January and April 2012, and placed in service with MSC as T-MLP 1 and T-MLP 2 in May 2013 and March 2014, respectively. On February 26, 2012, the Navy awarded NASSCO a detailed design and construction contract for the third T-MLP but the ship's configuration was changed midway through its construction in March 2014. T-MLP 3 entered service in June 2015. On December 19, 2014, NASSCO received a detail design and construction contract for the fourth ship and the Navy awarded the builder a construction contract for the fifth vessel on December 29, 2016.

The ships are based on the commercial Alaska-class tanker design (see Specifications). The first two were configured with what the Navy calls the Core Capability Set, which consists of "add-on modules that support a vehicle staging area, vehicle transfer ramp, large mooring fenders and up to three Landing Craft Air Cushion vessel lanes to support core transfer requirements."[1] In what are termed "skin-to-skin" operations, a cargo ship and the transfer dock navigate and moor alongside each other. After they are moored together, the cargo ship lifts the transfer dock's ramp and connects it to the cargo ship. Once the connection is secured, vehicles and cargo can be rolled on and off the cargo ship quickly. The transfer dock has a float-on/float-off capability, enabling it to ballast down or semi-submerge to about 50 feet, enabling LCACs and other craft to maneuver right up to the MLP's mission deck to pick up cargo.

In September 2015 the Navy reclassified mobile landing platforms T-MLP 1 and T-MLP 2 as expeditionary transfer docks and redesignated them as T-ESD 1 and T-ESD 2. They are assigned to MSC's Prepositioning (PM3) program and operate with deployed Maritime Prepositioning Ship squadrons. The ESDs can cruise 9,500 nautical miles at a sustained speed of 15 knots, contain 25,000 square feet of vehicle and equipment storage space, and stow 380,000 gallons of JP-5 fuel.

The next three ships in the program were reclassified as expeditionary mobile bases and redesignated as T-ESB 3–T-ESB 5 in September 2015. They differed from the original two MLPs by being designed to support a variety of maritime missions, including Special Operations Forces and Airborne Mine Countermeasures (AMCM). "The ESBs have a four spot flight deck and hanger, and are designed around four core capabilities: aviation facilities, berthing, equipment staging support, and command and control assets."[2] The ships' primary role is to serve as afloat forward staging bases [q.v.] (AFSB) to support AMCM and special operations. They can handle helicopters up to the size of the MH-53E Sea Dragon (and with future upgrades, the MV-22B Ospreys) and accommodate approximately 250 military personnel.

T-ESD 3 was delivered on June 12, 2015, for service with the MSC, and as such was initially termed a United States Naval Ship (USNS). However, when she deployed to the U.S. Fifth Fleet area of responsibility in August 2017, she was commissioned as a Navy ship and redesignated as USS *Louis B. Puller* (ESD 3) with a Navy captain in command and a permanently embarked Navy/MSC crew. According to the Navy, these changes "will provide combatant commanders greater operational flexibility on how the platform, is employed in accordance with the laws of armed conflict."[3] T-ESD 4 was delivered on February 22, 2018, and at this writing, T-ESD 5 is under construction by NASSCO in San Diego.

1. Combat Logistics and Fleet Support Ships

The Navy plans to fund the procurement of two additional T-ESBs: one each in Fiscal Year 2019 and Fiscal Year 2020, with $650 million to be requested in each of those two years. The service's current new construction and shipbuilding plan includes no T-ESB funding in Fiscal Years 2021–2023.[4]

The names of the five ESB and ESD ships refer to either a Marine Corps facility (Montfort Point) or notable Marines.

ESB / ESD Roster

T-ESD 1	*Montford Point* [A]	T-ESB 5	*Miguel Keith* [B]
T-ESD 2	*John Glenn* [A]	T-ESB 6[5]	
ESB 3	*Louis B. Puller* {A}	T-ESB 7[6]	
T-ESB 4	*Hershel "Woody" Williams* [B]		

SPECIFICATIONS

ESB/T-ESB

Length: 785 feet
Beam: 164 feet
Draft: 34.4 feet (full load)
Displacement: 90,000 tons (full load)
Propulsion: commercial diesel-electric; 2 shafts
Speed: 15 knots
Personnel: 34 MSC civilians & 250 military (depending on mission)

T-ESD

Length: 785 feet
Beam: 164 feet
Draft: 29.5 feet (full load)
Displacement: 78,000 tons (full load)
Propulsion: commercial diesel-electric; 2 shafts
Speed: 15 knots
Personnel: 34 MSC civilians

SUMMARY HISTORIES

USNS *Montford Point* (T-ESD 1)

- Built in 2012–2013 by General Dynamics/NASSCO in San Diego, California.
- Laid down on January 19, 2012, floated out on November 13, 2012, and christened on March 2, 2013.
- Completed builder's trials on March 20, 2013.
- Completed acceptance trials on April 19, 2013.
- Placed in service with MSC as mobile landing platform USNS *Montford Point* (T-MLP 1) on May 14, 2013.
- Assigned to Maritime Prepositioning Squadron 3 (MPSRON-3) based in the Guam-Saipan area of WestPac.
- Conducted mooring operations with the joint high-speed vessel *Millinocket* (JHSV 3) in October 2014.
- Reclassified as expeditionary transfer dock and redesignated as T-ESD 1 on September 4, 2015.

A few days after she was reclassified as an expeditionary transfer dock, USNS *Montford Point* is moored at a pier in Yokosuka, Japan, on September 22, 2015 (U.S. Navy photograph).

- In March 2016 performed "skin-to-skin" (S2S) operations with the cargo ship [q.v.] USNS *GYSGT Fred W. Stockham* (T-AK 3017) as part of Exercise Ssang Yong.
- In June 2016 participated in Exercise CARAT Thailand 2016, an eight-day training event in the Gulf of Thailand and ashore. T-ESD 1 supported LCAC operations during amphibious landings involving U.S. Marines and Royal Thai Marines.
- Conducted S2S maneuvers in July 2016 with vehicle cargo ship [q.v.] USNS *Dahl* (T-AKR 312).
- Participated in Exercise SEACAT 2016 in August 2016 along with naval and coast guard personnel from eight countries in Southeast Asia and the United States.
- Performed S2S drills in June 2017 with vehicle cargo ships [q.v.] USNS *Soderman* (T-AKR 317) and USNS *Red Cloud* (T-AKR 313) and cargo ship USNS *GYSGT Fred W. Stockham* (T-AK 3017).

USNS *John Glenn* (T-ESD 2)

- Built in 2012–2013 by General Dynamics/NASSCO in San Diego, California.
- Laid down on April 17, 2012, floated off on September 15, 2013, and christened on February 1, 2014.
- Completed builder's sea trials on January 13, 2014.
- Placed in service with MSC as mobile landing platform USNS *John Glenn* (T-MLP 2) on March 12, 2014.

The second of the Navy's two transfer expeditionary transfer docks, USNS *John Glenn* is underway, probably near San Diego, in this undated photograph (U.S. Navy photograph).

- Reclassified as expeditionary transfer dock and redesignated as T-ESD 2 on September 4, 2015.

USS *Lewis B. Puller* (ESB 3)

- Built in 2013–2015 by General Dynamics/NASSCO in San Diego, California.
- Laid down on November 5, 2013, and launched on November 6, 2014.
- Delivered to MSC on June 12, 2015, as mobile landing platform USNS *Lewis B. Puller* (T-MLP 3), the first afloat forward staging base [q.v.] variant of the MLP.[7]
- Reclassified as expeditionary transfer dock and redesignated as T-ESB 3 on September 4, 2015.
- Homeported in Norfolk, Virginia beginning October 13, 2015.
- Performed airborne countermine training with Helicopter Mine Countermeasures Squadron 15 in mid–June 2016.
- Deployed to U.S. Fifth Fleet area of responsibility in the Middle East on July 10, 2017 to support U.S. Navy and allied forces operating in the region.
- Commissioned as USS *Lewis B. Puller* (ESD 3) in Bahrain on August 17, 2017, the first ship to be commissioned outside the United States.
- Relieved USS *Ponce* (AFSB(I) 15) as afloat forward staging base [q.v.] in the summer of 2017.
- In February 2018 engaged in personnel cross-training with the guided missile destroyer USS *Preble* (DDG 88) in the Arabian Gulf.

Assisted by tugs shortly after she was floated off (launched) by her builder NASSCO, the future USS *Lewis B. Puller* is in San Diego on November 6, 2014 (NASSCO photograph courtesy of the U.S. Navy).

USNS *Hershel "Woody" Williams* (T-ESB 4)

An undated artist rendering of the expeditionary sea base USNS *Hershel "Woody" Williams* before her February 2018 delivery to the Military Sealift Command (U.S. Navy photograph).

- Built in 2016–2017 by General Dynamics/NASSCO in San Diego, California.
- Laid down on August 2, 2016, and christened on October 21, 2017.
- On February 15, 2018, the Marine Corps Commandant said his service would prefer ESB 4 to be deployed to the Mediterranean and the U.S. Central Command.[8]
- Delivered to MSC on February 22, 2018, as expeditionary sea base USNS *Hershel "Woody" Williams* (T-ESB 4).

USNS *Miguel Keith* (T-ESB 5)

This artist rendering illustrates the future expeditionary sea base USNS *Miguel Keith* (T-ESB 5) which is scheduled to be delivered to MSC in 2019 (U.S. Navy photograph).

- Under construction by General Dynamics/NASSCO in San Diego, California.
- Construction contract awarded on December 29, 2016.
- Named on November 4, 2017.
- Laid down on January 30, 2018.

NOTES

1. "Expeditionary Transfer Dock (ESD)/Expeditionary Mobile Base (ESB)," http://www.navy.mil/navydata/fact_display.asp?cid=4600&ct=4&source=GovDelivery&tid=675.
2. *Ibid.*
3. *Ibid.*
4. Report to Congress on the Annual Long-Range Plan for Construction of Naval Vessels for Fiscal Year 2019, Office of the Chief of Naval Operations, February 2018.

5. Planned.
6. *Ibid.*
7. In a November 2014 Navy photograph the ship is also designated as T-AFSB 1.
8. Were T-ESB 4 to be so deployed, it has not yet been determined whether she would be commissioned as a Navy warship—as was T-EFB 3—and change its designations from USNS to USS and from T-ESB 4 to ESB 4.

Command Ships (LCC)

The command ship USS *Blue Ridge* (LCC 19) is steaming off Oahu, Hawaii, on September 3, 1977, en route to joining the U.S. Seventh Fleet in the western Pacific (U.S. Navy photograph).

During World War II the Navy commissioned 16 amphibious force flagships (AGCs), with another two added in late 1945 (see AGC section in Chapter 3 for details). The AGCs carried Navy fleet and force commanders and their staffs, as well as Marine and Army headquarters units when conducting combined operations. These vessels were derived and converted from Maritime Commission cargo ship type hulls, a Navy transport and a small seaplane tender, and they were fitted with extensive communications equipment. Amphibious force flagships were originally placed in the fleet auxiliary category but were reclassified as amphibious command ships (LCCs) in the amphibious warfare category on January 1, 1969.

1. Combat Logistics and Fleet Support Ships

Between 1967 and 1970 the Navy constructed its first and only purpose-built amphibious command ships: LCC 19 and LCC 20.[1] Commissioned in 1970 and 1971, they were specifically designed to keep pace with 20-knot amphibious warfare vessels, and were equipped with a large landing pad for helicopters, and an array of electronic equipment, antennas and transmitters. In 1979 and 1981 these two LCCs assumed the role of fleet flagships previously filled by cruisers early in the Cold War. Accordingly, USS *Blue Ridge* (LCC 19) relieved the guided missile cruiser USS *Oklahoma City* (CG 5) as U.S. Seventh Fleet flagship in October 1979, while USS *Mount Whitney* (LCC 20) became fleet command ship of the U.S. Second Fleet in 1981, and later flagship of the U.S. Sixth Fleet in February 2005. Both vessels are now listed in the fleet support ship category, hence their inclusion in this chapter.[2]

USS *Blue Ridge* is forward-deployed and homeported in Yokosuka, Japan, and manned by an all-Navy crew of approximately 850 officers and enlisted personnel, including the Seventh Fleet commander and staff. USS *Mount Whitney* is forward-deployed and homeported in Gaeta, Italy. Unlike her sister ship, *Mount Whitney* is operated by a joint Navy-Military Sealift Command (MSC) crew of approximately 320 personnel. The Navy crew performs command, communications, and executive functions while the MSC civil service mariners perform in navigation, deck, engineering, laundry and mess functions.

The LCCs are armed with two Mk 15 Phalanx close-in weapons systems (CIWS) and they can carry any Navy helicopter other than the CH-53 Sea Stallion. On May 23, 2016, *Mount Whitney* became the first LCC to have a Marine Corps MV-22B Osprey land on its flight deck.

The two LCCs are now very "mature" ships; both are in their fourth decade of continuous service. In 2011 the Navy's Chief of Naval Operations pushed their projected "expiration date" out to 2039, which would make them nearly 70 years old when decommissioned! To help prolong their "shelf life," the Naval Sea Systems Command and MSC are undertaking an Extended Service Life Program (ELP) intended to ensure that the LCCs can support the full range of mission requirements for their embarked fleet commanders. The ELP "provides for the repair and overhaul of systems/equipment, replacement of obsolete equipment and modernization of selected systems, spaces and equipment." Major areas of focus in the ELP include "shipboard electrical generation and distribution, HVAC upgrades, operational space optimization, habitability and safety modifications, and corrosion control."[3]

The two command ships are named for a mountain range and a mountain, respectively.

LCC Roster

LCC 19   *Blue Ridge* [A]
LCC 20   *Mount Whitney* [A]

Specifications

Length: 634 feet (overall)
Beam: 108 feet
Draft: 28.8 feet
Displacement: 8,874 tons (full load)
Propulsion: 1 steam turbine; 22,000 shp; 1 shaft

Speed: 23 knots
Personnel[4]: 34 Navy officers & 564 Navy enlisted (LCC 19)
12 Navy officers, 161 Navy enlisted & 146 civilian MSC (LCC 20)

SUMMARY HISTORIES

USS *Blue Ridge* (LCC 19)

USS *Blue Ridge* (LCC 19) is underway in the Pacific on November 17, 2009, while participating with ships from the Japanese Maritime Self-Defense Force in the ANNUALEX 21G exercise (U.S. Navy photograph).

- Built by the Philadelphia Naval Shipyard in 1967–1970.
- Laid down as AGC 19 on February 27, 1967, and launched on January 4, 1969.
- Commissioned as USS *Blue Ridge* (LCC 19) on November 14, 1970.
- Transited from Philadelphia to her first homeport of San Diego, California, via the Strait of Magellan February 11–April 9, 1971.
- Conducted local operations, refresher training, and amphibious exercises before undergoing a post-shakedown availability October-December 1971.
- Began maiden deployment to the western Pacific (WestPac) on January 7, 1972, and relieved the amphibious command ship USS *Eldorado* (LCC 11) as the amphibious force flagship of the U.S. Seventh Fleet.
- Operated off Vietnam in the Gulf of Tonkin April–July 1972 while serving as a task force command ship. Engaged enemy shore batteries on Tiger Island on June 27.

- Returned home on August 18, 1972.
- Departed San Diego for second WestPac deployment on February 24, 1973, and relieved the amphibious transport USS *Paul Revere* (LPA 248) as flagship for the commander of Amphibious Group 1.
- During the 1973 deployment participated in various multilateral amphibious exercises, supported Operation End Sweep in North Vietnamese waters, and visited ports in the Asia. Returned to San Diego on October 23.
- Operated off California October 1973–October 1974.
- Deployed from San Diego to WestPac on October 18, 1974. During her service as Seventh Fleet Amphibious Force flagship, *Blue Ridge* provided aid and assistance to South Vietnamese refugees in April 1975. She was relieved by the amphibious assault ship (helicopter) USS *Denver* (LPH 9) the following month and returned to her homeport on May 22, 1975.
- Between November 1975 and June 1976 underwent an overhaul at the Long Beach Naval Shipyard.
- Engaged in refresher training during the summer of 1976.
- Deployed to WestPac on September 25, 1976. Exercised with Australian amphibious forces and performed various port calls and training evolutions during the deployment, and returned home on March 8, 1977.
- Deployed to WestPac on August 24, 1977, and returned to San Diego on November 15, 1977.
- Deployed to WestPac on August 3, 1978, and was back in her homeport on November 6, 1978.
- Transferred to her new and current homeport of Yokosuka, Japan in July 1979.
- Relieved the guided missile cruiser USS *Oklahoma City* (CG 5) as flagship of the Seventh Fleet in October 1979.
- Rescued refugees fleeing Vietnam in the South China Sea at various times during the 1979–1984 period.
- Visited Shanghai, China, in May 1989—one of three U.S. warships to visit that harbor for the first time since 1949.
- Served as flagship for U.S. Naval Forces Central Command in the Persian Gulf for nine and a half months during Operations Desert Shield and Desert Storm in 1990–1991.
- Visited Vladivostok, Russia, in July 1996, as part of events commemorating the 300th anniversary of the Russian Navy.
- Visited Vladivostok again in August 2002.
- In February 2004 paid a four-day port visit to Shanghai, China, her first visit there since March 2001. Returned to Yokosuka on March 16, 2004, after a seven-week cruise which included stops in Malaysia, Thailand, Okinawa, and the Philippines.
- Between March 15 and 22, 2005, visited Manila and the former Navy base at Subic Bay in the Philippines.
- *Blue Ridge* and her embarked Seventh Fleet staff paid a two-day visit to Manila February 8–9, 2007, and conducted shipboard tours, musical and cultural performances, and community service projects.

- Completed a two-month deployment on November 19, 2009, which included visits to South Korea, Guam, New Caledonia, Malaysia, Singapore, Australia and Vietnam. During the cruise, LCC 19 participated in a passing exercise with the French Navy and a combined training exercise with the Japan Maritime Self-Defense Force.
- On November 14, 2009, sailors and Marines celebrated the 39th birthday of the ship, while she was at sea on a deployment.
- Visited Pattaya, Thailand, in April 2010 during a spring deployment. She also made port visits to South Korea, Hong Kong, Malaysia and Indonesia on the cruise that began March 2.
- Participated in Exercise Ulchi Freedom Guardian with the South Korean Navy and visited Busan, South Korea in August 2010.
- As part of Operation Tomodachi, carried relief supplies from Singapore to Japan following the devastating March 11, 2011, earthquake and tsunami. Secretary of Defense Leon E. Panetta visited *Blue Ridge* on October 26, 2011, and thanked her personnel for their efforts during Tomodachi.
- Called on Manila on March 23, 2012. With more than 100 sailors and Marines with Filipino backgrounds on board, many members of the crew used the port visit to see their families.
- In May 2012 visited Jakarta, Indonesia, her first port call there since April 2010.
- Departed Yokosuka April 29, 2014, on a patrol in the Indo-Asia-Pacific region.
- When the amphibious transport dock USS *Denver* (LPD 9) decommissioned on August 14, 2014, *Blue Ridge* became the second oldest ship in the Navy's active duty fleet, just behind the frigate USS *Constitution* which was commissioned 173 years before her. (In August 2014 LCC 19 had been forward-deployed in Japan for 34 years.)
- Visited Zhanjiang, China, in April 2015.
- Completed a Mobility Damage Control Warfare assessment in May 2015 to demonstrate the crew's proficiency in responding to casualties and keeping the ship afloat in a simulated combat situation.
- Returned to homeport on September 2, 2015, after a three-month patrol in the Indo-Asia-Pacific region.
- Departed her homeport on February 22, 2016, to begin another patrol in the Seventh Fleet area of operations.
- Visited Shanghai, China, on May 6, 2016.
- In March 2017 *Blue Ridge* became the first ship in its class to obtain a large-scale upgrade to its network infrastructure. The ship's Consolidated Afloat Network and Enterprise Services (CANES) upgrade was the largest such installation in the Navy at that point.
- USS *Blue Ridge* earned two Battle Stars for her service during the Vietnam War.

USS *Mount Whitney* (LCC 20)[5]

- Built by Newport News Shipbuilding & Dry Dock Company in 1969–1970 as Blue Ridge-class amphibious force flagship.
- Laid down as AGC 20 on January 8, 1969 and launched as LCC 20 on January 8, 1970.

1. Combat Logistics and Fleet Support Ships 135

On October 6, 2005, USS *Mount Whitney* (LCC 20) is steaming in the Mediterranean Sea during the NATO exercise Destined Glory (Loyal Midas) 2005 (U.S. Navy photograph).

- Commissioned on January 16, 1971.
- Originally homeported in Norfolk, Virginia.
- Participated in various exercises and paid port calls in the Caribbean and the western Atlantic during the first half of 1972. Deployed to European waters in August and returned to Norfolk in October.
- Deployed to the U.S. Sixth Fleet area in the Mediterranean in May 1973 and returned home in July. Deployed for a second time that year on August 31 and returned home on December 6.
- Operated in the Caribbean early in 1974. Underwent dry-docking and yard availability July 1974–January 1975.
- Conducted various exercises early in 1975 and underwent an overhaul that summer.
- Participated in U.S. Bicentennial events in New York City in July 1976, and operated in the North Atlantic later that year.
- Remained in the western Atlantic early in 1977, deployed to Europe in September and returned home in December.
- Conducted various exercises early in 1978, deployed to Europe in September and was back in Norfolk the next month.
- Underwent a six-month $16.5 million regular overhaul at the Philadelphia Naval Shipyard June–December 1979.
- Operated in the North Atlantic in the second-half of 1980.
- From 1981 to 2005, served as flagship for the Commander of the U.S. Second Fleet and Commander Striking Fleet Atlantic.

- Participated in Operation Uphold Democracy in Haiti in 1994 with the commander of the joint task force embarked.
- Deployed to the U.S. Central Command area of responsibility on November 12, 2002, in support of Operation Enduring Freedom.
- In 2004, MSC civilian mariners joined the ship's crew, after which her complement consisted of approximately 170 Navy personnel and 155 civilians.
- In February 2005, *Mount Whitney*'s homeport was changed to Gaeta, Italy, and she relieved the amphibious transport dock USS *La Salle* (LPD 3) as flagship of the Sixth Fleet.
- Operated in the Black Sea in August 2008 and delivered humanitarian aid at the port of Poti, Georgia, during the Russo-Georgian War.
- During operations off Norway in September 2010, 242 sailors and MSC personnel were officially deemed "Bluenoses" in a ceremony inducting them into the royal and ancient order of the North Wind and as sons and daughters of Boreas Rex (i.e., first-timers who have crossed the boundary of the Arctic Circle).
- In 2011 operated as flagship for U.S. forces engaged in Operation Odyssey Dawn in Libya.
- Participated in August 19, 2012, events in Theoule-sur-Mer, France, commemorating the 68th anniversary of the August 1944 liberation of Provence.
- Underwent a 60-day overhaul and repair at the San Giorgio del Porto Shipyard in Genoa, Italy, February–April 2013. Following the overhaul, *Mount Whitney* deployed for two months to Portugal, Latvia and Germany, and participated in various community relations events, military exercises and port visits. She returned to Gaeta on July 3, 2013.
- Operated in the Black Sea in January 2014 during the Sochi Olympics in Russia.
- Entered the Viktor Lenac Shipyard in Rijeka, Croatia, on January 15, 2015. The nine-month yard availability was to enhance the ship's C4I (command, control, communications, computers and intelligence) capabilities, upgrade her shell plating, renew deck house steel and electrical power supply system, install new generators and control mechanisms, and refurbish her fuel systems. This work was intended to help extend *Mount Whitney*'s service life to 2039. Completed the availability in September 2015.
- Visited Glenmallan, Scotland, in October 2015.
- Returned to Gaeta on March 3, 2016, following a brief cruise to Cyprus and participation in command post exercise Juniper Cobra 2016.
- Departed her homeport on May 16, 2016, to prepare for BALTOPS 2016, an annual multinational exercise for U.S., allied and partner forces in the Baltic region of Europe. She led a flotilla of 43 ships participating in BALTOPS in Kiel, Germany, on June 23, and retuned to Gaeta on July 30, 2016.
- On May 23, 2016, a Marine Corps MV-22B Osprey made seven landings on the ship, the first time an Osprey had ever flown aboard an amphibious command ship.
- Along with personnel from 31 nations, participated in the eight-day March 2018 Obangame Express 2018 exercise in West Africa. The ship's operations in the Gulf of Guinea demonstrated U.S. support of regional efforts to counter various illegal activities at sea.

A MV-22B Osprey from Marine Medium Tiltroter Squadron 263 is taking off from *Mount Whitney*'s flight deck on May 23, 2016 (U.S. Navy photograph).

- Visited Tallinn, Estonia, on June 2, 2016; Helsinki, Finland, on July 8; and Aarhus, Denmark, on July 16, 2016.
- Made a return visit to Theoule-sur-Mer, France, on August 14, 2016, to commemorate the 72nd anniversary of Operation Dragoon, the allied liberation of Southern France in 1944.
- Departed Gaeta on October 7, 2016. After entering the Black Sea on October 10, conducted a bilateral PAASEX passing exercise with the Romanian Navy in the Black Sea ten days later.
- Entered a dry dock at the Viktor Lenac Shipyard in Croatia, on December 19, 2016, for a 10-month overhaul and upgrade as part of the ship' service life extension program. Celebrated her 46th birthday on January 16, 2017, while in the Croatian shipyard.
- Arrived in Valletta, Malta, on January 19, 2018, her first visit to that port since 2011.
- In June 2018, served as the flagship and communications platform for Naval Striking and Support Forces NATO during the two-week Baltic Operations (BALTOPS) 2018 exercise. The exercise involved 43 maritime units, 60aircraft and some 5,000 personnel.

Notes

1. The Navy had planned for a third Blue Ridge–class ship to be designated as AGC 21. However, that vessel was cancelled.

2. Navy press releases have referred to the two LCCs variously as flagships, command and control ships, command flagships, and amphibious command ships. Nevertheless, both the official Naval Vessel Register and the General Guidance for the Classification of Naval Vessels and Battle Force Counting Procedures (SECNAV Instruction 5030.8C), June 14, 2016, formally classify the LCCs simply as "command ships." It might be argued that after the LCCs assumed the full-time role of fleet flagships in 1979 and 1981 and were no longer strictly considered amphibious force vessels, they should have lost the "L" prefix in their hull classification symbol and been redesignated instead as CCs. As a precedent, "CC" was used to designate the cruiser USS *Northampton* (CC 1) when she served as a command ship for the Atlantic Fleet in the 1960s.

3. United States Navy Fact File, Amphibious Command Ships—LCC, Naval Sea Systems Command, January 9, 2017.

4. Various sources provide different data on the ships' complements. The data for LCC 19 was obtained from the document cited in Note 3 above.

5. Readers seeking official command histories and operations reports for this ship (covering the 1971–2002 period) can access those documents at https://www.history.navy.mil/research/archives/command-operations-reports/ships/m/mount-whitney-lcc-20-i.html.

Chapter 2

Support Ships

The U.S. Navy formally defines its support ships as "a grouping of ships designed to provide general support to either combatant forces or shore-based establishments; those auxiliary ships that provide support to naval operations, but are not involved with combatant forces, Navy warfighting, or support missions, and are not part of the battle force inventory."[1]

Currently, there are some 367 vessels in 14 different "active" hull classifications comprising the fleet's support ships. Each of these ship types are discussed below in alphabetical order of their hull classification symbols. In the roster listing each ship's name a bracketed letter indicates the vessel's most recently available status as follows: A = Active; C = Converted or reclassified to another vessel type; D = Disposed of; K = Struck from the Naval Vessel Register; L = Deactivated and laid up, generally in the National Defense Reserve Fleet; OS = Out of government service; R = In stand-by/reserve/reduced manning condition; S = Sold to unknown buyer; SC = Sold to a civilian operator or entity; SS = Sold for scrapping; SX = Expended as target; T = Transferred or sold to another U.S. agency, institution or nation; X = Cancelled; and Z = Sunk.

Note

1. "General Guidance for the Classification of Naval Vessels and Battle Force Counting Procedures" (SECNAV Instruction 5030.8C), June 14, 2016.

Crane Ships (T-ACS)

The Navy's crane ships included 10 former civilian container ships converted and fitted with three twin 30-ton-capacity pedestal cranes to lift containers and other cargo from themselves or adjacent vessels in forward ports where the usual heavy lift equipment is unavailable. The first T-ACS was completed in 1984 and the last in 1997. Five of the ships deployed to the Persian Gulf in 1990–1991. Four (T-ACS 7–T-ACS 10) have been deactivated and were transferred to the NDRF between 1989 and 1997, and six (T-ACS 1–T-ACS 6) are now in Reduced Operational Status (ROS)[1] in the MSC Ready Reserve Force and maintained by MARAD. The planned T-ACS 11 and T-ACS 12 contracts were not awarded. The T-ACS vessels carry state nicknames.

On June 5, 2009, the crane ship SS *Cornhusker State* (T-ACS 6) is arriving at the U.S. Naval Station in Guantanamo Bay, Cuba, to participate in a joint service exercise requiring ships to offload forces and supplies while offshore when port facilities are limited, damaged or undeveloped (U.S. Navy photograph).

ACS Roster

T-ACS 1	*Keystone State* [R]	T-ACS 6	*Cornhusker State* [R]
T-ACS 2	*Gem State* [R]	T-ACS 7	*Diamond State* [L]
T-ACS 3	*Grand Canyon State* [R]	T-ACS 8	*Equality State* [L]
T-ACS 4	*Gopher State* [R]	T-ACS 9	*Green Mountain State* [L]
T-ACS 5	*Flickertail State* [R]	T-ACS 10	*Beaver State* [C/T]

General Specifications—Keystone State–class

Length: 668.6 feet
Beam: 76.1 feet
Displacement: 31,500 tons (32,005.52 metric tons) full load
Propulsion: 2 boilers; 2 GE turbines; 19,250 shp; 1 shaft
Speed: 20 knots
Crew: 89 civilians

Histories

SS *Keystone State* (T-ACS 1)

Built by the National Steel & Shipbuilding Company in San Diego, California, *Keystone State* was laid down as the breakbulk container ship (C4-S-1aq type hull) *President Harrison* on January 23, 1965, and launched on October 2, 1965. She began her service with American President Lines, Inc., on April 25, 1966, and was acquired by MARAD on July 19, 1982, to be laid up in the NDRF in California and later in Virginia.

Between March 1983 and May 1984, *President Harrison* was converted to an auxiliary crane ship (C6-S-MA1qd hull type) by the Bay Shipbuilding Company in Sturgeon Bay, Wisconsin, during which time she was classified as T-ACS 1 on October 21, 1983, and renamed *Keystone State* on December 27, 1983.

T-ACS 1 was placed in service with MSC on May 8, 1984.

She has been activated and engaged in various missions, exercises, sea trials and drills from time to time over the years. For example, *Keystone State* was involved in Operation Risky Beach in August 1985, Operation Bold Eagle in September 1985, and Exercise Korean Retrograde 05 in 2005; and performed in activation drills in 1998, 2002, 2004, 2014, and 2016. The ship is assigned to Maritime Prepositioning Ship Squadron 3, berthed in Alameda, California, and maintained in a five-day readiness status (ROS 5).

2. Support Ships

SS *Gem State* (T-ACS 2)

- Former breakbulk container ship *President Monroe* built by National Steel & Shipbuilding Company.
- Laid down May 30, 1964, and launched May 22, 1965.
- Entered service with American President Lines, Inc. (APL), February 9, 1966.
- Traded by APL to MARAD on April 30, 1980, for credit on purchase price of new vessel and assigned to NDRF.
- Converted to C6-S-MA1qd auxiliary crane ship by Continental Marine in San Francisco beginning in October 1984 and renamed *Gem State* by MARAD the following month.
- Placed in service with MSC on October 31, 1985.
- Activated October 2, 1991, for MSC service in support of Operation Desert Storm. Later engaged in Operation Desert Sortie (removal of military equipment, supplies and ammunition out of Middle East).
- Returned to MARAD custody on February 14, 1992, after a 136-day activation.
- Currently berthed in Alameda assigned to Maritime Prepositioning Ship Squadron 3 and maintained in a five-day readiness status (ROS 5).

SS *Grand Canyon State* (T-ACS 3)

- Former breakbulk container ship *President Polk* built by National Steel & Shipbuilding Company.
- Laid down May 20, 1964, and launched January 23, 1965.
- Entered service with American President Lines, Inc., November 4, 1965.
- Acquired by MARAD in 1982 and laid up in NDRF in California.
- Converted to auxiliary crane ship by Dillingham Corp., in San Francisco from October 1985 to October 1987.
- Renamed *Grand Canyon State* on September 9, 1985 and placed in service with MSC on December 12, 1986.
- Currently berthed in Alameda assigned to Maritime Prepositioning Ship Squadron 3 and maintained in a five-day readiness status (ROS 5).

SS *Gopher State* (T-ACS 4)

- Former container ship (C5-S-73b hull type) *Export Leader* built by Bath Iron Works in Bath, Maine.
- Laid down on July 26, 1971, and launched July 8, 1972.
- Entered service with American Export–Isbrandtsen Lines, Inc. on January 22, 1973, and sold to Farrell Lines, Inc. in 1978.
- Acquired by MARAD in 1982.
- Served for 178 days as test ship for Project Arapaho (to demonstrate feasibility of operating ASW helicopters from merchant ships). Fitted with modular aviation facility, the ship conducted 45 night helicopter landings. Later laid up in NDRF in Virginia.
- Renamed *Gopher State* on June 13, 1986.
- Converted to auxiliary crane ship by Norfolk Shipbuilding & Drydock Corp. in Norfolk, Virginia, beginning October 21, 1986.

- Placed in service with MSC on October 12, 1987.
- Engaged in Operation Steel Box in September–November 1990 (transporting nerve agent artillery rounds from Wilhelmshaven, Germany, to Johnston Atoll in the Pacific for storage and disposal).
- Engaged in Operations Desert Shield, Desert Storm and Desert Sabre in 1990–1991.
- Currently berthed in Newport News, Virginia, and maintained in a five-day readiness status (ROS 5).

SS *Flickertail State* (T-ACS 5)

- Former container ship *Export Lightning* (C5-S-73b hull type) built by Bath Iron Works in Bath, Maine.
- Laid down on February 14, 1967, and launched on May 11, 1986.
- Entered service with American Export–Isbrandtsen Lines, Inc. on February 21, 1969, and sold to Farrell Lines, Inc. in 1978.
- Acquired by MARAD on December 15, 1986, and laid up in NDRF in Virginia.
- Renamed *Flickertail State* on June 13, 1986.
- Converted to auxiliary crane ship (C5-S-MA73c) by Norfolk Shipbuilding & Drydock Company in 1987–1988.
- Placed in service with MSC on February 6, 1988.
- Engaged in Operation Steel Box in September–November 1990 (transporting nerve agent artillery rounds from Wilhelmshaven, Germany, to Johnston Atoll in the Pacific for storage and disposal).
- Participated in Exercise Pacific Strike 2008, a joint logistics effort in 2008 involving more than 3,000 personnel to demonstrate a Joint Logistics Over the Shore (JLOTS) capability to deliver nearly 1,000 Army vehicles and more than 500 containers. *Flickertail State* carried more than 350 pieces of cargo for use by Navy Seabees in constructing a temporary pier.
- In 2009 a new large vessel interface lift on/lift off (LVI Lo/Lo) crane was installed on the ship to test its ability to transfer containers between two vessels while underway.
- Currently berthed in Newport News, Virginia, and maintained in a five-day readiness status (ROS 5).

SS *Cornhusker State* (T-ACS 6)

- Former container ship *Stag Hound* (C5-S-73b hull type) built by Bath Iron Works in Bath, Maine.
- Laid down on November 27, 1967, and launched on November 2, 1968.
- Delivered to MARAD on June 20, 1969, for service with American Export-Isbrandtsen Lines, Inc. and sold to Farrell Lines, Inc. in 1978.
- Acquired by MARAD on December 15, 1986, and laid up in NDRF in Virginia.
- Renamed *Cornhusker State* on June 13, 1986.
- Converted to auxiliary crane ship (C5-S-MA73c) by Norfolk Shipbuilding & Drydock Company in 1987–1988.
- Placed in service with MSC on February 6, 1988, and assigned to Ready Reserve Force.

- Currently berthed in Newport News, Virginia, and maintained in a five-day readiness status (ROS 5).

SS *Diamond State* (T-ACS 7)

- Former breakbulk cargo ship *Japan Mail* (C4-S-1s hull) built by Todd Shipyards in San Pedro, California, and launched August 8, 1971.
- Delivered to MARAD on April 19, 1962.
- Operated by American Mail Line as *Japan Mail* 1962–1975.
- Converted to a C6-S-1a container ship by Bethlehem Steel in San Francisco in 1971.
- Renamed *President Truman* on November 14, 1975, and operated by American President Lines 1975–1987.
- Returned to MARAD on January 21, 1987, and placed in NDRF.
- Converted to crane ship (C6-S-MA1xb) in 1988 and placed in service with MSC's Ready Reserve Force (RRF) on February 22, 1989.
- Removed from RRF and transferred to NDRF on July 28, 2006.
- Currently berthed in NDRF in Beaumont, Texas, as a parts source.

SS *Equality State* (T-ACS 8)

- Former breakbulk cargo ship (C4-S-1s) *Washington Mail* built by Todd Shipyards in San Pedro, California.
- Laid down July 6, 1960, and launched on May 11, 1961.
- Delivered to MARAD on January 2, 1962.
- Operated by American Mail Line 1962–1973. Lengthened in 1971 by Bethlehem Steel in San Francisco.
- Operated by American President Lines October 1, 1973, to August 30, 1983.
- Renamed *President Roosevelt* in November 1975.
- Sold to Delta Steamship Lines on August 30, 1983, and renamed *Santa Rosa*.
- Sold to United States Lines in 1985 and renamed *American Builder*.
- Acquired by MARAD on March 10, 1987.
- Converted to crane ship (C6-S-MA1xb) by Tampa Shipbuilding Company between January 1988 and February 1989.
- Renamed *Equality State* and assigned to MSC's RRF on May 24, 1989.
- Activated on August 31, 1990, and participated in Operation Desert Shield September 1990–May 1991 and in Operation Desert Sortie after the Gulf War.
- Deactivated September 1992–January 1993 at Bender Shipbuilding in Mobile, Alabama.
- Reactivated In September-October 2005 for relief operations in New Orleans following Hurricane Katrina.
- Returned to NDRF December 13, 2005.
- Currently berthed in NDRF in Beaumont, Texas, as parts source, and slated for disposal.

SS *Green Mountain State* (T-ACS 9)

- Former breakbulk cargo ship (C6-S-60a) *Mormacaltair* built by Ingalls Shipbuilding Inc. in Pascagoula, Mississippi.

- Laid down on December 2, 1963, launched on August 20, 1964, and delivered on March 26, 1965.
- Operated by Moore-McCormick Lines 1965–1983.
- Lengthened in 1975 by Todd Shipyard in Galveston, Texas.
- Sold to United States Lines in 1983 and renamed *American Altair*.
- Converted to crane ship (C6-S-MA60d hull) February 1989–September 1990 at National Steel and Shipbuilding in San Diego, California.
- Sold to MARAD in March 1992 and assigned to MSC's RRF. Placed in service as *Green Mountain State* on March 15, 1989, and berthed in Bremerton, Washington, in a five-day readiness status (ROS 5).
- Removed from RRF and transferred to NDRF on July 28, 2006.
- Currently berthed in NDRF in Suisun Bay, California, as parts source for sister ship *Pacific Tracker* (the former *Beaver State*, see below).

SS *Beaver State* (T-ACS 10)

- Former breakbulk cargo ship (C6-S-60a) *Mormacdraco* built by Ingalls Shipbuilding Inc. in Pascagoula, Mississippi.
- Laid down on April 13, 1964, launched on January 14, 1965, and delivered on May 28, 1965.
- Operated by Moore-McCormick Lines.
- Lengthened in 1976 by Todd Shipyard in Galveston, Texas.
- Sold to United States Lines in 1983 and renamed *American Draco* on September 13, 1983.
- Acquired by MARAD on April 2, 1987, and assigned to NDRF.
- Converted to crane ship (C6-S-MA60b hull) 1992–1997 by National Steel and Shipbuilding in San Diego, California.
- Renamed *Beaver State*. Placed in service with MSC's RRF on May 4, 1997, and berthed in Bremerton, Washington, in a five-day readiness status (ROS 5).
- Removed from RRF and transferred to NDRF on July 28, 2006.
- Converted to an X-band transportable radar ship (XTR 1) by Cascade General Shipyards in Portland, Oregon, for use in antiballistic missile testing by the U.S. Missile Defense Agency.
- Renamed *Pacific Tracker* on April 1, 2009.

Note

1. Laid up but with limited crews and ready to get underway with full crews in a few days.

Offshore Petroleum Distribution System (T-AG)

The Navy's offshore petroleum distribution system (OPDS) provides a capability for pumping out more than two million gallons of fuel oil a day from tankers anchored or moored off ports lacking suitable pierside facilities. Using up to eight miles of 8-inch-

USNS *VADM K. R. Wheeler* (T-AG 5001) is the Navy's only vessel capable of pumping diesel or aviation fuel to U.S. forces ashore from up to eight miles off the coast (U.S. Navy photograph).

diameter flexible pipes stored on five 35-foot spools on her weather deck, the OPDS vessel can "deploy a full length of pipe ashore, connect that pipe to the ship's bow discharge unit, run a float hose to a tanker from the ship's stern, and be ready to pump fuel at a rate of about 1,400 gallons per minute."[1] All this in less than 48 hours. The OPDS ship is supported by a 165-foot tender vessel, USNS *Fast Tempo*, which carries the float hose from the OPDS to the tanker to be pumped out. That tanker then pumps its cargo to holding tanks aboard the OPDS and from there the cargo is sent through her pipes to shore.

The OPDS, which is not a tanker herself, can connect up to any commercial or military tanker, pump 500,000 barrels per day, operate in currents of up to three knots and winds of up to 40 knots, and lay pipe in various ocean bottom conditions.

T-AG Roster

T-AG 5001   *VADM K. R. Wheeler* [A]

SPECIFICATIONS
Length: 348.5 feet
Beam: 70 feet
Draft: 26 feet

Displacement: 10,668 tons light
Propulsion: 2 diesel engines (MAK 12M32C); 16,314 bhp; 2 shafts
Speed: 15 knots
Personnel: 23–26 contract civilian mariners

History

USNS *Vice Admiral K.R. Wheeler* (T-AG 5001) was built in 2007 and originally owned by Edison Chouest Offshore of Cut Off, Louisiana—a provider of highly specialized offshore service and supply vessels. The ship was delivered to the Military Sealift Command at the Santa Rosa Island test range off the coast of Eglin Air Force Base, Florida, on September 20, 2007. MSC chartered the vessel for up to five years. (The NVR lists her charter date as March 31, 2010.) MSC purchased *Wheeler* in August 2012, making her a permanent unit in its fleet of auxiliaries. She then received six weeks of repairs and upgrades at Sembawang Wharves in Singapore, as part of a scheduled five-year maintenance cycle required by the U.S. Coast Guard and the American Bureau of Shipping. Repairs included removing and cleaning grid coolers, overhauling the ship's bow and stern thrusters, replacing the main propeller seal and painting the hull below the water line. This work was completed on October 17, 2012. The support vessel *Fast Tempo* received minor repairs at the same time.

USNS *Vice Admiral K.R. Wheeler*—the only active naval vessel with an "AG" hull number—is currently assigned to Maritime Prepositioning Ship Squadron 3 and operates out of the Guam/Saipan area of the Pacific.

Note

1. Laura M. Seal. "MSC Accepts New OPDS Platform—Improves Ability to Support U.S. Troops Ashore," *Sealift*, November 2007.

Missile Range Instrumentation Ships (T-AGM)

In the early 1960s the United States needed to extend the tracking coverage of missile tests and space flights offshore and beyond that usually provided by land-based facilities. The solution was to fit special electronics equipment and radars on board a small number of converted merchant-type vessels and one surveillance ship and deploy those vessels to sea as floating missile tracking ships. They were derived from a variety of sources, including former cargo ships, transports, and tankers. Designated as T-AGMs, the first missile range instrumentation ship—USNS *Range Tracker* (T-AGM 1)—entered the fleet in May 1961 and eventually was joined in this role over the years by some two dozen vessels. Ultimately the Navy acquired 13 merchant and naval ships and the Air Force another ten vessels (AGM 9–AGM 18) to support military and NASA missile and space requirements. All of them eventually were operated by MSC for the Navy, Air Force and NASA. The Air Force ships were transferred to MSC on April 28, 1964. The first AGMs began leaving service before the end of the 1960s and today there are only two remaining in operation—USNS *Invincible* (T-AGM 24) and USNS *Howard O. Lorenzen* (T-AGM 25)—

2. Support Ships

USNS *Howard O. Lorenzen* (T-AGM 25) is the Navy's newest missile range instrumentation ship, having replaced USNS *Observation Island* (T-AGM 23) in 2014 (U.S. Navy photograph).

both with the Navy's Military Sealift Command. AGMs have carried a variety of names, including cities, "range" names, and missile projects.

AGM Roster

T-AGM 1	*Range Tracker* [SS]	T-AGM 13	*Sword Knot* [SS]
T-AGM 2	*Range Recoverer*[1] [SS]	T-AGM 14	*Rose Knot* [D]
T-AGM 3	*Longview*[2] [SS]	T-AGM 15	*Coastal Sentry*[8] [SS]
T-AGM 4	*Richfield*[3] [SS]	T-AGM 16	*Coastal Crusader*[9] [SS]
T-AGM 5	*Sunnyvale*[4] [SS]	T-AGM 17	*Timber Hitch* [SS]
T-AGM 6	*Watertown* [SS]	T-AGM 18	*Sampan Hitch* [SS]
T-AGM 7	*Huntsville* [SS]	T-AGM 19	*Vanguard* [SS]
T-AGM 8	*Wheeling* [K/D]	T-AGM 20	*Redstone*[10] [SS]
T-AGM 9	*General H. H. Arnold*[5] [SS]	T-AGM 21	*Mercury*[11] [SC]
T-AGM 10	*General Hoyt S. Vanderberg*[6] [K]	T-AGM 22	*Range Sentinel*[12] [SS]
		T-AGM 23	*Observation Island* [L]
T-AGM 11	*Twin Falls*[7] [SS]	T-AGM 24	*Invincible* [A]
T-AGM 12	*American Mariner* [SX]	T-AGM 25	*Howard O. Lorenzen* [A]

Selected Specifications

Range Tracker (T-AGM 1) / VC2-S-AP3 type

Length: 455 feet
Beam: 62 feet

Draft: 22 feet
Displacement: 11,100 tons
Speed: 17 knots
Personnel: 89

Vanguard (T-AGM 19) / T2-SE-A2 type
Length: 595 feet
Beam: 75 feet
Draft: 25 feet
Displacement: 21,626 tons full load
Speed: 16 knots
Personnel: 86 + 108 technicians

Observation Island (T-AGM 23) / C4-S-1a type
Length: 563 feet
Beam: 76 feet
Draft: 28.58 feet
Displacement: 18,000 tons (full load)
Propulsion: 2 steam turbines; 22,000 shp; 1 shaft
Speed: 20 knots
Personnel: 66 civilians, 34 contractors & 20 Navy

Invincible (T-AGM 24)
Length: 224 feet
Beam: 43 feet
Draft: 15 feet
Displacement: 2,285 tons
Propulsion: 4 Caterpillar D-398B diesel generators with GE motors; 3,200 bhp; 2 shafts
Speed: 11 knots
Personnel: 18 civilians & 11 technicians

Howard O. Lorenzen (T-AGM 25)
Length: 534 feet overall
Beam: 89 feet
Draft: 21 feet
Displacement: 13,696 tons (full load)
Propulsion: 2 electric motors driven by 2 diesel generators; 1 shaft
Speed: 20 knots
Personnel: 88 civilian + Navy & technicians

SELECTED HISTORIES

USNS *Range Tracker* (T-AGM 1)

The Navy's first designated missile range instrumentation ship was derived from the former Victory ship SS *Skidmore Victory*. She had been laid down on April 6, 1945, by Oregon Shipbuilding Corporation, launched the following month, and delivered to Northland Transportation on June 18, 1945. The vessel was later operated by American President Lines as SS *President Buchanan*. As with so many of her sisters, she was laid up in the NDRF for a number of post-war years but unlike almost all of them, she was taken out of mothballs in the late 1950s to be converted into a seagoing tracker of space vehicles and missiles.

The conversion was performed by Ingalls Shipbuilding Corporation of Pascagoula, Mississippi, along with the Range System Division of the Chance-Vought Corporation in Dallas. The latter was responsible for installing the tracking and monitoring hardware, which included equipment for providing telemetry, navigation, timing, aerology, communications, radio command, and surveillance.[13] Other contractors supplying electronic components included Packard-Bell Company of Los Angeles and the Cubic Corporation of San Diego.

The new AGM was renamed *Range Tracker* and designated as the miscellaneous auxiliary T-AG 160 on July 12, 1960, but redesignated as the missile range instrumentation ship AGM 1 four months later on November 27. She was placed in service with MSTS in May 1961 and assigned to the 70 million-square mile Pacific Missile range, headquartered at Point Mugu, California. While homeported in Port Hueneme, California, USNS *Range Tracker*'s civil service crew supported Air Force missile and space programs from June 1961 until September 27, 1969, when she was withdrawn from service. The AGM was then transferred to MARAD and laid up in the NDRF mothballed group in Suisun Bay, California. She was struck from the Naval Register on April 28, 1970, and sold on July 10 of that year for scrapping by American Ship Dismantlers, Inc.

USNS *Vanguard* (T-AGM 19)

This versatile vessel carried oil for the fleet, operated as an AGM, and later tested advanced navigation systems for ballistic missile submarines (SSBNs). She has carried three different names and been placed in and out of service four different times during her career. That career began on February 29, 1944, when the T2-SE-A2 type tanker *Mission San Fernando* was delivered to the U.S. Maritime Commission. Her keel had been laid down on August 26, 1943, by Marine Ship Corporation and she was launched two months later on November 25. During World War II she carried fuel oil to U.S. forces in the Pacific under charter by Pacific Tankers Inc. Removed from service on May 10, 1946, the tanker was laid up in Olympia, Washington.

The Navy acquired her on October 21, 1947, and she was placed in service by the Naval Transportation Service as the oiler *Mission San Fernando*, designated as AO 122. Following the formation of MSTS on October 1, 1949, operational control of the oiler was transferred to it and the vessel was then known as USNS *Mission San Fernando* and designated as T-AO 122. On May 24, 1955, MSTS transferred her back to MARAD and she was laid up in Olympia for the second time. On June 22, 1955, her name was struck from the Vessel Register. But just briefly.

Just a year later, on June 21, the vessel was reacquired by the Navy, assigned to MSTS, and operated by Marine Transportation Lines under charter. Again, that did not last long because the oiler was transferred back to MARAD on September 4, 1957, and placed in the reserve fleet in the James River of Virginia.

Seven years later, she was recalled for service and reacquired by the Navy on September 28, 1964—not for duty as a tanker but in a new job as an AGM. Her conversion into that role was performed by the General Dynamics Corporation at Quincy, Massachusetts, between 1964 and 1966. The yard installed a new 72-foot section in the middle of the ship and outfitted her with various electronic systems, including three large dish antennas. She was renamed *Muscle Shoals* and designated as AGM 19 on April 8, 1965, but renamed again on September 1 as *Vanguard*. She began her service as an AGM on February 28, 1966, and supported NASA's July 1969 Apollo 11 mission—the first Moon landing.

Still another major change in the ship's life occurred on October 1, 1978, when she was assigned to the Navy's Strategic Systems Program to be converted to a navigation research ship as a replacement for USS *Compass Island* (AG 153). The Todd Shipyard in San Francisco performed the conversion work in 1980 by removing all of her high-profile missile tracking antennas. *Vanguard* was reclassified as miscellaneous auxiliary T-AG 194 on September 30, 1980, after which she steamed more than a quarter-million miles in two decades testing submarine navigation systems associated with the Poseidon and Trident SLBMs. Those operations came to an end on March 30, 1998, when she was placed "in service in reserve" and relieved by the oceanic survey ship [q.v.] USNS *Waters* (T-AGS 45).

Vanguard was laid up in the James River group of the NDRF on June 12, 1998, and her name was struck from the NVR on December 13, 1999. Title of the ship was transferred to MARAD on November 29, 2001, following which the Virginia State Historical Preservation Office undertook a review to determine whether she should be preserved or scrapped. On November 15, 2006, the office cleared the vessel for disposal. *Vanguard* was dismantled in the fall of 2013 at Marine Metal Inc. in Brownsville, Texas.[14]

USNS *Observation Island* (T-AGM 23)

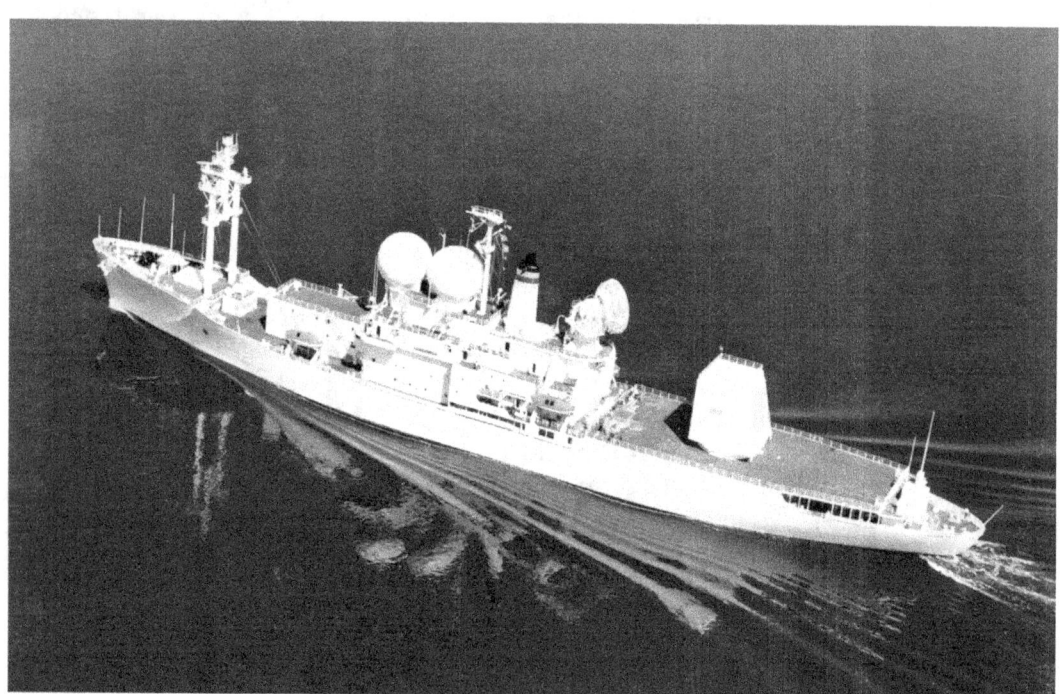

In July 2006 USNS *Observation Island* (T-AGM 23) is carrying an Air Force phased-array radar system for collecting missile test data. She was operated at the time by the Military Sealift Command for the U.S. Air Force Technical Applications Center in Florida (U.S. Navy photograph).

One of some 34 Mariner-class (C4-S-1A type) cargo vessels, SS *Empire State Mariner* was laid down by the New York Shipbuilding Corporation in Camden, New Jersey, on September 15, 1952, and launched on August 15, 1953. She was delivered to MARAD on February 24, 1954, for charter to United States Lines. The first phase of her three-phased career ran less than seven months, during which she made two voyages to the Europe and one to the Far East for MSTS. On November 9, 1954, she was deactivated and placed in the NDRF. But just two years later, the Navy selected *Empire State Mariner* to be the first ship to carry a fully integrated Fleet Ballistic Missile system and serve as a floating and mobile platform from which to fire prototype Polaris sea-launched ballistic missiles.

Originally designated as YAG 57, the cargo ship was transferred to the Navy on September 10, 1956, and reclassified as the miscellaneous auxiliary AG 154 nine days later. Her conversion was authorized on October 15, 1957, and performed at the Norfolk Naval Shipyard. She was formally commissioned on December 5, 1958, as USS *Observation Island* (EAG 154). During the next 13 years she conducted numerous test launches of the Polaris and Poseidon missiles, including one on November 16, 1963, with President John F. Kennedy on board (just six days before his death). Upon completion of the Poseidon development program, *Observation Island* was decommissioned on September 25, 1972, to be laid up in the NDRF for the second time.

The third phase of her career began August 18, 1977, when the ship was reacquired by the Navy for conversion to a missile range instrumentation ship and transferred to the MSC. Redesignated as T-AGM 23 on May 1, 1979, *Observation Island* underwent an extensive alteration at the Maryland Shipbuilding & Dry Dock Company in Baltimore between July 1979 and April 1981. The conversion involved installation of an AN/SPQ-11 250-ton, 40-foot high S-band phased-array Cobra Judy radar on the main deck aft and two large radar spheres on her superstructure. Cobra Judy had been developed to detect, track and record telemetry from U.S., Russian and Chinese missile launches in the Pacific.

As her role had been assumed by USNS *Howard O. Lorenzen* (T-AGM 25) [see below], USNS *Observation Island* was deactivated on March 25, 2014. She was struck from the NVR six days later after having served as an AGM for 33 years. Title to the ship was transferred to MARAD on May 8, 2014. During her more than half-century of government service, *Observation Island* had gradually worked her way up the seniority list to become very nearly the oldest commissioned ship on the Naval Vessel Register. At this writing she is currently moored in the NDRF in Beaumont, Texas, awaiting disposal.

USNS *Invincible* (T-AGM 24)

The only AGM derived from an ocean surveillance ship (AGOS) [q.v.], *Invincible* was laid down on May 2, 1986, and launched on November 8 of that year by Tacoma Boatbuilding Company in Tacoma, Washington. A member of the *Stalwart* class, the ship was placed in MSC service as T-AGOS 10 on January 30, 1987, and homeported in Little Creek, Virginia.

Her primary mission was to collect, process and transmit acoustic data using the AN/UQQ-2 surveillance towed array sensor—a passive underwater surveillance system. She was taken out of service on February 6, 1995, and her name struck from the NVR on May 9 of that year.

Three years later, on March 13, 1998, *Invincible* was reactivated for conversion into a missile range instrumentation ship, and reclassified as T-AGM 24 on April 4, 2000. According to the Navy's public history of the vessel, she "utilizes high-quality, dual-band Cobra Gemini S- and X-band phased arrays to support ballistic missile treaty verification worldwide." As a member of the MSC Special Mission fleet, she reportedly supports Air Force surveillance of Chinese and North Korean missile testing. In addition, in recent years she has been observed operating from Manama, Bahrain, apparently keeping an eye on Iranian activities in the Persian Gulf.[15]

USNS *Howard O. Lorenzen* (T-AGM 25)

The Navy's only purpose-built AGM, *Howard O. Lorenzen* was laid down on August 13, 2008, and launched on June 30, 2010, by Halter Marine, Inc., in Moss Point, Mississippi. She was placed in service with MSC as T-AGM 25 on January 10, 2012.

She carries the Cobra King radar suite consisting of steerable, instrument-quality S- and X-band phased arrays which significantly expand the data collection capabilities of the earlier Cobra Judy system which had been employed on board USNS *Observation Island* [q.v.] (T-AGM 23), the vessel *Howard O. Lorenzen* replaced in 2014. Initial operational capability of the Cobra Judy replacement was announced on March 31, 2014.

The ship is part of MSC's Special Missions fleet and operates in support of Air Force programs. She has been seen recently operating near Japan, most probably to monitor North Korean and Chinese missile testing.

Notes

1. Initially classified as miscellaneous auxiliary T-AG 161 in June 1960 and reclassified as AGM in November 1960.
2. Placed in service with MSTS as cargo ship *Haiti Victory* (T-AK 238) in March 1950 and reclassified as AGM in November 1960.
3. Placed in service with MSTS as *Private Joe E. Mann* (T-AK 253) in August 1950 and reclassified as AGM in October 1958.
4. Placed in service with MSTS as *Dalton Victory* (T-AK 256) in August 1950 and reclassified as AGM in October 1960.
5. Originally commissioned as transport [q.v.] USS *General R. E. Callan* (AP 139) in August 1944, converted to AGM for USAF in 1961, and reacquired by Navy in July 1964.
6. Originally commissioned as transport USS *General Harry Taylor* (AP 145) in May 1944, converted to AGM by USAF in 1961, and reacquired by Navy in July 1964.
7. Reclassified as survey ship AGS 37 after service as AGM.
8. Originally named *Somerset* (AK 212) but never commissioned as such. Converted to AGM in 1964.
9. Was to have been USS *Wexford* (AK 220) but construction contract cancelled in August 1945. Acquired by Navy in 1964 and placed in service as AGM.
10. Acquired in October 1947 as oiler *Mission De Pala* (AO 114), renamed *Johnstown* (AGM 20) in April 1965, and placed in service as *Redstone* (T-AGM 20) in June 1966.
11. Acquired in November 1947 as oiler *Mission San Juan* (AO 126), renamed *Flagstaff* (T-AGM 21) in April 1965, and renamed *Mercury* (T-AGM 21) in September 1965.
12. Commissioned as attack transport *Sherburne* (APA 205) in September 1944 and placed in service as T-AGM 22 in October 1971.
13. Robert M. Garrick, "USNS Range Tracker (T-AGM-1)," 168.
14. "USNS Vanguard T-AG-194," http://navy.memorieshop.com/Vanguard/index.html.
15. "USNS Invincible Back at Bahrain," https://www.bellingcat.com/news/mena/2016/09/28/usns-invincible-back-bahrain/.

Oceanographic Research Ships (AGOR)

Oceanographic research ships—designated as AGORs—perform a variety of basic research tasks at sea, including investigating the characteristics of ocean water at various depths, the seabed and the sea surface environment. The first ship designed from the hull up as an AGOR was the 208-foot, 1,300-ton USNS *Robert D. Conrad*, which was delivered in November 1962. Her design led to the larger 240-foot, 2,000-ton USNS *Melville* (T-AGOR 14). The design and construction of the most recent class of AGORs—*Neil Armstrong* (AGOR 27)—was competitively awarded to Dakota Creek Industries,

USNS *Lynch* (T-AGOR 7) is underway in Chesapeake Bay in 1966 (U.S. Navy photograph).

Inc., on October 14, 2011. An option for the construction of a second Armstrong-class vessel—*Sally Ride* (AGOR 28)—was exercised on February 3, 2012. The former was delivered on September 23, 2015, and the latter on July 1, 2016.

All of the six current Navy AGORs are part of the University National Oceanographic Laboratory System (UNOLS), an organization of more than 60 academic institutions and

The recently delivered oceanographic research vessel R/V *Sally Ride* (AGOR 28) is on a science verification cruise on December 15, 2016, to test her installed systems and readiness for conducting research missions (U.S. Navy photograph).

national laboratories who coordinate the activities of their respective oceanographic ship operations and facilities. (Some 23 civilian vessels operate under the UNOLS framework.) The Navy's AGORs, which are among the nation's largest, are affiliated with a university or oceanographic institution and are operated by civilians under contract with the Office of Naval Research. They support essential naval research in forward areas of the world's seas, as well as meet the needs of other federal agencies.

AGOR hull numbers are assigned to research vessels that were built under Navy contracts. Most of the Navy's oceanographic research ships were named for oceanographers and Navy oceanographic officers. The two most recent AGORs honor famous astronauts.

AGOR Roster

T-AGOR 1	*Josiah Willard Gibbs*[1] [T]	T-AGOR 13	*Bartlett* [T]
AGOR 2	*H. U. Sverdrup*[2]	T-AGOR 14	*Melville* [T]
T-AGOR 3	*Robert D. Conrad* [SS]	AGOR 15	*Knorr* [T]
T-AGOR 4	*James M. Gilliss* [T]	T-AGOR 16	*Hayes*[4] [K/L]
T-AGOR 5	*Charles H. Davis* [T]	T-AGOR 17	*Chain*[5] [SS]
T-AGOR 6	*Sands* [T]	AGOR 18	*Snatch*[6] [SS]
T-AGOR 7	*Lynch* [SS]	AGOR 19	[X]
T-AGOR 8	*Eltanin* [T/SS]	AGOR 20	[X]
AGOR 9	*Thomas G. Thompson*[3] [SX]	AGOR 21	*Gyre* [K]
		AGOR 22	*Moana Wave* [K]
AGOR 10	*Thomas Washington* [T]	AGOR 23	*Thomas G. Thompson*[7] [A]
T-AGOR 11	*Mizar* [SS]		
T-AGOR 12	*De Steiguer* [T]	AGOR 24	*Roger Revelle*[8] [A]

2. Support Ships

AGOR 25   Atlantis[9] [A]
AGOR 26   Kilo Moana[10] [A]
AGOR 27   Neil Armstrong[11] [A]
AGOR 28   Sally Ride[12] [A]

Selected Specifications

Conrad class: T-AGOR 3–T-AGOR 7, AGOR 9 and AGOR 10, and T-AGOR 12 and T-AGOR 13

Length: 208.83 feet
Beam: 37.41 feet
Draft: 16 feet
Displacement: 1,200 tons (standard); 1,380 tons (full load)
Propulsion: Diesel-electric (Caterpillar Tractor diesels); 2,500 bhp; 1 shaft
Speed: 13.5 knots
Personnel: 21–26 civilians & 15–19 scientists

Thompson class: AGOR 23–AGOR 25

Length: 274 feet overall
Beam: 53 feet
Draft: 19 feet
Displacement: 2,155 tons (light); 3,250 tons (full load)
Propulsion: Diesel-electric (3 diesel generators/Caterpillar 3516TA; 2 electric motors/General Motors CD6999); 6,000 shp; 2 azimuth propellers
Speed: 15 knots
Personnel: 20 civilian & 35–40 scientists & technicians

Armstrong class: AGOR 27 and AGOR 28

Length: 238 feet (overall)
Beam: 50 feet
Draft: 15 feet
Displacement: 3,043 tons
Propulsion: Two 876 kW Siemens AC electric motors (1175 hp each), 1752 kW total (2350 hp total); 2 controllable pitch propellers and bow & stern thrusters
Speed: 12 knots (sustained)
Personnel: 20 & 24 scientists

Selected Histories

USNS *Robert D. Conrad* (T-AGOR 3)

Laid down in January 1961, USNS *Robert D. Conrad* was launched on May 26, 1962, by Gibbs Shipyards, Inc., in Jacksonville, Florida. She was delivered to the Navy six months later.

The ship was assigned to Columbia University's Lamont Geological Observatory (later renamed the Lamont-Doherty Earth Observatory), the institution for which she worked her entire career. *Robert D. Conrad* was outfitted with wet and dry labs, a scientific and chart room, photo lab, scientific drafting room, machine shop, two 2-foot-diameter tubes for lowering instruments, and a retractable bow propeller for holding her position while using equipment over the side.

According to the Navy's public history of the ship, *Robert D. Conrad* "collected gravity and magnetic data on the seafloor, created seismic images of rock layers below the ocean floor, dredged rock samples, took ocean floor sentiment cores (creating what is now a collection of over 13,000 cores), mapped the ocean floor with sonar, and collected water samples to explore ocean currents, temperature, salinity, marine life and other data for a wide range of oceanographic research." Among her achievements was the assistance she rendered during the spring and summer of 1963 in the search for the wreckage of the lost nuclear attack submarine USS *Thresher* (SSN 593).

Conrad's contributions to oceanographic research came to an end on July 26, 1989, when she was taken out of service. Her name was struck from the NVR on October 4 of that year and she was sold to Bay Bridges Enterprises of Chesapeake, Virginia, on November 21, 2003. *Conrad* was officially dismantled by April 27, 2004.

USNS *Mizar* (T-AGOR 11)

This research vessel began life as a naval cargo ship, albeit a somewhat unique cargo ship. She was laid down by Avondale Marine Ways, Inc., of Avondale, Louisiana, in January 1957, launched on October 7, 1957, and placed in service with MSTS on March 7, 1958, as the cargo ship USNS *Mizar* (T-AK 272).

Built with an ice-strengthened hull, *Mizar* was used to resupply shore facilities along the Distant Early Warning (DEW) line and other U.S. installations in Greenland and the Canadian Arctic. In 1961, she headed south and carried helicopters and provisions to New Zealand and McMurdo Sound in Antarctica.

In 1963 *Mizar* began her conversion to an ocean research vessel and was redesignated as AGOR 11 on April 15, 1964. Two months after that by using her strobe lights, cameras, sonar and magnetometer, she was able to locate the wreckage of the lost submarine USS *Thresher* (SSN 593) which had sunk on April 10, 1963. *Mizar* later found and helped to recover a lost H-bomb off Palomares, Spain, and in October 1968, located the wreckage of the lost nuclear-powered submarine USS *Scorpion* (SSN 589) southwest of the Azores. The sub had been missing for five months.

Mizar was withdrawn from service and struck on February 16, 1990. The former AK 272/AGOR 11 was transferred to MARAD on February 7, 1992, to be laid up in the James River group of the NDRF in Virginia. Thirteen years later *Mizar* was sold on July 8, 2005, to Bay Bridge Enterprises of Chesapeake, Virginia, to be dismantled. She left the NDRF on August 16 to be cut up.

RV *Neil Armstrong* (T-AGOR 27)

Ordered in May 2010 as a replacement for the research vessel *Knorr* (AGOR 15), *Neil Armstrong*'s keel was laid down on August 17, 2012, by Dakota Creek Industries, Inc., in Anacortes, Washington. She was launched on February 22, 2014, and delivered to the Navy on September 23, 2015. The Woods Hole Oceanographic Institution of Woods Hole, Massachusetts, operates the ship under a renewable charter-party arrangement with ONR.

The ship is fitted with state of the art acoustic equipment capable of mapping the deepest areas of the oceans and is equipped with modular on-board laboratories to support a wide range of oceanographic research activities for both academic and government entities. She is powered by multi-drive, low-voltage diesel-electric propulsion systems which provide lower maintenance and fuel costs.

NOTES

1. Commissioned as small seaplane tender *San Carlos* (AVP 51) in March 1944, renamed and redesignated as T-AGOR and placed in service with MSTS in December 1958, taken out of service and struck in December 1971, and subsequently transferred to Greece.

An artist rendering of the general oceanic research vessel *Neil Armstrong* (U.S. Navy photograph).

2. Built for Norwegian government with U.S. offshore procurement funds; never served in U.S.
3. Delivered as AGOR in September 1965 and leased to University of Washington, returned to Navy and renamed *Pacific Escort II* and redesignated as unclassified miscellaneous vessel IX 517 in December 1989, renamed *Gosport* (IX 517) in May 1997, struck in February 2004, and expended as target in November of that year.
4. Delivered in July 1971, converted to acoustic research ship and placed in service as T-AG 195 in 1992, struck in December 2008, and laid up in Navy inactive ships maintenance facility in Philadelphia. An October 2016 entry in the NVR indicated that the Navy sought a determination of whether *Hayes* was eligible for inclusion in the National Register of Historic Places.
5. Commissioned as rescue and salvage ship ARS 20 in March 1944, reclassified as AGOR in April 1967, and struck in December 1977.
6. Commissioned as ARS 27 in December 1944, reclassified as AGOR in April 1967, unofficially renamed RV *Argo* in the late 1960s, struck in May 1970 and sold for scrapping.
7. Operated by University of Washington. Completed an 18-month, $52 million upgrade in April 2018 to extend the vessel's life by 15 to 20 years.
8. Operated by Scripps Institution of Oceanography.
9. Operated by Woods Hole Oceanographic Institution.
10. Operated by University of Hawaii.
11. Operated by Woods Hole Oceanographic Institution.
12. Operated by Scripps Institution of Oceanography.

SURVEYING SHIPS (AGS)

Surveying ships—designated as AGS—perform ocean surveys and collect various data to support fleet operations and the development of naval systems. They perform acoustical, biological, physical and geophysical surveys, thereby providing much of what the Navy needs to know about the ocean environment. The data they furnish help to enhance U.S. technology in undersea warfare and the detection of adversary vessels. Sur-

USNS *Maury* (T-AGS 39) was delivered to the Navy on March 31, 1989, and served with the Military Sealift Command for just five years before her retirement in September 1994. Acquired by the California Maritime Academy in May 1996 as the TS *Golden Bear III*, she makes two 2-month cruises a year to prepare students to become civilian mariners (U.S. Navy photograph).

veying ships have mapped 75 percent of the world's coastlines, aiding ship navigators in determining their positions and routes while traveling in unfamiliar waters.

All of the current Navy surveying ships are operated by the Military Sealift Command and sponsored by the Naval Oceanographic Command. There are at this writing six AGSs in operation. The AGS ships are typically named, as are AGORs, for oceanographers and naval oceanographic officers.

2. Support Ships

Surveying ships of the World War II era were converted from other ship types and reached hull number AGS 14. Three former VC2-S-AP3 type Victory ships were acquired by the Navy in 1957 to be converted as AGS 21–AGS 23 for seafloor charting and magnetic surveys to support the Navy's fleet ballistic missile programs. A fourth Victory ship—*Twin Falls* (AGS 37)—was never converted. The first purpose-built surveying ships were *Chauvenet* (T-AGS 29) and *Harkness* (T-AGS 32); both have been struck. Hull numbers AGS 41–44, 46–49, and 53–59 were not assigned.

The most recent class of surveying ships are the six members of the *Pathfinder* (T-AGS 60) class. The original contract for this class was awarded in January 1991 for two ships with an option for a third vessel (that option was exercised on May 29, 1992). A fourth ship was ordered in October 1994 with an option for two more. A fifth ship was ordered on January 15, 1997, and construction of a sixth *Pathfinder* vessel began in 1999. The six ships entered service between December 1994 and December 2001. The contract for a seventh ship—USNS *Maury* (T-AGS 66)—an improved *Pathfinder*, was awarded in December 2009 and she was delivered to MSC on February 16, 2016. In the interim, USNS *Sumner* (T-AGS 61) was taken out of service in August 2014, so *Maury*'s arrival restored the AGS fleet to six ships.

AGS Roster

AGS 1	*Pathfinder* [SS]	T-AGS 27	*Elisha Kent Kane* [S/T]
AGS 2	*Hydrographer*[1] [T]	AGS 28	*Towhee* [SS]
AGS 3	*Oceanographer*[2] [K/SS]	T-AGS 29	*Chauvenet*[21] [K/T]
AGS 4	*Bowditch*[3] [SS]	AGS 30	*San Pablo*[22] [SC]
AGS 5	*Sumner*[4] [SS]	T-AGS 31	*S. P. Lee*[23] [T]
AGS 6	*Derickson*[5] [SC]	T-AGS 32	*Harkness* [SS]
AGS 7	*Littlehales*[6] [SC]	T-AGS 33	*Wilkes* [T]
AGS 8	*Dutton*[7] [SC]	T-AGS 34	*Wyman*[24] [SS]
AGS 9	*Amistead Rust*[8] [T]	T-AGS 35	*Sgt. George D. Keathley*[25] [SX]
AGS 10	*John Blish*[9] [SS]		
AGS 11	*Chauvenet*[10] [SC]	AGS 36	*Coastal Crusader*[26] [SS]
AGS 12	*Harkness*[11] [S]	AGS 37	*Twin Falls*[27] [SS]
AGS 13	*James M. Gillis*[12] [SC]	T-AGS 38	*H.H. Hess* [SS]
AGS 14	*Simon Newcomb*[13] [SS]	T-AGS 39	*Maury* [T]
AGS 15	*Tanner*[14] [SS]	T-AGS 40	*Tanner* [T]
AGS 16	*Maury*[15] [SS]	T-AGS 45	*Waters* [A]
AGS 17	*Pursuit*[16] [SS]	AGS 50	*Rehobeth*[28] [SS]
AGS 18	*Requisite*[17] [K]	T-AGS 51	*John McDonnell*[29] [K/S]
AGS 19	*Sheldrake*[18] [SS]	T-AGS 52	*Littlehales* [T]
AGS 20	*Prevail*[19] [SS]	T-AGS 60	*Pathfinder* [A]
T-AGS 21	*Bowditch* [SS]	T-AGS 61	*Sumner* [K/L]
T-AGS 22	*Dutton* [SS]	T-AGS 62	*Bowditch* [A]
T-AGS 23	*Michelson* [SS]	T-AGS 63	*Henson* [A]
AGS 24	*Serrano*[20] [SS]	T-AGS 64	*Bruce C. Heezen* [A]
T-AGS 25	*Kellar* [T]	T-AGS 65	*Mary Sears* [A]
T-AGS 26	*Silas Bent* [T]	T-AGS 66	*Maury* [A]

Selected Specifications

Waters class: T-AGS 45

Length: 457 feet
Beam: 69 feet
Draft: 21 feet
Displacement: 12,208 tons (full load)
Propulsion: Diesel-electric; 7,400 shp; twin screws
Speed: 13 knots
Personnel: 32 civilians & 59 technicians

Pathfinder class: T-AGS 60–T-AGS 65

Length: 328.5 feet
Beam: 58 feet
Draft: 19 feet
Displacement: 4,762 long tons (full load)
Propulsion: Diesel-electric; 4 EMD/Baylor diesel generators; 11,425 hp (8.52 MV); 2 GE CDF 1944 motors; 8,000 h (5.96 MV) sustained; 6,000 hp (4.48 MV); 2 azimuth propellers; bow thruster with 1,500 hp (1.19 MV)
Speed: 16 knots
Personnel: 29 civilians & 27 scientists

Pathfinder class (Maury): T-AGS 66

Length: 353 feet
Beam: 58 feet
Draft: 18 feet
Displacement: 4,888 long tons (full load with margin)
Propulsion: Diesel-electric; 4 main diesel generator sets; 2 2865 kW KATO Model 8P10-3600 generators each coupled with an EMD Model L16-710G7C72, 16-cylinder diesel (3,600 bhp at 900 rpm); 2 1440 kW KATO Model 8P7-2600 generators, each coupled with an EMD Model L8-710GC72, 8-cylinder diesel; 2 azimuth propellers
Speed: 15 knots
Personnel: 28 civilians & 39 scientists

Selected Histories

USNS *Waters* (T-AGS 45)

Intended as a replacement for USNS *Mizar* (T-AGOR 11), *Waters* was laid down on May 1, 1991, by Avondale Industries, Inc., in New Orleans, Louisiana. She was launched on June 6, 1992 and placed in service as an oceanographic research ship [q.v.] (AGOR) with the Military Sealift Command on October 28, 1994.

Four years later, *Waters*'s mission was changed to support ballistic missile flight tests and to assist in evaluating submarine navigation systems. She was converted to that role in 1998 by Detyens Shipyards, Inc. in North Charleston, South Carolina. Accordingly, *Waters* replaced the missile range instrumentation ship USNS *Range Sentinel* (T-AGM 22) as a flight test navigation ship and USNS *Vanguard* (T-AG 194) as a submarine navigation test ship. Today she supports the Navy's Strategic Systems Program Office and is one of 24 vessels in MSC's special missions fleet. Her most recently publicly reported homeport is Cape Canaveral, Florida, although an MSC fact sheet updated in March 2017 states that no homeport is assigned.

USNS *Pathfinder* (T-AGS 60)

On November 8, 2011, the surveying ship USNS *Pathfinder* (T-AGS 60) is conducting a port visit to Veracruz, Mexico (U.S. Navy photograph).

The lead ship of the Pathfinder-class was built by Halter Marine, Inc., in Moss Point, Mississippi. Her keel was laid down on August 3, 1992, and she was launched 14 months later on October 4. *Pathfinder* was placed in service with MSC on October 28, 1994.

As part of the MSC Special Missions fleet, her crew of 28 civilian mariners and the ship's 27 scientists and technicians collect oceanographic and hydrographic survey data to improve the Navy's capabilities in undersea warfare. According to one unofficial source, *Pathfinder* is homeported in Norfolk, Virginia, but obviously she has operated in distant waters. For example, in September 2008 she embarked a Ukrainian oceanographic survey team from that nation's Department of Underwater Heritage to identify at least 15 shipwrecks in the Black Sea, including the lost World War II German submarine U-18 and the World War I Russian minelayer *Prut*.

USNS *Sumner* (T-AGS 61)

Halter Marine laid down the keel of *Sumner* on November 18, 1992, and launched the ship on February 28, 1994. She was placed in service with MSC on May 29, 1995.

Late in her career, she and sister USNS *Henson* (T-AGS 63) teamed up in Operation Unified Response in January 2010 to assist Haiti following the magnitude 7.3 earthquake that killed an estimated 20,000 people on January 12. At the time the earthquake struck, *Sumner* was moored in Port Canaveral, Florida, but got underway to transport 34-foot hydrographic survey launches and some technicians to the Guantanamo Bay naval facility in Cuba. There the launches and personnel were transferred to *Henson*, which had

Moored near the U.S. Naval Academy in Annapolis, Maryland, on April 28, 2010, USNS *Sumner* (T-AGS 61) is conducting tours on board for midshipmen and faculty to familiarize them with the various tools used in oceanographic missions (U.S. Navy photograph).

steamed in haste from the eastern Pacific for the rendezvous. Once equipped with the launches from *Sumner*, *Henson* continued on to Haiti to employ the launches in surveying safe navigational channels for arriving relief ships.

Press reports in May 2014 indicated that the U.S. Southern Command had requested $20.3 million to acquire *Sumner* and sail her around the Caribbean and South America in anti-drug smuggling operations. The House Armed Services Committee denied the request. *Sumner*'s active service came to an end not long thereafter when she was deactivated at Port Canaveral, and her name was struck from the Naval Vessel Register on August 29, 2014. Title to the ship was transferred from the Navy to MARAD on November 24, 2014. At last report, the ship is laid up in the NDRF in Beaumont, Texas, awaiting disposal by MARAD.

USNS *Bowditch* (T-AGS 62)

Built by Halter Marine, *Bowditch* was laid down on June 17, 1993, and launched on October 15, 1994. She began service with the MSC on July 19, 1996.

The AGS participated in Operation Damayan in November 2013 to provide humanitarian assistance to victims of Super Typhoon Haiyan (aka Yolanda) in the Philippines. Using her multi-beam contour-mapping system, she surveyed the approaches to San Pedro Bay at Tacloban, Leyte, to determine safe approach channels for ships arriving with relief supplies and equipment. *Bowditch* had performed in similar roles in the 2004 Banda Aceh tsunami and the 2010 devastating earthquake in Haiti.

Over the years *Bowditch* has had some contentious encounters with China. She was harassed by a Chinese frigate on March 23, 2001, in international waters which had been

The oceanographic survey ship USNS *Bowditch* (T-AGS 62) conducts deep-ocean and coastal surveys in Asian waters (U.S. Navy photograph).

declared by China as part of its Exclusive Economic Zone. On September 27, 2002, the Chinese government complained that "*Bowditch* was operating in China's exclusive economic zone in contravention of the international law of the sea." That same day a Pentagon spokesman dismissed reports in a Hong Kong newspaper that the ship had collided with a Chinese fishing boat eight days earlier in the Yellow Sea about 60 miles off China's coast. In the most serious incident, on December 15, 2016, the Chinese seized an unmanned underwater vehicle (UUV) that had been deployed from *Bowditch* in international waters some 50 miles northwest of Subic Bay in the Philippines. The UUV, referred to as a drone or "ocean glider," was used to collect oceanographic data, such as sea salinity, water clarity and ocean temperature—data that are useful in connection with the employment of sonar in ASW operations. The Chinese agreed to return the UUV two days later.

While her unofficial homeport is listed as Norfolk, Virginia, *Bowditch* in recent months has been operating in the Far East.

USNS *Henson* (T-AGS 63)

As one of the seven survey ships built by Halter Marine, *Henson* was laid down on October 13, 1995, and launched a year later on October 21. MSC placed her in service on February 20, 1998.

In January 2010 she, along with *Sumner* and *Bowditch*, took part in Operation Unified Response to assist in providing aid to the victims of a massive earthquake in Haiti. Later that year, *Henson* participated with the Royal Navy, French Navy and Ocean Technology Foundation in searching in the North Sea off Yorkshire, England, for John Paul Jones's historic *Bon Homme Richard*, lost in battle on September 23, 1779. *Henson* used her side-scan sonar, along with UUVs with side-scan and multi-beam sonar, in the search but, unfortunately, the September 2010 expedition failed to find the frigate's wreck.

In the most recent public reports at this writing, USNS *Henson* was operating in the Pacific near Guam.

USNS *Bruce C. Heezen* (T-AGS 64)

- Built by Halter Marine.
- Laid down August 19, 1997, and launched March 25, 1999.
- Placed in service with MSC January 13, 2000.
- Most recent operations at this writing have been in the Irish Sea.

USNS *Mary Sears* (T-AGS 65)

- Built by Halter Marine.
- Laid down July 28, 1999, and launched October 19, 2000.
- Placed in service with MSC December 17, 2001.
- Conducted hydrographic surveys of the ocean bottom off the Indonesian coast following the December 26, 2004, magnitude 9.0 earthquake near Sumatra, Indonesia. Collected data to be used in predicting natural disasters.
- Joined search for wreckage of downed Adam Air Flight KI-574, a Boeing 737–400, lost in the Makassar Strait on January 1, 2007. She found the aircraft's flight data recorder and cockpit voice recorder in more than 6,000 feet of water off West Sulawesi on January 21 and recovered scattered wreckage of the aircraft.
- Visited Tanjung Priok, Jakarta, Indonesia, in February 2008. (Since 1978 the U.S. and Indonesian navies have conducted more than 200 survey missions around the Indonesian archipelago.)
- Most recent operations at this writing have been off the Philippines.

USNS *Maury* (T-AGS 66)

- Built by VT Halter Marine, Inc., in Moss Point, Mississippi.
- Laid down February 1, 2011, and launched March 27, 2013.
- Completed acceptance trials in Gulf of Mexico on November 6, 2015.
- Delivered February 16, 2016.
- Differs from the other ships in the Pathfinder class—she's 25 feet longer than her sisters—by having an 18-by-18-foot "moon pool" that is used for launching and retrieving UUVs.
- Most recent operations at this writing have been near the U.S. East Coast. Completed her first operational oceanographic survey on November 8, 2017.

Notes

1. Originally patrol yacht PY 30, commissioned as AGS in May 1942, decommissioned in July 1946, and returned to USC&GS.
2. Former yacht *Corsair* and later *Natchez* (PG 85), commissioned as AGS in August 1942, and struck in October 1944.
3. Commissioned as miscellaneous auxiliary AG 30 in March 1940 and redesignated as AGS in December 1943.
4. Former submarine tender [q.v.] *Bushnell* (AS 2), reclassified as AG 32 in July 1940 and renamed the following month, and reclassified as AGS in December 1943.
5. Laid down as patrol craft sweeper PCS 1458 in April 1943 and reclassified as AGS in May 1944.
6. Commissioned as PCS 1388 in December 1943, reclassified as AGS in February 1945, and reclassified as coastal survey ship [q.v.] AGSC 7 in July 1946.
7. Commissioned as PCS 1396 in March 1944, reclassified as AGS in March 1945, and reclassified as AGSC in July 1946.
8. Commissioned as PCS 1404 in March 1944 and reclassified as AGS in March 1945.

9. Commissioned as PCS 1457 in February 1944, reclassified as AGS in March 1945, and reclassified as AGSC in July 1946.
10. Commissioned as motor minesweeper YMS 195 in March 1943 and reclassified as AGS in March 1945.
11. Commissioned as YMS 242 in March 1943, reclassified as AGS in March 1945, and reclassified as AGSC in July 1946.
12. Commissioned as YMS 262 in August 1943, reclassified as AGS in March 1945, and reclassified as AGSC in July 1946.
13. Commissioned as YMS 263 in August 1943, reclassified as AGS in March 1945, and reclassified as AGSC in July 1946.
14. Commissioned as attack cargo ship *Pamina* (AKA 34) in February 1945 and reclassified as AGS in May 1946.
15. Commissioned as *Renate* (AKA 36) in February 1945 and reclassified as AGS in July 1946.
16. Commissioned as minesweeper AM 108 in April 1943 and reclassified as AGS in August 1951.
17. Commissioned as AM 109 in June 1943 and reclassified as AGS in August 1951.
18. Commissioned as AM 62 in October 1942 and reclassified as AGS in April 1952.
19. Commissioned as AM 107 in April 1943 and reclassified as AGS in April 1952.
20. Commissioned as fleet ocean tug ATF 112 in September 1944 and recommissioned as AGS in June 1960.
21. Struck in 1992, transferred to MARAD and subsequently converted to training ship *Texas Clipper II* for Texas A&M University. Later used to house recovery workers and evacuees from Hurricane Rita in 2005–2006, and after that converted to missile instrumentation ship *Pacific Collector* for the U.S. Missile Defense Agency.
22. Commissioned as small seaplane tender AVP 30 in March 1943, recommissioned as AGS in September 1948, struck in January 1969, and loaned to Ocean Science Center of the Atlantic Conference in September 1971, and then sold.
23. Delivered as AGS 31 in December 1968, redesignated as miscellaneous auxiliary T-AG 192 in September 1970, placed out of service in January 1973, lent to National Geodetic Survey 1974–1992, struck in October 1992, and transferred to Mexico in December 1992.
24. Struck in May 1999 and transferred to MARAD custody in NDRF, sold for scrapping in March 2014 and dismantled by ESCO Marine by October of that year.
25. Acquired from the Army in July 1950 and assigned to MSTS as the small coastal transport T-APC 116, converted to hydrographic research ship T-AGS 35, taken out of service in December 1971, transferred to Taiwan in March 1972, and struck in April 1976.
26. Placed in service as missile range instrumentation ship T-AGM 16 in 1964, reclassified as AGS in 1969, struck in April 1976 and sold for scrapping by General Metals, Inc., of Tacoma, in April 1977.
27. Placed in service with MSTS as T-AGM 11, later redesignated as AGS 37, transferred to MARAD in May 1970 and laid up in NDRF group in Virginia, struck in November 1972, transferred to New York City's Board of Education and renamed SS *John W. Brown* in May 1973, and sold for scrapping in June 1982 to Union Metals & Alloys Corporation.
28. Commissioned as small seaplane tender AVP 50 in February 1944, reclassified as AGS in September 1948, struck in April 1970 and sold for scrapping in September 1970.
29. Struck on August 16, 2010, and sold by the Navy on June 3, 2014.

SUBMARINE ESCORT SHIPS (AGSE)

The submarine escort ship hull classification (AGSE) is one of the Navy's newest ship designations as it was first assigned in 2015. That classification encompasses only four craft: former type 250EDF offshore supply vessels (OSVs) previously owned by Hornbeck Offshore Services, Inc. (HOS) and chartered to the Navy by HOS since their construction in 2008 and 2009. As ordered by Congress, three of the OSVs were purchased by the Navy in March 2015 for $114 million. An option to acquire a fourth OSV—*HOS Black Powder*—which was also under charter to the Navy, was exercised later in 2015 for approximately $38 million. In addition to the sale, Hornbeck was contracted in March 2015 to provide maintenance and operations services for the initial three OSVs for a 10-year period and to continue to lease *HOS Black Powder* until she was acquired. That latter agreement was expected to last for 215 days beginning February 28 at an average daily rate of just over $30,000.

These four craft are part of the Military Sealift Command's Special Mission (PM2) fleet. They provide protection for transiting Trident fleet ballistic missile submarines (SSBNs) at two naval bases: *Arrowhead* and *Eagleview* operate out of Bangor, Washington,

USNS *Arrowhead* (T-AGSE 4) is seen here while under charter and prior to her March 2015 acquisition by the Navy's Military Sealift Command (U.S. Navy photograph).

and *Black Powder* and *Westwind* work out of Kings Bay, Georgia. According to the Naval Institute's authoritative reference work *Ships & Aircraft of the U.S. Fleet*, the AGSEs are the only MSC ships that are armed. Each is reported to carry one 25-mm Mk 38 Mod 2 Bushmaster cannon manned by Coast Guard personnel.

In addition to the AGSEs, MSC has employed other chartered vessels in the submarine and special warfare role. Because none of these are Navy-owned and are not designated as AGSEs, they are listed below separately from the AGSEs. As examples of their roles, MV *C-Champion* reportedly supports Navy SEAL training and can handle SEAL swimmer delivery vehicles (SDVs); MV *Dolores Chouest* had supported deep submergence rescue vehicles (DSRV)—which are no longer in service—and performs other Navy underwater work; and MV *Dominator* serves as a mother ship for submarine rescue chamber operations.

The Navy's AGSEs have retained the names assigned by their original owner.

AGSE Roster

| T-AGSE 1 | Black Powder [A] | T-AGSE 3 | Eagleview [A] |
| T-AGSE 2 | Westwind [A] | T-AGSE 4 | Arrowhead [A] |

Chartered/Civilian-Owned (Undesignated) Vessels[1]

MV *Carolyn Chouest*
MV *C-Champion*

MV *C-Commando*
MV *Dolores Chouest*

2. Support Ships

MV *Greystone*
MV *HOS Bluewater*
MV *HOS Dominator*
MV *HOS Gemstone*
MV *HOS Silverstar*
MV *Kellie Chouest*
MV *Malama*

Selected Specifications

USNS *Black Powder* (T-AGSE 1) class: T-AGSE 1–T-AGSE 4 (250EDF OSV)

Length: 250 feet
Beam: 54 feet
Draft: 14.6 feet
Displacement: 2,850 tons (full load)
Propulsion: 2 Caterpillar 3516 diesel engines; 3 Caterpillar C18 diesel generator sets; 3,600 shp; 2 shafts
Speed: 10–14 knots
Personnel: 11 civilians

MV HOS *Bluewater* & MV HOS *Greystone*

Length: 240 feet
Beam: 54 feet
Draft: 14.75 feet (max.)
Displacement: 1,863 tons (gross)
Propulsion: 2 Caterpillar 3516B diesel engines; 3 Caterpillar 3406 primary generators; 4,000 hp; 2 shafts
Speed: 13 knots (max.)

MV *C-Champion*

Length: 220 feet
Beam: 56 feet
Draft: 16.5 feet
Displacement: 2,106 tons (full load)
Propulsion: 2 diesel engines; 2 shafts
Speed: 12 knots
Personnel: 14 civilians and 30 Navy & technical

MV *C-Commando*

Length: 220 feet
Beam: 56 feet
Draft: 16.5 feet
Displacement: 1,903 tons (full load)
Propulsion: 2 diesel engines; 2 shafts
Speed: 12 knots
Personnel: 9 civilians and 32 Navy & technical

MV *Dolores Chouest*

Length: 240 feet
Beam: 40 feet
Draft: 11.83 feet
Displacement: 1,500 tons (full load)
Propulsion: 2 caterpillar D399-SCAC diesel engines; 2,250 shp; 2 shafts
Speed: 12 knots
Personnel: 8 civilians and 32 Navy & technical

MV *HOS Dominator*

Length: 240 feet
Beam: 54 feet
Draft: 13 feet
Displacement: 3,655 tons (full load)
Propulsion: 2 Caterpillar diesel engines; 2 shafts
Personnel: 12 civilians & 40 Navy & technical

Selected Summary Histories

USNS *Eagleview* (T-AGSE 3)

- Built in 2009 for Hornbeck Offshore Services, Inc., by Leevac Industries of Jennings, Louisiana.
- Delivered October 14, 2009, and chartered to MSC.
- Purchased by the Navy for approximately $38 million on March 2, 2015, and designated as T-AGSE 3.
- Supports Ohio-class SSBNs arriving and departing from Bangor Washington.
- On August 18, 2016, collided with USS *Louisiana* (SSBN 743) in the Strait of Juan de Fuca off the coast of Washington. Although each vessel was damaged, both returned safely to Bangor under their own power.

MV *Carolyn Chouest*[2]

- Built for Edison Chouest Offshore (ECO) by North American Shipbuilding—a wholly owned ECO subsidiary—of Larose, Louisiana, and in service in June 1994.
- Leased by MSC to support the Navy's nuclear-powered research submersible NR-1. Towed NR-1 to work sites, and carried additional crew and scientists and materials, and functioned as communications link. (NR-1 was taken out of service on November 21, 2008.)
- Recovered flight data recorder of downed EgyptAir Flight 990—a Boeing 767 aircraft—which crashed into the Atlantic about 60 miles south of Nantucket Island, Massachusetts, on October 31, 1999. Also recovered significant parts of the aircraft in 1999 and 2000.

MV *Kellie Chouest*[2]

- Built in 1996 for Edison Chouest Offshore (ECO) by North American Shipbuilding—a wholly owned ECO subsidiary—of Larose, Louisiana.
- Served as Deep Submergence Elevator Support Ship to assist search and rescue missions in deep water and as an escort for Navy submarine tests.
- Participated in June 1999 expedition to recover propeller and shaft of the historic USS *Monitor*, which sank in 1862 near Cape Hatteras, North Carolina. Navy divers recovered the pieces from the wreck on June 5 and placed them aboard *Kellie Chouest*.
- Recovered voice and data recorders of downed Alaska Airlines Flight 261—a McDonnell Douglas MD-83 aircraft—which crashed on January 31, 2000, in 700 feet of water near Anacapa Island, California.
- New lease by MSC awarded in June 2000. Reported to be valued at $19.9 million for four years.
- In June 2012 MSC awarded ECO an $8 million contract to charter the ship and a

crew for one year. The contract included two options to extend the charter period: one for a one-year extension and the other for six months. Exercising either option could bring the total contract up to $20.3 million.
- Most recent use is as platform for launch and recovery maintenance of small boats, and support of helicopter operations.³

NOTES

1. Includes craft both currently and previously listed as MSC submarine and special warfare support ships.
2. "Chouest." https://www.globalsecurity.org/military/systems/ship/chouest.htm.
3. Paul Pupora, *The Times-Picayune*, June 5, 2012, published online at http://www.nola.com/business/index.ssf/2012/06/navy_renews_charter_of_civilia.html.

HOSPITAL SHIPS (AH)

USNS *Mercy* (T-AH 19) is underway in the Pacific in September 2016 heading back to her homeport of San Diego. She was returning to California from her participation in Pacific Partnership 2016—an annual multilateral disaster relief mission in the Indo-Asia-Pacific region (U.S. Navy photograph).

The U.S. Navy has operated ships devoted to the care and treatment of sick and wounded personnel since the Civil War. In April 1862, the side-wheel steamer *Red Rover* was captured by the Union gunboat *Mound City* and converted into a "hospital boat." Although she technically belonged to the U.S. Army, *Red Rover* became part of the Navy on October 1, 1862, and was formally commissioned on December 26 of that year as the service's first hospital ship. She had a complement of 12 officers and 35 men along with some 30–40 medical department personnel. During her Union service, she treated 2,947 patients before being removed from duty in November 1865.

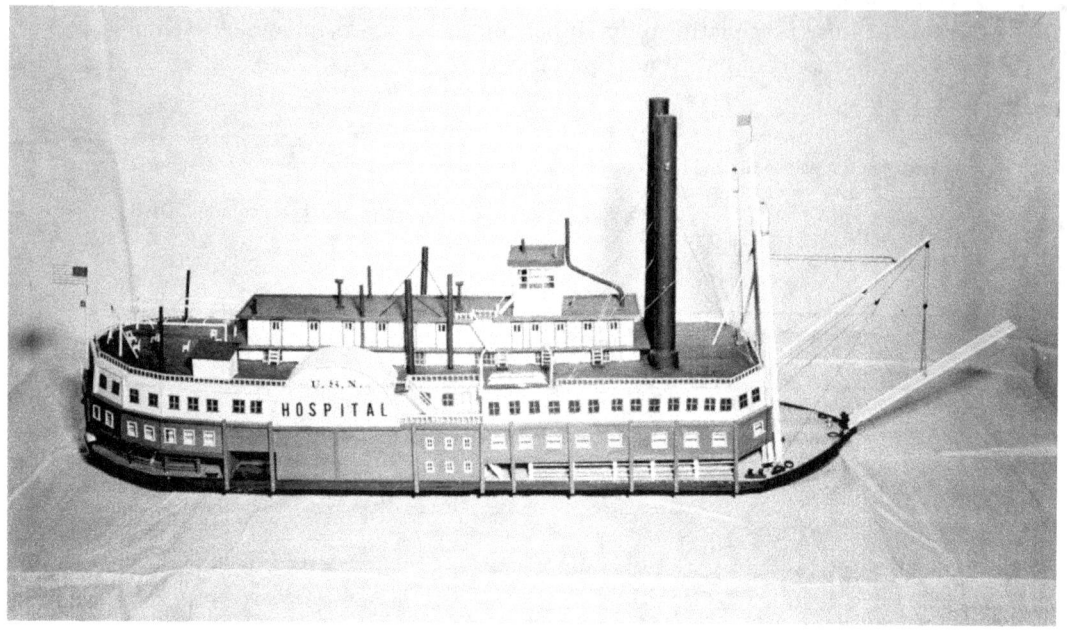

A model of USS *Red Rover* built by Doctor Victor Johnson (U.S. Navy photograph).

By early in the 20th century the Navy had acquired five vessels as hospital ships: USS *Relief*, commissioned in February 1908; USS *Relief* (AH 1), commissioned in December 1920; USS *Solace* (AH 2), commissioned in April 1898; USS *Comfort* (AH 3), commissioned in March 1918; and USS *Mercy* (AH 4), commissioned in January 1918. By the end of the 1930s, *Relief* (AH 1) was the only one of those still in commission. At the beginning of World War II, the AH inventory had doubled, as USS *Solace* (AH 5) had been commissioned in August 1941. When the Japanese surrendered in August 1945, the Navy's hospital ship roster had grown to 15 ships. As was typical of auxiliary vessels acquired during the war, the AH ships had not been specifically designed and built as hospital ships but had instead been converted from other ship types. AH 6–AH 8 (the Comfort class) were derived from Maritime Commission C1-B cargo ship type hulls; AH 9–AH 11 were converted from naval transport [q.v.] (AP) ships; AH 12–AH 17 (Haven class) were sourced from Maritime Commission C4-S-B2 cargo vessels; and AH 18 was originally a submarine tender [q.v.] (AS 21).

With postwar retirements, the AH roster had been cut back to six vessels shortly before the start of the Korean War. By January 1, 1958, there was only one active hospital ship—USS *Haven* (AH 12)—with another four laid up in reserve. A sixth ship—USS *Benevolence* (AH 13)—had sunk in August 1950 after being rammed off San Francisco. During the Vietnam War period, the Navy operated two hospital ships: USS *Repose* (AH 16) and USS *Sanctuary* (AH 17).

Today, there are still only two hospital ships—and they are "part-timers" at that. USNS *Mercy* (T-AH 19) and USNS *Comfort* (T-AH 20) are former commercial T8-S-100b type tankers that were converted in the mid–1980s and first placed in service in

1986 and 1987, respectively (see Selected Histories below). They have 12 operating rooms, four X-ray rooms, and up to 1,000 patient beds (although an additional 1,000 limited-care patients can be handled). The ships receive patients generally by helicopter but can also take aboard casualties from boats on the port side. The pair are based at U.S. ports in Reduced Operating Status (ROS) as part of the MSC Service Support (PM4) fleet. When called upon for a humanitarian crisis or wartime duty they acquire full civilian MSC crews along with medical staffs from military hospitals and then get underway with only five days' notice.

The Navy's hospital ships are given "benevolent" names. Perhaps reflecting an unfortunate paucity of benevolent synonyms, of the 21 AH ship names, five have been used more than once, viz., there have been two vessels each named *Relief*, *Repose* and *Solace* and three named *Comfort* and *Mercy*.

AH Roster

	Relief[1] [SC]	AH 11	*Refuge*[4] [SS]
AH 1	*Relief* [SS]	AH 12	*Haven*[5] [T/SS]
AH 2	*Solace* [SS]	AH 13	*Benevolence*[6] [Z]
AH 3	*Comfort* [SS]	AH 14	*Tranquility*[7] [SS]
AH 4	*Mercy* [SS]	AH 15	*Consolation* [SS]
AH 5	*Solace* [SC]	AH 16	*Repose* [SS]
AH 6	*Comfort* [SS]	AH 17	*Sanctuary* [SC/SS]
AH 7	*Hope* [SS]	AH 18	*Rescue*[8] [SS]
AH 8	*Mercy* [SS]	T-AH 19	*Mercy* [R]
AH 9	*Bountiful*[2] [SS]	T-AH 20	*Comfort* [R]
AH 10	*Samaritan*[3] [SS]		

SELECTED SPECIFICATIONS

Solace (AH 5)

Length: 409.3 feet
Bean: 62 feet
Draft: 20.6 feet
Propulsion: 2 Newport News geared turbines; 8,500 shp; 2 shafts
Speed: 18 knots (trial)
Personnel: 419 (ship's company) & 418 patients

Comfort class: AH 6–AH 8

Length: 418 feet
Beam: 60 feet
Draft: 27.6 feet
Displacement: 9,800 tons (full load)
Propulsion: geared turbine; 4,000 shp; 1 shaft
Speed: 15.5 knots (maximum)
Personnel: 486 (ship's company) & 400 patients

Haven class: AH 12–AH 17

Length: 529 feet
Beam: 71.5 feet
Draft: 23.5 feet
Displacement: 15,400 tons (full load)
Propulsion: twin steam geared turbines; 9,000 shp; 1 shaft

Speed: 17.5 knots (maximum)
Personnel: 309 Navy (ship's company)
   316 (hospital staff)
   560 beds (750 in emergencies)

Mercy class: T-AH 19 & T-AH 20

Length: 894 feet (overall)
Beam: 105.6 feet
Draft: 33 feet
Displacement: 69,360 tons (full load)
Propulsion: 1 steam turbine (General Electric); 24,500 shp; 1 shaft
Speed: 17.5 knots
Personnel: 16 civilian & 58 Navy (in ROS)
   61 civilian, 58 Navy & 1,000 medical/dental (when deployed); up to 1,000 patient beds

Selected Histories

USS *Repose* (AH 16)

USNS *Repose* (T-AH 16) is in San Diego harbor, California, on February 11, 1952, returning from her first deployment during the Korean War. The harbor tug *Cusseta* (YTB 405) is off her port bow ready to assist in mooring the hospital ship (U.S. Navy photograph).

Laid down on October 22, 1943, as the Maritime Commission type C4-S-B2 cargo ship *Marine Beaver*, *Repose* was built by Sun Shipbuilding & Dry Dock Company in Chester, Pennsylvania. She was launched on August 8, 1944, acquired by the Navy, and placed in service on September 14, 1944. The ship was immediately sent to the Bethlehem Steel Company's shipyard in Brooklyn, New York, to be converted into a hospital ship. She was commissioned as USS *Repose* on May 26, 1945.

Following testing, training and drills in the early summer of 1945, *Repose* transported patients from Pearl Harbor to San Francisco, operated as a base hospital in China, and served in Asian waters until July 5, 1949. She was deactivated in October 1949 and after her decommissioning on January 19, 1950, laid up in the San Francisco group of the Pacific Reserve Fleet.

The Navy shouldn't have bothered mothballing her because, with the outbreak of the Korean War, *Repose* was reactivated at the San Francisco Naval Shipyard and delivered to MSTS on August 26, 1950. Now designated as USNS *Repose* (T-AH 16), the hospital ship steamed for Pusan, Korea, arriving there on September 20. During the next four years, *Repose* served in Korea and Japan, with occasional visits to the U.S. West Coast for yard work.

On September 27, 1954, she was deactivated for a second time, decommissioned on December 21, 1954, and berthed in the Suisun Bay group of the Pacific Reserve Fleet. This time *Repose* remained in repose for a lot longer than the few months she spent in mothballs in 1950.

As the United States was increasing its involvement in the Vietnam conflict in the mid–1960s, *Repose* was summoned back to duty. In June 1965 she was towed to the Bethlehem Steel Shipyard and then to the Hunter's Point Naval Shipyard in San Francisco to be reactivated. *Repose* was recommissioned on October 16, 1965, left California on January 3, 1966, and arrived off Chu Lai, South Vietnam, on February 16.

Her hospital staff numbered 325, including 24 Medical Corps officers, three Dental Corps officers, seven Medical Service Corps officers, 29 Nurse Corps officers, 246 medical corpsmen, seven dental technicians, two Red Cross workers, two Vietnamese interpreters and a five-man Marine Corps liaison team. *Repose*'s ship's company during the war numbered 309 (19 officers and 290 enlisted). Among the equipment, capabilities and facilities that she had brought to the war were: a 250-unit frozen-blood bank (the first to be used at sea), automatic rapid x-ray film processing, a facility for the detection of brain hemorrhages, a machine that can rapidly measure a casualty's blood volume, a portable heart-lung machine and a recompression chamber for the treatment of diving and aviation accidents.[9]

The floating hospital provided almost constant medical services to American forces in Vietnam for four years. Primarily supporting the Third Marine Amphibious Force in the I Corps Tactical Zone, *Repose* shuttled between Chu Lai and Da Nang and up to Dong Ha, near the DMZ. In April 1967 she was joined by USS *Sanctuary* (AH 17). The two AHs provided about half of the U.S. medical capability in I Corps. On one occasion in 1967, 100 new patients were admitted on a single day, bringing the total number of patients on board to nearly 650. Wounded personnel brought to *Repose* had a better than 98 percent probability of survival. During her deployment, *Repose* treated more than 9,000 battlefield casualties and admitted over 24,000 patients for inpatient care. About three-quarters of the patients returned directly to duty; the remainder were transferred out or evacuated to hospitals ashore for further treatment.[10]

After four years in country, *Repose* left Vietnam on March 14, 1970, and was decommissioned two months later. Placed back in the Pacific Reserve Fleet, her name was struck from the Naval Vessel Register on March 15, 1974. Title to the ship was transferred to MARAD on June 3 of that year, and on April 18, 1975, the vessel was sold for $344,889.78 to the Nicolai Joffe Corporation to be dismantled.

Over the course of her career, USS *Repose* earned nine battle stars for Korean War service and ten campaign stars for Vietnam service.

USS *Solace* (AH 5)

The hospital ship USS *Solace* (AH 5) is anchored in Hawaiian waters shortly after her commissioning in 1941 (U.S. Navy photograph).

- Originally passenger liner SS *Iroquois*.
- Built in 1927 by Newport News Shipbuilding and Dry Dock Company in Newport News, Virginia.
- Acquired by Navy on July 22, 1940, from Clyde-Mallory Steamship Line.
- Converted to hospital ship by Atlantic Basin Iron Works in Brooklyn, New York.
- Renamed *Solace* on July 18, 1940.
- Commissioned on August 9, 1941.
- At Pearl Harbor on December 7, 1941, *Solace* treated many wounded and dying personnel during and immediately after the Japanese attack.
- Operated in the Pacific 1942–1945, served as hospital ship at Noumea and Ulithi, and cared for casualties from battles in the Marshall Islands, Saipan, Guadalcanal, Peleliu, Iwo Jima and Okinawa.

- As an element of Operation Magic Carpet at war's end, transported personnel from Pearl Harbor to San Francisco in 1945 and early 1946.
- Decommissioned on March 27, 1946, and struck on May 21, 1946.
- Returned to custody of War Shipping Administration on July 18, 1946.
- Sold in April 1948 for $300,000 to Turkish Maritime Lines, renamed SS *Ankara*, and converted back to a passenger liner.
- Retired in 1977 and dismantled in 1981.

USS *Consolation* (AH 15)

On March 30, 1955, USS *Consolation* (AH 15) is approaching and about to pass under the Golden Gate Bridge in San Francisco as she returns from her last Navy deployment to the western Pacific. Five years later she would become SS *Hope* employed in humanitarian missions around the world (U.S. Navy photograph).

- Haven-class hospital ship built by Sun Shipbuilding and Dry Dock Company, of Chester, Pennsylvania.
- Launched as *Marine Walrus* on August 1, 1944.
- Acquired by Navy August 30, 1944, converted to AH by Bethlehem Steel Company, in Hoboken, New Jersey, and commissioned on May 22, 1945.
- Served as station hospital for 5th and 6th Fleets in October 1945.
- Operated in Caribbean and eastern Atlantic in the late 1940s.

- Cared for wounded in Korea 1950–1955.
- Pioneered in the first use of helicopters to evacuate wounded from battlefield to hospital ship.
- Participated in Operation Passage to Freedom to evacuate North Vietnamese nationals in French Indo-China in 1954.
- Placed out of commission in reserve on December 30, 1955.
- Leased to People to People Health Foundation on March 16, 1960 and renamed SS *Hope* for use in Project HOPE humanitarian assistance operations. Made 11 Project HOPE voyages to Southeast Asia, Africa, Central and South America, and Mideast in 1960–1974.
- Struck September 15, 1974, and sold for scrapping that same month.

USNS *Mercy* (T-AH 19)

- Built by the National Steel and Shipbuilding Company of San Diego, California. Laid down as the San Clemente-class T8-S-100b tanker *Worth* on December 1, 1974, and launched July 1, 1975.
- Acquired by MSC and placed in service as *Mercy* (T-AH 19) on November 8, 1986.
- Maintained in Reduced Operating Status (ROS), capable of deployment within five days from receipt of sailing orders. Operational readiness is maintained by a reduced civilian crew and cadre of medical technicians. Ship gets underway twice a year for a week of training.
- Deployed for Operations Desert Shield, Desert Sword and Desert Sabre from August 9, 1990, to April 23, 1991.
- Engaged in Operation Unified Assistance following the December 26, 2004, magnitude 9.0 earthquake off the west coast of Sumatra, Indonesia.
- Participated in humanitarian and other exercises including Medical Civil Action Program 2006; Pacific Partnerships 2008, 2010, 2012, 2015, and 2016; MERCEX 02–15; and RIMPAC Exercise 2014.
- In February 2018 deployed to the Indo-Asia-Pacific region to participate in Pacific Partnership 2018 and support disaster response and preparedness missions in visits to Indonesia, Sri Lanka, Malaysia and Vietnam.
- Departed San Diego on February 23, 2018, to participate in Pacific Partnership 2018. During the five-month mission, *Mercy* was scheduled to visit Indonesia, Malaysia, Sri Lanka and Vietnam.
- On March 20, 2018, delivered medical supplies to Ulithi Atoll, part of the Caroline Islands in the Federated States of Micronesia.
- Arrived in Nha Trang, Vietnam, on May 17, 2018, and in Yokosuka, Japan, on June 10, as part of Pacific Partnership 2018.
- Homeported in San Diego, California.

USNS *Comfort* (T-AH 20)

- Built by the National Steel and Shipbuilding Company of San Diego, California. Laid down as the San Clemente-class T8-S-100b tanker *Rose City* on May 1, 1975, and launched February 1, 1976.
- Acquired by MSC and placed in service as *Comfort* (T-AH 20) on December 1, 1987.

Moored in San Juan, Puerto Rico, on October 27, 2017, USNS *Comfort* (T-AH 20) is on the scene to provide humanitarian relief following Hurricane Maria (U.S. Navy photograph).

- Deployed August 1990–April 1991 to Mideast on Operations Desert Shield and Desert Storm. Ship saw more than 8,000 outpatients, admitted 700 inpatients and performed 337 surgeries that were typically beyond the capability of shore-based hospitals.
- In June 1994 deployed to Jamaica to serve as afloat migrant processing center for Haitian migrants. Served off Port-au-Prince, Haiti, in late 1994 to provide surgical support for U.S. operations ashore.
- Rendered aid and support to relief workers in New York City following the terrorist attack of September 11, 2001. Provided nearly 17,000 meals and washed 4,400 pounds of laundry for embarked workers.
- Served as trauma center in Arabian Gulf during Operation Iraqi Freedom (January–June 2003). Provided medical care to nearly 700 people.
- Following Hurricane Katrina, treated nearly 1,500 people in New Orleans in September-October 2005.
- Sailed in Latin American waters in June–October 2007 on Partnership for the Americas humanitarian assistance mission and helped treat more than 98,000 people in 12 countries.
- In April–July 2009 participated in Continuing Promise training mission during which the ship's medical teams treated more than 100,000 patients in seven countries in the Caribbean.
- Provided humanitarian assistance in 2010 to Haitian victims of a magnitude 7.3 earthquake.
- Deployed to Puerto Rico on September 29, 2017, to furnish aid and assistance following the devastating Hurricane Maria. Treated more than 1,900 patients,

performed 191 surgeries and delivered two newborns (a girl on October 14 and a boy on November 3). Returned home on November 21.
- Berthed in Norfolk, Virginia.

NOTES

1. Originally passenger liner SS *John Englis* built in 1895–96, acquired by Navy in 1902, commissioned as USS *Relief* in February 1908, renamed *Repose* in April 1918, and sold in May 1919 for commercial service.
2. Commissioned as transport [q.v.] *Henderson* in May 1917, classified as AP 1 in July 1920, converted to hospital ship in 1943–1944, recommissioned as *Bountiful* in March 1944, decommissioned September 1946, and sold for scrapping in January 1948.
3. Commissioned as transport *Chaumont* (AP 5) in November 1921, converted to AH in 1943–1944, recommissioned as *Samaritan* in March 1944, decommissioned in June 1946, and sold for scrapping in December 1947.
4. Originally SS *Blue Hen State* built in 1920–1921, acquired in April 1942, commissioned as transport *Kenmore* (AP 62) in August 1942, converted to AH in 1943–1944, recommissioned as *Refuge* in February 1944, decommissioned in April 1946 and struck the next month, and sold for scrapping in February 1948.
5. Built as cargo vessel SS *Marine Hawk* in 1944, acquired in June 1944, converted to hospital ship in 1944–1945, commissioned in May 1945, reclassified as evacuation transport [q.v.] APH 112 in June 1946 and reclassified back to AH 12 in October 1946, decommissioned in July 1947 and laid up, recommissioned in September 1950 for Korean War duty, decommissioned in June 1957, struck in March 1967, transferred to MARAD in June 1967, and transferred to Union Carbide Corporation in January 1968. Ultimately sold for scrapping in December 1988.
6. Built as cargo ship *Marine Lion*, acquired July 1944, commissioned as AH 13 in May 1945, decommissioned September 1947 and laid up, reactivated in 1950 and assigned to MSTS as T-AH 13, rammed by SS *Mary Luckenbach* during sea trials on August 25, 1950, and sunk off San Francisco.
7. Built as cargo ship SS *Marine Dolphin* in 1943–1944, acquired in August 1944, converted to AH in 1944–1945, commissioned as AH 14 in April 1945, reclassified as APH 114 in November 1945, reclassified as AH 14 in March 1946, decommissioned in July 1946 and laid up, struck in September 1961, transferred to MARAD in September 1962, and sold for scrapping in July 1974.
8. Built in 1932 as passenger liner *St. John*, acquired in April 1941 and commissioned as submarine tender *Antaeus* (AS 21) in May 1941, reclassified as miscellaneous auxiliary AG 67 in September 1943, converted to hospital ship and renamed *Rescue* (AH 18) in January 1945, decommissioned in June 1946, and struck in August 1946. Later operated as merchant ship in 1946–1959, and then dismantled.
9. Moeser and Edwards "USS *Repose* (AH-16)."
10. *Ibid.*

CARGO SHIPS (T-AK)

Ships currently classified as cargo ships (designated as "T-AK"—with the "T" prefix signifying that they are either government-owned or a bareboat chartered ship assigned to the Military Sealift Command) differ from their mid–20th century AK predecessors. The earlier "straight" AKs were relatively simple in design and conventional in purpose, i.e., they transported freight, materials and supplies from place to place and were manned by Navy personnel. (The last of these straight cargo ships was sold off in 2003. See Chapter 3 for information about the earlier AKs.) Today's AKs, on the other hand, have morphed into relatively more exotic ship types, such as container ships, container-Roll On/Roll Off (RO/RO) vehicle ships, Lighter-Aboard Ship (LASH) barge-carrying vessels, and container-RO/RO-tanker ships. No longer manned by Navy personnel, current T-AKs are typically operated by civilian mariners who work for private companies under contract to MSC. The ships are employed in one of two MSC programs: Prepositioning (PM3) or Sealift (PM5).

Maritime Prepositioning Ships (MPS) are assigned to MPS squadrons located at Diego Garcia in the Indian Ocean, and at Guam and Saipan in the western Pacific. Each squadron consists of four to six ships as well additional prepositioning ships dedicated to other military services. These ships carry enough equipment, supplies and muni-

The container-RO/RO vessel USNS *LCPL Roy M. Wheat* (T-AK 3016) is undergoing sea trials in the Gulf of Mexico following her conversion in 2003 (U.S. Navy photograph).

tions—including tanks, food, water, cargo, hospital equipment, petroleum products and spare parts—to support a Marine Expeditionary Brigade of about 16,000 personnel for a month. Their ability to rapidly move military gear between distant operating areas enables the United States to respond quickly to distant humanitarian or military crises. In such a crisis, the "user" personnel are flown out to the MPS's operating area to link up with and utilize the cargo carried by the vessel.

T-AKs employed in the Sealift program provide cost-effective point-to-point ocean transportation for the Department of Defense and other federal agencies during either peacetime or wartime.

Early cargo ships were named for astronomical bodies and U.S. counties; later AKs have been named for Medal of Honor recipients and war heroes, geographic promontories and various other sources.

T-AK Roster (Active)

The following cargo ships are listed in the current MSC vessel inventory. Footnotes refer to the role of the ship as defined by MSC.

T-AK 3005 *SGT Matej Kocak*[1]
T-AK 3006 *PFC Eugene A. Obregon*[2]
T-AK 3007 *MAJ Stephen W. Pless*[3]
T-AK 3008 *2ND LT John P. Bobo*[4]
T-AK 3009 *PFC Dewayne T. Williams*[5]

USNS *SGT William R. Button* (T-AK 3012) is moored off the coast of Latvia on May 25, 2017, in support of the Saber Strike 17 maritime prepositioning force operations (U.S. Navy photograph).

T-AK 3010	1ST LT Baldomero Lopez[6]	T-AK 4396	MAJ Bernard F. Fisher[12]
T-AK 3011	1ST LT Jack Lummus[7]	T-AK 4543	LTC John U. D. Page[13]
T-AK 3012	SGT William R. Button[8]	T-AK 4544	SSG Edward A, Carter, Jr.[14]
T-AK 3015	1ST LT Harry L. Martin[9]		
T-AK 3016	LCPL Roy M. Wheat[10]	T-AK 5307	Ocean Crescent[15]
T-AK 3017	GYSGT Fred W. Stockham[11]	T-AK 5362	CAPT David I. Lyon[16]

AK / T-AK Roster (Inactive)

The following MSC vessels are currently in MARAD custody for various purposes, such as training, cannibalization or disposal.

The former cargo ships T-AK 287–T-AK 294 were reclassified as T-AKR 287–T-AKR 294, respectively, and are currently in the MARAD Ready Reserve Force (RRF). See the vehicle cargo ship (AKR) section for details.

Footnotes below provide the ship's Maritime Administration design or type, its present Ready Reserve Force location (viz., BRF—Beaumont, Texas; JRRF—James River, Virginia; and SBRF—Suisun Bay, California) and its status (viz., Disposal—vessel available for disposal or in the process of being disposed of; Logistics Support—vessel reserved for cannibalization or material stripping to support other Ready Reserve Force vessels; Militarily Useful—vessel reserved for future military or strategic use as determined by Defense Department sponsors; Stripping—being stripped of useful material prior to becoming available for disposal; and Training—vessel reserved as training platform for one or more federal agencies).

AK 1014	*Cape Nome*[17]		AK 5056	*Cape Breton*[27]
AK 2039	*Cape Girardeau*[18]		AK 5057	*Cape Bover*[28]
AK 5009	*Cape Ann*[19]		AK 5058	*Cape Borda*[29]
AK 5010	*Cape Alexander*[20]		AK 5061	*Cape Fear*[30]
AK 5011	*Cape Archway*[21]		AK 5070	*Cape Flattery*[31]
AK 5012	*Cape Alava*[22]		AK 5071	*Cape Florida*[32]
AK 5013	*Cape Avinoff*[23]		AK 5073	*Cape Farewell*[33]
AK 5029	*Cape Jacob*[24]		AK 5075	*Cape Johnson*[34]
AK 5036	*Cape Chalmers*[25]		AK 5077	*Cape Juby*[35]
AK 5051	*Cape Gibson*[26]			

AK / T-AK Roster (Discarded)

The following vessels are neither listed in the current MSC inventory nor in the current MARAD NDRF.

T-AK 323	*TSGT John A. Chapman*		AK 5016	*Lake* [SS]
AK 851	*Cleveland*		AK 5017	*Pride* [SS]
AK 1005	*Austral Rainbow*		AK 5018	*Scan* [SS]
AK 2005	*Transcolorado*		AK 5019	*Courier*
AK 2016	*Pioneer Commander* [SS]		AK 5022	*Cape John*
AK 2018	*Pioneer Contractor* [SS]		AK 5026	*Del Viento* [SS]
AK 2019	*Pioneer Crusader* [SS]		AK 5037	*Cape Canso* [SS]
AK 2033	*Buyer*		AK 5038	*Cape Charles* [SS]
AK 2035	*Gulf Shipper* [SS]		AK 5039	*Cape Clear* [SS]
AK 2036	*Gulf Trader*		AK 5040	*Cape Canaveral* [SS]
T-AK 2049	*Green Valley*		AK 5041	*Cape Cod* [SS]
T-AK 2050	*Green Wave*		AK 5042	*Cape Carthage* [SS]
AK 2062	*American Cormorant*		AK 5044	*Gulf Banker* [SS]
AK 2064	*Green Harbour*		AK 5045	*Gulf Farmer* [SS]
T-AK 3000	*CPL Louis J. Hauge*		AK 5046	*Gulf Merchant*
T-AK 3001	*PFC William B. Baugh*		AK 5049	*Del Monte*
T-AK 3002	*PFC James Anderson, Jr.*		AK 5050	*Del Valle* [SS]
T-AK 3003	*1ST LT Alex Bonnyman, Jr.*		AK 5059	*Cape Bon* [T]
			AK 5060	*Cape Blanco* [SS]
T-AK 3004	*PVT Franklin J. Phillips*		AK 5074	*Cape Catawba* [SS]
AK 4638	*A1C William H. Pitsenbarger*		AK 9204	*Jeb Stuart*
			AK 9301	*Buffalo Soldier*
AK 4729	*American Tern*		AK 9302	*American Merlin*
AK 5005	*Adventurer* [SS]		AK 9519	*Baffin Strait*
AK 5006	*Aide* [SS]		AK 9651	*American Kestrel* [SS]
AK 5007	*Ambassador* [SS]		AK 9653	*Noble Star*
AK 5008	*Banner* [SS]		AK 9655	*Green Ridge*
AK 5015	*Agent*		AK 9682	*Advantage*

Selected General Specifications

SGT Matej Kocak class: T-AK 3005—T-AK 3007

Length: 821 feet
Beam: 105.6 feet
Draft: 32 feet
Displacement: 48,754 tons (full load)
Propulsion: 2 steam turbines (General Electric); 30,000 shp; 1 shaft
Speed: 20 knots
Personnel: 34 civilians & 10 technicians

2LT John P. Bobo class: T-AK 3008—T-AK 3012

Length: 675.2 feet
Beam: 105.5 feet
Draft: 29.5 feet
Displacement: 44,330 tons (full load)
Propulsion: 2 Stork-Wartsilia Werkspoor 16TM410 diesels; 27,000 bhp; 1 shaft
Speed: 18 knots
Personnel: 38 civilians & 10 technicians

Selected Summary Histories

USNS *SGT Matej Kocak* (T-AK 3005)

- Maritime Administration C7-S-133a type container-RO/RO vehicle ship.
- Built as *John B. Waterman* by Sun Shipbuilding and Dry Dock, in Chester, Pennsylvania, and delivered March 23, 1983.
- First owned by Waterman Steamship Corporation.
- Initially acquired by Navy under 25-year charter for use as MPS vessel.
- Converted by National Steel and Shipbuilding Company in San Diego with addition of 157-foot amidships section and helicopter platform.
- Placed in service with MSC in October 1984 and operated by Waterman.
- Purchased by government for MSC as T-AK 3005 on January 15, 2009.
- Supported Exercise Phoenix Express 2012 in the Mediterranean in May 2012.
- Based at Mediterranean as member of Maritime Prepositioning Ship Squadron 1 (which was disestablished September 28, 2012).
- Performed in various surge sealift operations and military exercises such as Pacific Pathways 2015 and 2016 to promote military interoperability in Southeast Asia, and Epic Guardian 2016 to promote interoperability with African partner nations.
- Ran aground off Okinawa on January 22, 2015, and refloated nine days later.
- Performed test and evaluation sea trials in August 2016 prior to receiving a new civilian operator.
- Berthed in Hampton Roads, Virginia, in Reduced Operational Status.

USNS *PFC Eugene A. Obregon* (T-AK 3006)

- Maritime Administration C7-S-133a type container-RO/RO vehicle ship.
- Built as SS *Thomas Heywood* by Sun Shipbuilding and Dry Dock, in Chester, Pennsylvania, and delivered February 11, 1983.
- First owned by Waterman Steamship Corporation.

2. Support Ships

USNS *PFC Eugene A. Obregon* (T-AK 3006) is just getting underway in Newport News, Virginia, on December 4, 2016, to participate in training exercise Resolute Endeavor II (U.S. Navy photograph).

- Initially acquired under 25-year charter for use as MPS vessel.
- Converted by National Steel and Shipbuilding Company in San Diego with addition of 157-foot amidships section and helicopter platform.
- Placed in service with MSC in January 1985 and operated by Waterman.
- Purchased by MSC in January 2010 as T-AK 3006.
- Assigned to Prepositioning program.
- Participated in Exercise Baltic Operations in June 2010.
- Engaged in Bold Alligator 2012 exercise in January-February and in Joint-Logistics-Over-the-Shore 2012 exercise in August 2012.
- Was based at Mediterranean as member of Maritime Prepositioning Ship Squadron 1 (which was disestablished September 28, 2012).
- Performed test and evaluation sea trials in August 2016 prior to receiving a new civilian operator.
- Berthed in Hampton Roads, Virginia, in Reduced Operational Status.

USNS *MAJ Stephen W. Pless* (T-AK 3007)

- Maritime Administration C7-S-133a type container-RO/RO vehicle ship.
- Built as SS *Charles Carroll* by Sun Shipbuilding and Dry Dock (some sources list General Dynamics in Quincy, Massachusetts as the builder) and delivered in 1983.

On February 20, 2016, USNS *MAJ Stephen W. Pless* (T-AK 3007) is anchored in the Gulf of Thailand while participating in Exercise Cobra Gold 2016, one of the largest multilateral exercises in the Asia-Pacific region (U.S. Navy photograph).

- First owned by Waterman Steamship Corporation.
- Initially acquired under 25-year charter for use as MPS vessel.
- Converted by National Steel and Shipbuilding Company in San Diego with addition of 157-foot amidships section and helicopter platform.
- Placed in service with MSC in 1985 and operated by Waterman.
- Purchased by MSC in January 2009 as T-AK 3007 and assigned to Maritime Prepositioning Ship Squadron 3 in western Pacific.
- Participated in Exercise Cobra Gold 2009 in February 2009 and offloaded 100 pieces of Marine cargo in Thailand.
- In February and April 2010 delivered Marine cargo during Exercise Freedom Banner in South Korea.
- Current role is to provide services when called upon as a dry cargo-carrying surge sealift ship.
- Supported Exercise Balikatan 16 in the Philippines and participated in multiple transportation operations in three Asian countries during a five-month mini-deployment in 2016.
- Performed test and evaluation sea trials in August 2016 prior to receiving a new civilian operator.
- Currently maintained In Reduced Operational Status.

USNS *2ND LT John P. Bobo* (T-AK 3008)

- Built in 1984–1985 by General Dynamics at Quincy, Massachusetts.

- Acquired in long-term charter by Navy on February 14, 1985.
- Deployed in support of Operation Iraqi Freedom in January 2003.
- Purchased by MSC on January 16, 2007.
- Flagship of Maritime Prepositioning Ship Squadron 1 in the Mediterranean (which was disestablished September 28, 2012).

USNS *1LT Harry L. Martin* (T-AK 3015)

Sailors are offloading a boat from the container roll-on/roll-off vessel USNS *1LT Harry L. Martin* (T-AK 3015) at the Marine Corps Blount Island Command in Jacksonville, Florida, on September 11, 2012 (U.S. Navy photograph).

- Container-RO/RO Vehicle ship
- Built in 1979 as MV *Tarago* by Bremer Vulkan AG in Bremen, Germany.
- Delivered in January 1980.
- Acquired by Navy in 1995.
- Converted in 1999 at Atlantic Drydock in Jacksonville, Florida, for duty as MPS.
- Placed in MSC service on April 20, 2000, and assigned to Maritime Prepositioning Ship Squadron 3 in western Pacific.
- Participated in humanitarian mission following December 20004 tsunami in South Asia.
- Participated in Cobra Gold exercise in Thailand in April-May 2008.
- Currently assigned to MSC's Sealift program.

Notes

1. Navy-owned Maritime Administration C7-S-133a design container-RO/RO vehicle ship to provide services when called upon as a dry cargo-carrying surge sealift ship.
2. Ibid.
3. Ibid.
4. Navy-owned Maritime Administration C8-M-MA134 design container-RO/RO vehicle ship to provide equipment to sustain a Marine Corps Air Ground Task Force for up to 30 days by discharging cargo in port or at sea using organic lighterage (barges).
5. Ibid.
6. Ibid.
7. Ibid.
8. Ibid.
9. Navy-owned Maritime Administration C7-S-133a design container-RO/RO vehicle ship to provide services when called upon as a dry cargo-carrying surge sealift ship.
10. Ibid.
11. Navy-owned Large, Medium-Speed RO/RO (LMSR) vehicle ship combining enhanced prepositioning capabilities with modifications to provide a multi-mission vessel to unified commanders.
12. Chartered vessel to provide the Air Force with prepositioned ammunition stocks.
13. Chartered vessel to provide 30 days sustainment for an Army brigade combat team.
14. Ibid.
15. Chartered vessel to provide port-to-port dry cargo shipping worldwide.
16. Chartered vessel to provide the Air Force with prepositioned ammunition stocks.
17. C5-S-78a/JRRF/Logistics Support.
18. C5-S-75a/SBRF/Logistics Support.
19. C4-S-58a/JRRF/Disposal.
20. C4-S-58a/JRRF/Disposal.
21. Ibid.
22. Ibid.
23. C4-S-58a/JRRF/Disposal.
24. C4-S-1u/SBRF/Logistics Support.
25. C3-S-37c/Charleston, SC/Training.
26. C5-S-75a/BRF/Disposal.
27. C4-S-66a/Brownsville, TX/Disposal.
28. C4-S-66a/SBRF/Logistics Support.
29. C4-S-1u/SBRF/Logistics Support.
30. C8-S-81b/SBRF/Logistics Support.
31. C9-S-81d/BRF/Military.
32. C8-S-81b/BRF/Stripping.
33. C9-S-81d/BRF/Militarily Useful.
34. C4-S-1u/JRRF/Disposal.
35. C4-S-1u/JRRF/Logistics Support.

Vehicle Cargo Ships (AKR / T-AKR)

Vehicle cargo ships (AKRs) carry military equipment—primarily tanks and wheeled vehicles—to deployed U.S. forces around the globe. Operated by civilian mariners under the aegis of the Military Sealift Command (MSC), the AKRs are usually maintained in port by a small nucleus crew of about 10 mariners in a reduced operational status (ROS) but when called upon and fully activated with a full crew can be sent to sea in a just a few days.

The Navy's first purpose-built oceangoing Roll-on/Roll-off vessel was USNS *Comet* (T-AKR 7), which was placed in service with MSTS in January 1958. She could accommodate 700 vehicles. *Comet* was followed by USNS *Meteor* (T-AKR 9) in May 1967, and by USNS *Mercury* (T-AKR 10) and USNS *Jupiter* (T-AKR 11) in June and May 1980, respectively. Between June 1984 and November 1985 the Navy acquired eight converted SL-7 type high-speed merchant ships—the fastest cargo ships ever built for the U.S. merchant marine. Designated T-AKR 287–T-AKR 294, all eight participated in Operations Desert Shield, Desert Storm and Iraqi Freedom. They are now in the MSC Ready Reserve Force.

A seagull perched on a bollard observes USNS *Soderman* (T-AKR 317) preparing to moor at the Naval Station in Everett, Washington, on February 23, 2007 (U.S. Navy photograph).

A Joint Chiefs of Staff study in the early 1990s found that additional sealift ships were needed to provide greater carrying-capacity to transport military supplies and equipment during wartime and international crises. That requirement led to the acquisition of 19 Large, Medium-Speed, Roll-on/Roll-off Ships (LSMRs) which gave the Navy five million square feet of new capacity. These new LSMRs can carry an entire U.S. Army task force, including 58 tanks, 48 other tracked vehicles and more than 900 trucks and other wheeled vehicles. They have a cargo-carrying capacity of more than 380,000 square feet (the equivalent of nearly eight football fields). Equipped with a slewing stern ramp and a removable ramp that services two side ports, these vessels can quickly load and unload vehicles from the ship. In addition, interior ramps facilitate traffic movement after cargo is loaded aboard. The LSMR AKRs are fitted with two 110-ton single-pedestal twin cranes to allow for loading and unloading cargo in ports with poor or no pierside infrastructure.

The largest group of vehicle cargo ships today belong to the eight-vessel Watson class (T-AKR 310–T-AKR 317), which entered service between June 1998 and September 2002. At about the same time, the Navy acquired seven LSMRs of the Bob Hope class (T-AKV 300–T-AKV 306), which were placed in service between November 1998 and September 2003. Ships of those two classes can each carry more than 1,000 vehicles, including about 60 Army M1 Abrams tanks.

The first USNS *Soderman* (T-AKR 299) was transferred to the MSC's Prepositioning

The lead ship of the Bob Hope (T-AKR 300) class is anchored in Souda Bay off the Greek island of Crete on January 20, 2004 (U.S. Navy photograph).

program, converted in 2000–2001, and placed in service as USNS *GYSGT Fred W. Stockham* (T-AK 3017) in March 2001. Her original name was given to a new *Soderman* (T-AKR 317) in September 2002.

Eight AKRs are assigned to the MSC Prepositioning program (PM3) and 11 others belong to MSC's Sealift program (PM5). At this writing, there are 35 AKRs designated as Ready Reserve Force vessels in the National Defense Reserve Fleet (NDRF) which is maintained by MARAD.

AKR names are derived from a variety of sources, including celestial bodies, geographic promontories, Medal of Honor recipients and a famous comedian who entertained the troops.

AKR Roster

T-AKR 7	*Comet* [SS]	AKR 289	*Denebola*[7] [R]
T-AKR 9	*Meteor* [SS]	AKR 290	*Pollux*[8] [R]
T-AKR 10	*Mercury/Cape Island*[1] [R]	AKR 291	*Altair*[9] [R]
T-AKR 11	*Jupiter/Cape Intrepid*[2] [R]	AKR 292	*Regulus*[10] [R]
		AKR 293	*Capella*[11] [R]
AKR 112	*Cape Texas*[3] [R]	AKR 294	*Antares*[12] [R]
AKR 113	*Cape Taylor*[4] [R]	T-AKR 295	*Shugart*[13]
AKR 287	*Algol*[5] [R]	T-AKR 296	*Gordon*[14]
AKR 288	*Bellatrix*[6] [R]	T-AKR 297	*Yano*[15]

2. Support Ships

T-AKR 298	*Gilliland*[16]	AKR 5062	*Cape Isabel*[40] [R]
T-AKR 299	*Soderman*[17]	AKR 5063	*Cape May*[41] [R]
T-AKR 300	*Bob Hope*[18]	AKR 5064	*Cape Mendocino*[42] [L]
T-AKR 301	*Fisher*[19]	AKR 5065	*Cape Mohican*[43] [R]
T-AKR 302	*Seay*[20]	AKR 5066	*Cape Hudson*[44] [R]
T-AKR 303	*Mendonca*[21]	AKR 5067	*Cape Henry*[45] [R]
T-AKR 304	*Pililaau*[22]	AKR 5068	*Cape Horn*[46] [R]
T-AKR 305	*Brittin*[23]	AKR 5069	*Cape Edmont*[47] [R]
T-AKR 306	*Benavidez*[24] [R]	AKR 5076	*Cape Inscription*[48] [R]
T-AKR 310	*Watson*[25]	AKR 5077	*Cape Lambert* [SS]
T-AKR 311	*Sisler*[26] [R]	AKR 5078	*Cape Lobos*[49] [L/D]
T-AKR 312	*Dahl*[27]	AKR 5082	*Cape Knox*[50] [R]
T-AKR 313	*Red Cloud*[28]	AKR 5083	*Cape Kennedy*[51] [R]
T-AKR 314	*Charlton*[29]	AKR 9205	*Virginian*[52] [SS]
T-AKR 315	*Watkins*[30]	AKR 9666	*Cape Vincent*[53] [R]
T-AKR 316	*Pomeroy*[31]	AKR 9670	*Strong Texan*
T-AKR 317	*Soderman*[32]	AKR 9672	*American Falcon*
AKR 1001	*Admiral W. M. Callaghan*[33] [R]	AKR 9673	*American Condor*
		AKR 9678	*Cape Rise*[54] [R]
AKR 2044	*Cape Orlando*[34] [R]	AKR 9679	*Cape Ray*[55] [R]
AKR 5051	*Cape Ducato*[35] [R]	AKR 9701	*Cape Victory*[56] [R]
AKR 5052	*Cape Douglas*[36] [R]	AKR 9711	*Cape Trinity*[57] [R]
AKR 5053	*Cape Domingo*[37] [R]	AKR 9960	*Cape Race*[58] [R]
AKR 5054	*Cape Decision*[38] [R]	AKR 9961	*Cape Washington*[59] [R]
AKR 5055	*Cape Diamond*[39] [R]	AKR 9962	*Cape Wrath*[60] [R]

SELECTED SPECIFICATIONS

Shugart class: T-AKR 295 & T-AKR 297

Length: 906.75 feet
Beam: 105.5 feet
Draft: 34.6 feet
Displacement: 55,298 tons (full load)
Propulsion: 1 Burmeister & Wain 12L90 GFCA diesel; 46,663 bhp; 1 shaft; bow & stern thrusters
Speed: 24 knots
Personnel: 26 civilians (45 max.) & up to 50 active duty

Gordon class: T-AKR 296 & T-AKR 298

Length: 956 feet
Beam: 105.9 feet
Draft: 35.75 feet
Displacement: 55,422 tons (full load)
Propulsion: 1 Burmeister & Wain 12K84EF diesel, 26,000 bhp; 2 Burmeister & Wain 9K84EF diesels, 39,000 bhp; 3 shafts
Speed: 24 knots
Personnel: 26 civilian & up to 50 active duty

Bob Hope class: T-AKR 300–T-AKR 306

Length: 951.4 feet
Beam: 106 feet
Draft: 34.6 feet
Displacement: 62,968 tons (full load)
Propulsion: 4 Colt Pielstick 10 PC4 2V diesels; 65,160 bhp; 1 shaft

Speed: 24 knots
Personnel: 26 civilians (45 max.) & up to 50 active duty

Watson class: T-AKR 310–T-AK 317

Length: 951.4 feet
Beam: 106 feet
Draft: 34 feet
Displacement: 62,968 tons (full load)
Propulsion: 2 General Electric LM2500-30 gas turbines; 64,000 shp; 2 shafts
Speed: 24 knots
Personnel: 26–30 civilians, 5 maintenance & up to 50 active duty

Selected Histories

USNS *Comet* (T-AKR 7)

Designated at the time as the vehicle landing ship T-LSV 7, USNS *Comet* is moored to a pier in Naha, Okinawa, on June 19, 1965 (U.S. Navy photograph).

Considered to be the first vessel built specifically as a roll-on/roll-off vessel, *Comet* was laid down by the Sun Shipbuilding and Dry Dock Company on May 15, 1956, as a MARAD C3-ST-14a design dry cargo ship. She was launched in Chester, Pennsylvania, on July 31, 1957, and delivered to the Navy on January 24, 1958. *Comet* entered service with MSTS as a cargo ship designated as T-AK 269 and participated in the U.S. response to the Lebanon crisis later that year.

In October 1961 the Defense Department planned for the construction of five Comet-class ships to begin in fiscal year 1963 but that plan was scrubbed. *Comet* herself was reclassified as a vehicle landing ship and redesignated as T-LSV 7 on January 1, 1963, and six years later redesignated again as the vehicle cargo ship AKR 7.

Comet was assigned to the MSC Ready Reserve Force (RRF) and berthed in San

Francisco in fiscal year 1984 under the administrative control of MARAD. From time to time she engaged in various RRF exercises and deployed to the Mideast in Operations Desert Shield and Desert Storm in 1990–1991. In 2003 she made her last major deployment—in support of Operation Iraqi Freedom.

After returning to the United States, *Comet* was placed in reduced operational status (ROS) in Alameda, California. She was subsequently downgraded from the RRF and laid up in MARAD's Suisun Bay group of the NDRF in July 2006. Her career was ended on May 26, 2016, when she was sold to All Star Metals, LLC. to be dismantled.

USNS *Meteor* (T-AKR 9)

Seven years before she was renamed *Meteor*, the vehicle landing ship USNS *Sea Lift* (T-LSV 9) is steaming in the East China Sea in July 1968 (U.S. Navy photograph).

Built as an improved version of the Navy's first RO/RO vessel, *Meteor* was laid down on May 18, 1964, by the Lockheed Shipbuilding and Construction Company in Seattle, Washington. She was launched on April 17, 1965, as SS *Sea Lift*, a Maritime Administration C4-ST-67a type hull. When construction was completed two years later, the vessel had a cargo capacity of 77,578 square feet and could accommodate 700 vehicles in two after holds and general cargo in her two forward holds. *Sea Lift* was placed in service with MSTS designated as the vehicle landing ship T-LSV 9 on May 19, 1967.

Operating in the Pacific, *Sea Lift* transported military vehicles throughout East Asia, including deliveries to South Vietnam during the war. She was reclassified as a vehicle cargo ship and redesignated T-AKR 9 on August 14, 1969, and on September 12, 1975, took on a new identity as USNS *Meteor*. That same year, *Meteor* became one of seven vessels to comprise the first prepositioning squadron based in Diego Garcia in the Indian Ocean.

On October 30, 1985, she was assigned to the Ready Reserve Force, with administrative control passing to MARAD. As one of the 31 RO/RO ships and one of the 55 vessels in the RRF, *Meteor* was berthed in Oakland, California, in a reduced operational status to be ready for active duty in 10 days. As such, the ship participated in various RRF exercises and like her predecessor *Comet*, took part in Operations Desert Shield and Desert Storm.

In 2003 *Meteor* was shifted to the Suisun Bay group of the NDRF still in ROS-10 status. But three years later, she was removed from the RRF program and identified as a "militarily useful" vessel, i.e., reserved for future military or strategic use as determined by Defense Department sponsors. Even that "tentative" status was changed in January 2008 when the ship was determined to be no longer required for retention. On July 29, 2015, *Meteor* left Suisun Bay for Brownsville, Texas, where she was to be dismantled by All Star Metals, the same shipbreaker who cut up *Comet*. By April 4, 2016, *Meteor* had been totally scrapped.

Notes

1. Renamed *Cape Island* in November 1993; now RRF vessel berthed in Tacoma, Washington.
2. Renamed *Cape Intrepid* in November 1993; now RRF vessel in Tacoma.
3. RRF vessel in Beaumont, Texas.
4. *Ibid.*
5. Laid down as SS *Sea-Land Exchange* in November 1971, placed in service as cargo ship USNS *Algol* (T-AK 287), redesignated as T-AKR in September 1982; now RRF vessel in Alameda, California.
6. Laid down as SS *Sea-Land Trade,* placed in service as cargo ship *Bellatrix* (T-AK 288), redesignated as T-AKR in September 1982; now RRF vessel in Marrerro, Louisiana.
7. Laid down as SS *Sea-Land Resource,* placed in service as cargo ship *Denebola* (T-AK 289), redesignated as T-AKR in September 1982; now RRF vessel in Baltimore, Maryland.
8. Laid down as SS *Sea-Land Market,* placed in service as cargo ship *Pollux* (T-AK 290), redesignated as T-AKR 290 in September 1982; now RRF vessel in Orange, Texas.
9. Laid down as SS *Sea-Land Finance,* placed in service as cargo ship *Altair* (T-AK 291), redesignated as T-AKR 291 in November 1983; now RRF vessel in Marrerro, Louisiana.
10. Laid down as SS *Sea-Land Commerce,* placed in service as cargo ship *Regulus* (T-AK 292), redesignated as T-AKR 292 in November 1983; now RRF vessel in Orange, Texas.
11. Laid down as SS *Sea-Land McLean,* placed in service as cargo ship *Capella* (T-AK 293), redesignated as T-AKR 293 in November 1983; now RRF vessel in Alameda, California.
12. Laid down as SS *Sea-Land Galloway,* placed in service as cargo ship *Antares* (T-AK 294), redesignated as T-AKR 294 in November 1983; now RRF vessel in Baltimore, Maryland.
13. Assigned to MSC Sealift (PM5) program.
14. *Ibid.*
15. *Ibid.*
16. *Ibid.*
17. Originally MV *Lica Maersk*, acquired in November 1997, placed in service in 1998 as *Soderman* (T-AKR 299), taken out of service in 2000 for conversion to an enhanced prepositioning ship, placed back in service in March 2001 as USNS *GYSGT Fred W. Stockham* (T-AKR 3017), and now operates out of Diego Garcia.
18. Assigned to MSC Sealift (PM5) program.
19. *Ibid.*
20. Assigned to MSC Prepositioning (PM3) program.
21. Assigned to MSC Sealift (PM5) program.
22. Assigned to MSC Prepositioning (PM3) program. T-AK 304 is in Maritime Prepositioning Ships Squadron 3 based in the Guam-Saipan area of the western Pacific and participated in Exercise Cobra Gold 2018 in Thailand in February 2018.
23. Assigned to MSC Sealift (PM5) program.
24. *Ibid.*
25. Assigned to MSC Sealift (PM5) program.
26. Assigned to MSC Prepositioning (PM3) program.
27. *Ibid.*
28. *Ibid.*
29. *Ibid.*
30. *Ibid.*
31. *Ibid.*
32. *Ibid.*

33. RRF vessel in Alameda, California.
34. Ibid.
35. RRF vessel in Charleston, South Carolina.
36. Ibid.
37. Ibid.
38. Ibid.
39. Ibid.
40. RRF vessel in Long Beach, California.
41. RRF vessel in Norfolk, Virginia.
42. RRF vessel in San Francisco, California.
43. RRF vessel in Alameda, California.
44. RRF vessel in San Francisco, California.
45. RRF vessel in San Francisco, California.
46. RRF vessel in San Francisco, California.
47. RRF vessel in Charleston, South Carolina.
48. RRF vessel in Long Beach, California.
49. Laid up in Beaumont, Texas, group of NDRF awaiting disposal.
50. RRF vessel in New Orleans, Louisiana.
51. Ibid.
52. Laid down as MV *Saint Magnus-85*, renamed *Jolly Indaco* and *Strong Virginian*, chartered by MSC in 1992 and placed in service as MV *Strong Virginian* (AK 9205), charter ended in 2002, sold to Sealift Inc. in 2003 and renamed MV *Virginian*, chartered by MSC as AKR 9205; reportedly sold for scrap in August 2012.
53. RRF vessel in Beaumont, Texas.
54. RRF vessel in Portsmouth, Virginia. *Cape Ray* was modified in late 2013 to contribute to United Nations and Organization for the Prohibition of Chemical Weapons joint mission to eliminate Syria's chemical weapons materials. She departed for the mission on January 27, 2014. *Cape Race* was deployed in 2014 to support Air Force mission to transport two CV-22 Osprey aircraft out of Djibouti. *Cape Rise* deployed to West Africa in October 2014 as part of United Assistance to stop the spread of the Ebola virus.
55. Ibid.
56. RRF vessel in Beaumont, Texas.
57. Ibid.
58. RRF vessel in Portsmouth, Virginia. *Cape Ray* was modified in late 2013 to contribute to United Nations and Organization for the Prohibition of Chemical Weapons joint mission to eliminate Syria's chemical weapons materials. She departed for the mission on January 27, 2014. *Cape Race* was deployed in 2014 to support Air Force mission to transport two CV-22 Osprey aircraft out of Djibouti. *Cape Rise* deployed to West Africa in October 2014 as part of United Assistance to stop the spread of the Ebola virus.
59. RRF vessel in Baltimore, Maryland.
60. Ibid.

Transport Oilers (AOT / T-AOT)

Transport oilers carry fuel to ports and depots to support U.S. forces globally. Operated by civilian crews, these vessels do not transfer their cargos to naval ships while underway but instead deliver petroleum products to shore-based storage and distribution facilities.

The transport oiler hull type classification was established on September 30, 1978, when the Navy changed the designation of 18 tankers operated by the Military Sealift Command (MSC) and seven Navy oilers laid up in the National Defense Reserve Fleet (NDRF) from AO to AOT. (The mothballed Navy vessels were AOs 50, 67, 73, 75, 76, 78 and 134.)

In the 1970s the Navy acquired nine Sealift-class transport oilers (T-AOT 168–T-AOT 176) to replace World War-Ii-vintage tankers of the Maritime Administration T-2 type. With a cargo capacity of 220,000 barrels, they entered service in 1974–1975 and were deactivated in 1995. The Sealift class was joined by four transport oilers of the Falcon class (T-AOT 182–T-AOT 185), which began their service in 1976. Those ships could carry 310,000 barrels and have since been discarded.

The more recent Champion-class ships (T-AOT 1121–T-AOT 1125) were "build-and-

USNS *Sealift China Sea* (T-AOT 170) began her naval service in May 1975 and is seen here later in that decade. She was taken out of service in April 1995, sold to a Greek shipping company, and ultimately scrapped in March 2000 (U.S. Navy photograph).

charter" T-5 type tankers, i.e., vessels built for private ownership but long-term chartered to MSC. Although initially constructed for commercial service, four of the ships (T-AOT 1122–T-AOT 1125) were subsequently purchased by MSC in January 2003. USNS *Lawrence H. Gianella* (T-AOT 1125) was later assigned to MSC's Maritime Prepositioning (PM3) Force in 2009–2011 but is now listed by MSC as a unit in its Sealift (PM5) fleet. The other three Champions are now out of service and laid up in the NDRF in Beaumont, Texas.

All but one of the current AOTs are chartered vessels. For example, during Fiscal Year 2015 four long-term chartered U.S. flagged tankers—MT *Empire State* (AOT 5193), MT *Evergreen State* (T-AOT 5205), MT *Maersk Peary* (T-AOT 5246) and MT *SLNC Pax* (T-AOT 5356)—and one government-owned tanker—USNS *Lawrence H. Gianella* (T-AOT 1125)—were the primary carriers of 35.5 million barrels (or 1.49 billion gallons) of Defense Department petroleum products on more than 192 voyages. *Maersk Peary*—the only long-term chartered tanker with an ice-strengthened hull—delivered 118,916 barrels of fuel to the National Science Foundation station at McMurdo Sound in Antarctica (Operation Deep Freeze) and another chartered tanker brought 207,790 barrels of fuel to the Air Force installation at Thule, Greenland (Operation Pacer Goose). Those operations were supplemented by numerous short-term voyage and time-chartered commercial tankers, both U.S. and foreign flag.

Many AOTs were named for rivers but several carry names derived from various sources.

AOT Roster

In the listing below a single asterisk indicates a former Navy oiler (AO) reclassified as an AOT with the same hull number. A double asterisk indicates a commercial vessel currently chartered by MSC.

2. Support Ships

The transport oiler USNS *Lawrence H. Gianella* (T-AOT 1125) is maneuvering alongside the fleet replenishment oiler USNS *Laramie* (T-AO 203) on November 28, 2017, to perform a skin-to-skin (moored alongside each other) fuel lightering (transfer) operation (U.S. Navy photograph).

T-AOT 50	*Tallulah** [SS]	T-AOT 185	*Susquehanna** [K]
T-AOT 67	*Cache** [SS]	AOT 1001	*Patriot* [OS]
T-AOT 73	*Millicoma** [SS]	AOT 1002	*Ranger* [SC]
T-AOT 75	*Saugatuck** [SS]	AOT 1006	*Rover* [OS]
T-AOT 76	*Schuykill** [SS]	AOT 1007	*Courier* [OS]
T-AOT 77	*Cassatot** [SS]	AOT 1012	*Mission Buenaventura* [SS]
T-AOT 78	*Chepachet**[1] [T]		
T-AOT 79	*Cowanesque** [SS]	AOT 1121	*Gus W. Darnell*[2] [OS]
T-AOT 109	*Waccamaw** [SS]	T-AOT 1122	*Paul Buck*[3] [L]
T-AOT 134	*Mission Santa Ynez** [SS]	T-AOT 1123	*Samuel L. Cobb*[4] [L]
T-AOT 149	*Maumee** [SS]	T-AOT 1124	*Richard G. Matthiesen*[5] [L]
T-AOT 151	*Shoshone** [SS]		
T-AOT 152	*Yukon** [SS]	T-AOT 1125	*Lawrence H. Gianella*[6] [A]
T-AOT 165	*American Explorer** [SS]		
T-AOT 168	*Sealift Pacific** [SC]	AOT 1201	*New York Sun/Allegiance* [OS]
T-AOT 169	*Sealift Arabian Sea** [SC]		
T-AOT 170	*Sealift China Sea** [SC]	AOT 1203	*Overseas Alice* [OS]
T-AOT 171	*Sealift Indian Ocean** [SC]	AOT 1204	*Overseas Valdez* [OS]
		AOT 1205	*Overseas Vivian* [OS]
T-AOT 172	*Sealift Atlantic** [SC]	AOT 5075	*American Osprey* [SS]
T-AOT 173	*Sealift Mediterranean** [SC]	AOT 5076	*Mount Washington* [SS]
		AOT 5083	*Mount Vernon* [SS]
T-AOT 174	*Sealift Caribbean** [SC]	AOT 5084	*Chesapeake*[7] [L]
T-AOT 175	*Sealift Arctic** [SC]	T-AOT 5193	*Empire State*** [A]
T-AOT 176	*Sealift Antarctic** [SC]	T-AOT 5205	*Evergreen State*[8] [OS]
T-AOT 181	*Potomac** [SS]	AOT 5246	*Maersk Peary*** [A]
T-AOT 182	*Columbia** [SS]	T-AOT 5356	*SLNC Pax*** [A]
T-AOT 183	*Neches** [K]	T-AOT 5406	*Galveston/Petroleum Producer*** [A]
T-AOT 184	*Hudson** [K]		

T-AOT 5419   SLNC *Goodwill*** [A]
AOT 9101   *Petersburg*[9] [R]
(no number) *Falcon Champion*[10] [SC]
(no number) *Falcon Leader*[11][SC]
(no number) *Montauk* [OS]

Selected Specifications

Suamico class: T-AOT 50—T-AOT 78, inclusive (T2-SE-A1 design)
Length: 523.5 feet
Beam: 68 feet
Draft: 30.8 feet
Displacement: 22,380 tons (full load)
Propulsion: turbo-electric; 6,000 shp, 1 shaft
Speed: 15 knots

Sealift class: T-AOT 168–T-AOT 176
Length: 587 feet
Beam: 84 feet
Draft: 34.3 feet
Displacement: 32,000 tons (full load)
Propulsion: Pielstick turbo-charged diesels; 14,000 shp; 1 shaft
Speed: 16 knots
Personnel: 30 civilians

USNS *Potomac* (T-AOT 181) (originally T5-S-12a design)
Length: 661 feet
Beam: 89 feet
Draft: 36 feet
Displacement: 34,800 tons (full load)
Propulsion: steam turbine; 18,600 shp
Speed: 18 knots

Falcon class: T-AOT 182–T-AOT 185
Length: 672 feet
Beam: 89 feet
Draft: 36 feet
Displacement: 45,877 tons (full load)
Propulsion: Pielstick diesel; 15,000 shp; 1 shaft
Speed: 16.5 knots
Personnel: 23 civilians

Champion class: T-AOT 1121–T-AOT 1125 (T5 design)
Length: 615 feet
Beam: 90 feet
Draft: 24.6 feet
Displacement: 39,624 tons (full load)
Propulsion: 1 Sulzer 5RTA 76 diesel; 18,400 hp; 1 shaft
Personnel: 24 civilians

MT *Empire State* (T-AOT 5193)
Length: 600.4 feet
Beam: 105.6 feet
Displacement: 49,000 tons
Speed: 14.8 knots
Personnel: 21 civilians

MT *Maersk Peary* (T-AOT 5246)

Length: 592 feet
Beam: 105.6 feet
Displacement: 47,876 tons
Speed: 14.8 knots
Personnel: 21 civilians

MT *SLNC Pax* (T-AOT 5356) & MT *SLNC Goodwill* (T-AOT 5419)

Length: 621 feet
Beam: 62 feet
Displacement: 62,174 tons
Speed: 15 knots

ATB *Galveston/Petrochem Producer* (T-AOT 5406)

Length: 604 feet
Beam: 71 feet
Displacement: 26,884 tons
Speed: 14.8 knots

SELECTED HISTORY

USNS *Potomac* (T-AOT 181)

This ship has perhaps the most fascinating history of any of the transport oilers, if for no other reason than she was in effect two ships joined at the hip.

Her story begins with the construction of the oiler USNS *Potomac* (T-AO 150) in 1957. Built as a T3-S-12a tanker by Sun Shipbuilding and Dry Dock Company of Chester, Pennsylvania, *Potomac* was launched on October 8, 1956, and delivered to the Navy on January 30, 1957. She was assigned to the Military Sea Transportation Service (MSTS), predecessor to today's Military Sealift Command (MSC), and put to work supplying fuel to U.S. military installations at home and overseas. During the summer of 1961, *Potomac* delivered petroleum products to American bases in Greenland. On September 26 of that year, while pumping fuel ashore for the Marine Corps Air Station Cherry Point in Morehead City, North Carolina, a fire broke out in aviation gas that had spilled from an open suction valve. In the ensuing blaze, the ship's bow and amidships areas were destroyed while 200 feet of the stern section remained generally intact. That after section was cut from the wreck and towed to the Newport News Shipbuilding & Dry Dock Company in Newport News, Virginia. The totaled remainder of the ship was scrapped and her name struck from the Vessel Register.

The surviving stern section and its propulsion machinery was then incorporated into another tanker christened as SS *Shenandoah*, which as a result of the mating was approximately the same length and capacity of the destroyed *Potomac*. The completed *Shenandoah* was delivered to the Keystone Shipping Company on December 11, 1964, and immediately placed on bareboat charter to MSTS. She delivered fuel to installations in Asia, and in August 1967, helped save the injured crew of the Japanese fishing vessel *Shoichi Maru*, which had caught fire 100 miles north of Wake Island.

In 1976 the Navy reacquired *Shenandoah* from Keystone Shipping and assigned her to MSC. As there was already a ship of the same name in the fleet—the destroyer tender [q.v.] AD 26—the tanker was renamed *Potomac* and designated as T-AOT 181. As a result, the new *Potomac* was reunited with a major part of the old *Potomac*. During her MSC service over the next seven years she delivered fuel in support of military operations around the world.

On May 3, 1984, the ship was laid up in the Ready Reserve Fleet (RRF) group in Beaumont, Texas. But her service was not yet ended. In 1985, *Potomac* served as the platform to demonstrate the new Offshore Petroleum Distribution System (OPDS) whereby a tanker standing offshore can transfer petroleum products to onshore storage facilities via a flexible pipeline run to the beach from a mooring buoy to which the tanker is attached. OPDS thus permits tankers which are unable to tie up at fuel piers to deliver up to 1.7 million gallons of fuel per day. *Potomac* was converted for the demonstration in Mobile, Alabama, and put the OPDS to the test there and in Cape Charles, Virginia. That work completed, the ship returned to the Beaumont Reserve Fleet on April 29, 1986.[12]

But once again *Potomac*'s service was not yet over. She was ordered back to active duty on December 9, 1990, to support Operations Desert Shield and Desert Storm. The reactivation work was performed by Houston Ship Repair in Orange, Texas, and in 1991 *Potomac* was sent to Diego Garcia in the Indian Ocean where she served in MSC's Prepositioning Force for the next 10 years. During 1994 *Potomac* assisted in humanitarian relief efforts in Rwanda and later supported military operations in Bosnia by transporting fuel from Kuwait. She departed her base in Diego Garcia on April 6, 2001, for the return home, and arrived in Galveston, Texas, on June 13. Prior to being placed in mothballs in Beaumont, the ship was dry-docked in Tampa, Florida, in November 2001. She was briefly reactivated again in March 2005 for sea trials and in September 2005 to assist in Hurricane Katrina relief efforts. *Potomac* was placed back in the Beaumont RRF one month later and administratively downgraded to the NDRF on August 11, 2008. She was withdrawn from the NDRF on September 5, 2012, after being sold to ESCO Marine, Inc., in Brownsville, Texas, to be dismantled after almost 50 years of service.

NOTES

1. Built as the Maritime Commission T2-SE-A1 tanker SS *Eutaw Springs* in 1943, commissioned as the oiler USS *Chepachet* (AO 78) in April 1943, decommissioned in May 1946, reclassified as a transport oiler and placed in service with MSTS as AOT 78, reinstated on the Naval Register in January 1948, taken out of service in July 1950 and laid up in NDRF in Suisun Bay, transferred to MARAD in March 1972, transferred and leased to U.S. Department of Energy in November 1978, struck in January 1980, transferred again to state of Hawaii in February 1982, and ultimately scrapped later that year.
2. Transferred to owner—Ocean Spirit Inc.—in September 2005.
3. Laid up in BRF Beaumont, Texas, in "interim hold" for future determination of status.
4. Ditto.
5. Laid up in BRF Beaumont as "militarily useful," i.e., reserved for future military or strategic use as determined by Defense Department sponsors.
6. Listed by MSC as part of its Sealift (PM5) program. Conducted a skin-to-skin lightering fuel transfer with the fleet replenishment oiler ISNS Laramie (T-AO 203) on November 28, 2017.
7. Laid up in BRF Beaumont as "stripping" vessel. i.e., being stripped of useful material prior to becoming available for disposal.
8. Chartered by MSC in 2011 but not currently listed by MSC as a long-term chartered tanker.
9. Ready Reserve Force ship in San Francisco, California.
10. Placed in service January 19, 1984, laid up in NDRF April 3, 1990, and sold in 1996.
11. Placed in service August 18, 1983, transferred to MARAD June 5, 1990, and sold June 14, 2001
12. Among the tankers in MARAD's inventory that were fitted with OPDS are: *American Osprey* (AOT 5075), *Chesapeake* (AOT 5084), *Mount Washington* (AOT 5083), *Petersburg* (AOT 9101), *Potomac* (T-AOT 181), and, of course, the currently active USNS *VADM K. R. Wheeler* (T-AG 5001) [q.v.].

CABLE REPAIRING SHIPS (ARC / T-ARC)

The Navy's cable repairing ships install and maintain underwater cable systems, including the nation's array of subsurface sonar sensors known as the Sound Surveillance

System (SOSUS) which detects and tracks submarines. In addition, cable repair ships–designated as ARCs–perform oceanographic and acoustic surveys for the Naval Electronic Systems Command under the aegis of the Oceanographer of the Navy.

USNS *Zeus* (T-ARC 7) is the first vessel built specifically for the Navy as a cable ship and is currently the only ARC now in service. She is operated by the Navy's Military Sealift Command (MSC) on behalf of the Space and Naval Warfare Systems Command. *Zeus* was ordered on August 17, 1979, but not laid down at the National Steel & Shipbuilding Company in San Diego, until June 1, 1981. She was launched on October 30, 1982, and placed in service with the MSC on March 19, 1984.

Zeus is propelled by an advanced system that uses bow- and stern-mounted thrusters for precise track-keeping and position-holding employed in cable laying and repair, laying sound arrays, projector towing and related functions. According to the Navy, the ship carries a variety of "cable handling equipment, including five cable tanks, cable transporters, cable tension machines, self-fleeting cable drums, overboarding sheaves, and a dynamometer cable fairleader."[1] She has centralized integrated displays for monitoring various ship and cable machinery functions, passive stabilization to reduce her rolling motion at sea when operating at slow speeds, and high-performance survey equipment. These features give *Zeus* the ability to lay up to 1,000 miles of cable in depths down to 9,000 feet in a single deployment before heading back to port for additional cable supplies.

Among the ship's electronic equipment are single-beam and multi-beam sonars for profiling the ocean bottom, deployable sidescan sonars and camera sleds, and deployable acoustic measurement buoys and environmental measurement (current, temperature and density) buoys used in oceanic survey operations.

Zeus is part of MSC's "afloat staging command support" force (PM7) and operates out of Cheatham Annex of the Naval Weapons Station in Yorktown, Virginia. Now the only active cable laying/repair ship in the Navy, she is typically at sea 300 days a year.

Most of the ARCs were named for mythological characters, and all but one were originally built for other purposes and served in other roles before becoming cable repair ships.

ARC Roster

ARC 1	*Portunus* [T]	ARC 5	*Yamacraw* [SS]
T-ARC 2	*Neptune* [SS]	T-ARC 6	*Albert J. Myer* [SS]
T-ARC 3	*Aeolus* [Z]	T-ARC 7	*Zeus* [A]
T-ARC 4	*Thor* [SS]		

SELECTED SPECIFICATIONS

Neptune class: T-ARC 2 & T-ARC 6

Length: 369 feet
Beam: 47 feet
Draft: 18 feet
Displacement: 7,400 tons (full load)
Propulsion: turbo-electric; 4,000 shp; 2 shafts
Speed: 14 knots
Personnel: 71 civilians, 6 Navy & 25 technicians

Aeolus (T-ARC 3)
Length: 438 feet
Beam: 58 feet
Draft: 19.25 feet
Displacement: 7,040 tons
Propulsion: turbo-electric; 6,000 shp; 2 shafts
Speed: 16.9 knots
Personnel: 80 civilians & 2 Navy technicians

Zeus (T-ARC 7)
Length: 513 feet overall; 464 feet waterline
Beam: 73 feet
Draft: 24 feet
Displacement: 15,700 tons (full load)
Propulsion: Diesel-electric; 5 diesel generators (General Motors EMD); 12,500 shp; twin shafts; 2 bow and 2 stern side thrusters
Speed: 15 knots
Personnel: 51 civilians, 6 Navy and 32 civilian technicians

SUMMARY HISTORIES

USS *Portunus* (ARC 1)

- Keel laid on August 1, 1944; launched September 11, 1944; and commissioned as a medium landing ship (LSM 275) on October 6, 1944.
- Operated in the Pacific during World War II and participated in the Okinawa campaign.
- Decommissioned on April 21, 1947, in San Pedro, California, and laid up in the Pacific Reserve Fleet.
- Reactivated during the Korean War, LSM 275 was reclassified as a cable laying and repair ship on December 14, 1951; converted to an ARC between January and August 1952; and commissioned as ARC 1 on July 2, 1952.
- Operated off the U.S. West Coast in late 1952 and early 1953. Transferred to the East Coast in June 1953.
- Named USS *Portunus* on July 13, 1953, and assigned to the 3rd Naval District headquartered in New York. Laid cable off Cape May, New Jersey, and off Bermuda; conducted ocean bottom surveys and cable operations off Colombia's Atlantic and Pacific coasts in October 1953.
- Overhauled in early 1954, followed by cable operations during 1955–1959 off Sandy Hook, New Jersey; Bermuda; Wood Island, Maine; Nantucket; Rhode Island; and Little Creek, Virginia.
- Decommissioned on April 30, 1959, and struck from the Vessel Register on May 1 of that year.
- Transferred to Portugal on November 16, 1959, under the Military Assistance Program. Commissioned by Portugal two days later as the diver tender NRP *Medusa* (A 5214). Disposed of in 1976.

USNS *Neptune* (T-ARC 2)

- Built in 1945, delivered to the U.S. Army in February 1946, and commissioned by that service as USACS *William H.G. Bullard*.

2. Support Ships

- Acquired by the Navy in 1953 and converted in Baltimore with the addition of new electric cable machinery, precision navigational instrumentation and a helicopter platform over the fantail.
- Commissioned on June 1, 1953, as USS *Neptune* (ARC 2).
- Engaged in Project Caesar for the Sound Surveillance System (SOSUS) by placing permanent underwater surveillance equipment to monitor surface and submerged vessels. She operated in the Atlantic from Canada to the Caribbean, and completed more than 50 cable laying and repair projects. Also installed underwater facilities used in R&D and training, and conducted acoustic surveys and testing.
- Operated in the Pacific in 1954, 1957, 1960 and 1964.
- Overhauled in Boston between December 1965 and March 1966.
- Homeport changed from Portsmouth, New Hampshire, to San Francisco on January 1, 1967.
- Decommissioned in 1973 and assigned to MSC as USNS *Neptune* (T-ARC 2).
- Placed out of service January 1, 1991, struck on August 20, 1992, transferred to the MARAD on April 1, 1998, and laid up in the James River of Virginia.
- Sold on November 3, 2005, to International Shipbreaking Ltd. In Brownsville, Texas, for dismantling.

USNS *Aeolus* (T-ARC 3)

In this bow-on view USS *Aeolus* (ARC 3) is seen underway off the U.S. East Coast in May 1961. She was decommissioned and transferred to MSC in 1973, which operated her for 12 years (U.S. Navy photograph).

- Laid down on March 29, 1945; launched on May 20, 1945; and commissioned as the assault cargo ship USS *Turandot* (AKA 47) on June 18, 1945.
- Transported 172 Army personnel to the New Hebrides in September 1945 and carried troops back to the United States on two cruises later that year.
- Decommissioned on March 21, 1946; transferred to the Maritime Commission on June 25 of that year; and struck on April 17, 1947.
- Reacquired by the Navy on November 4, 1954, for conversion to a cable repair ship. Converted in Baltimore; renamed USS *Aeolus* and designated as ARC 3 on March 17, 1955. Commissioned two months later on May 14.
- Operated in both the Atlantic (out of Norfolk) and Pacific (out of San Francisco) 1956–1959.
- From 1959 to June 1962 while based in Portsmouth, New Hampshire, worked along East Coast and in the West Indies.
- Damaged in a collision with a civilian oil tanker in September 1962 and repaired the next month.
- Overhauled in the spring of 1963. Performed cable laying and repair in both the Atlantic and Pacific from 1963 to 1973.
- Decommissioned on October 1, 1973, and transferred to MSC to be manned by civilian crew as USNS *Aeolus* (T-ARC 3).
- Placed out of service in May 1985 and transferred to Maritime Commission for layup in the National Defense Reserve Fleet in the James River of Virginia.
- Struck on February 28, 1985, and transferred to the North Carolina division of marine fisheries in August the following year.
- Sunk on July 29, 1988, to become part of artificial reef in 110 feet of water about 22 miles from the Beaufort inlet.

USNS *Thor* (T-ARC 4)

- Laid down on April 18, 1945; launched on June 8, 1945; acquired by the Navy on July 9, 1945; and commissioned that same day as the assault cargo ship USS *Vanadis* (AKA 49).
- Decommissioned on March 27, 1946; struck on June 5, 1946; transferred to the Maritime Commission a month later on July 2 for layup in the James River National Defense Reserve Fleet in Virginia.
- Reacquired by the Navy on April 14, 1955, and reinstated on the Vessel Register as AKA 49.
- Converted in 1955 to a cable repair ship (ARC 4) in Baltimore.
- Renamed USS *Thor* on November 14, 1955, and commissioned on January 3, 1956.
- Operated in both the Atlantic and Pacific in 1956 to 1968. Conducted "special operations" around Midway Island in the spring of 1968.
- Underwent a year-long overhaul in Boston from February 1970 to February 1971, following which *Thor* deployed to the Pacific. Returned to the East Coast of the U.S. early in 1972 and then operated back in the Pacific Ocean later that year.
- In early 1972 the ship performed cable operations near the Arctic Circle.
- Decommissioned in Portsmouth, New Hampshire, on July 2, 1973, and transferred that day to MSC, becoming USNS *Thor* (T-ARC 4).
- Operated for MSC in the Pacific until April 1974, when she was placed out of

USNS *Thor* began her naval service in World War II as a commissioned assault cargo ship but later worked as a cable repair ship for 20 years before her retirement in 1974 (U.S. Navy Photo).

   service and returned to the Maritime Commission for a July 31, 1975, layup in the National Defense Reserve Fleet at Suisun Bay off Benicia, California.
- Sold for dismantling on September 22, 1977, and withdrawn from NDRF on October 13, 1977.

USS *Yamacraw* (ARC 5)

- Laid down in Point Pleasant, West Virginia, as USAMP *Major General Arthur Murray* for service in the U.S. Army's Mine Planter Service of the Coast Artillery Corps, which was then responsible for the coastal defense of the United States. (Responsibility for controlled coastal defensive mine fields was transferred to the Navy in 1949.)
- Acquired by the Navy on January 2, 1945, converted to an auxiliary minelayer in Charleston, South Carolina, and commissioned as USS *Trapper* (ACM 9) on March 15, 1945.
- Deployed to the Pacific in late 1945 and operated out of Kobe, Japan.
- Decommissioned and transferred to the U.S. Coast Guard on June 20, 1946. Renamed USCGC *Yamacraw* and designated WARC 333.

- Featured in *Onionhead*, a 1958 comedy-drama film with Andy Griffith and Walter Matthau on a Coast Guard ship during World War II.
- Reacquired by the Navy on May 17, 1959; converted to a cable repair ship, and commissioned as USS *Yamacraw* (ARC 5) on April 30, 1959.
- Assigned to 3rd Naval District headquartered in New York; operated out of Portsmouth, New Hampshire, and conducted research projects for Office of Naval Research and for Bell Telephone Laboratories.
- Decommissioned on July 2, 1965, transferred to the Maritime Administration on July 21, 1965, and struck from the Naval Vessel Register.
- Sold for scrapping to American Smelting Company in 1967.

USNS *Albert J. Meyer* (T-ARC 6)

- Laid down as a S3-S2-BP1 hull in Wilmington, Delaware, on April 14, 1945; launched on November 7, 1945; and delivered to the Maritime Commission on May 17, 1946, for layup in the James River group of the National Defense Reserve Fleet (NRDF).
- Acquired by the Army on February 7, 1952, as USACS *Albert J. Myer* and operated by the Army Transport Service.
- Returned to the Maritime Administration on June 13, 1966, and transferred to the Navy.
- Converted to a cable laying and repair ship and assigned to the Navy's Military Sea Transportation Service (MSTS) as USNS *Albert J. Myer* (T-ARC 6).
- Manned by a civilian crew and operated globally.
- Placed out of service and struck from the Naval Vessel Register on November 7, 1994.
- Transferred to the Maritime Administration on April 1, 1998, and laid up in the James River group of the NRDF.
- Ultimately returned to the Navy and removed from the NDRF on August 24, 2005, to be dismantled by International Shipbreaking in Brownsville, Texas.

Note

1. https://www.history.navy.mil/research/histories/ship-histories/danfs/z/zeus-ii—t-arc-7-.html

Advanced Aviation Base Ship / Aviation Logistics Support Ship (AVB / T-AVB)

The Navy's first advanced aviation base ships were two former tank landing ships (LSTs) converted in the late 1950s and early 1960s. Designated as AVB 1 and AVB 2, they supported land-based Navy patrol aircraft operating from unimproved airfields as well as seaplanes based in the Mediterranean area. They were succeeded by two former C5-S-78a type (Seabridge class) combination Roll-On/Roll-Off container ships that were converted in the mid–1980s to provide maintenance and logistics support for land-based Marine aircraft in forward areas. Designated as T-AVB 3 and T-AVB 4, these aviation logistics support ships are assigned to the Ready Reserve Force (RRF) and are maintained

2. Support Ships

The aviation logistic support ship SS *Curtiss* (T-AVB 4) is in Reduced Operational Status while moored at the Naval Base San Diego in California on February 15, 2011 (U.S. Navy photograph).

by small nucleus crews in Reduced Operational Status (ROS). When fully reactivated and ready for sea within 120 hours after call up, the AVBs are manned by some 37 MSC civilian personnel and a Marine aircraft maintenance detachment along with communications and other support personnel totaling about 362 Marines. All of the equipment, vehicles, spare parts and supplies needed to support a forward-based Marine aviation unit are then transported by the AVB to the deployed Marine unit's operating area and quickly offloaded ashore.

The ships are fitted with both a stern ramp and side ports, and when equipped with mobile facilities, can service aircraft while anchored offshore. The AVBs have 35,000 square feet of vehicle storage space and can carry between 300 and 684 containers depending on the mission they are performing—either maintenance or supply For handling containers and equipment, the AVBs can employ ten 30-ton-capacity booms and a single 70-ton boom.

The first two AVBs were named for U.S. counties and the last two for aviation pioneers.

AVB Roster

AVB 1	*Alameda County* [T]	T-AVB 4 *Curtiss* [R]
AVB 2	*Tallahatchie County* [SS]	
T-AVB 3	*Wright* [R]	

Specifications

Alameda County (LST 32/AVB 1)
Length: 328 feet
Beam: 50 feet
Draft: 14 feet
Displacement: 1,625 tons (light)
Propulsion: 2 General Motors 12–567A 900hp diesel engines; 1,700 shp; 2 shafts
Speed: 11.6 knots
Personnel: 119

Tallahatchie County (LST 1154/AVB 2)
Length: 382 feet
Beam: 54 feet
Draft: 14.5 feet
Displacement: 6,000 tons
Propulsion: two 450 psi boilers; two geared turbines
Speed: 14 knots
Personnel: 272 (LST) or 190 (AVB) and 382 in aircraft maintenance detachment

Wright class: T-AVB 3 & T-AVB 4
Length: 600.9 feet (overall)
Beam: 90 feet
Draft: 34 feet
Displacement: 27,580 tons (full load)
Propulsion: 2 steam turbines; 30,000 shp; 1 shaft
Speed: 23.6 knots
Personnel: 40 civilians & more than 300 troops

Histories

USS Alameda County (AVB 1)
- Built as tank landing ship LST 32 in 1943 by Dravo Corporation in Pittsburgh, Pennsylvania.
- Laid down on February 17, 1943, launched on May 22, and commissioned on July 12, 1943.
- Deployed to Mediterranean in March 1944.
- Attacked by German bombers on April 1, resupplied Anzio beachhead in summer and participated in invasion of southern France in August 1944.
- Transported troops, prisoners, railroad cars and other vehicles in Italy, France and North Africa in 1945.
- Returned to U.S. in July 1945.
- Decommissioned in July 1946 and laid up at Green Cove Springs, Florida.
- With the start of the Korean War, recommissioned on March 7, 1951.
- Beginning in September 1953 served as advanced base support ship operating out of Naples, Italy. Provided Navy with capability of establishing forward air bases in the Mediterranean.
- LST 32 was named USS Alameda County on July 1, 1955.
- In response to Suez crisis of October 1956 she shifted to Souda Bay, Crete, and established emergency air base in November 1955.
- Redesignated as AVB 1 on September 28, 1957.

The advanced aviation base ship USS *Alameda County* (AVB 1) was a converted tank landing ship. She is seen here as an AVB while maneuvering slowly in the harbor at Malta during the 1950s (U.S. Navy photograph).

- In July–September 1958 supported air squadrons assisting the Marine landing force ashore in Beirut, Lebanon.
- Decommissioned in Naples, Italy, on June 25, 1962, and struck five days later.
- Sold to Italy on November 20, 1962.
- Renamed *Anteo* (A-5306). Later redesignated as L-9869. Decommissioned in August 1973.

USS *Tallahatchie County* (AVB 2)

- Built in 1945–1946 as tank landing ship LST 1154 by Boston Navy Yard in Boston, Massachusetts.
- Laid down on August 4, 1945; launched on July 19, 1946; and commissioned on May 24, 1949.
- Between December 1949 and May 1958 operated in the western Atlantic and Caribbean.
- Named USS *Tallahatchie County* on July 1, 1955.
- Operated with Sixth Fleet in the Mediterranean in May–December 1958 and July 1959–February 1960.
- Converted to advance aviation base ship at Charleston Naval Shipyard in early 1962.
- Redesignated as AVB 2 on February 3, 1962.
- Deployed to Mediterranean on May 15, 1962, with Naples, Italy, as new homeport.
- Operated in Crete and Sardinia late 1962 and early 1963.
- In November–December 1963 undertook a 4,800-mile cruise of eastern Mediterranean for Naval Oceanographic Office.

In November 1968, USS *Tallahatchie County* (AVB 2) is beached in Souda Bay on the Greek island of Crete, with a mechanized landing craft (LCM) on her port side (U.S. Navy photograph).

- Overhauled in Italian shipyard in early 1964.
- Participated in advance base exercise associated with NATO Operation Fallex in September 1964.
- Salvaged downed aircraft in waters off Libya in February 1965.
- Supported Patrol Squadron 24 (VP-24) in Souda Bay, Crete, July–September 1965.
- Operated out of Naples late 1965 to January 1970.
- Decommissioned and struck January 15, 1970.
- Sold for scrapping in July 1970 to Contieri Navali Santa Maria of Genoa, Italy.

SS *Wright* (T-AVB 3)

- Built by Ingalls Shipbuilding, Inc., of Pascagoula, Mississippi, as C5-S-78a type breakbulk, container ship SS *Mormacsun*.
- Laid down on June 24, 1968, and launched on July 29, 1969.
- Began service with Moore-McCormack Lines, Inc., on February 2, 1970.
- Renamed *Young America* and delivered to American Export–Isbrandtsen Lines, Inc. (Mediterranean Marine Line, Inc.) on October 19, 1970.
- Acquired by American Export Lines, Inc., on August 31, 1977.
- Sold to Farrell Lines, Inc., in March 1978.
- Acquired by MARAD on December 15, 1981 and laid up in James River, Virginia, group of NDRF.
- Began conversion to AVB at Todd Shipyards in Galveston, Texas, on June 12, 1984.

2. Support Ships

- Renamed USNS *Wright* and designated as T-AVB 3 on May 14, 1986.
- Placed in service with MSC on September 7, 1986.
- Participated in Operation Iraqi Freedom January–July 2003 with some 330 Marines embarked.
- Following Hurricane Sandy in October 2012, provided berthing for government and non-government relief workers in New York City.
- Participated in 14-nation Exercise Bold Alligator 16 in the Atlantic in August 2016.
- Assisted in relief efforts in the Caribbean following Hurricane Irma in September 2017.
- Berthed in Philadelphia, Pennsylvania, as part of the Ready Reserve Force of the NDRF with small nucleus crew in five-day Reduced Operational status (ROS).

SS *Curtiss* (T-AVB 4)

- Built by Ingalls Shipbuilding, Inc., of Pascagoula, Mississippi, as C5-S-78a type breakbulk, container ship SS *Mormacsky*.
- Laid down on April 16, 1968, and launched on December 28, 1968.
- Began service with Moore-McCormack Lines, Inc., on July 21, 1969.
- Renamed SS *Great Republic* on October 19, 1970.
- Acquired by MARAD in 1981.
- Renamed *Curtiss* and designated as AVB 4 on January 27, 1986.
- Converted to AVB at Todd Shipyards in Galveston, Texas.
- Placed in service with MSC on April 11, 1987.
- Marine Aviation Logistics Squadron 16 deployed on board for Operations Desert Shield and Desert Storm August 1990–March 1991.
- In April 2001 participated in Exercise Pacific Provider 21, a month-long logistics exercise off California.
- In March 2011 engaged in Exercise Pacific Horizon 2011 to evaluate the movement of combat equipment from ship to shore in the absence of developed port facilities.
- In June 2013 participated in Exercise Dawn Blitz off Port Hueneme. California.
- Berthed in San Diego, California, as part of the Ready Reserve Force of the NDRF with small nucleus crew in five-day Reduced Operational status (ROS).

High Speed Transports (HST / T-HST)

The Navy owns two high-speed catamaran ferries that were originally built for commercial service between Oahu and Maui in Hawaii. One of the vessels—USNS *Guam* (T-HST 1)—has been undergoing testing and evaluation for her planned service with U.S. Marine units in Okinawa and in Japan; the other vessel—HST 2 (the former USNS *Puerto Rico*)—is currently on long-term lease to Bay Ferries Limited for commercial service in the Gulf of Maine between Portland, Maine, and Yarmouth, Nova Scotia.

The HSTs are named for U.S. territories.

The high speed transport USNS *Guam* (T-HST 1) is getting underway from the Joint Expeditionary Base Little Creek–Fort Story in Virginia Beach, Virginia, on October 5, 2017 (U.S. Navy photograph).

HST Roster

    T-HST 1   *Guam* [A]
    HST 2   ex–*Puerto Rico* [OS]

SPECIFICATIONS

Guam (T-HST 1)
Length: 373 feet (HST 2 is 349 feet long)
Beam: 78 feet
Draft: 12 feet
Displacement: 2,437 tons (full load)
Propulsion: 4 MTU 20V8000 M70 diesel engines; 4 Rolls-Royce waterjets
Speed: 33 knots
Personnel: 15–18 civilians

HISTORIES

USNS *Guam* (T-HST 1)
- Built by Austral USA, in Mobile, Alabama, as high-speed ferry *Huakai* ("Journey") at a cost of $88 million.
- Launched January 18, 2007, for ownership of Hawaii Superferry, which ceased operations in March 2009.
- In April 2009 Defense Department stated intention to charter high-speed ferries

in 2009–2011 to transport troops and equipment from Okinawa to training areas and other locations pending availability of new-construction high-speed vessels.
- Participated in Operation Unified Response in early 2010 to deliver humanitarian aid to victims of January 12 magnitude 7.3 earthquake in Haiti.
- Acquired by MARAD in September 13, 2010, for $25 million as a result of foreclosure action against owner which had defaulted on loan guaranteed by MARAD.
- Transferred to MSC on January 27, 2010 (the Navy provided $35 million in funding for both HST 1 and HST 2).
- Renamed *Guam* (T-HST 1) on May 9, 2012. Navy Secretary stated the two vessels "will be used for peacetime operations such as troop transport, exercise missions and humanitarian and disaster relief."
- Intended to replace MSC-chartered high-speed vessel *Westpac Express* (HSV 4676) to provide high-speed transport for III Marine Expeditionary Force.
- At this writing *Guam* is berthed in Okinawa as a unit in MSC Prepositioning (PM3) force.

HST 2
- Built by Austral USA, in Mobile, Alabama, as high-speed ferry *Alakai* ("Sea Path") at a cost of $88 million.
- Launched September 29, 2008, for ownership of Hawaii Superferry, which ceased operations in March 2009.
- In April 2009 Defense Department stated intention to charter high-speed ferries in 2009–2011 to transport troops and equipment from Okinawa to training areas and other locations pending availability of new-construction high-speed vessels.
- Participated in Operation Unified Response in early 2010 to deliver humanitarian aid to victims of January 12 magnitude 7.3 earthquake in Haiti.
- Acquired by MARAD in September 13, 2010, for $25 million as a result of foreclosure action against owner.
- Transferred to MSC on January 27, 2010 (the Navy provided $35 million for both HST 1 and HST 2).
- Renamed *Puerto Rico* (T-HST 2) on May 9, 2012. Navy Secretary stated the two vessels "will be used for peacetime operations such as troop transport, exercise missions and humanitarian and disaster relief."
- In August 2012 towed from Norfolk, Virginia, to Philadelphia, Pennsylvania, for layup.
- Name withdrawn on February 6, 2016, and reassigned on December 14, 2016, to expeditionary fast transport [q.v.] USNS *Puerto Rico* (T-EPF 11).
- On March 24, 2016, Bay Ferries Limited announced agreement with MARAD and Navy for long-term charter of HST 2. She would be branded as "The CAT" for her service carrying passengers and vehicles between Portland, Maine, and Yarmouth, Nova Scotia. (NVR lists lease date of March 31, 2016.)
- Began service for Bay Ferries on June 15, 2016. Carried approximately 35,500 passengers that year (typically 850 passengers, 20 trucks and 90 cars per run).
- Engine problems in 2017 resulted in cancellation of about 25 percent of its trips but nevertheless vessel carried some 41,500 passengers.

Relic/Museum Ship

America's Ship of State—USS *Constitution*—fires her starboard guns while underway in Massachusetts Bay, Massachusetts, on July 20, 1997 (U.S. Navy photograph).

The reader might rightfully wonder why an eighteenth-century frigate appears in these pages in the same company as contemporary missile range instrumentation vessels and high speed transports. Actually, there are several reasons for that. First, this particular vessel is today the world's oldest commissioned warship afloat and the only surviving veteran of the War of 1812. Second, she is this nation's most venerated naval vessel. Third, she is officially America's "Ship of State." And fourth, and more to the point, the Navy has officially classified her as a "Support Ship," i.e., an auxiliary.

USS *Constitution* first put to sea in 1798. She has fought against the Barbary pirates and the Royal Navy. In an August 1812 engagement with a British frigate, her oak-planked hull proved so resistant to cannon balls, she subsequently earned the sobriquet of "Old Ironsides."

Moored in Boston since May 1934 as an historic relic and museum ship, *Constitution* is visited by a half-million people every year. Once annually, typically on Independence Day, she is taken out under tow into Boston Harbor and turned around before being moored again, a maneuver intended to ensure that she weathers equally on her port and starboard sides.

SPECIFICATIONS

Length: 305 feet (overall)
Beam: 43.5 feet
Draft: 22.5 feet
Displacement: 1,900+ tons
Propulsion: 48 sails (c. 1812)
Speed: 13 knots (c. 1812)
Personnel: 3 officers and more than 85 enlisted[1]

SUMMARY HISTORY

With a history spanning more than two centuries, it is not possible to provide a comprehensive account of *Constitution*'s past within the confines of this volume. The following list includes just a few of the significant events in her career.[2]

- Launched on October 21, 1797, at Hartt's Shipyard in Boston.
- Underway for first time on July 23, 1798.
- Conducted operations against Barbary States of North Africa 1803–1807.
- Fought against and defeated Royal Navy frigate HMS *Guerriere* on August 19, 1812. Destroyed frigate HMS *Java* on December 29, 1812.
- Sailed around the world 1844–1846.
- Began service as a museum ship in 1907.
- Renamed *Old Constitution* 1917–1925.
- Classified as an unclassified (IX) ship with no hull number in 1920.
- Designated as IX 21 on January 8, 1941, and placed in permanent commission.
- Designated as National Historic Landmark on December 19, 1960.
- Added to National Register of Historic Places in 1966.
- Designation of IX 21 withdrawn on September 1, 1975, by direction of Secretary of the Navy.
- Sailed on her own on July 20, 1997—for the first time in 116 years.
- Officially designated as America's Ship of State on October 28, 2009.
- Completed a two-year restoration on July 23, 2017.

NOTES

1. 1812 complement was over 450 sailors and Marines.
2. For more information about the ship's history, readers can consult the entry in the online Dictionary of American Naval Fighting Ships (https://www.history.navy.mil/research/histories/ship-histories/danfs/c/constitution.html), a selected bibliography of books and articles about the vessel (https://www.history.navy.mil/research/histories/ship-histories/danfs/c/constitution/constitution-bibliography.html), a collection of materials https://www.history.navy.mil/browse-by-topic/ships/uss-constitution-americas-ship-of-state.html, and Sayers, *Uncommon Warriors*, 108–13.

CHAPTER 3

Directory of Inactive U.S. Navy Auxiliary Ships

Gathered together in the pages that follow are the more than 3,500 ships, boats and other vessels that were classified by the Navy as auxiliaries at one time or another in the past 100 years. This chapter's enormous roster is made up of 103 auxiliary hull types that are no longer in active service; auxiliary types currently serving the fleet are covered in Chapters 1 and 2.

As reflected in the following roster, there has been considerable flux in the auxiliary vessel family over the years. Some auxiliary hull classifications have been moved to other categories. For example, the attack cargo ship (AKA) classification, which had been considered as a fleet auxiliary in 1945 was rerated as an amphibious vessel on the January 1950 Navy List and redefined as amphibious cargo ship (LKA) in 1969. As another example, the labor transport or barracks ship (APL) classification which had been rated as a fleet auxiliary in 1945 was subsequently reclassified as a barracks craft (non-self-propelled) and moved to the service craft category. And the tide has sometimes moved in the other direction, whereby ship types formerly rated as combatant vessels have been rerated as auxiliary types. For instance, several diesel fleet submarines (SS) were reclassified in the 1960s as auxiliary submarines (AGSS) and listed in the auxiliary vessel category, and a number of older aircraft carriers (CV/CVL) joined the auxiliary family in 1959 when they were reclassified as auxiliary aircraft transports (AVT).

In addition to these sorts of "paper" or administrative changes, the Navy has also produced fluctuations in the all-time auxiliary roster by reclassifying the same vessel in various auxiliary hull types.

As an illustration, USS *Panther* was commissioned as an auxiliary cruiser in 1898 and later reclassified as an auxiliary repair ship in 1907 and then as a destroyer tender (AD) in 1917 and then again as a submarine tender (AS) in 1920. As a second example, USS *Glover* was authorized as a miscellaneous auxiliary but was commissioned as an escort research ship (AGDE) in 1965, reclassified as a frigate research ship (AGFF) in 1975 and then as a "regular" frigate (FF) later that year, and ultimately reclassified as a sonar trials ship designated as T-AGFF 1 in 1990.

In addition, the Navy has sometimes given more than one auxiliary vessel the same name (but not concurrently). For example, there have been three ships known as USS

Mars in the fleet. The first was a collier (AC) commissioned in 1900, the second was to have been a repair ship (AR) of which construction was cancelled in 1945, and the third was a combat store ship (AFS) commissioned in 1963. Or take the case of USS *Wright*. The first was commissioned as a lighter-than-air aircraft tender (AZ) in 1921, later reclassified as heavier-than-air aircraft tender (AV) in 1926 and then changed to seaplane tender (AV) in the mid–1930s, reclassified as a miscellaneous auxiliary (AG) in 1944, and ultimately renamed *San Clemente* in 1945. The second *Wright* was commissioned in 1947 as a light aircraft carrier (CVL), reclassified as an auxiliary aircraft transport (AVT) in 1959, and finally reclassified as a command ship (CC) in 1963. The third *Wright* is an aviation logistic support ship (AVB) placed in service in 1986.

The following directory of inactive auxiliary ships is organized in alphabetical order of their hull classification symbols, i.e., usually a two- or three-letter abbreviation, e.g., "AD" (for destroyer tender) and "ADG" (for degaussing ship). In all there are more than 100 such classifications listed in these pages. Some classifications have multiple terms for the ship type, as the Navy changed the nomenclature over the years, e.g., the AFDB has been variously termed the "Auxiliary Floating Dry Dock—Big," "Large Auxiliary Floating Dry Dock," and "Large Auxiliary Floating Dry Dock (non-self-propelled)" at different times. Finally, the naming convention or "style" itself has sometimes been scrambled, clumsy or inconsistent, especially with regards to suffixes which were used to distinguish one variant of a basic ship type from another. Wherever it makes sense, this directory irons out and standardizes such nomenclature for clarity.

Crane Ship (AB)

Crane Ship No. 1 awaits her next lifting assignment at the Puget Sound Navy Yard in Bremerton, Washington (U.S. Navy photograph).

The former battleship USS *Kearsarge* (BB 5) was commissioned February 20, 1900, and converted to a floating crane ship in 1920 (designated as IX 16). Redesignated as AB 1 on August 15, 1939, she was named *Crane Ship No. 1* on November 6, 1941, performed heavy lift operations at various naval shipyards (including Puget Sound, Norfolk and Boston), struck on June 22, 1955, and sold to Patapsco Scrap Company and dismantled in 1955–1956.

See also Auxiliary Crane Ships (ACS) in Chapter 2.

Advanced Base Docks (ABD)

ABD 1–ABD 30 (no names) were floating non-self-propelled dry docks. Completed in 1943 and 1944, they were 256 feet long and 80 feet wide. ABD 31–ABD 58 (no names) were 240 feet long and 101 feet wide, and completed in 1944. Some ABDs were used to assemble an Advanced Base Sectional Dock [q.v.] in 1945.

Advanced Base Sectional Docks (ABSD)

Completed and commissioned in 1943–1945, ABSD 1 and ABSD 2 were 10-section dry docks that were 927 feet long and 256 wide. ABSD 3 was a nine-section dock that

The battleship USS *West Virginia* (BB 48) is being repaired in ABSD 1 off Aessi Island, Espiritu Santo, New Hebrides on November 13, 1944 (U.S. Navy photograph).

was 844 feet long and 256 feet wide. ABSD 4 through ABSD 7 were seven-section docks measuring 825 feet long and 240 feet wide. All of these docks were non-self-propelled and armed with 40-mm and 20-mm guns. They were later reclassified as Auxiliary Floating Dry Dock—Big (AFDB) [q.v.] and redesignated AFDB 1–AFDB 7, respectively. ABSD 7 was assembled from ABDs 37, 38, 39, 40, 51, 52 and 58.

Colliers (AC)

USS *Cyclops* (AC 4) is anchored in New York's Hudson River on October 3, 1911, six years before she disappeared in the Bermuda Triangle (U.S. Navy).

Colliers were bulk cargo ships that carried coal for use as fuel by the Navy's coal-fired, steam-powered warships.

EARLY COLLIERS

All of the following 17 colliers were acquired in 1898 except for *Quincy*, which was acquired in 1917. Most were disposed of by 1923 except for *Southerly*, which was decommissioned in 1933.

Alexander	*Marcellus*[4]	*Scandia*[10]
Cassius	*Merrimac*[5]	*Southery*[11]
Hannibal[1]	*Nanshan*[6]	*Sterling*
Justin	*Pompey*[7]	*Zafiro*
Lebanon[2]	*Quincy*[8]	
Leonidas[3]	*Saturn*[9]	

Later Colliers

The following colliers were acquired and commissioned between 1898 and 1917. While most of the ships were discarded in the 1920s, several of them—as noted below—continued to serve in other roles in the 1930s and a few lasted until 1946. Two vessels—*Proteus* and *Nereus*—were the longest-serving "pure" colliers, remaining as such until December 1940.

AC 1 *Vestal*[12]
AC 2 *Prometheus*[13]
AC 3 *Jupiter*[14]
AC 4 *Cyclops*[15]
AC 5 *Vulcan*
AC 6 *Mars*
AC 7 *Hector*
AC 8 *Neptune*
AC 9 *Proteus*
AC 10 *Nereus*
AC 11 *Orion*
AC 12 *Jason*[16]
AC 13 *Abarenda*[17]
AC 14 *Ajax*[18]
AC 15 *Brutus*
AC 16 *Caesar*
AC 17 *Nero*

Notes

1. Reclassified as a miscellaneous auxiliary [q.v.] (AG 1) in 1921, decommissioned in August 1944, and expended as a target in March 1945.
2. Reclassified as a miscellaneous auxiliary (AG 2) in July 1920 and decommissioned two years later.
3. Reclassified as a survey ship in 1914, reclassified as a sub chaser/destroyer tender [q.v.] (AD 7) in 1917, and decommissioned in November 1921.
4. Sunk in a collision in August 1912.
5. The second ship of her name. Scuttled on June 3, 1898.
6. Reclassified as a miscellaneous auxiliary (AG 3) in July 1920, and decommissioned and sold in 1922.
7. Converted to a torpedo boat tender in 1911 and decommissioned in 1922.
8. Reclassified as a cargo ship [q.v.] (AK 10) in 1920, and decommissioned and sold in 1922.
9. Reclassified as a miscellaneous auxiliary (AG 4) in July 1920, and decommissioned and sold in 1922.
10. Renamed USS *Ajax* in 1901 and designated AC 14 [*see below*] in 1920.
11. Designated as unclassified miscellaneous vessel IX 26 in 1922 and struck and sold in 1933.
12. Acquired in 1909, reclassified as a repair ship [q.v.] (AR 4) in 1913, and struck in 1946.
13. Commissioned in 1910 as *Ontario*, reclassified as a repair ship (AR 3) in 1913, and struck in 1946.
14. Commissioned in 1913, converted to aircraft carrier and renamed *Langley* (CV 1) in 1922, reclassified as seaplane tender AV 3 [q.v.] in 1937, and sunk by Japanese in battle on February 27, 1942.
15. Acquired in 1910, commissioned in 1917, and disappeared with no survivors or wreckage in the Bermuda Triangle in early March 1918.
16. Commissioned as Fuel Ship #12 in 1913, reclassified as a seaplane tender (AV 2) in 1930, and struck in 1936.
17. Acquired in 1898, reclassified as a miscellaneous auxiliary [q.v.] (AG 14) in 1924, and struck in 1926.
18. Former *Scandia* [*see above*]. Reclassified as a miscellaneous auxiliary (AG 15) in 1924 and decommissioned the following year.

Destroyer Tenders (AD)

These ships provided maintenance and other support to destroyers and small surface warships. They were equipped with various facilities to repair and maintain destroyers' equipment, including a foundry, a large machine shop and an electrical shop; and several other shops, such as blacksmith, pipe, welding, boiler, sheet-metal, torpedo, canvas and gyro repair, pattern, carpenter, typewriter, fire control and optical gear, and even a shop for watch repair. Also on board were a photographic lab and a design and blueprint room. To administer to the medical needs of destroyer crews, the ADs were outfitted with an operating room, sick bay and dental office.

Destroyer tenders served in the Navy from 1909 until 1996. The first ship built specifically as a destroyer tender was USS *Melville* (AD 2), commissioned in December 1913 and decommissioned 33 years later. AD 20 and AD 21 were converted from Maritime Commission C3 type cargo ships, AD 34 had been a repair ship, and AD 16 was a C3-S1-N2 type vessel. The last active AD was USS *Shenandoah* (AD 44), commissioned in August 1983, decommissioned in September 1996, and struck in April 1999.

3. Directory of U.S. Navy Auxiliary Ships

USS *Yellowstone* (AD 41) is maneuvering in sea trials off California on May 29, 1980 (U.S. Navy photograph).

AD 1 *Dixie*[1]
AD 2 *Melville*[2]
AD 3 Dobbin
AD 4 Whitney
AD 5 Prairie
AD 6 Panther[3]
AD 7 Leonidas
AD 8 Buffalo
AD 9 Black Hawk
AD 10 Bridgeport[4]
AD 11 Altair[5]
AD 12 Denebola[6]
AD 13 Rigel[7]
AD 14 Dixie
AD 15 Prairie
AD 16 Cascade
AD 17 Piedmont
AD 18 Sierra
AD 19 Yosemite[8]
AD 20 Hamul[9]
AD 21 Markab[10]
AD 22 Klondike[11]
AD 23 Arcadia
AD 24 Everglades
AD 25 Frontier
AD 26 Shenandoah
AD 27 Yellowstone
AD 28 Grand Canyon[12]
AD 29 Isle Royal
AD 30 Great Lakes[13]
AD 31 Tidewater[14]
AD 32 New England[15]
AD 33 Canopus[16]
AD 34 Alcor[17]
AD 35 Arrowhead
AD 36 Bryce Canyon
AD 37 Samuel Gompers[18]
AD 38 Puget Sound
AD 39[19]
AD 40[20]
AD 41 Yellowstone
AD 42 Acadia[21]
AD 43 Cape Cod
AD 44 Shenandoah

Notes

1. Commissioned as auxiliary cruiser in April 1898, recommissioned as a transport in November 1899, reclassified as a destroyer tender in February 1909, and decommissioned in June 1922 and scrapped.

2. Decommissioned in August 1946, struck April 1947, sold in July 1948 for dismantling.
3. Commissioned as auxiliary cruiser in April 1898, reclassified as auxiliary repair ship in November 1907, reclassified as a destroyer tender in April 1917, designated AD 6 in 1920, and struck May 1922.
4. Acquired in 1917 as repair ship [q.v.] but reclassified as destroyer tender and designated as such in 1920, struck in October 1941 and transferred to U.S. Army the next year.
5. Commissioned in November 1921, decommissioned in April 1946 and scrapped in 1950.
6. *Ibid.*
7. Commissioned as AD 13 in February 1922, classified as base repair ship (ARb 1) [q.v.] in April 1941 and redesignated as repair ship [q.v.] AR 11 the same month.
8. Commissioned in March 1944, decommissioned and struck January 1994, and expended as target in November 2003.
9. Commissioned as cargo ship [q.v.] AK 30 in June 1941, reclassified as AD 20 in January 1943, decommissioned in June 1962 and sold for scrapping in October 1975.
10. Commissioned as cargo ship AK 31 in June 1941, reclassified as AD 21 in January 1942, and reclassified as repair ship AR 23 in April 1960.
11. Commissioned in July 1945 and reclassified as repair ship AR 22 in February 1960.
12. Commissioned in April 1946 and reclassified as repair ship AR 28 in March 1971.
13. Laid down in April 1945 but cancelled January 7, 1946.
14. Commissioned in February 1946, transferred to Indonesia in 1971, and struck in June 1978.
15. Laid down in October 1944 as submarine tender [q.v.] AS 28, reclassified as AD 32 in August 1944 but cancelled August 12, 1945.
16. Cancelled August 12, 1945.
17. Commissioned in September 1941 as miscellaneous auxiliary [q.v.] AG 34, reclassified as repair ship AR 10 in December 1941, reclassified as AD 34 in November 1944, and struck in August 1946.
18. Expended as target July 2003.
19. Authorized but not built.
20. *Ibid.*
21. Expended as target in September 2010.

Degaussing Vessels / Degaussing Ships[1] (ADG)

Degaussing ships were used to reduce the magnetic signature of a naval vessel by dragging a large electrical cable along the vessel's side to defend against magnetic mines.

USS *Surfbird* (ADG 383) is underway in the western Pacific in August 1967 (U.S. Navy photograph).

3. Directory of U.S. Navy Auxiliary Ships

The first degaussing vessels (comprising four former yard patrol craft and three former auxiliary minesweepers) were classified as service craft and designated as YDG 1–YDG 7). They served as degaussing vessels between 1942 and 1946. The five vessels listed below (of which four were former YDGs redesignated as ADGs in November 1947) were considered auxiliary ships. The four ex–YDGs operated as degaussing vessels between 1943 and 1946, received names in February 1955, and were disposed of by 1982 (through sale for either civilian use or scrapping or by sinking). The fifth ship, USS *Surfbird*, was reclassified as an ADG in 1957 and struck and sold in 1975. She became the cargo ship MV *Helenka B*, and is still in service.

- ADG 8 *Lodestone* (ex-PCE 876 / ex–YDG 8)
- ADG 9 *Magnet* (ex-PCE 879 / ex–YDG 9)[2]
- ADG 10 *Deperm* (ex-PCE 883 / ex–YDG 10)[3]
- ADG 11 *Ampere* (ex-USS Drake [AM 359] / ex–YDG 11)
- ADG 383 *Surfbird* (ex–AM 383 / ex–MSF 383)

Notes

1. The nomenclature of the degaussing type "vessel" was changed to "ship" in 1960.
2. Expended as target.
3. Expended as target.

Ammunition Ships (AE)

Following an overhaul, the Atlantic Fleet ammunition ship USS *Nitro* (AE 23) is steaming off Virginia in January 1978 (U.S. Navy photograph).

Fitted with specialized cargo-handling equipment and compartmentation, ammunition ships delivered munitions and ordnance of various types, including shells and missiles, to the Navy's surface warships, usually while underway. They also carried ammunition from one shore-based depot to another. The first ammunition ship, USS *Pyro* (AE 1), was commissioned in August 1920 and the last, USS *Kiska* (AE 35), was commissioned in December 1972. AE 3–AE 6, AE 8, AE 9 and AE 13 were converted from Maritime Commission C2 cargo ship hulls, AE 10 was a C1-A type, and AE 11, AE 12, and AE 14–AE 19 were converted from C2-S-AJ1 types.

During World War II—the high water mark for the AEs—the Navy operated 19 ammunition ships of the Pyro, Lassen and Wrangell classes. After the war the total number of active AEs declined despite the addition of newer vessels. The two Suribachi-class ships (AE 21–AE 22) were commissioned in the late 1950s specifically for UNREP delivery. In the mid–1960s, the Navy commissioned two former attack cargo ships [q.v.] as AEs—*Virgo* (AE 30) and *Chara* (AE 30)—for use in the Vietnam War. The Kilauea-class ships (AE 26–AE 35) were the last AEs built. They were commissioned between 1968 and 1972, and struck from the NVR beginning in August 1999. The last AE to go was USNS *Flint* (T-AE 32), commissioned in November 1971, struck in November 2013, and then transferred to MARAD and sold for scrapping. The ordnance delivery mission is now being performed by ammunition cargo ships (AKE) operated by MSC personnel (see Chapter 1).

AE 1 *Pyro*
AE 2 *Nitro*
AE 3 *Lassen*
AE 4 *Mount Baker*[1]
AE 5 *Rainier*
AE 6 *Shasta*
AE 7[2]
AE 8 *Mauna Loa*
AE 9 *Mazama*
AE 10 *Sangay*
AE 11 *Mount Hood*[3]
AE 12 *Wrangell*

AE 13 *Akutan*
AE 14 *Firedrake*
AE 15 *Vesuvius*
AE 16 Mount Katmai
AE 17 Great Sitkin
AE 18 *Paricutin*
AE 19 *Diamond Head*
AE 20 *Fomalhaut*[4]
AE 21 *Suribachi*
AE 22 *Mauna Kea*
AE 23 *Nitro*
AE 24 *Pyro*

AE 25 *Haleakala*
AE 26 *Kilauea*[5]
AE 27 *Butte*[6]
AE 28 *Santa Barbara*[7]
AE 29 *Mount Hood*
AE 30 *Virgo*[8]
AE 31 *Chara*[9]
AE 32 *Flint*
AE 33 *Shasta*[10]
AE 34 *Mount Baker*[11]
AE 35 *Kiska*[12]

Notes

1. Commissioned as USS *Kilauea* in May 1941, renamed in March 1943, struck in December 1969, and sold for scrapping in March 1974.
2. Army transport *Henry Gibbons* was to have become AE 7 but was sunk in June 1942 by a submarine in the Gulf of Mexico.
3. Exploded on November 10, 1944, with the loss of the ship and almost all of her crew.
4. Commissioned in March 1942 as cargo ship [q.v.] AK 22, reclassified as an AE in December 1948, and sold for scrapping in April 1970.
5. Commissioned in August 1968, transferred to MSC and redesignated T-AE 26 in October 1980, struck in September 2008, and expended as a target in July 2012.
6. Commissioned in December 1968, transferred to MSC and redesignated T-AE 27 in June 1996, struck in May 2004, and expended as a target in June 2006.
7. Commissioned in July 1970, transferred to MSC and redesignated T-AE 28 in October 1998, struck in August 2005, and sold for scrapping in November 2006.
8. Commissioned as attack cargo ship [q.v.] AKA 20 in July 1943, reclassified as an AE in November 1965, decommissioned in February 1971, and sold for scrapping in November 1973.
9. Commissioned as AKA 58 in June 1944, reclassified as an AE in November 1965, decommissioned in March 1972, and sold for scrapping in November 1972.

10. Commissioned in February 1972, transferred to MSC and redesignated T-AE 33 in October 1997, and struck in April 2011.
11. Commissioned in July 1972, transferred to MSC and redesignated T-AE 34 in December 1996, and sold for scrapping in August 2012.
12. Transferred to MSC and redesignated T-AE 35 in August 1996, struck in January 2011, and sold for scrapping in 2013.

Storeships / Provisions Store Ships / Store Ships (AF)

The store ship USS *Denebola* (AF 56) is underway in Hampton Roads, Virginia, in March 1971 (U.S. Navy photograph).

Store ships—sometimes informally referred to as reefers or beef boats—delivered supplies, including frozen, chilled and dry provisions, to the Navy's warships and other vessels, sometimes while underway at sea. The first store ships were commissioned in 1898 and the first vessel to be formally designated as a store ship—USS *Bridge* (AF 1)—was commissioned in June 1917. AF 10 and AF 11 were Maritime Commission C2 cargo vessels, AF 28 and AF 29 were C2-S-E1 types, and AF 30–AF 39, and AF 41–AF 47 were R1-M-AV3 types. The final reefer to be commissioned during World War II was USS *Valentine* (AF 47).

Although many of the AFs were struck from the Vessel Register en masse in 1946, a few were recalled to service during the Korean conflict. The last AFs joined the fleet in 1961–1962 but by the late 1970s there were only two active store ships. The very last store ship operating in naval service—USNS *Rigel* (T-AF 58)—was decommissioned in September 1992, struck in May 1994 and transferred to MARAD in April 1998. The role previously performed by AFs was assumed by combat store ships (AFS) [q.v.] and later by fast combat support ships (AOE) [q.v.].

AF 1	*Bridge*	AF 34	*Kerstin*
AF 2	*Celtic*	AF 35	*Latona*
AF 3	*Culgoa*	AF 36	*Lioba*
AF 4	*Glacier*	AF 37	*Malabar*
AF 5	*Pompey*[1]	AF 38	*Merapi*
AF 6	*Rappahannock*	AF 39	*Palisana*
AF 7	*Arctic*	AF 40	*Saturn* (ex–AK 49)[4]
AF 8	*Boreas*	AF 41	*Athanasia*
AF 9	*Yukon*	AF 42	*Bondia* (later T-AF 42)[5]
AF 10	*Aldebaran*	AF 43	*Gordonia*
AF 11	*Polaris*	AF 44	*Laurentia*[6]
AF 12	*Mizar*	AF 45	*Lucidor*
AF 13	*Tarazed*	AF 46	*Octavia*
AF 14	*Uranus*	AF 47	*Valentine* (later T-AF 47)[7]
AF 15	*Talamanca*	AF 48	*Alstede*
AF 16	*Pastores*	AF 49	*Zelima*
AF 17	*Antigua*	T-AF 50	*Bald Eagle*
AF 18	*Calamares*	T-AF 51	*Blue Jacket*
AF 19	*Roamer*	T-AF 52	*Golden Eagle* (later Arcturus AF 52)[8]
AF 20	*Pontiac*[x]		
AF 21	*Merak*	T-AF 53	*Grommet Reefer*[9]
AF 22	*Ariel*	AF 54	*Pictor*
AF 23	*Cygnus*	AF 55	*Aludra*
AF 24	*Delphinus*	AF 56	*Denebola*
AF 25	*Taurus*	AF 57	*Regulus*[10]
AF 26	*Octans*	AF 58	*Rigel* (later T-AF 58)[11]
AF 27	*Pictor*[2]	AF 59	*Vega*
AF 28	*Hyades*	AF 60	*Sirius*
AF 29	*Graffias*[3]	AF 61	*Procyon*
AF 30	*Adria*	AF 62	*Bellatrix*
AF 31	*Arequipa*	T-AF 63	*Asterion*
AF 32	*Corbuda*	T-AF 64	*Perseus*
AF 33	*Karin*		

NOTES

X = Lost during World War II.
 1. Commissioned in 1898 and served as a collier [q.v.] and later as a torpedo boat tender.
 2. Named in April 1943 but acquisition cancelled in May 1944.
 3. Served in World War II, and the Korean and Vietnam Wars.
 4. Originally cargo ship [q.v.] AK 49 commissioned in 1942 but reclassified as store ship AF 40 in April 1944 and struck in 1946.
 5. Assigned to MSTS in July 1951 and redesignated as T-AF 42, and struck in 1973.
 6. Assigned to MSTS 1950–1969 and redesignated as T-AF 44, and transferred to MARAD in 1970.
 7. Assigned to MSTS in 1951–1959 and redesignated as T-AF 47, and sold in 1967.
 8. Operated by MSTS 1950–1961. Renamed USS *Arcturus* and commissioned as AF 52 in November 1961, struck in 1985, and expended as a target in July 1997.
 9. Ran aground in Italy in December 1952, stern sank and bow transferred to MARAD in July 1953 for disposal.

10. Struck on September 10, 1971, after grounding in Hong Kong.
11. Commissioned as AF 58 in 1955, assigned to MSTS in 1975 and redesignated T-AF 58, and struck in May 1994.

Auxiliary Floating Docks (AFD)

These were 1,000-ton one-piece welded steel docks, 200 feet long and 64 feet wide, with an inside wing wall width of 45 feet and draft of 14.5 feet. They serviced minesweepers, tugs, small landing ships and patrol craft and similar vessels. The first AFDs were completed in 1943 and all were on hand by the end of World War II. Designated AFD 1–AFD 34. In 1946, the AFD was reclassified as an Auxiliary Floating Drydock–Little (AFDL) [q.v.] and redesignated AFDL 1–AFDL 34 respectively.

Auxiliary Floating Dry Docks–Big / Large Auxiliary Floating Dry Docks / Large Auxiliary Floating Dry Docks (non-self-propelled) (AFDB)

Seven former Advanced Base Sectional Docks (ABSD) [q.v.] were reclassified as AFDBs in 1946 and an AFDB was acquired in 1980. The AFDBs were capable of handling vessels with displacements of 30,000 tons or more, such as aircraft carriers and battleships. The docks consisted of seven to 10 steel sections that were detachable for towing and maintenance. By the late 1970s, only two AFDBs were in service (AFDB 1 and AFDB 7); the remainder were in reserve. None are left today.

AFDB 1 *Artisan* (ex–ABSD 1)[1]
AFDB 2 (ex–AFSB 2)[2]
AFDB 3 (ex–AFSB 3)[3]
AFDB 4 (ex–AFSB 4)[4]
AFDB 5 (ex–ABSD 5)[5]
AFDB 6 (ex–ABSD 6)[6]
AFDB 7 *Los Alamos*[7]
AFDB 8 *Machinist*[8]

Notes

1. Ten-section dock initially commissioned on May 10, 1943, as AFDB 1. In and out of commission and periodically assembled and disassembled 1945–1970. Named in June 1979. Sections A, G, H, I and J struck in June 1977 and sold for scrapping on June 1, 1978. Section B reclassified as the unclassified miscellaneous vessel IX 534 (no name), struck on January 4, 2007, and "disposed of/sold" on September 17 of that year. Section C redesignated as IX 525 on April 2, 1998, and assigned to Pacific Missile Facility in Hawaii, struck on June 22, 2009, and "disposed of/sold" on March 17, 2010. Section D redesignated as IX 521 on August 16, 1996, and "disposed of/sold" on September 17, 2007. Section E struck on November 26, 2003, and "disposed of/sold" on September 6, 2005. Section F struck on November 1, 1981, and expended as target on January 1, 1982.
2. Ten-section dock commissioned on August 14, 1943. Sections A and G sold for dismantling in 1987. Sections B and C expended as targets in 1987. Section D reclassified as IX 522 on August 16, 1996. Sections E and I sold in July 1990. Section F reclassified as IX 524 on April 25, 1997, and assigned to Pacific Missile Facility. Section H reclassified as IX 535 on October 10, 2002, and "disposed of/sold for reuse/conversion" on September 19, 2007. Section J expended as a target on July 13, 1990.
3. Nine-section dock commissioned on October 27, 1944. Struck August 1, 1981. Transferred to Bath Iron Works in Maine on April 1, 1982, and ultimately sold to a shipyard in Croatia.
4. Seven-section dock commissioned on March 30, 1944, struck on April 15, 1989, and sunk as a reef.
5. Seven-section dock commissioned in November 1944, transferred to Todd Shipyards in Port Arthur, Texas, and struck in 1984.
6. Seven-section dock commissioned September 28, 1944, and sold on January 1, 1976, for dismantling.
7. Seven-section dock commissioned on January 6, 1945. Sections A, B, C and D towed in 1961 to Holy Loch, Scotland, and placed in service as *Los Alamos* on November 10 that year. One section transferred to U.S. Army in 1968. Sections A through D deactivated in 1992 and placed in NDRF. Six sections transferred to Brownsville Texas, in 1995.
8. Placed in service in June 1980, struck on April 23, 1997, and sold the next year for commercial service in Guam.

Auxiliary Floating Dry Docks—Little (Concrete) (AFDC)

Beginning in 1943, the Navy constructed thirteen 2800-ton reinforced concrete docks classified as Auxiliary Repair Docks-Concrete (ARDC) [q.v.] They were 389 feet long, 84 feet wide and 40 feet deep overall, with pontoons 14 feet deep and wing walls tapering from 13.5 feet at the base to 10 feet at the top deck. A crane with a lifting capacity of five tons was installed on top of each wing wall. The ARDCs were reclassified in 1946 as Auxiliary Floating Dry Docks–Little [q.v.] and designated AFDL 35–AFDL 46. They have since been disposed of, including transfers to other navies, sales to commercial shipyards, scrapping, and in one case—AFDL 46 (ex-ARDC 13)—as a target in an A-bomb test in 1946.

Auxiliary Floating Dry Docks—Little / Auxiliary Floating Docks—Lengthened / Small Auxiliary Floating Dry Docks / Small Auxiliary Floating Dry Docks (non–self-propelled) (AFDL)

AFDL 21 has just been launched on February 22, 1965, from the auxiliary floating dock—medium *Richland* (AFDM 8) to be put in service at the Naval Ship Repair Facility in Agana, Guam (U.S. Navy photograph).

3. Directory of U.S. Navy Auxiliary Ships

AFDLs were mobile, steel trough type, unit docks, similar to AFDs [q.v.]. Because new World War II destroyer escorts were too long and heavy for docking in existing AFDs, five AFDs were lengthened by inserting an 88-foot section amidships, extending their length to 288 feet and their lifting capacity to 1,900 tons. In 1946 all of the AFDs were redesignated as AFDLs and the type was reclassified as Auxiliary Floating Drydock–Little. Also in 1946, 13 former Auxiliary Repair Docks—Concrete (ARDC) [q.v.] were reclassified as Auxiliary Floating Dry Docks—Little and redesignated as AFDL 35–AFDL 46. In the mid–1960s AFDLs were known as Small Auxiliary Floating Dry Docks and in the mid–1970s as Small Auxiliary Floating Dry Docks (non-self-propelled). The final AFDL, *Diligence* (AFDL 48), was completed in 1956. AFDL 49 was cancelled in 1958. The only AFDL still in service is *Dynamic* (AFDL 6) which had been commissioned in March 1944.

AFDL 1   *Endeavor* (ex–AFD)[1]
AFDL 2   (ex–AFD 2)[2]
AFDL 3   (ex–AFD 3)
AFDL 4   (ex–AFD 4)[3]
AFDL 5   (ex–AFD 5)[4]
AFDL 6   *Dynamic* (ex–AFD 6)[5]
AFDL 7   *Ability* (ex–AFD 7)[6]
AFDL 8   (ex–AFD 8)[7]
AFDL 9   (ex–AFD 9)[8]
AFDL 10 (ex–AFD 10)[9]
AFDL 11 (ex–AFD 11)[10]
AFDL 12 (ex–AFD 12)[11]
AFDL 13 (ex–AFD 13)[12]
AFDL 14 (ex–AFD 14)[13]
AFDL 15 (ex–AFD 15)[14]
AFDL 16 (ex–AFD 16)[15]
AFDL 17 (ex–AFD 17)[16]
AFDL 18 (ex–AFD 18)[17]
AFDL 19 (ex–AFD 19)[18]
AFDL 20 (ex–AFD 20)[19]
AFDL 21 (ex–AFD 21)[20]
AFDL 22 (ex–AFD 22)[21]
AFDL 23 *Adept* (ex–AFD 23)[22]
AFDL 24 (ex–AFD 24)[23]
AFDL 25 *Undaunted* (ex–AFD 25)[24]
AFDL 26 (ex–AFD 26)[25]
AFDL 27 (ex–AFD 27)[26]
AFDL 28 (ex–AFD 28)[27]
AFDL 29 (ex–AFD 29)[28]
AFDL 30 (ex–AFD 30)[29]
AFDL 31 (ex–AFD 31)[30]
AFDL 32 (ex–AFD 32)[31]
AFDL 33 (ex–AFD 33)[32]
AFDL 34 (ex–AFD 34)[33]
AFDL 35 (ex–ARDC 2)[34]
AFDL 36 (ex–ARDC 3)[35]
AFDL 37 (ex–ARDC 4)[36]
AFDL 38 (ex–ARDC 5)[37]
AFDL 39 (ex–ARDC 6)[38]
AFDL 40 (ex–ARDC 7)[39]
AFDL 41 (ex–ARDC 8)[40]
AFDL 42 (ex–ARDC 9)[41]
AFDL 43 (ex–ARDC 10)[42]
AFDL 44 (ex–ARDC 11)[43]
AFDL 45 (ex–ARDC 12)[44]
AFDL 46 (ex–ARDC 13)[45]
AFDL 47 *Reliance* (ex–ARD 33)[46]
AFDL 48 *Diligence*[47]

Notes

1. Struck in 1985 and transferred to Dominican Republic in 1986.
2. Struck in 1981 and sold in 1986.
3. Transferred to Brazil in 1966 and sold in 1977.
4. Transferred to Taiwan in 1958.
5. In service in Little Creek, Virginia.
6. Named in June 1979, struck and sold in 1981, and scrapped.
7. Struck and sunk as a reef in 1981.
8. Struck and dismantled in 1982.
9. Stuck and transferred to the Philippines in 1987.
10. Transferred to Cambodia in 1971.
11. Disposed of in July 1984.
12. Transferred to South Vietnam in 1975 and struck in October 1983.
13. Reportedly transferred in 1947.
14. Struck in 1983.
15. Disposed of in June 1982.
16. Sold in January 1971 and dismantled.
17. Struck in December 1962.
18. Struck and transferred in 1983.
19. Transferred to Philippines in 1961 and sold in 1980.
20. Struck in March 1989. Now in commercial service.
21. Transferred to South Vietnam and struck in July 1985.

22. Named in June 1979, leased to commercial shipyard, and sold in March 2010.
23. Transferred to the Philippines in 1948 and sold in 1980.
24. Struck in May 1997 and sold.
25. Transferred to Paraguay in 1965, struck in September 1976, and sold to Paraguay in February 1977.
26. Sold in May 1961 and dismantled.
27. Transferred to Mexico in January 1973 and sold to Mexico in 1978.
28. Sold in August 1983 and dismantled.
29. Sold in June 1979.
30. Transferred in 1947 to USCG as YFD 83 and struck in April 2006.
31. Struck in 1946.
32. Transferred to Peru in 1959 and sold in September 1980.
33. Transferred to Taiwan in 1959.
34. Struck in June 1973 and dismantled in 1974.
35. Transferred to Taiwan in March 1947.
36. Sold and dismantled in December 1981.
37. Transferred to San Francisco Maritime National Historical Park (n.d.) and sold in 1981.
38. Transferred to Brazil in 1980 and sold in 1981.
39. Struck in June 1987 and transferred to the Philippines in June 1990.
40. Sold in 1983 to a commercial shipyard.
41. Struck in May 1974, sold in January 1975, and dismantled.
42. Sold in April 1979 and dismantled.
43. Transferred to the Philippines in September 1969 and sold in August 1980.
44. Sold in 1981.
45. Expended as a target in 1946 and struck in 1947.
46. Leased to commercial shipyard in 1980s and 1990s; struck and sold December 5, 2007.
47. Named in June 1979, struck in August 1986 and transferred in November 1986.

Auxiliary Floating Dry Docks—Medium / Medium Auxiliary Floating Dry Docks / Medium Auxiliary Floating Dry Docks (non-self-propelled) (AFDM)

Beginning in 1941 and continuing through 1944, the Navy acquired 66 yard floating dry docks (designated as YFDs) for shipyard and harbor use. Their lifting capacity varied between 400 and 20,000 tons. The latter were 659 feet long and 132.5 feet wide overall and composed of six sections. Other YFDs constructed of timber were built with capacities of 7,000, 10,500, 12,000 and 16,000 tons. Still other YFDs were steel-built in three sections: 14,000-tons (598 feet long), 15,000-tons (615 feet long) and 18,000-tons (622 feet long). Some 25 one-piece timber docks were acquired with 1,000-ton capacity and a few were delivered with lifting capacities of 3,000, 3,500 and 5,000 tons. Eventually 14 YFDs were reclassified as Auxiliary Floating Dry Docks–Medium (AFDM) but by 1950 there were just six AFDMs in service. The AFDM type was reclassified as Medium Auxiliary Floating Dry Docks (non-self-propelled) in the mid–1970s.

AFDM 1 (ex–YFD 3)[1]
AFDM 2 (ex–YFD 4)[2]
AFDM 3 (ex–YFD 6)[3]
AFDM 4 (ex–YFD 10)[4]
AFDM 5 *Resourceful* (ex–YFD 21)[5]
AFDM 6 *Competent* (ex–YFD 62)[6]
AFDM 7 *Sustain* (ex–YFD 63)[7]
AFDM 8 *Richland* (ex–YFD 64)[8]
AFDM 9 (ex–YFD 65)[9]
AFDM 10 *Resolute* (ex–YFD 67)[10]
AFDM 11 (ex–YFD 68)[11]
AFDM 12 (ex–YFD 69)[12]
AFDM 13 (ex–YFD 70)[13]
AFDM 14 *Steadfast* (ex–YFD 71)[14]

NOTES

1. Redesignated as AFDM 1 in 1946 and struck in September 1986.
2. Struck in September 2006.

In June 1967 the destroyer USS *Edson* (DD 946) is undergoing repairs in the medium auxiliary floating dry dock *Resourceful* (AFDM 5) at the Subic Bay Naval Base in the Philippines (U.S. Navy photograph).

   3. Commissioned in December 1943, redesignated as AFDM 3 in 1946, struck in November 2000, and sold in April 2002.
   4. Transferred to Mexico in 1948.
   5. Commissioned in February 1943, named in 1979, struck in August 1997, and sold in April 1999.
   6. Commissioned in June 1944, named in June 1979, struck in August 1997, and sold in October 2005.
   7. Named in May 1979, struck in January 2007, and sold in February 2008.
   8. Commissioned on November 28, 1944, redesignated as AFDM 8 in 1946, named in April 1968, struck in August 1997 and transferred to Guam.
   9. Sold in August 1989.
   10. Listed on NVR as leased as of December 16, 2004.
   11. Dismantled in 1990.
   12. Transferred to Port of Portland in 1969.
   13. Transferred to Todd Seattle in 1969.
   14. Reclassified as AFDM 14 in 1981, named in 1984 and struck in February 1999.

Combat Store Ships (AFS)

Combat store ships delivered refrigerated and dry provisions, parts, general stores, mail and personnel to naval vessels while underway at sea. The deliveries were made either by transferring the cargo while operating alongside the receiving vessel or by vertical replenishment, i.e., using helicopters to ferry the freight to the recipient. The AFS

On July 3, 1969, a UH-46 Seaknight helicopter carries a net load of supplies from combat store ship USS *Niagara Falls* (AFS 3) over to the aircraft carrier USS *Kearsarge* (CVS 33) in the South China Sea (U.S. Navy photograph).

vessels combined the capabilities of store ships (AF) [q.v.], stores issue ships (AKS) [q.v.] and aviation store ships (AVS) [q.v.]. They were operated by the Navy's Military Sealift Command (MSC) with both civilian mariners and Navy personnel on board. The first seven combat stores ships were commissioned between 1963 and 1970, and the last three—former Royal Navy replenishment ships–were acquired in 1981 and 1984. The AFS ships are no longer in the fleet, having been replaced by ammunition cargo ships (AKE).

AFS 1 *Mars*[1]
AFS 2 *Sylvania*[2]
AFS 3 *Niagara Falls*[3]
AFS 4 *White Plains*[4]

AFS 5 *Concord*[5]
AFS 6 *San Diego*[6]
AFS 7 *San Jose*[7]
T-AFS 8 *Sirius*[8]

T-AFS 9 *Spica*[9]
T-AFS 10 *Saturn*[10]

Notes

1. Decommissioned in December 1993 and assigned to MSC and designated as T-AFS 1, out of service in February 1998 and struck in May 2004, and expended as a target in July 2006.
2. Decommissioned in May 1994, struck in January 1995, and sold for scrapping in October 2012.
3. Decommissioned and assigned to MSC as T-AFS 3 in September 1994, struck in September 2008, and expended as a target in July 2012.
4. Decommissioned in April 1995, struck in August 1995, and expended as a target in July 2002.
5. Decommissioned and assigned to MSC as T-AFS 5 in October 1992, struck in August 2009, and expended as a target in July 2012.
6. Decommissioned and assigned to MSC as T-AFS 5 in August 1993, struck in September 2003, and sold for scrapping in May 2006.
7. Decommissioned and assigned to MSC as T-AFS 7 in November 1993; struck in January 2010, and sold for scrapping in October 2013.

8. Former Royal Fleet Auxiliary (RFA) *Lyness* (A-339) purchased by U.S. Navy and renamed USNS *Sirius* in January 1981, and struck and transferred to MARAD in July 2005.
9. Former RFA *Tarbatness* (A-345) purchased by USN in November 1981 and renamed USNS *Spica*, struck in January 2008, and expended as a target in May 2009.
10. Former RFA *Stromness* (A-344) purchased by USN in January 1983 and renamed USNS *Saturn*, struck in April 2009, and expended as a target in October 2010.

Afloat Forward Staging Base (AFSB)

See Chapter 1.

Miscellaneous Auxiliaries (AG)

The miscellaneous auxiliary hull classification encompassed a disparate collection of vessels that did not fit neatly into a more obvious or clearly defined specific ship type, such as ammunition ship (AE) or oiler (AO). As a catch-all hull classification, AGs included everything from former battleships, cruisers and destroyers to former minesweepers, small freighters and presidential yachts. Hull numbers between AG 50 and AG 66 and between AG 195 and AG 335 were not assigned. There is now only one extant AG listed on the NVR: the offshore petroleum distribution ship *VADM K.R. Wheeler* (T-AG 5001), chartered by MSC on March 31, 2010 (see Chapter 2). Specific histories of the AGs may be found in the AG pages of Navsource.org, and in *Uncommon Warriors* (see Bibliography for full citations of those sources). In the listing below, an "x" following the ship's name indicates a vessel lost in World War II.

AG 1	*Hannibal*	AG 28	*Manley*
AG 2	*Lebanon*	AG 29	*Bear*
AG 3	*Nanshan*	AG 30	*Bowditch*
AG 4	*Saturn*	AG 31	*Argonne*
AG 5	*General Alava*	AG 32	*Sumner*
AG 6	*Dubuque*	AG 33	*Kaula*
AG 7	*Paducah*	AG 34	*Alcor*
AG 8	*Mahanna*	AG 35	*Calypso*
AG 9	*Great Northern/Columbia*	AG 36	*Manasquan*
AG 10	*Antares*	AG 37	*Manomet*
AG 11	*Procyon*	AG 38	*Matinicus*
AG 12	*Gold Star*	AG 39	*Menemsha*
AG 13	*Pensacola*	AG 40	*Monomoy*
AG 14	*Abarenda*	AG 41	*Midway/Panay*
AG 15	*Ajax*	AG 42	*Camanga*
AG 16	*Utah* (ex–BB 31)[x]	AG 43	*Majaba*
AG 17	*Wyoming*	AG 44	*Malanao*
AG 18	*Stoddert*	AG 45	*Taganak*
AG 19	*Boggs*	AG 46	*Tuluran*
AG 20	*Kilty*	AG 47	*Manhasset*
AG 21	*Lamberton*	AG 48	*Muskeget*
AG 22	*Radford*	AG 49	*Anacapa*
AG 23	*Sequoia*	AG 50	*Kopara*
AG 24	*Semmes*	AG 66	*Besboro*
AG 25	*Potomac*	AG 67	*Antaeus*
AG 26	*Cuyahoga*	AG 68	*Basilan*
AG 27	*Robert L. Barnes*[x]	AG 69	*Burias*

AG 70	*Zaniah*	AG 123	*Rockaway*
AG 71	*Baham*	AG 124	*Maumee*
AG 72	*Parris Island*	AG 125	*Patoka*
AG 73	*Belle Isle*	AG 126	*McDougal*
AG 74	*Coasters Harbor*	AG 127	*Winslow*
AG 75	*Cuttyhunk Island*	AG 128	*Mississippi*
AG 76	*Avery Island*	AG 129	*Whitewood*
AG 77	*Indian Island*	AG 130	*Camano*
AG 78	*Kent Island*	AG 131	*Deal*
AG 79	*San Clemente*	AG 132	*Elba*
AG 80	*Du Pont*	AG 133	*Errol*
AG 81	*J. Fred Talbott*	AG 134	*Estero*
AG 82	*Schenck*	AG 135	*Jekyl*
AG 83	*Kennison*	AG 136	*Metomkin*
AG 84	*Hatfield*	AG 137	*Roque*
AG 85	*Fox*	AG 138	*Ryer*
AG 86	*Bulmer*	AG 139	*Sharps*
AG 87	*MacLeish*	AG 140	*Torry*
AG 88	*Burton Island*	AG 141	*Whidbey*
AG 89	*Edisto*	AG 142	*Nashawena*
AG 90	*Atka*	AG 143	*Mark*
AG 91	*Dahlgren*	AG 144	*Tingles*
AG 92	*Gwinnett*	AG 145	*Hewell*
AG 93	*Nicollet*	AG 146	*Electron*
AG 94	*Pontotoc*	AG 147	*Proton*
AG 95	*Litchfield*	AG 148	*Colington*
AG 96	*Broome*	AG 149	*League Island*
AG 97	*Simpson*	AG 150	*Chimon*
AG 98	*Ramsay*	AG 151	*Richard E. Kraus*
AG 99	*Preble*	AG 152	*Timmerman*
AG 100	*Sicard*	AG 153	*Compass Island*
AG 101	*Pruitt*	AG 154	*Observation Island*
AG 102	*Babbitt*	AG 157	*King County*
AG 103	*Upshur*	AG 159	*Oxford*
AG 104	*Elliot*	T-AG 160	*Range Tracker*
AG 105	*Hogan*	T-AG 161	*Range Recoverer*
AG 106	*Howard*	T-AG 162	*Mission Capistrano*
AG 107	*Stansbury*	AGDE 163	*Glover*
AG 108	*Chandler*	AG 164	*Kingsport*
AG 109	*Zane*	AG 165	*Georgetown*
AG 110	*Trever*	AG 166	*Jamestown*
AG 111	*Hamilton*	AG 167	*Belmont*
AG 112	*Breckinridge*	AG 168	*Liberty*
AG 113	*Barney*	T-AG 169	*Private Jose F. Valdez*
AG 114	*Biddle*	T-AG 170	*Lt. James E. Robinson*
AG 115	*Ellis*	T-AG 171	*Sgt. Joseph E. Muller*
AG 116	*Cole*	AG 172	*Phoenix*
AG 117	*Whipple*	AG 173	*Provo*
AG 118	*McCormick*	T-AG 174	*Cheyenne*
AG 119	*John D. Ford*	T-AG 175	*Sgt. Curtis F. Shoup*
AG 120	*Paul Jones*	AG 176	*Peregrine*
AG 121	*Humboldt*	AG 177	*Shearwater*
AG 122	*Matagorda*	T-AG 178	*Flyer*

3. Directory of U.S. Navy Auxiliary Ships

T-AG 179	*Havenford*	T-AG 190	*Webster*
T-AG 180	*Antioch*	AG 191	*Spokane*
T-AG 181	*Adelphi*	AG 192	*S.P. Lee*
T-AG 182	*Lynn*	AG 193	*Glomar Explorer*
T-AG 183	*Clarksburg*	T-AG 194	*Vanguard*
T-AG 184	*Clemson*	T-AG 195	*Hayes*
T-AG 185	*Carthage*	T-AG 335	(no name)
T-AG 186	*Bessemer*	EAG 398	*Hunting*
T-AG 187	*Milford*	AG 520	*Alacrity*
T-AG 188	*Radcliffe*	AG 521	*Assurance*
T-AG 189	*Rollins*	T-AG 5001	*VADM. K.R. Wheeler*

Icebreakers (AGB)

Viewed left to right, three Navy icebreakers—USS *Burton Island* (AGB 1), USS *Atka* (AGB 3) and USS *Glacier* (AGB 4)—are pushing a large iceberg that was blocking the channel to McMurdo Station in Antarctica on the last day of 1965 (U.S. Navy photograph).

Built for the purpose of moving through ice-covered waters and opening channels for other ships, the Navy's six AGBs were commissioned between 1944 and 1955 and transferred to the Coast Guard between 1953 and 1966.

U.S. Navy Auxiliary Vessels

AGB 1	*Burton Island* (ex–AG 88)[1]	AGB 4	*Glacier*[4]
AGB 2	*Edisto* (ex–AG 89)[2]	AGB 5	*Staten Island*[5]
AGB 3	*Atka* (ex–AG 90)[3]	AGB 6	*Westwind*[6]

Notes

1. Originally commissioned in December 1946 and reclassified as AGB 1 in March 1949; transferred to USCG in December 1966 as USCGC *Burton Island* (WAGB 283), and sold for scrapping in August 1980.
2. Originally commissioned in March 1947 and reclassified as AGB 2 in March 1949; transferred to USCG as USCG *Edisto* (WAGB 284) in October 1965, decommissioned in November 1974, and sold for scrapping in September 1977.
3. Originally commissioned as USCGC *Southwind* (WAGB 280) in July 1944, transferred to USSR in March 1945, commissioned as USS *Atka* in October 1950, transferred back to the Coast Guard in October 1966, and struck in November 1966.
4. Commissioned as USS *Glacier* in May 1955, transferred to USCG as USCGC *Glacier* (WAGB 4) in June 1966, decommissioned in July 1987, and sold for scrapping in February 2012.
5. Commissioned by the Coast Guard as USCGC *Staten Island* (WAG 278) in February 1944, transferred to USN as USS *Northwind* (AGB 5) in January 1952, renamed *Staten Island* in February 1952, decommissioned and transferred to USCG as USCGC *Staten island* (WAGB 278) in February 1966, decommissioned in November 1974, and sold for scrapping.
6. Commissioned by USCG as *Westwind* (WAG 281) in September 1944, transferred to USSR in 1945, commissioned as USS *Westwind* (AGB 6) in February 1952, transferred back to USCG as USCGC *Westwin*d (WAGB 281) in September 1952, and decommissioned in February 1988.

Amphibious Force Flagships (AGC) / Amphibious Command Ships (LCC)

USS *Pocono* (AGC 16) is underway in the early 1960s (U.S. Navy photograph).

3. Directory of U.S. Navy Auxiliary Ships

Originally called "combined operations—communications—headquarters ships," the AGCs carried Navy fleet and force commanders and their staffs, and when conducting combined operations, Army or Marine headquarters units. The AGCs were fitted with extensive communications equipment for this purpose. Public information about the AGCs was not disclosed until the end of World War II. During that conflict the Navy commissioned 16 AGCs, with another two added in late 1945. Six Coast Guard Treasury-class vessels—*Bibb, Campbell, Duane, Ingham, Spencer* and *Taney*—were converted to amphibious force flagships (WAGC) in 1944.

Amphibious force flagships in the fleet auxiliary category were reclassified as amphibious command ships (LCC) in the amphibious warfare category in 1969, and the two LCCs commissioned after that date—USS *Blue Ridge* (LCC 19) and USS *Mount Whitney* (LCC 20)—are covered in Chapter 1.

AGC 1	*Appalachian*[1]		AGC 11	*Eldorado*[11]
AGC 2	*Blue Ridge*[2]		AGC 12	*Estes*[12]
AGC 3	*Rocky Mount*[3]		AGC 13	*Panamint*[13]
AGC 4	*Ancon*[4]		AGC 14	*Teton*[14]
AGC 5	*Catoctin*[5]		AGC 15	*Adirondack*[15]
AGC 6	*Duane*[6]		AGC 16	*Pocono*[16]
AGC 7	*Mount Whitney*[7]		AGC 17	*Taconic*[17]
AGC 8	*Mount Olympus*[8]		AGC 18	*Biscayne*[18]
AGC 9	*Wasatch*[9]		AGC 369	*Williamsburg*[19]
AGC 10	*Auburn*[10]			
WAGC 31	*Bibb*		WAGC 35	*Ingham*
WAGC 32	*Campbell*		WAGC 36	*Spencer*
WAGC 33	*Duane*		WAGC 37	*Taney*

Notes

1. Decommissioned in May 1947, struck in March 1959, and sold for scrapping in 1960.
2. Decommissioned in March 1947, struck in January 1960, and sold for scrapping in August 1960.
3. Decommissioned in March 1947, struck in July 1960, and sold for scrapping in March 1973.
4. Commissioned in August 1942 as transport [q.v.] AP 66, reclassified as AGC in February 1943, decommissioned in February 1946, struck in April 1946, served as training ship *State of Maine* 1962–1973, and sold for scrapping in May 1973.
5. Decommissioned in April 1947, transferred to MARAD in December 1959, and dismantled in May 1960.
6. Was to have been AGC 6 but was renamed USCGC *Duane* (WAGC 33) and later redesignated as WPC 33. Sunk as reef in November 1987.
7. Redesignated as LCC 7 in January 1969, struck in March 1970, and sold for scrapping in September 1977.
8. Decommissioned in April 1956 and sold for scrapping in January 1973.
9. Decommissioned in August 1946, struck in January 1960, and sold for scrapping.
10. Decommissioned in May 1947, struck in August 1960, and sold for scrapping in February 1961.
11. Redesignated LCC 11 in January 1969, decommissioned and struck in November 1972, and sold in August 1973.
12. Redesignated LCC 12 in January 1969, decommissioned in October 1969, struck in July 1976, and sold for scrapping in December 1977.
13. Decommissioned in January 1947, struck in July 1960, and sold for scrapping in March 1961.
14. Decommissioned in August 1946, struck in June 1961, and sold for scrapping in March 1962.
15. Decommissioned in February 1955, struck in June 1961, and sold for scrapping in November 1972.
16. Redesignated as LCC 16 in November 1968, struck in December 1976, and sold in December 1981.
17. Redesignated as LCC 17 in January 1969, decommissioned in December 1969, and struck in December 1976.
18. Commissioned in March 1941 as small seaplane tender [q.v.] AVP 11, reclassified as AGC 18 in October 1944, transferred to USCG in July 1946 as USCGC *Dexter* (WAGC 18) and redesignated as WHEC 385 in May 1966, decommissioned in July 1968, transferred back to USN, and expended as a target in 1968.
19. Commissioned in October 1941 as patrol gunboat PG 56, reclassified as AGC 369 in November 1945, served as presidential yacht from November 1945 to decommissioning in June 1953, struck in April 1962, and sold in 1968.

Escort Research Ship (AGDE) / Frigate Research Ship (AGFF)

Seen early in her career in January 1968, USS *Glover* (AGDE 1) is underway in Narragansett Bay, Rhode Island (U.S. Navy photograph).

USS *Glover* was authorized as the miscellaneous auxiliary AG 163 but was commissioned as an escort research ship designated as AGDE 1 on November 3, 1965. She had been equipped with a modified propeller configuration and advanced sonar and antisubmarine weapons to test state of the art ASW equipment and procedures. *Glover* was reclassified as a frigate research ship (AGFF 1) on June 30, 1975, and then as a "regular" frigate (FF 1098) on October 1, 1975. A decade later, she was configured with a wide-aperture array sonar, decommissioned, reclassified as a sonar trials ship designated as T-AGFF 1, and placed in service with the MSC on June 15, 1990. *Glover* was taken out of service and transferred to NDRF on September 28, 1992, struck on November 20 of that year, and reportedly sold for $80,743.79 on April 15, 1994, to N.R. Acquisitions and subsequently dismantled in North Carolina.

Auxiliary Deep Submergence Support Ships (AGDS)

USS *Point Loma* (AGDS 2) is ballasted down in this January 16, 1977, view of the ship off Santa Catalina, California (U.S. Navy photograph).

USS *White Sands* was initially commissioned as the auxiliary repair dock [q.v.] USS ARD 20 on March 31, 1944. She was converted to a bathyscaph support auxiliary repair dock (ARD [BS] 20) in 1965–1966, named *White Sands* on March 9, 1968, and supported the bathyscaphe *Trieste II* in California. *White Sands* also participated in the 1969 search for the lost attack submarine USS *Scorpion* (SSN 589). She was reclassified as an auxiliary deep submergence research ship and designated as AGDS 1 on August 1, 1973. Decommissioned and struck in 1974, she was sold on September 1 of that year for commercial service as a dry dock in Seattle.

USS *Point Loma* (AGDS 2) was the former cargo ship dock (AKD) [q.v.] USNS *Point Barrow* (T-AKD 1), which had been taken out of mothballs in 1974 and converted to a deep submergence support ship in 1974–1976. Commissioned on July 3, 1976, *Point Loma* was used to carry, launch, recover and service the submersible *Trieste*. She was decommissioned in September 1986 and assigned that same month to MSC as USNS *Point Loma* (T-AGDS 2). The ship was struck in September 1993 and sold for scrapping in December 2005.

AGDS 1 *White Sands*   T-AGDS 2 *Point Loma*

Hydrofoil Research Ship (AGEH)

"Flying" with her hull out of the water, USS *Plainview* (AGEH 1) is engaged in tests and evaluation in the waters of Puget Sound, Washington, probably in May 1968 (U.S. Navy photograph).

USS *Plainview* (AGEH 1) was laid down in May 1964, launched in June 1965 and placed in service on March 3, 1969, as the Navy's first hydrofoil research ship. Reportedly, she was the world's largest hydrofoil at the time. She served for nine years and was placed out of service on September 22, 1978, and struck eight days later. *Plainview* was sold for dismantling on July 1, 1979, and partially dismantled. At last report (c. 2014) the hulk is located in the Columbia River in Washington.

Environmental Research Ships (AGER)

Three former U.S. Army freight and supply ships (FS) were acquired by the Navy and first used as light cargo ships [q.v.] (AKL) but converted during the 1960s to meet naval intelligence requirements, with a secondary role of responding to National Security Agency needs. Designated as AGERs, two of the vessels were out of service and struck by 1970; USS *Pueblo* (AGER 2) was captured with her crew by North Korea on January 23, 1968. Although the crew was later released, the ship remains in North Korean hands today.

AGER 1	*Banner* (ex–FS-345)[1]	
AGER 2	*Pueblo* (ex–FS-344)[2]	
AGER 3	*Palm Beach* (ex–FS 217)[3]	

USS *Pueblo* (AGER 2) is underway off San Diego, California, on October 19, 1967—just three months before she was captured by North Korea (U.S. Navy photograph).

NOTES

1. Acquired in July 1950 as AKL 25, named in September 1952, converted to AGER in 1965, decommissioned and struck in November 1969, and sold for scrapping in June 1970.
2. Transferred to Navy in April 1966 as AKL 44, named in June 1966, commissioned as AGER in May 1967, and now listed on NVR as "active, in commission" while held by North Korea.
3. Acquired in June 1966 as AKL 45, redesignated as AGER in May 1967, decommissioned and struck in December 1969, and sold. Ran aground in Cayman Islands reportedly while drug running and sunk.

Miscellaneous Command Ships (AGF)

After World War II until 1972 small seaplane tenders (AVP) [q.v.] served as flagships for U.S. forces in the Persian Gulf area. One of those vessels, USS *Valcour* (AVP 55) was reclassified as the Navy's first miscellaneous command ship (AGF) in 1965 and performed that role while based in Bahrain. She was succeeded by USS *La Salle* in 1972. Two purpose-built command ships—USS *Blue Ridge* (LCC 19) and USS *Mount Whitney* (LCC 20)—are classified as fleet support ships in the combatant ship category and are covered in Chapter 1. USS *Coronado*, although also an amphibious warfare ship, is listed below because she was modified to serve as a flagship to relieve *La Salle* while AGF 3 was overhauled in the United States.

AGF 1   *Valcour*[1]
AGF 3   *La Salle*[2]
AGF 11   *Coronado*[3]

NOTES

1. Commissioned in July 1946 as AVP 55, reclassified as AGF 1 in December 1965, decommissioned and struck in June 1973, and sold for scrapping in May 1977.
2. Commissioned in February 1964 as amphibious transport dock LPD 3, converted in 1981–1982 to AGF 3 to serve as flagship for Commander, Middle East Force, decommissioned and struck in May 2005, and expended as a target in April 2007.
3. Commissioned in May 1970 as amphibious transport dock LPD 11, converted to AGF 11 as flagship for Commander, U.S. Third Fleet in August 1980, decommissioned in February 2005 and transferred to MSC as USNS *Coronado* (T-AGF 11), struck in September 2006, and expended as a target in September 2012.

Frigate Research Ship / Auxiliary General Frigate (AGFF)

See Escort Research Ship (AGDE) above.

Electronic-Deception Hydrofoil Craft (AGHR)

Hydrofoil vessel proposed in the 1962–1963 period to operate at high speeds distant from a task force and employ its electronic warfare equipment to deceive enemy naval units. Tentatively designated as AGHR, this vessel was never built.[1]

NOTE

1. Friedman, *U.S. Small Combatants*, 510.

Patrol Combatant Support Ship (AGHS)

The tank landing ship USS *Wood County* (LST 1178) was to have been converted into a patrol combatant support ship (AGHS) to act as a tender for the Navy's patrol combatant–missile (hydrofoil) (PHM) boats. The planned 30-boat PHM program was later cut back to only six units leading to the cancellation of the AGHS conversion in 1977. *Wood County* was struck in February 1989 and dismantled in 2002. The AGHS hull classification is listed as "inactive" on the NVR.

Missile Range Instrumentation Ships (AGM)

See Chapter 2.

Major Communications Relay Ships (AGMR)

The two AGMR ships were former aircraft carriers converted and fitted with massive antenna arrays and extensive communications equipment for receiving, processing and sending messages to and from local ships and distant shore-based communications facilities. They served as AGMRs in the 1960s.

AGMR 1   *Annapolis*[1]
AGMR 2   *Arlington*[2]

NOTES

1. Commissioned in February 1945 as escort aircraft carrier USS *Gilbert Islands* (CVE 107), reclassified as cargo ship and aircraft ferry [q.v.] AKV 39 in May 1959, converted to AGMR in 1963 and renamed *Annapolis* on June 22, 1963, recommissioned as AGMR 1 in March 1964, decommissioned in December 1969, struck in October 1976, and sold for scrapping in November 1979.

2. Commissioned in July 1946 as light aircraft carrier USS *Saipan* (CVL 48), reclassified as an auxiliary aircraft carrier landing training ship [q.v.] and designated AVT 6 in May 1959, converted to AGMR in 1963–1966, commissioned as USS *Arlington* in August 1966, decommissioned in January 1970, struck in August 1975, and sold for scrapping in June 1976.

Oceanographic Research Ships (AGOR)

See Chapter 2.

Ocean Surveillance Ships (AGOS)

See Chapter 1.

Motor Torpedo Boat Tenders / Patrol Craft Tenders (AGP)

In June 1968 USS *Garrett County* is supporting Operation Game Warden units in the Co Chien River in South Vietnam's Mekong Delta. Three Navy river patrol boats (PBR) are moored along the ship's port side while a Navy UH-1B helicopter is landing on her deck (U.S. Navy photograph).

The AGPs provided support in the form of repairs, fuel and provisions for PT boats during World War II and for various riverine patrol craft during the Vietnam War. AGPs 1–3 were converted from gunboats; AGPs 4, 5, 10, 11 and 14–18 were converted from tank landing ships (LST); AGPs 6–9 were converted from small seaplane tenders [q.v.] (AVP); and AGPs 12 and 13 were derived from Maritime Commission C1-A vessels. All of these motor torpedo boat tenders served as AGPs in 1943–1945 and were struck from the Vessel Register in 1946–1947. (The hull number AGP 19 was to have been assigned to LST 1152 but that conversion was cancelled in July 1944.) The last four AGPs listed below were classified as patrol craft tenders and were converted from LSTs in 1966 and 1970. Three went on to serve in other navies and the last tender, AGP 1176, was scrapped in 1977. (Two 19th century colliers—USS *Iris* and USS *Pompey*—served as torpedo boat tenders in 1909–1916 and 1911–1921, respectively, and were discarded thereafter.)

AGP 1	*Niagara* (ex–PG 52)	AGP 14	*Alecto* (ex–LST 977)
AGP 2	*Hilo* (ex–PG 58)	AGP 15	*Callisto* (ex–LST 966)
AGP 3	*Jamestown* (ex–PG 55)	AGP 16	*Antigone* (ex–LST 773)
AGP 4	*Portunus* (ex–LST 330)	AGP 17	*Brontes* (ex–LST 1125)
AGP 5	*Varuna* (ex–LST 14)	AGP 18	*Chiron* (ex–LST 1133)
AGP 6	*Oyster Bay* (ex–AVP 28)	AGP 20	*Pontus* (ex–LST 201)
AGP 7	*Mobjack* (ex–AVP 27)	AGP 786	*Garrett County* (ex–LST 786)[1]
AGP 8	*Wachapreague* (ex–AVP 56)	AGP 821	*Harnett County* (ex–LST 821)[2]
AGP 9	*Willoughby* (ex–AVP 57)		
AGP 10	*Orestes* (ex–LST 135)	AGP 838	*Hunterdon County* (ex–LST 838)[3]
AGP 11	*Silenus* (ex–LST 604)		
AGP 12	*Acontius*	AGP 1176	*Graham County* (ex–LST 1176)[4]
AGP 13	*Cyrene*		

Notes

1. Commissioned in August 1944 as LST, decommissioned in July 1946, recommissioned in October 1966 as AGP, served in Vietnam 1967–1971, decommissioned and transferred to South Vietnam in April 1971 as RVNS *Can Tho* (HQ 801), and later transferred to the Philippines as BPK *Kalinga Apayao* (LT 516) and now decommissioned.
2. Commissioned in November 1944 as LST, decommissioned in July 1946, recommissioned in August 1966, served in Vietnam, 1967–1970, reclassified as AGP in 1970, decommissioned in 1970 and transferred to South Vietnam as RVNS *My Tho* (HQ 800) in October 1970, transferred to the Philippines in April 1976 as BRP *Sierra Madre* (LT 57), now grounded on a shoal and used as an outpost.
3. Commissioned in December 1944 as LST, decommissioned in August 1946, named in July 1955, recommissioned in September 1966, served in Vietnam in 1967–1971, reclassified as an AGP in August 1971, and decommissioned and transferred to Malaysia in August 1971 as KD *Sri Langaw* (A-1500).
4. Commissioned in April 1958, reclassified as AGP in 1972 to support Asheville (PG 84)-class gunboats in the Mediterranean, struck in March 1977 and dismantled.

Radar Picket Ships (AGR)

Converted from civilian Liberty (Z-EC2-S-C5) ships in 1954–1958, the Navy's radar picket ships served as sea-based extensions of the U.S. Distant Early Warning (DEW) line and were intended to detect possible attacks by Soviet bombers. They were equipped with long-range air search, height-finding, and air/surface search radars and IFF equipment. AGRs 1–13 were initially designated as YAGRs and redesignated as AGRs in 1958. The AGRs steamed on 30–45-day patrols and racked up 220 to 250 days at sea annually. They were withdrawn from service in 1965 and most were laid up in the NDRF for a period and subsequently sold for scrapping, with a few sold to commercial users.

3. Directory of U.S. Navy Auxiliary Ships

USS *Picket* (AGR 7), which guarded the U.S. Pacific Coast, is in San Francisco Bay in 1965 (U.S. Navy photograph).

AGR 1	*Guardian*	AGR 9	*Investigator*
AGR 2	*Lookout*	AGR 10	*Outpost*
AGR 3	*Skywatcher*	AGR 11	*Protector*
AGR 4	*Searcher*	AGR 12	*Vigil*
AGR 5	*Scanner*	AGR 13	*Interdictor*
AGR 6	*Locator*	ARR 14	*Interpreter*
AGR 7	*Picket*	AGR 15	*Interrupter/Tracer*[1]
AGR 8	*Interceptor*	AGR 16	*Watchman*

NOTE

1. Renamed in September 1959.

Surveying Ships (AGS)

See Chapter 2.

Coastal Surveying Ships (AGSC)

The AGSC ships performed hydrographic research and surveys in coastal waters. All of them were derived from other ship types in the postwar years, almost all served only briefly as coastal surveying ships, and all were struck by 1969.

The former self-propelled lighter YF 854, USS *Littlehales* (AGSC 15) is operating off Little Creek, Virginia, on October 11, 1963 (U.S. Navy photograph).

AGSC 8	*Dutton*[1]	AGSC 14	*Simon Newcomb*[5]
AGSC 10	*John Blish*[2]	AGSC 15	*Littlehales*[6]
AGSC 12	*Harkness*[3]	AGSC 16	*Requisite*[7]
AGSC 13	*James M. Gillis*[4]		

Notes

1. Commissioned in March 1944 as the submarine chaser sweeper PCS 1386, reclassified as hydrographic surveying ship AGS 8 in March 1945, reclassified as AGSC 8 in July 1946, decommissioned in August 1949 and sold in 1954.

2. Commissioned in February 1944 as submarine chaser sweeper PCS 1437, reclassified as hydrographic research ship AGS 10 and named in March 1945, reclassified as AGSC in July 1946, decommissioned in August 1949, and sold for scrapping in February 1950.

3. Commissioned in March 1943 as motor minesweeper YMS 242, converted to surveying ship and redesignated as AGS 12 in March 1945, reclassified as AGSC in July 1946, converted to coastal minesweeper—underwater locator AMCU 12 in 1951, struck in November 1959, and sold in 1960.

4. Commissioned in August 1943 as YMS 262, reclassified as AGS 13 and named in March 1945, reclassified as AGSC in July 1946, converted to AMCU 13 in March 1951, reclassified as coastal minehunter MHC 13 in February 1955, struck in January 1960, and sold in 1960.

5. Commissioned in August 1943 as YMS 263, reclassified as AGS 14 and named in March 1945, reclassified as AGSC in July 1946, decommissioned in November 1949, struck in January 1950, and sold for scrapping in April 1950.

6. Commissioned in December 1952 as self-propelled lighter YF 854, reclassified as AGSC and named in February 1959, and struck in February 1968.

7. Commissioned as minesweeper USS *Requisite* (AM 109) in June 1943, reclassified as AGS 18 in August 1951, and decommissioned in April 1964. (Information on specific dates of service as an AGCS is unavailable.)

Submarine Escort Ship (AGSE)

See Chapter 2.

Satellite Launching Ship (AGSL)

An inactive auxiliary ship type classification that was never assigned to a specific vessel.

Miscellaneous Auxiliary Submarines / Auxiliary Research Submarines (AGSS)

After World War II the Navy modified several of its fleet submarines (designated as SS) for various research and auxiliary assignments, and reclassified those boats as miscellaneous auxiliary submarines (designated as AGSS). The first of those was USS *Manta* (AGSS 299) which, beginning in 1949, was used as a submerged target fitted with large blisters to absorb hits from dummy torpedoes. She later served as a Naval Reserve training vessel in the 1960s and was expended as a target in 1969. The Navy acquired two purpose-built research submarines: USS *Albacore* (AGSS 569), commissioned in 1953, to test a high-speed hull form, and USS *Dolphin* (AGSS 555), commissioned in 1968, for special deep-diving operations. In addition, scores of fleet boats were administratively redesignated as AGSS vessels in the 1960s to avoid having them counted as first-line attack submarines. Other fleet boats that had served as dockside training vessels were redesignated as AGSS beginning in 1962. Eventually, all AGSS boats were discarded, with the only survivors serving as memorials and floating museums.

AGSS 214	*Grouper*[1]	AGSS 292	*Devilfish*	AGSS 342	*Chopper*
AGSS 224	*Cod*	AGSS 295	*Hackleback*	AGSS 348	*Cusk*
AGSS 225	*Cero*	AGSS 298	*Lionfish*	AGSS 374	*Loggerhead*
AGSS 228	*Drum*	AGSS 299	*Manta*	AGSS 383	*Pampanito*
AGSS 229	*Flying Fish*[2]	AGSS 300	*Moray*	AGSS 384	*Parche*
AGSS 236	*Silversides*	AGSS 301	*Roncador*	AGSS 387	*Pintado*
AGSS 240	*Angler*	AGSS 303	*Sablefish*	AGSS 388	*Pipefish*
AGSS 241	*Bashaw*	AGSS 304	*Seahorse*	AGSS 389	*Piranha*
AGSS 242	*Bluegill*	AGSS 310	*Batfish*	AGSS 395	*Redfish*
AGSS 243	*Bream*	AGSS 311	*Archerfish*[3]	AGSS 399	*Sea Cat*[5]
AGSS 244	*Cavalla*	AGSS 318	*Baya*[4]	AGSS 401	*Sea Dog*
AGSS 245	*Cobia*	AGSS 319	*Becuna*	AGSS 403	*Atule*
AGSS 246	*Croaker*	AGSS 321	*Besugo*	AGSS 405	*Sea Owl*
AGSS 256	*Hake*	AGSS 324	*Blenny*	AGSS 406	*Sea Poacher*
AGSS 269	*Rasher*	AGSS 328	*Charr*	AGSS 409	*Piper*
AGSS 270	*Raton*	AGSS 331	*Bugara*	AGSS 411	*Spadefish*
AGSS 272	*Redfin*	AGSS 334	*Cabezon*	AGSS 412	*Trepang*
AGSS 274	*Rock*	AGSS 335	*Dentuda*	AGSS 417	*Tench*
AGSS 286	*Billfish*	AGSS 336	*Capitaine*	AGSS 419	*Tigrone*[6]
AGSS 288	*Cabrilla*	AGSS 337	*Carbonero*	AGSS 423	*Torsk*
AGSS 291	*Crevalle*	AGSS 338	*Carp*	AGSS 476	*Runner*

U.S. Navy Auxiliary Vessels

AGSS 479	*Diablo*[7]		AGSS 563	*Tang*
AGSS 480	*Medregal*		AGSS 567	*Gudgeon*[9]
AGSS 481	*Requin*		AGSS 569	*Albacore*[10]
AGSS 482	*Irex*		AGSS 570	*Mackerel*/SST 1[11]
AGSS 489	*Spinax*		AGSS 573	*Salmon*
AGSS 555	*Dolphin*[8]		AGSS 574	*Grayback*

Notes

1. Employed in acoustic research.
2. Employed in acoustic research.
3. Employed in oceanographic research.
4. Employed in acoustic research.
5. Fitted with special equipment 1949–1952 and struck in 1968.
6. Employed in acoustic research.
7. Transferred to Pakistan in June 1964.
8. Conducted numerous deep-ocean research missions, decommissioned in September 2006, and now at San Diego Maritime Museum in California.
9. Later redesignated as SSAG 567.
10. Diesel submarine built with very low length-to-beam ratio, capable of submerged speeds of more than 30 knots (making her world's fastest submarine at the time), struck in May 1980, and dedicated as memorial in Portsmouth, N.H., in 1983.
11. Planned as AGSS but placed in service as USS SST 1 in 1953, named in July 1956, decommissioned and struck in January 1973, and expended as a target in October 1978.

Technical Research Ships (AGTR)

USS *Liberty* (AGTR 5) intercepted radio and other electronic traffic off Africa and in the Middle East before she was attacked by Israel in June 1967 (U.S. Navy photograph).

To support the expanding collection requirements of the National Security Agency in the 1960s, the Navy assembled a small group of secret vessels to gather and process foreign communications and other electronic emissions (called signals intelligence or SIGINT). Three of these vessels were classified as Environmental Research Ships [q.v.] (AGER) and five larger retired civilian vessels were classified as Technical Research Ships (AGTR).

AGTR 1	*Oxford*[1]		AGTR 4	*Belmont*[4]
AGTR 2	*Georgetown*[2]		AGTR 5	*Liberty*[5]
AGTR 3	*Jamestown*[3]			

NOTES

1. Former Liberty ship (Z-EC2-S-C5) SS *Samuel R. Allen*, acquired in October 1960, commissioned as AG 159 in July 1961, reclassified as AGTR in April 1964, decommissioned and struck in December 1969, and sold for scrapping in May 1970.
2. Former Liberty ship *Robert W. Hart* acquired in August 1962, named and classified as AG 165 in March 1963, commissioned in November 1963, reclassified as AGTR in April 1964, decommissioned and struck in 1969, and sold for scrapping in 1970.
3. Former Liberty ship SS *J. Howland Gardner* acquired in August 1962, named and designated as AG 166 in March 1963, commissioned in December 1963, reclassified as AGTR 3 in April 1964, struck in January 1970, and sold for scrapping in 1970.
4. Former Victory ship SS *Iran Victory* acquired in February 1963, classified as AG 167 in June 1963, reclassified AGTR 4 in April 1964, commissioned in November 1964, decommissioned and struck in January 1970, and sold for scrapping in June 1970.
5. Former Victory ship SS *Simmons Victory* acquired in February 1963, named and designated as AG 168 in June 1963, reclassified as AGTR 5 in April 1964, and commissioned in December 1964. Attacked by Israeli aircraft and patrol boats on June 8, 1967, with 34 men killed and 169 wounded. Struck in June 1970, and sold for scrapping in December 1970.

Hospital Ships (AH)

See Chapter 2.

Heavy Salvage Lift Craft (AHLC)

An official Navy model of the heavy salvage lift craft *Crandall* illustrates some of her special equipment after she had been classified as YHLC 2 (U.S. Navy photograph).

These vessels were the former German salvage lift craft *Energie* and *Ausdauer* acquired by the Navy in 1967 and initially designated AHLC 1 and AHLC 2, respectively. They were subsequently renamed *Crilley* and *Crandall* and classified as the service craft YHLC 1 and YHLC 2, respectively. The pair had been used to lift sunken vessels.

| AHLC 1 | *Crilley*[1] | AHLC 2 | *Crandall*[2] |

NOTES

1. Transferred to MARAD in December 1977 and sold in November 2001 for scrapping.
2. Transferred to MARAD in February 1976 and sold in November 2001 for scrapping.

Cargo Ships (AK)

The cargo ship USS *Spica* (AK 16) was acquired by the Navy in November 1921. Seen here off Boston on April 26, 1940, she operated in the Pacific during World War II. *Spica* was decommissioned in January 1946, sold to a civilian operator in June 1947 and renamed SS *Pleamar* (U.S. Navy photograph).

The Navy has employed cargo ships to transport freight, materials and supplies from point to point since before the Civil War, and over the years their numbers have fluctuated widely in times of war and peace. During World War I, for example, the Navy used 354 cargo ships to ferry supplies and equipment to U.S. forces in Europe and then, after the November 1918 armistice, to bring the soldiers and materials back to the United States. The first vessels specifically designated as cargo ships in the Navy's 1920 ship classification system were eight cargo vessels commissioned in 1917 and another three commissioned in 1918 (designated AK 1–AK 11). All were decommissioned between 1921 and 1933.

At the beginning of World War II there were only 33 cargo ships on Navy list. In

1942, 20 of the newer AKs were converted to attack cargo ships [q.v.] (AKA) and seven older cargo ships were transferred to the Army in 1943. But by late 1944 there were 160 AKs, including a number of Victory ships on loan from the Maritime Commission and nine coastal cargo ships lent by the Army and Great Britain. At war's end, the cargo ship hull numbers had reached AK 236. With massive post-war retirements, mothballing, sell offs and scrapping, there were just six AKs listed on the Vessel Register by January 1950. Eight years later, there were 41 AKs but only about half of that number remained by 1965.

There are no longer any "straight" cargo ships in active service or on the Naval Vessel Register. The last such AK was USS *Mirfak* (T-AK 271), which had been built in 1957, worked for the MSTS, and was sold for scrapping in 2003. Her sister ships *Eltanin* (AK 270) and *Mizar* (AK 272) were converted to oceanographic research ships [q.v.] in the early 1960s.

EARLY CARGO SHIPS

AK 1	*Houston*		AK 38	*Edenton*
AK 2	*Kittery*		AK 39	*Mendocino**
AK 3	*Newport News*		AK 40	*Will H. Point**
AK 4	*Bath*		AK 41	*Hercules*
AK 5	*Gulfport*		AK 42	*Mercury*[17]
AK 6	*Beaufort*		AK 43	*Jupiter*[18]
AK 7	*Pensacola*[1]		AK 44	*Aroostock*
AK 8	*Astoria*		AK 45	*Stratford*[19]
AK 9	*Long Beach*		AK 46	*Pleiades*
AK 10	*Quincy*		AK 47	*Aquilla*
AK 11	*Robert L. Barnes*[2]		AK 48	*Pegasus*[20]
AK 12	*Arcturus*[3]		AK 49	*Saturn*[21]
AK 13	*Capella*		AK 50	*Alcoa Pennant*
AK 14	*Regulus*		AK 51	*Aries*[22]
AK 15	*Sirius*		AK 52	*Matinicus*[23]
AK 16	*Spica*		AK 53	*Libra*[24]
AK 17	*Vega*		AK 55	*Titania*[25]
AK 18	*Arcturus*[4]		AK 56	*Oberon*[26]
AK 19	*Procyon*[5]		AK 57	*Thomas Jefferson*
AK 20	*Bellatrix*[6]		AK 58	*Malantic*
AK 21	*Electra*[7]		AK 59	*Larranga*
AK 22	*Fomalhaut*[8]		AK 60	*El Costan*
AK 23	*Alchiba*		AK 61	*Mana*
AK 24	*Alcyone*[9]		AK 62	*Kopara*[27]
AK 25	*Algorab*[10]		AK 63	*Asterion*
AK 26	*Alhena*[11]		AK 64	*Andromeda*[28]
AK 27	*Almaack*[12]		AK 65	*Aquarius*[29]
AK 28	*Betelgeuse*[13]		AK 66	*Centaurus*[30]
AK 29	*Delta*[14]		AK 67	*Cepheus*[31]
AK 30	*Hamul*[15]		AK 68	*Thuban*[32]
AK 31	*Markab*[16]		AK 69	*Virgo*[33]
AK 32	*John R.R. Hannay**		AK 70	*Crater*
AK 33	*West Elasco**		AK 71	*Adhara*
AK 34	*Meigs**		AK 72	*Aludra*[x]
AK 35	*Liberty*		AK 73	*Arided*
AK 36	*William R. Gibson**		AK 74	*Carina*
AK 37	*Ludington**		AK 75	*Cassiopeia*

AK 76	Celeno	AK 128	Leonis
AK 77	Cetus	AK 129	Phobus
AK 78	Deimos[x]	AK 130	Arkab
AK 79	Draco	AK 131	Melucta
AK 80	Enceladus	AK 132	Propus
AK 81	Europa	AK 133	Seginus
AK 82	Hydra	AK 134	Syrma
AK 83	Media	AK 135	Venus
AK 84	Mira	AK 136	Ara
AK 85	Nashira	AK 137	Ascella
AK 86	Norma	AK 138	Cheleb
T-AK 87	Sagitta	AK 139	Pavo
AK 88	Tucana	AK 140	Situla
T-AK 89	Vela	AK 141	—
AK 90	Albireo	AK 155	(cancelled)
AK 91	Cor Caroli	AK 156	Alamosa
AK 92	Eridanus	AK 157	Alcona
AK 93	Etamin[34]	AK 158	Amador
AK 94	Mintaka	AK 159	Antrim
AK 95	Murzim	AK 160	Autauga
AK 96	Sterope	AK 161	Beaverhead
AK 97	Serpens[x]	AK 162	Beltrami
AK 98	Auriga	AK 163	Blount
AK 99	Bootes	AK 164	Brevard
AK 100	Lynx	AK 165	Bullock
AK 101	Lyra	AK 166	Cabell
AK 101	Atik	AK 167	Caledonia
AK 102	Triangulum	AK 168	Charlevoix
AK 103	Sculptor	AK 169	Chatham
AK 104	Ganymede	AK 170	Chicot
AK 105	Naos	AK 171	Claiborne
AK 106	Caelum	AK 172	Clarion
AK 107	Hyperion	AK 173	Codington
AK 108	Rotanin	AK 174	Colquitt
AK 109	Allioth[35]	AK 175	Craighead
AK 110	Alkes	AK 176	Dodridge[39]
AK 111	Giansar	AK 177	Duval[40]
AK 112	Grumium[36]	AK 178	Fairfield
AK 113	Rutilicus	AK 179	Faribault
AK 114	Alkaid	AK 180	Fentress
AK 115	Crux	AK 181	Flagler
AK 116	Alderamin	AK 182	Gadsden
AK 117	Zaurak	AK 183	Glacier
AK 118	Shaula	AK 184	Grainger
AK 119	Matur	AK 185	Gwinnett[41]
AK 120	Zaniah[37]	AK 186	Habersham
AK 121	Sabik	AK 187	Hennepin
AK 122	Baham[38]	AK 188	Herkimer
AK 123	Menkar	AK 189	Hidalgo
AK 124	Azimech	AK 190	Kenosha
AK 125	Lesuth	AK 191	Lebanon
AK 126	Megrez	AK 192	Lehigh
AK 127	Alnitah	AK 193	Lancaster

3. Directory of U.S. Navy Auxiliary Ships

AK 194	Marengo	T-AK 240	Private John R. Towle
AK 195	Midland	T-AK 241	Pvt. Francis X. McGraw
AK 196	Minidoka	T-AK 242	Sgt. Andrew Miller
AK 197	Muscatine	T-AK 243	Sgt. Archer T. Gammon
AK 198	Muskingum	T-AK 244	Sgt. Morris E. Crain
AK 199	Nicollet[42]	T-AK 245	Capt. Arlo L. Olson
AK 200	Pembina	T-AK 246	Col. William J. O'Brien
AK 201	Pemiscot	T-AK 247	Pvt. John F. Thorson
AK 202	Pinellas	T-AK 248	Sgt. George Peterson
AK 203	Pipestone	T-AK 249	Short Splice
AK 204	Pitkin	T-AK 250	Pvt. Frank J. Petrarca
AK 205	Poinsett	T-AK 251	Lt. George W.G. Boyce
AK 206	Pontotoc[43]	T-AK 252	Lt. Robert Craig
AK 207	Richland	T-AK 253	Pvt. Joe E. Mann[55]
AK 208	Rockdale	T-AK 254	Sgt. Truman Kimbro
AK 209	Schuyler	T-AK 255	Pvt. Leonard C. Bostrom
AK 210	Screven	T-AK 256	Dalton Victory[56]
AK 211	Sebastian	AK 257	Altair[57]
AK 212	Somerset	AK 258	Antares[58]
AK 213	Sussex	AK 259	Alcor
AK 214	Tarrant	AK 260	Betelgeuse
AK 215	Tipton	AK 261	Alchiba
AK 216	Traverse[44]	AK 262	Algorab
AK 217	Tulare[45]	AK 263	Aquarius
AK 218	Washtenaw[46]	AK 264	Centauris
AK 219	Westchester[47]	AK 265	Cepheus
AK 220	Wexford[48]	AK 266	Serpens
AK 221	Kenmore[49]	T-AK 267	Marine Fiddler
AK 222	Livingston[50]	T-AK 269	Comet[59]
AK 223	De Grasse[51]	T-AK 270	Eltanin[60]
AK 224	Prince Georges[52]	T-AK 271	Mirfak
AK 225	Allegan	T-AK 272	Mizar[61]
AK 226	Appanoose	T-AK 273	Taurus[62]
AK 227	Boulder Victory	T-AK 274	Lt. James E. Robinson[63]
AK 228	Provo Victory	T-AK 275	Pvt. Joseph F. Merrell[64]
AK 229	Las Vegas Victory	T-AK 276	Sgt. Jack J. Pendleton[65]
AK 230	Manderson Victory	T-AK 277	Schuyler Otis Bland
AK 231	Bedford Victory	T-AK 279	Norwalk
AK 232	Mayfield Victory	T-AK 280	Furman
AK 233	Newcastle Victory	T-AK 281	Victoria
AK 234	Bucyrus Victory	T-AK 282	Marshfield
AK 235	Red Oak Victory	T-AK 283	Wyandot[66]
AK 236	Lakewood Victory	T-AK 284	Northern Light
T-AK 237	Greenville Victory	T-AK 285	Southern Cross
T-AK 238	Haiti Victory[53]	T-AK 286	Vega
T-AK 239	Kingsport Victory[54]		

LATER CARGO SHIPS

In recent years a number of MSC specialized cargo-type vessels, including container ships and roll-on/roll-off (RO/RO) ships, have been assigned "AK" hull numbers. Although they are not "straight" cargo vessels per se, these newer AKs are listed below. AK-designated vessels in the current inventory of the Navy's Military Sealift Command are indicated with an asterisk and their assignment is provided in a footnote (and they are further discussed in Chapter 2). AK-designated vessels currently in MARAD custody—for training purposes or reserved either for cannibalization or for future military use—are indicated with two asterisks.

T-AK 287	*Algol*[67]	AK 4638	*A1C William H. Pitsenbarger*
T-AK 288	*Bellatrix*[68]		
T-AK 289	*Denebola*[69]	AK 4729	*American Tern*
T-AK 290	*Pollux*[70]	AK 5005	*Adventurer*
T-AK 291	*Altair*[71]	AK 5006	*Aide*
T-AK 292	*Regulus*[72]	AK 5007	*Ambassador*
T-AK 293	*Capella*[73]	AK 5008	*Banner*
T-AK 294	*Antares*[74]	AK 5009	*Cape Ann***
AK 323	*TSgt. John A. Chapman*[75]	AK 5010	*Cape Alexander*
AK 851	*Cleveland*	AK 5011	*Cape Archway*
AK 1005	*Austral Rainbow*	AK 5012	*Cape Alava*
AK 1014	*Cape Nome*	AK 5013	*Cape Avinoff***
AK 2005	*Transcolorado*[76]	AK 5015	*Agent*
AK 2016	*Pioneer Commander*	AK 5016	*Lake*
AK 2018	*Pioneer Contractor*	AK 5017	*Pride*
AK 2019	*Pioneer Crusader*	AK 5018	*Scan*
AK 2033	*Buyer*	AK 5019	*Courier*
AK 2035	*Gulf Shipper*	AK 5022	*Cape John*
AK 2036	*Gulf Trader*	AK 5026	*Del Viento*
AK 2039	*Cape Girardeau***	AK 5029	*Cape Jacob*
AK 2049	*Green Valley*	AK 5036	*Cape Chalmers***
AK 2050	*Green Wave*	AK 5037	*Cape Canso*
AK 2062	*American Cormorant*	AK 5038	*Cape Charles*
AK 2064	*Green Harbour*	AK 5039	*Cape Clear*
AK 3000	*CPL Louis J. Hauge Jr.*	AK 5040	*Cape Canaveral*
AK 3001	*PFC William B. Baugh*	AK 5041	*Cape Cod*
AK 3002	*PFC James Anderson, Jr.*	AK 5042	*Cape Carthage*
AK 3003	*1st LT Alex Bonnyman*	AK 5043	*Cape Catoche*
AK 3004	*PVT Franklin J. Phillips*	AK 5044	*Gulf Banker*
T-AK 3005	*SGT Matej Kocak**[77]	AK 5045	*Gulf Farmer*
T-AK 3006	*PFC Eugene A. Obregon**[78]	AK 5046	*Gulf Merchant*
T-AK 3007	*MAJ Stephen W. Pless**[79]	AK 5049	*Del Monte*
T-AK 3008	*2nd LT John P. Bobo**[80]	AK 5050	*Del Valle*
T-AK 3009	*PFC Dewayne T. Williams**[81]	AK 5051	*Cape Gibson*
		AK 5056	*Cape Breton*
T-AK 3010	*1st LT Baldomero Lopez**[82]	AK 5057	*Cape Bover***
T-AK 3011	*1st LT Jack Lummus**[83]	AK 5058	*Cape Borda*
T-AK 3012	*SGT William R. Button**[84]	AK 5059	*Cape Bon*[91]**
T-AK 3015	*1st LT Harry L. Martin**[85]	AK 5060	*Cape Blanco*
T-AK 3016	*LCPL Roy M. Wheat**[86]	AK 5061	*Cape Fear***
T-AK 3017	*GYSGT Fred W. Stockham**[87]	AK 5070	*Cape Flattery***
		AK 5071	*Cape Florida*
AK 4296	*CAPT Stephen L. Bennett*	AK 5073	*Cape Farewell***
AK 4396	*MAJ Benard F. Fisher**[88]	AK 5074	*Cape Catawba*
T-AK 4543	*LTC John U.D. Page**[89]	AK 5075	*Cape Johnson*
T-AK 4544	*SSG Edward A. Carter, Jr.**[90]	AK 5077	*Cape Juby*
		AK 5089	*LTC Calvin P. Tutus*

3. Directory of U.S. Navy Auxiliary Ships

AK 5091	*SP5 Eric C. Gibson*	AK 9302	*American Merlin*[94]
T-AK 5307	*Ocean Crescent**[92]	AK-W9519	*Baffin Strait*
T-AK 5362	*CAPT David I. Lyon**[93]	AK 9651	*American Kestrel*
AK 9204	*Jeb Stuart*	AK 9653	*Noble Star*
AK 9205	*Strong Virginian*	AK 9655	*Green Ridge*
AK 9301	*Buffalo Soldier*	AK 9682	*Advantage*

NOTES

* = Army vessel intended for naval use but was not so employed; its Navy hull number therefore was officially "not used."
X = Lost during World War II.
1. Reclassified as miscellaneous auxiliary [q.v.] AG 13 in June 1922.
2. Reclassified as fleet oiler [q.v.] AO 14 in July 1920.
3. Reclassified as AG 12 in May 1922.
4. Reclassified as an attack cargo ship [q.v.] in February 1943.
5. *Ibid.*
6. *Ibid.*
7. *Ibid.*
8. *Ibid.*
9. *Ibid.*
10. *Ibid.*
11. *Ibid.*
12. *Ibid.*
13. *Ibid.*
14. Reclassified as repair ship [q.v.] AR 9 in March 1943.
15. Reclassified as destroyer tender [q.v.] AD 20 in January 1943.
16. Reclassified as destroyer tender [q.v.] AD 21 in January 1942.
17. Reclassified as general stores issue ship [q.v.] AKS 20 in July 1945.
18. Reclassified as aviation stores issue ship [q.v.] AVS 8 in July 1945.
19. Reclassified as transport [q.v.] AP 41 in 1941.
20. Reclassified as unclassified miscellaneous vessel IX 222 in May 1945.
21. Reclassified as stores ship [q.v.] AF 40 in April 1944.
22. The former USS *Manomet* (AG 37) renamed and reclassified as AK 51 in January 1942.
23. The former USS *Matinicus* (AG 38) reclassified as AK 52 in January 1942 and subsequently reclassified as a transport and renamed *Gemini* in August 1942.
24. Reclassified as an attack cargo ship [q.v.] in February 1943.
25. Reclassified as an attack cargo ship [q.v.] in February 1943.
26. Reclassified as an attack cargo ship [q.v.] in February 1943.
27. Reclassified as a miscellaneous auxiliary ship.
28. Reclassified as an attack cargo ship [q.v.] in February 1943.
29. *Ibid.*
30. *Ibid.*
31. *Ibid.*
32. *Ibid.*
33. *Ibid.*
34. Reclassified as IX 173 in August 1944.
35. Reclassified as IX 204 in March 1945.
36. Reclassified as IX 174 in June 1944.
37. Reclassified as an attack cargo ship [q.v.] in February 1943.
38. *Ibid.*
39. Cancelled in August 1945.
40. *Ibid.*
41. Reclassified as an attack cargo ship [q.v.] in February 1943.
42. *Ibid.*
43. *Ibid.*
44. Cancelled in August 1945.
45. Cancelled in August 1945.
46. Cancelled in August 1945.
47. Cancelled in August 1945.
48. Cancelled in August 1945.
49. Former transport (AP).
50. Former transport (AP).
51. Former transport (AP).
52. Former transport (AP).

53. Reclassified as missile range instrumentation ship [q.v.] in November 1960 and renamed USNS *Longview* (T-AGM 3) in January 1961.
54. Reclassified as an AG and renamed USNS *Kingsport* (T-AG 164) in November 1961.
55. Reclassified an AGM in October 1958 and renamed USNS *Richfield* (T-AGM 4) in November 1960.
56. Reclassified as an AGM and renamed USNS *Sunnyvale* (T-AGM 5) in October 1960.
57. Reclassified as an AKS.
58. Reclassified as an AKS.
59. Reclassified as vehicle landing ship T-LSV 7 in January 1963.
60. Reclassified as an oceanographic research ship [q.v.].
61. Reclassified as an oceanographic research ship [q.v.].
62. Reclassified as T-LSV 8 in January 1963.
63. Former aircraft transport T-AKV 3 reclassified as T-AG 170 in December 1962 and subsequently reclassified as T-AK 274 in July 1964.
64. Former T-AKV 4.
65. Former T-AKV 5 reclassified as T-AK 276 in May 1956.
66. Former T-AKA 92 subsequently redesignated as T-AK 283.
67. Reclassified as a vehicle cargo ship (AKR) [see Chapter 2].
68. *Ibid.*
69. *Ibid.*
70. *Ibid.*
71. *Ibid.*
72 *Ibid.*
73. *Ibid.*
74. *Ibid.*
75. Originally MV *American Merlin* (AK 9302), and renamed and redesignated as AK 323 in April 2005.
76. Former transport [q.v.] *Marine Adder* (T-AP 193).
77. Assigned to the MSC Sealift Program to provide "services when called upon as dry cargo-carrying surge sealift ship."
78. Assigned to the MSC Sealift Program to provide "services when called upon as dry cargo-carrying surge sealift ship."
79. Assigned to the MSC Sealift Program to provide "services when called upon as dry cargo-carrying surge sealift ship."
80. Assigned to the MSC Prepositioning Program to provide "equipment to sustain a Marine Corps Air Ground Task Force for up to 30 days" and able to discharge her cargo in port or at sea using organic lighterage.
81. *Ibid.*
82. *Ibid.*
83. *Ibid.*
84. *Ibid.*
85. Assigned to the MSC Sealift Program to provide "services when called upon as dry cargo-carrying surge sealift ship."
86. *Ibid.*
87. Former USNS *Soderman* (T-AKR 299) assigned to the MSC Prepositioning Program to preposition Army stocks and be available to move common user cargo.
88. Assigned to the MSC Prepositioning Program to provide the Air Force with prepositioned ammunition stocks.
89. Assigned to the MSC Prepositioning Program with Army containers.
90. Assigned to the MSC Prepositioning Program with Army containers.
91. Renamed *Enterprise*.
92. Assigned to the MSC Sealift Program to carry dry cargo.
93. Assigned to the MSC Prepositioning Program to provide the Air Force with prepositioned ammunition stocks.
94. Renamed MV *TSgt John A. Chapman* (AK 323) in April 2005.

Attack Cargo Ships (AKA) / Amphibious Cargo Ships (AKA / LKA)

Beginning in 1943, the Navy converted 16 of its ordinary cargo ships (AK) [q.v.] into specialized vessels to transport heavy equipment, supplies and troops employed in amphibious assaults on enemy beaches. These converted vessels were classified as attack cargo ships, designated with AKA-series hull numbers, and typically armed with one 5-inch/38, four twin 40-mm and twelve 20-mm guns. AKA 1, AKA 2, AKA 6–AKA 8 and AKA 11 were Maritime Commission C1 cargo ships, AKA 3 and AKA 4 were C2-T types, AKA 5 was a C1-A type, AKA 9 was a C2-S, and AKA 10 was a C3-E. The AKAs were equipped with landing craft for ferrying their embarked troops and cargo ashore. The

The Charleston-class amphibious cargo ship *St. Louis* (LKA 116) is performing sea trials off the Virginia coast on October 1, 1969. She was commissioned the following month (U.S. Navy photograph).

first 16 AKAs were supplemented by another 88 attack cargo ships during the war, including 32 vessels of the *Artemis* (AKA 21) class (MC S4-SE2-BE1 type). The largest single group of AKAs was of the 62-ship *Andromeda* (AKA 15) class (MC C2-S-B1 type).

After 1945 the attack cargo ships were no longer considered fleet auxiliaries but were then classified as amphibious warfare vessels. Some of the World War II veterans were later converted to other ship types, such as surveying ships, and others were later returned to active service during the Korean and Vietnam wars. Between 1954 and 1969 six new purpose-built AKAs—USS *Tulare* (AKA 112) and five Charleston (AKA 113–AKA 117) class—joined the fleet as the first AKAs constructed as such from the keel up. They were the final additions to the AKA inventory. In 1969 the Navy reclassified the attack cargo ships as amphibious cargo ships, and redesignated those still on hand as LKAs. The LKA role was assumed by newer amphibious transport docks (LPDs), and the last amphibious cargo ship–USS *El Paso* (LKA 117)–was decommissioned in April 1994 and struck in August 2015. At this writing, she and her four Charleston-class sisters are mothballed in Philadelphia and Pearl Harbor.

AKA 1	Arcturus (ex–AK 18)	AKA 48	Valeria
AKA 2	Procyon (ex–AK 19)	AKA 49	Vanadis[7]
AKA 3	Bellatrix (ex–AK 20)	AKA 50	Veritas
AKA 4	Electra (ex–AK 21)	AKA 51	Xenia[8]
AKA 5	Fomalhaut (ex–AK 22)[1]	AKA 52	Zenobia[9]
AKA 6	Alchiba (ex–AK 23)	AKA 53	Achernar
AKA 7	Alcyone (ex–AK 24)	AKA 54	Algol*
AKA 8	Algorab (ex–AK 25)	AKA 55	Alshain
AKA 9	Alhena (ex–AK 26)	AKA 56	Arneb*
AKA 10	Almaack (ex–AK 27)	AKA 57	Capricornus*
AKA 11	Betelgeuse (ex–AK 28)	AKA 58	Chara[10]
AKA 12	Libra* (ex–AK 53)	AKA 59	Diphda
AKA 13	Titania (ex–AK 55)	AKA 60	Leo
AKA 14	Oberon (ex–AK 56)	AKA 61	Muliphen*
AKA 15	Andromeda (ex–AK 64)	AKA 62	Sheliak
AKA 16	Aquarius (ex–AK 65)	AKA 63	Theenim
AKA 17	Centaurus (ex–AK 66)	AKA 64	Tolland
AKA 18	Cepheus (ex–AK 67)	AKA 65	Shoshone
AKA 19	Thuban[2]	AKA 66	Southampton
AKA 20	Virgo[3]	AKA 67	Starr
AKA 21	Artemis	AKA 68	Stokes
AKA 22	Athene	AKA 69	Suffolk
AKA 23	Aurelia	AKA 70	Tate
AKA 24	Birgit	AKA 71	Todd
AKA 25	Circe	AKA 72	Caswell
AKA 26	Corvus	AKA 73	New Hanover
AKA 27	Devosa	AKA 74	Lenoir
AKA 28	Hydrus	AKA 75	Alamance
AKA 29	Lacerta	AKA 76	Torrance
AKA 30	Lumen	AKA 77	Towner
AKA 31	Medea	AKA 78	Trego
AKA 32	Mellena	AKA 79	Trousdale
AKA 33	Ostara	AKA 80	Tyrrell
AKA 34	Pamina[4]	AKA 81	Valencia
AKA 35	Polana	AKA 82	Venango
AKA 36	Renate[5]	AKA 83	Vinton
AKA 37	Roxane	AKA 84	Waukesha
AKA 38	Sappho	AKA 85	Wheatland
AKA 39	Sarita	AKA 86	Woodford
AKA 40	Scania	AKA 87	Duplin
AKA 41	Selinur	AKA 88	Uvalde
AKA 42	Sidonia	AKA 89	Warrick
AKA 43	Sirona	AKA 90	Whiteside
AKA 44	Sylvania	AKA 91	Whitley
AKA 45	Tabora	AKA 92	Wyandot[11]
AKA 46	Troilus	AKA 93	Yancey*
AKA 47	Turandot[6]	AKA 94	Winston*

3. Directory of U.S. Navy Auxiliary Ships

AKA 95	*Marquette*		AKA 107	*Vermilion**
AKA 96	*Mathews*		AKA 108	*Washburn**
AKA 97	*Merrick**		AKA 109	*San Joaquin*[12]
AKA 98	*Montague*		AKA 110	*Segwick*[13]
AKA 99	*Rolette*		AKA 111	*Whitfield*[14]
AKA 100	*Ogelthorpe*		AKA 112	*Tulare**[15]
AKA 101	*Ottawa*		AKA 113	*Charleston**
AKA 102	*Prentiss*		AKA 114	*Durham**
AKA 103	*Rankin**		AKA 115	*Mobile**
AKA 104	*Seminole**		AKA 116	*St. Louis**
AKA 105	*Skagit**		AKA 117	*El Paso**
AKA 106	*Union**			

Notes

* Redesignated in 1969 as LKA with same hull number.

1. Commissioned as cargo ship [q.v.] AK 22 in March 1942, reclassified as attack cargo ship AKA 5 in February 1943, reclassified as ammunition ship [q.v.] AE 20 in December 1948, and sold for scrapping in April 1970.
2. Laid down as cargo ship AK 68 in February 1943 but commissioned as AKA 19 four months later, struck in January 1977, and disposed of by MARAD in September 1984.
3. First commissioned in July 1943, recommissioned as ammunition ship AE 30 in August 1966, decommissioned in February 1971, and sold for scrapping in November 1973.
4. Commissioned in February 1945, reclassified as a surveying ship [q.v.] and renamed USS *Tanner* (AGS 15) in May 1946, struck in August 1969, and sold for scrapping in August 1970.
5. Commissioned in February 1945, reclassified as a surveying ship and renamed USS *Maury* (AGS 16) in July 1946, struck in December 1969 and sold for scrapping in August 1973.
6. Commissioned in June 1945, converted to a cable repair/laying ship [q.v.] and recommissioned as USS *Aeolus* (ARC 3) in March 1955, transferred to MSC as USNS *Aeolus* (T-ARC 3) in October 1973, struck in February 1985, and sunk as an artificial reef in July 1988.
7. Commissioned in July 1945, recommissioned as a cable repair ship USS *Thor* (ARC 4) in January 1956, transferred to MSC as USNS *Thor* (T-ARC 4) in July 1973, and sold for scrapping in September 1977.
8. Transferred to Chile in December 1946.
9. *Ibid.*
10. Commissioned in June 1944, reclassified as ammunition ship AE 31 in November 1965, struck in March 1972, and sold for scrapping eight months later.
11. Commissioned in September 1944, transferred to MSTS as USNS *Wyandot* (T-AKA 92) in December 1962, later redesignated T-AK 283, laid up in 1976, and sold for scrapping in November 1987.
12. Cancelled in August 1945.
13. *Ibid.*
14. *Ibid.*
15. Commissioned in January 1956, decommissioned in March 1986, struck in August 1992, transferred to NDRF, and sold for scrapping in November 2011.

Auxiliary Cargo Barge/Lighter Ship (AKB)

The Navy formally established the AKB ship classification in January 1993 (in Secretary of the Navy Instruction 5030.1L) but it was omitted from the official listing of ship types in 2006. Similarly, the AKB designation does not appear in the Naval Vessel Register's listing of either active or inactive classification symbols. Apparently no vessel was ever actually designated as an AKB.

Cargo Ship Dock (AKD)

Resembling a Navy amphibious transport dock (LPD), USNS *Point Barrow* (T-AKD 1) was placed in service with MSTS on May 29, 1958. She transported vehicles, supplies and landing craft to U.S. radar stations in the Arctic until 1965. Between 1965 and 1970 the

Constructed with a strengthened hull and bow and fitted with special insulation for Arctic operations, USNS *Point Barrow* (T-AKD 1) is underway on April 18, 1959 (U.S. Navy photograph).

ship hauled NASA Saturn rockets and other Apollo space program equipment from California to Florida, and she also occasionally ferried landing craft to Vietnam. *Point Barrow* was taken out of service in September 1972 and deactivated. Two years later, she was acquired by the Navy and reclassified on March 8, 1974, as an auxiliary deep submergence support ship [q.v.]. She was the only vessel built to a S2-ST-23A hull design and was the Navy's sole AKD.

Dry Cargo and Ammunition Ships / Ammunition Cargo Ships (AKE)

See Chapter 1.

Auxiliary Cargo Float-On/Float-Off Ship (AKF)

FLO/FLO ships have long and low well decks that can be semi-submerged using ballast tanks so that other vessels or large floating cargo can be moved on board for transport. When the FLO/FLO ship's ballast tanks are pumped out, the well deck rises above the water and the cargo is lifted with it. The Navy listed an AKF classification for this type of vessel in the 1990s but it was omitted from the official listing of ship types in 2006. Similarly, the AKF designation does not appear in the Naval Vessel Register's listing of either active or inactive classification symbols. Apparently no vessel was ever actually designated as an AKF.

General Store Ship Issue (AKI)

This is an inactive ship classification in the Naval Vessel Register. See the Stores Issue Ship (AKS) section below for information about this type of auxiliary.

Light Cargo Ships (AKL)

The light cargo ship USS *Banner* (AKL 25) is underway in Pearl Harbor on January 13, 1953. Fourteen years later she was serving as a spy ship designated as AGER 1 (U.S. Navy photograph).

The Navy's 46 light cargo ships were former Army coastal freighters (designated by the Army with FS hull numbers) acquired for naval service generally between 1947 and 1952. Some of the ex-FS vessels were initially classified by the Navy as miscellaneous auxiliaries (AG) [q.v.] before later becoming AKLs. Several of the light cargo ships were never named (AKL 18–AKL 24, for example), three AKLs later became intelligence-gathering spy ships (see the Environmental Research Ships section above), including the ill-fated USS *Pueblo* (AGER 2, ex-AKL 44), and one–USS *Hewell* (AKL 14)–stared in a major motion picture.[1] The last AKL operated by the Navy was USNS *Redbud* (T-AKL 398). She had been acquired from the Coast Guard in July 1949 and operated by MSTS. *Redbud* was struck and returned to USCG in November 1970, and then transferred to the Philippines in March 1972.

AKL 1	*Camano*[2] (ex–FS 256)	AKL 24	(ex–FS 309)
AKL 2	*Deal*[3] (ex–FS 263)	AKL 25	*Banner*[16] (ex–FS 345)
AKL 3	*Elba*[4] (ex–FS 267)	T-AKL 26	(ex–FS 368)
AKL 4	*Errol*[5] (ex–FS 274)	T-AKL 27	(ex–FS 369)
AKL 5	*Estero*[6] (ex–FS 275)	AKL 28	*Brule* (ex–FS 370)
AKL 6	*Jekyl*[7] (ex–FS 282)	AKL 29	(ex–FS 371)
AKL 7	*Metomkin*[8] (ex–FS 316)	AKL 30	(ex–FS 400)
AKL 8	*Rogue*[9] (ex–FS 347)	T-AKL 31	(ex–FS 407)
AKL 9	*Ryer*[10] (ex–FS 361)	AKL 32	(ex–FS 548)
AKL 10	*Sharps*[11] (ex–FS 385)	AKL 33	(ex–FS 238)
AKL 11	*Torry*[12] (ex–FS 394)	AKL 34	(ex–FS 343)
AKL 12	*Mark*[13] (ex–FS 214)	AKL 35	(ex–FS 383)
T-AKL 13	*Tingles*[14] (ex–FS 266)	AKL 36	(ex–FS 398)
AKL 14	*Hewell* (ex–FS 391)	AKL 37	*Alcyone* (ex–FS 195)
T-AKL 15	(ex–FS 230)	AKL 38	*Alhena* (ex–FS 257)
T-AKL 16	(ex–FS 233)	AKL 39	*Almaack* (ex–FS 283)
AKL 17	*New Bedford*[15] (ex–FS 289)	AKL 40	*Deimos* (ex–FS 390)
		AKL 41	(ex–FS 528)
AKL 18	(ex–FS 174)	AKL 42	*Renate* (ex–FS 547)
AKL 19	(ex–FS 175)	AKL 43	(ex–FS 219)
T-AKL 20	(ex–FS 193)	AKL 44	*Pueblo*[17] (ex–FS 344)
AKL 21	(ex–FS 259)	AKL 45	*Palm Beach*[18] (ex–FS 217)
AKL 22	(ex–FS 256)	AKL 398	*Redbud*[19]
AKL 23	(ex–FS 288)		

Notes

1. In the summer of 1954 *Hewell* played the part of the fictitious USS *Reluctant* (AKL 601) in the film "Mister Roberts."
2. AKL 1–AKL 11 were previously designated as the Navy's AG 130–AG 140, respectively.
3. *Ibid.*
4. *Ibid.*
5. *Ibid.*
6. *Ibid.*
7. *Ibid.*
8. *Ibid.*
9. *Ibid.*
10. *Ibid.*
11. *Ibid.*
12. *Ibid.*
13. *Mark* and *Tingles* were previously designated as the Navy's AG 144 and AG 145, respectively.
14. *Ibid.*
15. Reclassified as IX 308 in October 1971, struck in April 1995, and sold to commercial buyer in May 1996.
16. Redesignated as AGER 1 in June 1967.
17. Reclassified as AGER 2 in May 1967.
18. Reclassified as AGER 3 in May 1967.
19. Former Coast Guard lighthouse tender WLB-398.

Net Cargo Ships (AKN)

During World War II the Navy converted four civilian (EC2-S-C1 "Liberty") vessels and one minelayer into net cargo ships (AKN). These ships served as floating depots and transports for large nets intended to defend harbors and anchorages against submarine attack. Commissioned between 1943 and 1946, all of the AKNs but one were sold for scrapping by 1973; *Keokuk*, the oldest net cargo ship by far, was sold in 1947 to a steamship operator.

The net cargo ship USS *Keokuk* (AKN 4) had been a net layer and minelayer before becoming a net cargo ship. She is seen here a year or two before her 1945 decommissioning (U.S. Navy photograph).

AKN 1	*Indus*	AKN 4	*Keokuk*[1]
AKN 2	*Sagittarius*	AKN 5	*Zebra*[2]
AKN 3	*Tuscana*	AKN 6	*Galilea*[3]

NOTES

1. Originally laid down as the steamship *Henry M. Flagler* in 1914, later SS *Columbia Heights*, acquired by the Navy in July 1941 to become a coastal minelayer but reclassified as a net layer and renamed *Keokuk* (AN 5) the next month. She was reclassified as a minelayer (CM 8) in May 1942, reclassified as AKN 4 in November 1943, decommissioned in December 1945, and sold in March 1947 to a commercial operator.

2. Acquired in October 1943 as unclassified miscellaneous vessel IX 107, reclassified as AKN 5 in February 1944, decommissioned in January 1946, struck the next month, and sold for scrapping in March 1972.

3. Laid down as a net layer *Montauck* (AN 2) in April 1942, reclassified as transport [q.v.] AP 161 in August 1943, reclassified as landing ship vehicle (LSV 6) in April 1944, reclassified as AKN 6 and renamed *Galilea* in October 1946, decommissioned in July 1947, struck in September 1961, and sold for scrapping in June 1973.

Vehicle Cargo Ships (AKR)

See Chapter 2.

Stores Issue Ships / General Stores Issue Ships (AKS)

Between 1941 and 1952 the Navy created nearly three dozen mobile warehouses for general stores (e.g., office supplies, toilet paper and canned goods) by converting existing naval and Maritime Commission vessels into general stores issue ships (designated as AKS). AKS 3 was converted from a miscellaneous auxiliary, AKS 20 from a former cargo ship, AKS 1 and AKS 2 were Maritime Commission C2 cargo ships, AKS 4 was a C2-F, and AKS 5–AKS 15 were EC2-S-C1 "Liberty" ships. During World War II these ships were usually stationed in rear areas, distributed their stores piecemeal to requisitioning

USS *Gratia* (AKS 11) was commissioned in November 1944, carried stores and passengers in the Pacific, decommissioned in July 1946, struck in the following year, and dismantled in 1964 (U.S. Navy photograph).

ships and shore facilities, and were resupplied in turn by cargo ships [q.v.] (AKs) deployed from the United States to re-provision the store issue ships. During the 1960s and early 1970s the surviving AKS vessels still left in the NDRF were slowly sold off for dismantling until, by 1973, none were left.

AKS 1	*Castor*	AKS 16	*Blackford*[3]	AKS 27	*Electron*[14]
AKS 2	*Pollux*[1]	AKS 17	*Dorchester*[4]	AKS 28	*Proton*[15]
AKS 3	*Antares*[2]	AKS 18	*Kingman*[5]	AKS 29	*Colington*[16]
AKS 4	*Pollux*	AKS 19	*Presque Isle*[6]	AKS 30	*League Island*[17]
AKS 5	*Acubens*	AKS 20	*Mercury*[7]		
AKS 6	*Kochab*	AKS 21	*Belle Isle*[8]	AKS 31	*Chimon*[18]
AKS 7	*Luna*	AKS 22	*Coasters Harbor*[9]	AKS 32	*Altair*[19]
AKS 8	*Talita*			AKS 33	*Antares*[20]
AKS 9	*Volans*	AKS 23	*Cuttyhunk Island*[10]		
AKS 10	*Cybele*				
AKS 11	*Gratia*	AKS 24	*Avery Island*[11]		
AKS 12	*Hecuba*				
AKS 13	*Hesperia*	AKS 25	*Indian Island*[12]		
AKS 14	*Iolanda*				
AKS 15	*Liguria*	AKS 26	*Kent Island*[13]		

Notes

1. Commissioned in May 1941 and lost after grounding in February 1942. Struck the following month.
2. Commissioned as miscellaneous auxiliary [q.v.] AG 10 in February 1922, reclassified as AKS 3 in November 1940, decommissioned in August 1946, and sold for scrapping in September 1947.
3. AKS 16–AKS 18 reclassified as self-propelled barracks ships [q.v.] APB 45–APB 47, respectively, in 1945.

4. *Ibid.*
5. *Ibid.*
6. Renamed *Vanderburgh* and reclassified APB 48 in 1945.
7. Formerly classified as cargo ship [q.v.] AK 42, reclassified as AKS 20 in July 1945, decommissioned in May 1959, and sold for scrapping in May 1975.
8. AKS 21–AKS 26 were formerly miscellaneous auxiliary ships AG 73–AG 78, respectively.
9. *Ibid.*
10. *Ibid.*
11. *Ibid.*
12. *Ibid.*
13. *Ibid.*
14. AKS 27–AK 31 were formerly miscellaneous auxiliary ships AG 146–AG 150, respectively.
15. *Ibid.*
16. *Ibid.*
17. *Ibid.*
18. *Ibid.*
19. Commissioned in January 1952 as cargo ship AK 257, reclassified as AKS 32 in December 1953, decommissioned in May 1969, and sold for scrapping in January 1975.
20. Commissioned in February 1952 as cargo ship AK 258, reclassified as AKS 33 in April 1959, decommissioned in December 1964, and sold for scrapping in April 1974.

Aircraft Transports / Aircraft Cargo Ships / Cargo Ship and Aircraft Ferries (AKV)

On June 15, 1943, the aircraft transport USS *Card* (ACV 11) is in the Atlantic ferrying six F4F Wildcat fighters and seven TBF/TBM Avenger torpedo bombers on her flight deck. She would later be redesignated as T-AKV 40, sunk during the Vietnam War and returned to service (U.S. Navy photograph).

During World War II and into the 1960s the Navy employed a few former merchant ships and some *Casablanca* (CVE 55)- and *Commencement Bay* (CVE 108)-class escort aircraft carriers (CVEs) to transport aircraft as ordinary cargo over long distances. Initially classified as "transport and aircraft ferries" [q.v.] and designated as APVs, these vessels were reclassified as "aircraft transports" (AKV) in September 1943 and later as "aircraft cargo ships." On May 7, 1959, the classification of 32 inactive and four active CVEs then in the fleet—which had previously been designated as escort aircraft carriers (CVE), helicopter escort aircraft carriers (CVHE), and utility aircraft carriers (CVU)— was changed to "cargo ship and aircraft ferry" and redesignated as AKV 8–AKV 43. None of the AKVs remain afloat today; almost all were disposed of by government sale to be cut up for scrap.

AKV 1	Kitty Hawk[1]	AKV 23	Tinian[23]
AKV 2	Hammondsport[2]	AKV 24	Nehenta Bay[24]
T-AKV 3	LT. James E. Robinson[3]	AKV 25	Hoggatt Bay[25]
T-AKV 4	Pvt. Joseph F. Merrell[4]	AKV 26	Kadashan Bay[26]
T-AKV 5	Sgt. Jack J. Pendelton[5]	AKV 27	Marcus Island[27]
T-AKV 6	Albert M. Boe[6]	AKV 28	Savo Island[28]
T-AKV 7	Cardinal O'Connell[7]	AKV 29	Rudyerd Bay[29]
AKV 8	Kula Gulf[8]	AKV 30	Sitkoh Bay[30]
AKV 9	Cape Gloucester[9]	AKV 31	Takanis Bay[31]
AKV 10	Salerno Bay[10]	AKV 32	Lunga Point[32]
AKV 11	Vela Gulf[11]	AKV 33	Hollandia[33]
AKV 12	Siboney[12]	AKV 34	Kwajalein[34]
AKV 13	Puget Sound[13]	AKV 35	Bougainville[35]
AKV 14	Rendova[14]	AKV 36	Matanikau[36]
AKV 15	Bairoko[15]	AKV 37	Commencement Bay[37]
AKV 16	Badoneng Strait[16]	AKV 38	Block Island[38]
AKV 17	Saidor[17]	AKV 39	Gilbert Islands[39]
AKV 18	Sicily[18]	AKV 40	Card[40]
AKV 19	Point Cruz[19]	AKV 41	Core[41]
AKV 20	Mindoro[20]	AKV 42	Breton[42]
AKV 21	Rabaul[21]	AKV 43	Croatan[43]
AKV 22	Palau[22]		

Notes

1. Acquired in June 1941 and commissioned as transport and aircraft ferry [q.v.] APV 1 in November 1941, reclassified as aircraft transport AKV 1 in September 1943, decommissioned in January 1946, and struck the next month.
2. Commissioned in December 1941 as APV 2, reclassified as AKV 2 in September 1943, decommissioned in March 1946, and struck the next month.
3. Acquired in March 1950 and assigned to MSTS as T-AKV 3, reclassified as miscellaneous auxiliary [q.v.] T-AG 170 in December 1962, reclassified as cargo ship [q.v.] T-AK 274 in January 1964, and struck in January 1981.
4. Acquired in March 1950 and assigned to MSTS as T-AKV 4, reclassified as T-AK 275, and struck in August 1974.
5. Acquired in March 1950 and assigned to MSTS as T-AKV 5, reclassified as T-AK 276, ran aground in 1973 and lost.
6. T-AKV 6–T-AKV 7 acquired in March 1950 and struck in March 1954.
7. Ibid.
8. AKV 8–AKV 23 were formerly CVE 108–CVE 123, respectively.
9. Ibid.
10. Ibid.
11. Ibid.
12. Ibid.
13. Ibid.
14. Ibid.
15. Ibid.
16. Ibid.
17. Ibid.
18. Ibid.
19. Ibid.

20. *Ibid.*
21. *Ibid.*
22. *Ibid.*
23. *Ibid.*
24. AKV 24–AKV 28 were formerly CVE 74–CVE 78, respectively.
25. *Ibid.*
26. *Ibid.*
27. *Ibid.*
28. *Ibid.*
29. Former CVE 81.
30. Former CVE 86.
31. Former CVE 89.
32. Former CVE 94.
33. AKV 33–AKV 34 were formerly CVE 97–CVE 98, respectively.
34. *Ibid.*
35. AKV 35–AKV 36 were formerly CVE 100–CVE 101, respectively.
36. *Ibid.*
37. AKV 37–AKV 38 were formerly CVE 105–CVE 106, respectively.
38. *Ibid.*
39. Former CVE 107, renamed *Annapolis* and reclassified as major communications relay ship [q.v.] AGMR 1 in June 1963.
40. Formerly designated as AVG 11, CVE 11 and CVHE 11; reclassified as cargo ship and aircraft ferry T-AKV 40, sunk in Saigon, South Vietnam, on May 3, 1964, raised on May 19 and returned to service on December 11, 1964; transferred to NDRF in March 1970, and sold for scrapping in May 1971.
41. Formerly designated as AVG 13, ACV 13, CVE 13, CVHE 13 and T-CVU 13; reclassified as T-AKV 41 in May 1959, removed from service in November 1969, and sold for scrapping in April 1971.
42. Formerly designated as AVG 23, ACV 23, CVE 23, CVHE 23 and T-CVU 23; reclassified as T-AKV 42 in May 1959, and sold for scrapping in February 1972.
43. Formerly designated as AGV 25, ACV 25, CVE 25, CVHE 25 and T-CVU 25; reclassified as T-AKV 43 in May 1959, removed from service in October 1969, and sold for scrapping in February 1971.

Net Tenders (AN) / Net Laying Ships (AN) / Net Laying Ships (ANL)

With her distinctive "horns" marking her as a net layer, USS *Winterberry* (AN 56) is engaged in sea trials in San Francisco Bay in 1944 (U.S. Navy photograph).

The job of laying out and maintaining floating steel nets in channels and anchorages was performed during World War II by the Navy's net tenders. The net arrays were used to prevent enemy submarines and small craft from entering a protected harbor or anchorage. Later in the war smaller nets were placed around individual ships at anchor to defend against torpedoes.

The first net tenders of the Aloe class (YN 1–YN 32) were put in service in 1941 and in full commission in 1942, and were rated at the time as yard and district craft, not auxiliaries. They were followed in 1943 by the Ailanthus class (AN 38–AN 74) and in 1945 by the Cohoes class (AN 78–AN 92).[1] In January 1944, the net tenders were rated as auxiliary ships, reclassified as "net laying ships" and redesignated with an "AN" hull classification symbol. In January 1969, that symbol was changed to "ANL."

Net tenders typically were diesel-powered with about 1,200 shp, displaced from 700 to 1,200 tons, manned by four officers and 44 enlisted personnel, and cruised some 5,000 miles at 10 knots. Their most distinctive identifying feature was a double bowsprit—called "the horns"—between which nets and gear could be streamed out or brought on board.

Most members of the Ailanthus class were sold in 1947 and most vessels of the Aloe class were sold or transferred to other navies in the 1970s. Vessels of the Cohoe class were decommissioned over a 25-year period beginning in 1946 and struck between 1962 and 1977. USS *Cohoes* (ANL 78) was the last of the net layers to be decommissioned (on June 30, 1972).

USS *Cohoes* (AN 78) is underway near Pearl Harbor in Hawaii on May 6, 1968 (U.S. Navy photograph).

3. Directory of U.S. Navy Auxiliary Ships

AN 1	Monitor[2]	AN 33	Nutmeg	AN 65	Palo Verde[29]
AN 2	Montauk[3]	AN 34	Teaberry	AN 66	Pinon
AN 3	Osage[4]	AN 35	Teak	AN 67	Shellbark
AN 4	Saugus[5]	AN 36	Pepperwood[17]	AN 68	Silverleaf
AN 5	Keokuk[6]	AN 37	Yew[18]	AN 69	Stagbush
AN 6	Aloe	AN 38	Ailanthus[19]	AN 70	Allthorn[30]
AN 7	Ash	AN 39	Bitterbush	AN 71	Tesota[31]
AN 8	Boxwood	AN 40	Anagua	AN 72	Yaupon[32]
AN 9	Butternut[7]	AN 41	Baretta	AN 73	Precept[33]
AN 10	Catalpa	AN 42	Cliffrose[20]	AN 74	Boxelder[34]
AN 11	Chestnut	AN 43	Satinleaf	AN 75	Prefect[35]
AN 12	Cinchona	AN 44	Corkwood	AN 76	Satinwood[36]
AN 13	Buckeye[8]	AN 45	Cornel	AN 77	Preventer[37]
AN 14	Buckthorn	AN 46	Mastic	AN 78	Cohoes
AN 15	Ebony	AN 47	Canotia	AN 79	Etlah[38]
AN 16	Eucalyptus	AN 48	Lancewood[21]	AN 80	Suncock
AN 17	Chinquapin[9]	AN 49	Papaya	AN 81	Manayunk
AN 18	Gum Tree	AN 50	Cinnamon[22]	AN 82	Marietta[39]
AN 19	Holly	AN 51	Silverbell[23]	AN 83	Nahant
AN 20	Elder	AN 52	Snowbell[24]	AN 84	Naubuc[40]
AN 21	Larch[10]	AN 53	Spicewood	AN 85	Oneota
AN 22	Locust[11]	AN 54	Manchineel	AN 86	Passaconaway[41]
AN 23	Mahogany	AN 55	Torchwood[25]		
AN 24	Mango	AN 56	Winterberry	AN 87	Passaic[42]
AN 25	Hackberry[12]	AN 57	Viburnum	AN 88	Shakamaxon
AN 26	Mimosa	AN 58	Abele	AN 89	Tonawanda[43]
AN 27	Mulberry[13]	AN 59	Terebinth	AN 90	Tunxis[44]
AN 28	Palm	AN 60	Catclaw[26]	AN 91	Waxsaw[45]
AN 29	Hazel[14]	AN 61	Chinaberry	AN 92	Yazoo
AN 30	Redwood	AN 62	Hoptree	AN 93[46]	
AN 31	Rosewood[15]	AN 63	Whitewood[27]		
AN 32	Sandalwood[16]	AN 64	Palo Blanco[28]		

Notes

1. AN 6–AN 37 were formerly YN 1–YN 32, AN 38–AN 59 were formerly YN 57–YN 78, AN 60–AN 66 were formerly YN 81–YN 87, AN 67–AN 72 were formerly YN 91–YN 96, and AN 78–AN 83 were formerly YN 97–YN 102, respectively.
2. AN 1–AN 2 reclassified as transports [q.v.] AP 160–AP 161, respectively, in August 1943.
3. Ibid.
4. AN 3–AN 4 reclassified as transports AP 108–AP 109, respectively, in May 1943.
5. Ibid.
6. Commissioned as AN 5 in February 1942, reclassified as minelayer CM 8 in May 1942, and reclassified as net cargo ship [q.v.] AKN 4 in November 1943.
7. Redesignated as ANL 9 in January 1969, reclassified as miscellaneous auxiliary (yard craft) YAG 60, struck in July 1971, and expended as a target in June 1977.
8. Authorized as *Cottonwood* (YN 8) but commissioned as USS *Buckeye* (YN 8) in December 1942, reclassified as net layer AN 13 in January 1944, decommissioned in March 1947, struck in July 1963 and used as a salvage training hulk in Hawaii.
9. Laid down as *Fir* (YN 120) in March 1941, commissioned as *Chinquapin* (AN 12) in January 1943, redesignated as AN 17 in January 1944, and decommissioned in March 1946.
10. Transferred to Turkey in May 1948.
11. Transferred to France in 1966.
12. Sold to France in March 1949.
13. Sold to Ecuador in August 1978.
14. Laid down as *Poplar* (YN 24) but commissioned as *Hazel* in December 1942, redesignated as AN 29 in January 1944, struck in September 1962, and sold for scrapping.
15. Sold to France in 1969.
16. Transferred to France in September 1967.

17. Sold to France in March 1949.
18. *Ibid.*
19. Ran aground in Alaska in February 1944 and lost.
20. Transferred to Republic of China (Taiwan) in 1947.
21. Laid down as *Ironwood* (YN 67) in October 1942 but commissioned as USS *Lancewood* (YN 67) in October 1943, reclassified as AN 48 in January 1944, decommissioned in February 1946, and sold in April 1947.
22. Laid down in November 1942 as *Royal Palm* (YN 69) but commissioned as *Cinnamon* (YN 69) and reclassified as AN 50 in January 1944, and decommissioned and transferred to Republic of China in March 1947.
23. Transferred to Republic of China (Taiwan) in 1947.
24. *Ibid.*
25. *Ibid.*
26. Transferred to Republic of China in 1946.
27. Converted for ice operations and reclassified as miscellaneous auxiliary [q.v.] AG 129 in January 1947, and sold in 1950.
28. Laid down as YN 85 in May 1943 but commissioned as auxiliary fleet tug [q.v.] ATA 214 in September 1944, and sold in April 1947.
29. Laid down as YN 86 in July 1943 but commissioned as ATA 215 in December 1944, decommissioned in June 1946, struck in December 1948, and sold in February 1949.
30. Laid down as YN 74 in October 1943 but commissioned as ATA 216 in October 1944.
31. Laid down as YN 95 in December 1943 but commissioned as ATA 217 in January 1945.
32. Laid down as AN 72 in January 1944 but commissioned as ATA 218 in March 1945.
33. Transferred under Lend Lease to U.K. in October 1944, returned in January 1945, and struck in March 1946.
34. Transferred to U.K. in December 1944, returned in December 1945, and struck in March 1946.
35. Transferred to U.K. in June 1944, returned in December 1945, and struck in March 1946.
36. Transferred to U.K. in August 1944, returned in November 1945, struck in March 1946, and sold in July 1947.
37. Transferred to U.K. in September 1944, returned in January 1946, and struck in March 1946.
38. Decommissioned in May 1960 and sold to Dominican Republic in September 1976.
39. Transferred to Venezuela in 1962 and sold to that nation in December 1977.
40. Reclassified as non-self-propelled salvage craft tender YRST 4 in April 1968, and sold for scrapping in September 1975.
41. Sold to Dominican Republic in September 1976.
42. *Ibid.*
43. Transferred to Haiti in May 1960 and sold to that nation in 1979.
44. Transferred to Venezuela in 1963.
45. *Ibid.*
46. Never entered U.S. service when built, transferred to the Netherlands in 1952 (1952–1969) and subsequently to Turkey in September 1970.

Oilers (AO)

See Chapter 1.

Fast Combat Support Ships (AOE)

See Chapter 1.

Gasoline Tankers (AOG)

Serving between 1943 and the 1970, the Navy's AOGs transported from point to point thousands of gallons of aviation gasoline and light petroleum products. The majority of these gasoline tankers belonged to the *Patatpsco* (AOG 1) and *Mettawee* (AOG 17) classes. The former vessels, AOG 1–AOG 11 and AOG 48–AOG 59, were completed in 1943, 311-feet long, displaced 4,130 tons (full load) and carried 2,120 tons of gasoline as cargo. The latter grouping, AOG 17–AOG 63, were completed in 1943–1945, 221-feet long, displaced 2,280 tons (full load) and carried 1,228 tons of gasoline as cargo. AOG 17–AOG 46 and AOG 60–AOG 63 were Maritime Commission T1-M-A2 coastal tankers. Members of a third AOG class, Klickitat (AOG 64–AOG 75), were MC T1-M-BT1 coastal tankers completed in 1945, 325-feet long, displaced 5,940 tons (full load), and carried 30,000 barrels of gasoline. AOG 47 was converted from an oiler. Seven AOGs were transferred to other countries (France, Taiwan, New Zealand and Argentina) between 1948 and 1967.

Commissioned in July 1944, the gasoline tanker USS *Calamus* (AOG 25) is operating off San Francisco two months before her May 1946 decommissioning (U.S. Navy photograph).

Some of the World War II-era AOGs went on to serve during the Korean and Vietnam wars. The last three of those veterans—USS *Chewaucan* (AOG 50), USS *Nespelen* (AOG 55) and USS *Noxubee* (AOG 56)—were struck in 1975.

In 1949–1950, the Navy acquired five former merchant tankers (T-AOG 76–T-AOG 80), which were assigned to MSTS. They were later either transferred to other navies or sold for scrapping by March 1982, although USNS *Nodaway* (T-AOG 78) remained in the MSC Ready Reserve Force until September 2006. She was sold to a Japanese company three months later. Finally, in the summer of 1957, the two most recent gasoline tankers—T-AOG 81 and T-AOG 82—began operating with MSC to support U.S. activities in the Arctic. They were sold in December 2006.

AOG 1	*Patapsco*	AOG 12	*Halawa*	AOG 22	*Wautauga*[12]
AOG 2	*Kern*[1]	AOG 13	*Kaloli*	AOG 23	*Ammonusuc*
AOG 3	*Rio Grande*	AOG 14	*Aroostook*[7]		
AOG 4	*Wabash*[2]	AOG 15	*Conusauga*	AOG 24	*Sheepscot*[13]
AOG 5	*Susquehanna*[3]	AOG 16	*Guyandot*[8]	AOG 25	*Calamus*
		AOG 17	*Mettawee*[9]	AOG 26	*Chiwaukum*[14]
AOG 6	*Agawam*	AOG 18	*Pasquetank*[10]		
AOG 7	*Elkhorn*[4]			AUG 27	*Escatawpa*
AOG 8	*Genesee*[5]	AOG 19	*Sakatonchee*[11]	AUG 28	*Gualala*[15]
AOG 9	*Kishwaukee*			AOG 29	*Hiwassee*
AOG 10	*Nemasket*	AOG 20	*Seekonk*	AOG 30	*Kalamazoo*[16]
AOG 11	*Tombigbee*[6]	AOG 21	*Sequatchie*		

AOG 31	Kanawha	AOG 49	Chestatee[22]	AOG 67	Nodaway		
AOG 32	Narraguagas	AOG 50	Chewaucan	AOG 68	Peconic[34]		
AOG 33	Ochlockonee	AOG 51	Maquoketa[23]	AOG 69	Petaluma		
AOG 34	Oconee	AOG 52	Mattabesset	AOG 70	Piscataqua		
AOG 35	Ogeechee	AOG 53	Namakagon[24]	AOG 71	Quinnebaug[35]		
AOG 36	Ontonagon[17]	AOG 54	Natchaug[25]	AOG 72	Sebasticook[36]		
AOG 37	Yahara	AOG 55	Nespelen[26]	AOG 73	Kiamichi[37]		
AOG 38	Ponchatoula	AOG 56	Noxubee[27]	AOG 74	Tellico[38]		
AOG 39	Quastinet	AOG 57	Pecatonica[28]	AOG 75	Truckee[39]		
AOG 40	Sacandaga[18]	AOG 58	Pinnebog[29]	T-AOG 76	Tonti[40]		
AOG 41	Tetonkaha	AOG 59	Wacissa[30]	T-AOG 77	Rincon[41]		
AOG 42	Towaliga[19]	AOG 60	Manokin	T-AOG 78	Nodaway[42]		
AOG 43	Tularosa	AOG 61	Sakonnet	T-AOG 79	Petaluma[43]		
AOG 44	Wakulla	AOG 62	Conemaugh	T-AOG 80	Piscataqua		
AOG 45	Yacona	AOG 63	Klaskanine[31]	T-AOG 81	Alatna		
AOG 46	Waupaca	AOG 64	Klickitat	T-AOG 82	Chattahoochee		
AOG 47	Shikellamy[20]	AOG 65	Michigamme[32]				
AOG 48	Chehalis[21]	AOG 66	Nanticoke[33]				

Notes

1. Commissioned in March 1943, assigned to MSTS and redesignated as T-AOG 2 in July 1950, and sold for scrapping in December 1975.
2. Commissioned in May 1943, assigned to MSTS as T-AOG 4 in 1950, removed from service in September 1957, and struck in May 1958.
3. Commissioned in June 1943, assigned to MSTS as T-AOG 5 in July 1950, struck in March 1959, and sold for scrapping in August 1973.
4. Sold to Taiwan in May 1972.
5. Transferred to Chile in November 1987.
6. Sold to Greece in July 1978.
7. Sold to France in March 1949.
8. Ibid.
9. Laid down as self-propelled gasoline barge Clearwater (YOG 47) but commissioned as Mettawee (AOG 17) in August 1943, and sold for scrapping in January 1964.
10. Formerly designated as YOG 48 and reclassified as AOG 18 in March 1943.
11. Formerly YOG 49 and commissioned as AOG 19 in January 1944.
12. Transferred to Republic of China in 1948.
13. Ran aground in June 1945 and scrapped.
14. Transferred to Turkey in May 1948.
15. Sold to Brazil in 1948.
16. Sold to Colombia in 1947.
17. Commissioned in September 1944, transferred to U.S. Army in 1946, assigned to MSTS as T-AOG 36 in 1952, taken out of service in September 1956, and sold for scrapping in January 1964.
18. Ran aground in October 1945 and struck two months later.
19. Transferred to Republic of China in 1948.
20. Commissioned as oiler [q.v.] AO 90 in April 1943, reclassified as AOG 47 in July 1943, decommissioned in January 1946 and struck the next month.
21. Exploded and lost on October 7, 1949.
22. Commissioned in December 1944, assigned to MSTS as T-AOG 49 in March 1952, taken out of service in November 1956, and sold for scrapping in October 1975.
23. Commissioned in February 1945, assigned to MSTS as T-AOG 51 in March 1952, taken out of service in October 1957, and sold in December 1975.
24. Transferred to New Zealand in June 1962 and to Taiwan in May 1976.
25. Transferred to Greece in 1959.
26. Sold for scrapping in March 1976.
27. Ibid.

28. Transferred to Taiwan in April 1961.
29. Assigned to MSTS as T-AOG 58 in March 1952, taken out of service in July 1954, and sold for scrapping in December 1987.
30. Assigned to MSTS as T-AOG 59 in February 1952, transferred to USAF in September 1957, and sold for scrapping in May 1964.
31. Sold to Brazil in 1948.
32. Sold to Argentina in 1948.
33. Sold to Argentina in 1946.
34. Assigned to MSTS as T-AOG 68 in October 1949, taken out of service in November 1957, and sold for scrapping in December 1982.
35. Navy acquisition cancelled in August 1945.
36. *Ibid.*
37. *Ibid.*
38. *Ibid.*
39. *Ibid.*
40. Assigned to MSTS in October 1949, taken out of service in July 1960, and transferred to Colombia in January 1965.
41. Assigned to MSTS in 1950 and transferred to South Korea in February 1982.
42. Sold in December 2006.
43. Assigned to MSTS in 1950 and transferred to South Korea in February 1982.

Replenishment Oilers (AOR)

The replenishment oiler USS *Milwaukee* (AOR 2) is engaged in sea trials off Massachusetts in October 1969 (U.S. Navy photograph).

The seven *Wichita* (AOR 1)-class replenishment oilers combined the role of fleet oiler (AO), with a lesser capability as an ammunition ship (AE) and combat stores ship (AKS). The AORs delivered petroleum and munitions to warships employing fuel hoses and UH-46 Sea Knight helicopters while underway. Commissioned between June 1969 and October 1976, these vessels were 659 feet long with a beam of 96 feet and a draft of 37 feet. They could carry 160,000 barrels of petroleum, 600 tons of munitions, 200 tons of dry stores and 100 tons of refrigerated stores. The Wichita class was decommissioned between March 1993 and October 1995, and all were sold for scrapping between July 2008 and June 2013.

The atypical USS *Conecuh* (AOR 110) had been built for the German Navy in 1938 as the combination oil and supply U-boat tender *Dithmarschen*. She was allocated to the United States as a war prize in January 1946 and went into U.S. service designated as the unclassified miscellaneous vessel IX 301. She was used to evaluate the concept of "one-stop" oil and supply replenishment. IX 301 was renamed *Conecuh* and reclassified as a fleet oiler (AO 110) in October 1946, reclassified as a replenishment oiler (AOR 110) in September 1952, commissioned as such in February 1953, decommissioned in April 1956, struck in June 1960, and sold five months later to be dismantled.

AOR 1	Wichita	AOR 4	Savannah	AOR 7	Roanoke
AOR 2	Milwaukee	AOR 5	Wabash	AOR 110	Conecuh
AOR 3	Kansas City	AOR 6	Kalamazoo		

Submarine Oiler (AOSS)

The submarine USS *Guavina* is refueling a seaplane at sea in 1955 (U.S. Navy photograph).

USS *Guavina* (SS 362) was commissioned in December 1943 as a Gato-class fleet submarine. Between March 1949 and February 1950, she was converted into a submarine oiler and redesignated as SSO 362. The conversion entailed fitting the sub with side blisters which enabled her to carry 160,000 gallons of fuel and increased her beam by ten feet. *Guavina* was then used to test the feasibility of refueling seaplanes (such as the planned P6M SeaMaster) and other submarines. At one point during the testing, she refueled the submarine USS *Dogfish* (SS 350)—while both boats were submerged.[1] *Guavina* was reclassified as an auxiliary submarine (AGSS 362) in December 1951 and then back to submarine oiler (AOSS 362) in June 1957. Following this last redesignation, she continued evaluating various procedures for both submarine and seaplane refueling until early 1959, when she was decommissioned. Struck from the Naval Register in June 1967, the former AOSS 362 was sunk as a target by USS *Cubera* (SS 347) on November 14, 1967.

NOTE

1. Polmar. *The American Submarine*, 91.

Transport Oilers (AOT)

See Chapter 2.

Transports (AP)

The transport USS *War Hawk* (AP 168) spent her career in the Pacific war. She is seen here in San Francisco Bay in 1945–1946 (U.S. Navy photograph).

The Navy's transports carried troops (and sometimes their dependents) between the United States and distant ports, primarily in Europe and Asia.

EARLY TRANSPORTS

During and immediately following the Spanish-American War of 1898, for example, the transports *Lawton*, *City of Peking*, and *Manila* delivered soldiers to the Far East. Other ships designated as transports early in the 20th century included USS *Buffalo* (between 1906 and 1915; later reclassified as destroyer tender [q.v.] AD 8), USS *Dixie* (1899–1902; later reclassified as AD 1), and USS *Prairie* (1906–1917; later reclassified as AD 5). In World War I, the Navy operated 45 commissioned vessels to ferry American doughboys to the battlefields in Europe. Almost all of those transports were former civilian passenger ships, including 16 German vessels appropriated in U.S. harbors. At war's end in 1918, the flow of troops to the front was reversed and 80 additional ex–civilian vessels were added to the Navy's own transport force to help bring home more than 2 million troops.[1]

LATER TRANSPORTS

During the interwar years, the transport force shrank considerably such that by 1939 there were just two troopships in commission: USS *Henderson* (AP 1) and USS *Chaumont* (AP 5). Two years later, when the Japanese attacked Pearl Harbor, the Navy had 44 APs on hand. That number doubled during the war; there were 85 APs on the Navy List by January 1945, including a number of Maritime Commission P2 and C4 types then being built. (Several older Navy transports had been transferred to the Army Transportation Corps in 1943 and 1944. In addition, three APs had been reconfigured into hospital ships [q.v.], six were converted to vehicle landing ships [LSV] and 58 APs had been reclassified as attack transports [q.v.] in 1942.)

The largest group of World War II transports belonged to the 30-vessel General Squier class (AP 130–AP 159). These Maritime Commission C4-S-A1 type ships were 523 feet long, could steam at 17 knots, and carried 3,000–3,800 troops. The "General" class (AP 110–AP 119 and AP 176) were MC P2-S2-R2 types, 62-feet long, capable of 19 knots, with a capacity of more than 5,500 troops. The "Admiral" class (AP 120–AP 127) was comprised of P2-SE2-R1 vessels. They had a top speed of 19 knots and could carry some 4,500 troops. When the Japanese surrendered in September 1945, more than 90 AP transports were in service, with a combined capacity of more than 300,000 troops.

During the postwar period, the transport force shrank again, with only eight APs on the Navy's Vessel Register in January 1950. The Korean War changed all that, when a number of transports were pulled out of the mothball fleet for active service. By January 1958, there were 53 APs left on the Register, many of which were still active. In 1965, with the Vietnam War underway, seven P2-SE2-R1, four P2-S2-R2 and three P2-S1-DN3 type transports were in service with the Navy's MSTS. USNS *Geiger* (T-AP 197), commissioned in September 1952, was the last of the troopships. She was taken out of service and transferred to MARAD for layup in April 1971. After a stint with the Massachusetts Maritime Academy in the early 1980s as TS *Bay State* (IV), she was sold for scrapping in October 1986.

AP 1	*Henderson*[2]	AP 11	*Barnett*[10]
AP 2	*Doyan*[3]	AP 12	*Heywood*[11]
AP 3	*Hancock*[4]	AP 13	*George F. Elliott*[x]
AP 4	*Argonne*[5]	AP 14	*Fuller*[12]
AP 5	*Chaumont*[6]	AP 15	*William P. Biddle*
AP 6	*William Ward Burrows*	AP 16	*Neville*[13]
AP 7	*Wharton*	AP 17	*Harry Lee*[14]
AP 8	*Harris*[7]	AP 18	*Feland*[15]
AP 9	*Zeilin*[8]	AP 19	*Catlin*[16]
AP 10	*McCawley*[9]	AP 20	*Munargo*

3. Directory of U.S. Navy Auxiliary Ships

AP 21	Wakefield	AP 74	Lejeune
AP 22	Mount Vernon	AP 75	Gemini[47]
AP 23	West Point	AP 76	Anne Arundel
AP 24	Orizaba	AP 77	Thurston
AP 25	Leonard Wood[17]	AP 78	Bayfield[48]
AP 26	Joseph T. Dickman[18]	AP 79	Bolivar[49]
AP 27	Hunter Liggett[19]	AP 80	Callaway[50]
AP 28	Kent	AP 81	Cambria[51]
AP 29	U.S. Grant	AP 82	Cavalier[52]
AP 30	Henry T. Allen[20]	AP 83	Chilton[53]
AP 31	Chateau Thierry	AP 84	Clay[54]
AP 32	St. Mihiel	AP 85	Custer[55]
AP 33	Republic	AP 86	DuPage[56]
AP 34	J. Franklin Bell[21]	AP 87	Elmore[57]
AP 35	American Legion[22]	AP 88	Fayette[58]
AP 36	John L. Clem[23]	AP 89	Fremont[59]
AP 37	President Jackson[24]	AP 90	Henrico[60]
AP 38	President Adams[25]	AP 91	Knox[61]
AP 39	President Hayes[26]	AP 92	Lamar[62]
AP 40	Crescent City[27]	AP 93	Leon[63]
AP 41	Stratford[28]	AP 94	Ormsby[64]
AP 42	Tusker H. Bliss[x]	AP 95	Pierce[65]
AP 43	Hugh L. Scott[x]	AP 96	Sheridan[66]
AP 44	Willard A. Holbrook[29]	AP 97	Sumter[67]
AP 45	Thomas H. Barry[30]	AP 98	Warren[68]
AP 46	James Parker[31]	AP 99	Wayne[69]
AP 47	J.W. McAndrew[32]	AP 100	Windsor[70]
AP 48	Frederick Funston[33]	AP 101	Wood[71]
AP 49	James O'Hara[34]	AP 102	Hotspur/La Salle[72]
AP 50	Joseph Hewes[x]	AP 103	President Polk
AP 51	John Penn[35]	AP 104	President Monroe
AP 52	Edward Rutledge[x]	AP 105	George F. Elliott
AP 53	Lafayette[36]	AP 106	Catskill[73]
AP 54	Hermitage	AP 107	Ozark[74]
AP 55	Arthur Middleton[37]	AP 108	Osage[75]
AP 56	Samuel Chase[38]	AP 109	Saugus[76]
AP 57	George Clymer[39]	AP 110	General John Pope
AP 58	Charles Carroll[40]	AP 111	General A. E. Anderson
AP 59	Thomas Stone[41]	AP 112	General W. A. Mann
AP 60	Thomas Jefferson[42]	AP 113	General Henry W. Butner
AP 61	Monticello	AP 114	General William Mitchell
AP 62	Kenmore[43]	AP 115	General George M. Randall
AP 63	Rochambeau	AP 116	General M. C. Meigs
AP 64	Monrovia[44]	AP 117	General Walter H. Gordon
AP 65	Calvert[45]	AP 118	General W. P. Richardson
AP 66	Ancon[46]	AP 119	General William Weigel
AP 67	Dorothea L. Dix	AP 120	Admiral W.S. Benson[77]
AP 68	Alameda	AP 121	Admiral W.L. Capps[78]
AP 69	Elizabeth C. Stanton	AP 122	Admiral R.E. Coontz[79]
AP 70	Florence Nightingale	AP 123	Admiral E.W. Eberle[80]
AP 71	Lyon	AP 124	Admiral C.E. Hughes[81]
AP 72	Susan B. Anthony[x]	AP 125	Admiral H.T. Mayo[82]
AP 73	Leedstown[x]	AP 126	Admiral Hugh Rodman[83]

276 U.S. Navy Auxiliary Vessels

AP 127	Admiral William S. Sims[84]	AP 166	Comet
AP 128	Admiral David W. Taylor[85]	AP 167	John Land
AP 129	Admiral F.B. Upham[86]	AP 168	War Hawk
AP 130	General G.O. Squier	AP 169	Golden City
AP 131	General T.H. Bliss	AP 170	Winged Arrow
AP 132	General J.R. Brooke	AP 171	Storm King
AP 133	General Oswald H. Ernst	AP 172	Cape Johnson
AP 134	General R.L. Howze	AP 173	Herald of the Morning
AP 135	General W.M. Black	AP 174	Arlington
AP 136	General H.L. Scott	AP 175	Starlight
AP 137	General S.D. Sturgis	AP 176	General J.C. Breckenridge
AP 138	General C.G. Morton	AP 177	Europa
AP 139	General R.E. Callan[87]	T-AP 178	Frederick Funston[95]
AP 140	General M.B. Stewart	T-AP 179	James O'Hara[96]
AP 141	General A.W. Greely	T-AP 180	David C. Shanks
AP 142	General C.H. Muir	T-AP 181	Fred C. Ainsworth
AP 143	General H.B. Freeman	T-AP 182	George W. Goethels
AP 144	General H.F. Hodges	T-AP 183	Henry Gibbons
AP 145	General Harry Taylor[88]	T-AP 184	Pvt. Elden H. Johnson[97]
AP 146	General W.F. Hase	T-AP 185	Pvt. William H. Thomas[98]
AP 147	General Edgar T. Collins	T-AP 186	Sgt. Charles E. Mower[99]
AP 148	General M.L. Hersey	T-AP 187	Pvt. Joe P. Martinez
AP 149	General J.H. McRae	T-AP 188	Aiken Victory
AP 150	General M.M. Patrick	T-AP 189	LT. Raymond O. Beaudoin
AP 151	General W.C. Langfit		
AP 152	General Omar Bradley	T-AP 190	Pvt. Sadeo S. Munemori
AP 153	General R.M. Blatchford	T-AP 191	Sgt. Howard E. Woodford
AP 154	General LeRoy Eltinge	T-AP 192	Sgt. Sylvester Antolak
AP 155	General A.W. Brewster	T-AP 193	Marine Adder[100]
AP 156	General D.E. Aultman	T-AP 194	Marine Lynx
AP 157	General C.C. Ballou	T-AP 195	Marine Phoenix
AP 158	General W.G. Haan	T-AP 196	Barrett
AP 159	General Stuart Heintzelman	T-AP 197	Geiger
		T-AP 198	Upshur
AP 160	Monitor[89]	T-AP 199	Marine Carp
AP 161	Montauck[90]	T-AP 200	Marine Jumper
AP 162	Kenmore[91]	T-AP 201	Marine Marlin
AP 163	Livingston[92]	T-AP 202	Marine Serpent
AP 164	De Grasse[93]	T-AP 1001	Empire State VI[101]
AP 165	Prince Georges[94]		

Notes

Note: AP 134, AP 135, AP 137–AP 151, and AP 153–AP 159 were redesignated as T-APs with same hull numbers when assigned to MSTS beginning in 1950.

X = Lost during World War II.

1. Steven S. Roberts notes on his Shipscribe website that the additional vessels included eight appropriated German liners, more than 20 passenger ships, two hospital ships, a coastal passenger steamer, four former minelayers and 45 converted freighters.
2. Reclassified as the hospital ship [q.v.] *Bountiful* (AH 9) in March 1944.
3. Reclassified as the attack transport APA 1 in February 1943.
4. Reclassified as the unclassified miscellaneous vessel IX 12 in April 1922 and sold in 1926.
5. Reclassified as the submarine tender [q.v.] AS 10 in July 1924.
6. Reclassified as the hospital ship *Samaritan* (AH 10) in March 1944.
7. AP 8–AP 12 later reclassified as APA 2–APA 6, respectively.
8. *Ibid.*

3. Directory of U.S. Navy Auxiliary Ships

9. *Ibid.*
10. *Ibid.*
11. *Ibid.*
12. AP 14–AP 18 later reclassified as APA 7–APA 11, respectively.
13. *Ibid.*
14. *Ibid.*
15. *Ibid.*
16. Commissioned as USS *George Washington* in September 1917; later commissioned as *Catlin* in March 1941.
17. AP 25–AP 27 later reclassified as APA 12–APA 14, respectively.
18. *Ibid.*
19. *Ibid.*
20. Reclassified as APA 15 in February 1943.
21. AP 34 and AP 35 later reclassified as APA 16 and APA 17, respectively.
22. *Ibid.*
23. The former USS *Santa Ana* was assigned an AP designation in 1941 but did not subsequently serve as a Navy vessel.
24. AP 37–AP 40 later reclassified as APA 18–APA 21, respectively.
25. *Ibid.*
26. *Ibid.*
27. *Ibid.*
28. Originally classified as cargo ship [q.v.] AK 45 but commissioned as AP 41 in August 1941.
29. Although designated AP 44–AP 47 respectively, by the Navy, these ships were operated by the Army Transportation Service during World War II.
30. *Ibid.*
31. *Ibid.*
32. *Ibid.*
33. AP 48 and AP 49 were reclassified as APA 89 and APA 90, respectively, in April 1943.
34. *Ibid.*
35. Reclassified as APA 23 in February 1943.
36. Former SS *Normandie* acquired in December 1941, severely damaged in a fire and capsized at a New York City pier in February 1942, refloated in August 1943, reclassified as transport and aircraft ferry [q.v.] APV 4 in September 1943, struck in October 1945, and sold for scrapping in October 1946.
37. AP 55–AP 60 reclassified as APA 25–APA 30, respectively, in February 1943.
38. *Ibid.*
39. *Ibid.*
40. *Ibid.*
41. *Ibid.*
42. *Ibid.*
43. Renamed *Refuge* and reclassified as hospital ship AH 11 in February 1944.
44. AP 64 and AP 65 reclassified as APA 31 and APA 32, respectively, in February 1943.
45. *Ibid.*
46. Reclassified as amphibious force flagship [q.v.] AGC 4 in February 1943.
47. Commissioned as cargo ship *Matinicus* (AK 52) in August 1942, renamed *Gemini* and reclassified as transport AP 75 in August 1942.
48. AP 78–AP 101 reclassified as APA 33–APA 56, respectively, in February 1943. *Wood* (AP 101) renamed *Leedstown* (APA 56) in March 1943. *Hotspur* (AP 102) renamed *La Salle* in April 1943.
49. *Ibid.*
50. *Ibid.*
51. *Ibid.*
52. *Ibid.*
53. *Ibid.*
54. *Ibid.*
55. *Ibid.*
56. *Ibid.*
57. *Ibid.*
58. *Ibid.*
59. *Ibid.*
60. *Ibid.*
61. *Ibid.*
62. *Ibid.*
63. *Ibid.*
64. *Ibid.*
65. *Ibid.*
66. *Ibid.*
67. *Ibid.*
68. *Ibid.*
69. *Ibid.*
70. *Ibid.*

71. *Ibid.*
72. *Ibid.*
73. AP 106–AP 109 reclassified as vehicle landing ships LSV 1–LSV 4, respectively, in April 1944. AP 108 and AP 109 were originally laid down as net layers AN 3 and AN 4, respectively.
74. *Ibid.*
75. *Ibid.*
76. *Ibid.*
77. Renamed *General Daniel I. Sultan,* assigned to MSTS as T-AP 120 in March 1950, served during Vietnam War, and dismantled in 1987.
78. Renamed *General Hugh J. Gaffey* and assigned to MSTS as T-AP 121 in March 1950, struck in October 1969, reinstated in November 1978, used as a non-self-propelled barracks ship and designated as IX 507, and expended as a target in June 2000.
79. Renamed *General Alexander M. Patch* and assigned to MSTS as T-AP 122 in March 1950, served during Vietnam War and sold for scrapping in June 2001.
80. Renamed *General Simon B. Buckner* and assigned to MSTS as T-AP 123 in March 1950, served during Vietnam War and dismantled in May 1999.
81. Renamed *General Edwin D. Patrick* and assigned to MSTS as T-AP 124 in March 1950, served during Korean War, and sold for scrapping in April 2010.
82. Renamed *General Nelson M. Walker* and assigned to MSTS as T-AP 125 in March 1950, served during Vietnam War, and sold for scrapping in September 2004.
83. Renamed *General Maurice Rose* and assigned to MSTS as T-AP 126 in March 1950, served during Vietnam War, and struck in August 1990 and scrapped in 1997.
84. Renamed *General William O. Darby* and assigned to MSTS as T-AP 127 in April 1950, served during Vietnam War, reclassified as IX 510 in October 1981 and used to house crews of ships undergoing conversion and modernization in Norfolk, Va., and sold for scrapping in September 2004.
85. Never commissioned; acquisition cancelled in December 1944.
86. *Ibid.*
87. Commissioned in August 1944, assigned to MSTS as T-AP 139 in April 1950, transferred to Air Force in June 1961, converted to missile range instrumentation ship [q.v.], reacquired by Navy in July 1964 and assigned to MSTS as USNS *General H. H. Arnold* (T-AGM 9), and sold for scrapping in October 1982.
88. Commissioned in May 1944, assigned to MSTS as T-AP 145 in March 1950, transferred to Air Force in July 1961, converted to a missile range instrumentation ship, reacquired by Navy in July 1964 and assigned to MSTS as USNS *Hoyt S. Vandenberg* (T-AGM 10).
89. AP 160 and AP 161 were formerly net layers AN 1 and AN 2, respectively, and were reclassified as LSV 5 and LSV 6, respectively, in April 1944.
90. *Ibid.*
91. AP 162–AP 165 reclassified as AK 221–AK 224, respectively, in August 1944.
92. *Ibid.*
93. *Ibid.*
94. *Ibid.*
95. T-AP 178 and T-AP 179 were originally commissioned in April 1943 as the attack transports APA 89 and APA 90, respectively. They were assigned to MSTS in April 1950.
96. *Ibid.*
97. T-AP 184 and T-AP 185 were originally commissioned as the evacuation transports [q.v.] USS *Pinkney* (APH 2) in November 1942 and USS *Rixey* (APH 3) in December 1942, respectively. They were assigned to MSTS as T-APs in March 1950 and sold for scrapping in 1970.
98. *Ibid.*
99. Originally commissioned as USS *Tyron* (APH 1) in September 1942, assigned to MSTS as T-AP 186 in March 1950, and sold for scrapping in March 1969.
100. Acquired in July 1950 and assigned to MSTS the next month. Sold to commercial operator in August 1967, chartered by MSC in July 1968 and renamed *Transcolorado* and designated as cargo ship T-AK 2005.
101. Originally civilian cargo ship SS *Oregon.* Never commissioned or operated in Navy service. Converted to training ship *Empire State VI* and transferred in December 1989 to the State University of New York Maritime College at Fort Schuyler, N.Y.

Attack Transports (APA) / Amphibious Transports (LPA)

The need in World War II for specialized vessels to deliver troops ashore in amphibious assaults led to the development and commissioning of hundreds of attack transports (APAs). These ships were equipped with their own landing craft to carry Marines and Army personnel directly onto enemy-held beaches and they were armed with one or two 5-inch/38 dual purpose guns for shore-bombardment and self-protection, along with 20-

Commissioned in August 1945, the attack transport USS *Bronx* (APA 236) carried hundreds of servicemen in the Pacific theater back to the United States in the months immediately following the Japanese surrender. She was decommissioned in 1949 (U.S. Navy photograph).

and 40-mm guns for anti-aircraft defense. The first attack transports (APA 1–APA 56) were derived by converting existing transport ships (APs) [q.v.] (essentially AP 2–AP 101, with some exceptions) in 1943. The largest group of attack transports belonged to the Haskell class (APA 117–APA 180 and APA 187–APA 239). They were Maritime Commission VC2-S-AP5 "Victory" types commissioned in 1944 and 1945, 455-feet long, and carried 25–27 landing craft. Two other large APA classes that entered the fleet during the war were Bayfield (APA 33–APA 48 and APA 92–APA 116), made up of MC C3-S-A2 types which carried 1,650 troops, and Gilliam (APA 57–APA 88), consisting of MC S4-SE2-BD1 types. All but 18 of the Navy's attack transports had been built under Maritime Commission contracts. Four of the older APAs (*McCawley*, *Joseph Hewes*, *John Penn*, and *Edward Rutledge*), all former APs, were lost during the conflict. At the end of World War II the Navy had classified 230 ships as APAs (the never-named APA 181–AP 186 were cancelled in 1944 and APA 240–APA 247 were cancelled in 1945).

After 1945 the attack transports were no longer considered fleet auxiliaries but were then classified as amphibious warfare vessels. In 1969 the Navy reclassified the attack transport ships still on hand as amphibious transports and redesignated them as LPAs (retaining their APA hull numbers). Beginning in the 1960s, the role formerly performed by the attack transport was gradually assumed by newer types of amphibious vessels, such as the amphibious transport dock (LPD) and dock landing ship (LSD). The final two vessels to become attack transports were USS *Paul Revere* (APA 248, later LKA 248), commissioned in September 1956, and USS *Francis Marion* (APA 249, later LKA 249), commissioned in July 1961, both of which were C4-S-1A "Mariner" types. They were decommissioned in January 1980 and sold to Spain.

USS *Paul Revere* (LPA 248) is entering Pearl Harbor on July 2, 1969 (U.S. Navy photograph).

APA 1	*Doyen*	APA 22	*Joseph Hewes*
APA 2	*Harris*	APA 23	*John Penn*[x]
APA 3	*Zeilin*	APA 24	*Edward Rutledge*
APA 4	*McCawley*[x]	APA 25	*Arthur Middleton*
APA 5	*Barnett*	APA 26	*Samuel Chase*
APA 6	*Heywood*	APA 27	*George Clymer*
APA 7	*Fuller*	APA 28	*Charles Carroll*
APA 8	*William P. Biddle*	APA 29	*Thomas Stone*[x]
APA 9	*Neville*	APA 30	*Thomas Jefferson*
APA 10	*Harry Lee*	APA 31	*Monrovia*
APA 11	*Feland*	APA 32	*Calvert*
APA 12	*Leonard Wood*	APA 33	*Bayfield*
APA 13	*Joseph T. Dickman*	APA 34	*Bolivar*
APA 14	*Hunter Liggett*	APA 35	*Callaway*
APA 15	*Henry T. Allen*	APA 36	*Cambria*
APA 16	*J. Franklin Bell*	APA 37	*Cavalier*
APA 17	*American Legion*	APA 38	*Chilton**
APA 18	*President Jackson*	APA 39	*Clay*
APA 19	*President Adams*	APA 40	*Custer*
APA 20	*President Hayes*	APA 41	*DuPage*
APA 21	*Crescent City*	APA 42	*Elmore*

3. Directory of U.S. Navy Auxiliary Ships

APA 43	*Fayette*	APA 96	*Cecil*
APA 44	*Fremont**	APA 97	*Dauphin*
APA 45	*Henrico**	APA 98	*Dutchess*
APA 46	*Knox*	APA 99	*Dade*
APA 47	*Lamar*	APA 100	*Mendocino*
APA 48	*Leon*	APA 101	*Montour*
APA 49	*Ormsby*	APA 102	*Riverside*
APA 50	*Pierce*	APA 103	*Queens*
APA 51	*Sheridan*	APA 104	*Westmoreland*
APA 52	*Sumter*	APA 105	*Shelby*
APA 53	*Warren*	APA 106	*Hansford*
APA 54	*Wayne*	APA 107	*Goodhue*
APA 55	*Windsor*	APA 108	*Goshen*
APA 56	*Leedstown*[1]	APA 109	*Grafton*
APA 57	*Gilliam*	APA 110	*Griggs*
APA 58	*Appling*	APA 111	*Grundy*
APA 59	*Audrain*	APA 112	*Guilford*
APA 60	*Banner*	APA 113	*Sitka*
APA 61	*Barrow*	APA 114	*Hamblen*
APA 62	*Berrien*	APA 115	*Hampton*
APA 63	*Bladen*	APA 116	*Hanover*
APA 64	*Bracken*	APA 117	*Haskell*
APA 65	*Briscoe*	APA 118	*Hendry*
APA 66	*Brule*	APA 119	*Highlands*
APA 67	*Burleson*	APA 120	*Hinsdale*
APA 68	*Butte*	APA 121	*Hocking*
APA 69	*Carlisle*	APA 122	*Kenton*
APA 70	*Carteret*	APA 123	*Kittson*
APA 71	*Catron*	APA 124	*LaGrange*
APA 72	*Clarendon*	APA 125	*Lanier*
APA 73	*Cleburne*	APA 126	*St. Mary's*
APA 74	*Colusa*	APA 127	*Allendale*
APA 75	*Cortland*	APA 128	*Arenac*
APA 76	*Crenshaw*	APA 129	*Marvin H. McIntyre*
APA 77	*Crittenden*	APA 130	*Attala*
APA 78	*Cullman*	APA 132	*Barnwell**
APA 79	*Dawson*	APA 133	*Beckham*
APA 80	*Elkhart*	APA 134	*Bland*
APA 81	*Fallon*	APA 135	*Bosque*
APA 82	*Fergus*	APA 136	*Botetourt*
APA 83	*Fillmore*	APA 137	*Bowie*
APA 84	*Garrard*	APA 138	*Braxton*
APA 85	*Gasconade*	APA 139	*Broadwater*
APA 86	*Geneva*	APA 140	*Brookings*
APA 87	*Niagara*	APA 141	*Buckingham*
APA 88	*Presidio*	APA 142	*Clearfield*
APA 89	*Frederick Funston*[2]	APA 143	*Clermont*
APA 90	*James O'Hara*[3]	APA 144	*Clinton**
APA 91	*Adair*	APA 145	*Colbert*
APA 92	*Alpine*	APA 146	*Collingsworth**
APA 93	*Barnstable*	APA 147	*Cottle*
APA 94	*Baxter*	APA 148	*Crockett*
APA 95	*Burleigh*	APA 149	*Audubon*

APA 150	*Bergen*	APA 203	*Meriwether*
APA 151	*La Porte*	APA 204	*Sarasota**
APA 152	*Latimer*	APA 205	*Sherburne*[5]
APA 153	*Laurens*	APA 206	*Sibley*
APA 154	*Lowndes**	APA 207	*Mifflin*
APA 155	*Mellette*	APA 208	*Talladega**
APA 157	*Napa**	APA 209	*Tazewell*
APA 158	*Newberry*	APA 210	*Telfair**
APA 159	*Darke*	APA 211	*Missoula*
APA 160	*Deuel*	APA 212	*Montrose**
APA 161	*Dickens*	APA 213	*Mountrail**
APA 162	*Drew*	APA 214	*Natrona*
APA 163	*Eastland*	APA 215	*Navarro**
APA 164	*Edgecombe*	APA 216	*Neshoba*
APA 165	*Effingham*	APA 217	*New Kent*
APA 166	*Fond Du Lac*	APA 218	*Noble*
APA 167	*Freestone*	APA 219	*Okaloosa*
APA 168	*Gage*	APA 220	*Okanogan**
APA 169	*Gallatin**	APA 221	*Oneida*
APA 170	*Gosper*	APA 222	*Pickaway**
APA 171	*Granville*	APA 223	*Pitt**
APA 172	*Grimes*	APA 224	*Randall*
APA 173	*Hyde**	APA 225*	*Bingham**
APA 174	*Jerauld*	APA 226	*Rawlins*
APA 175	*Karnes*	APA 227	*Renville**
APA 176	*Kershaw*	APA 228	*Rockbridge**
APA 177	*Kingsbury**	APA 229	*Rockingham**
APA 178	*Lander**	APA 230	*Rockwall*
APA 179	*Lauderdale**	APA 231	*Saint Croix**
APA 180	*Lavaca*	APA 232	*San Saba*
APA 181–		APA 233	*Sevier**
APA 186[4]		APA 234	*Bollinger**
APA 187	*Oconto*	APA 235	*Bottineau**
APA 188	*Olmsted**	APA 236	*Bronx**
APA 189	*Oxford*	APA 237	*Bexar**
APA 190	*Pickens*	APA 238	*Dane*
APA 191	*Pondera*	APA 239	*Glynn**
APA 192	*Rutland**	APA 240	*Harnett*[6]
APA 193	*Sanborn*	APA 241	*Hempstead*[7]
APA 194	*Sandoval**	APA 242	*Iredell*[8]
APA 195	*Lenawee*	APA 243	*Luzerne*[9]
APA 196	*Logan**	APA 244	*Medera*[10]
APA 197	*Lubbock*	APA 245	*Maricopa*[11]
APA 198	*McCracken*	APA 246	*McLennon*[12]
APA 199	*Magoffin**	APA 247	*Mecklenburg*[13]
APA 200	*Marathon*	APA 248	*Paul Revere**
APA 201	*Menard*	APA 249	*Francis Marion**
APA 202	*Menifee*		

NOTES

* Redesignated in January 1969 as LKA with same hull number.
X = Lost during World War II.

3. Directory of U.S. Navy Auxiliary Ships 283

    1. Assigned to the Navy in August 1942 as transport *Wood* (AP 101) but commissioned in July 1943 as *Leedstown* (APA 56), decommissioned in March 1946, and sold I July 1947 for commercial service.
    2. Commissioned in April 1943, decommissioned in April 1946, assigned in May 1950 to MSTS as transport T-AP 178 and T-AP 179, respectively, and sold for scrapping in May 1969 and January 1968, respectively.
    3. *Ibid.*
    4. Unnamed and cancelled in 1944.
    5. Commissioned in September 1944, decommissioned in August 1946, converted to missile range instrumentation ship [q.v.], and placed in service with MSC in October 1971 as USNS *Range Sentinel* (T-AGM 22).
    6. Cancelled in 1945.
    7. *Ibid.*
    8. *Ibid.*
    9. *Ibid.*
  10. *Ibid.*
  11. *Ibid.*
  12. *Ibid.*
  13. *Ibid.*

Self-Propelled Barracks Ships (APB)

The self-propelled barracks ship USS *Benewah* (APB 35) is anchored in South Vietnam's Soi Rap River on October 24, 1967, with ten riverine warfare ships moored alongside (U.S. Navy photograph).

    First commissioned just as World War II was ending, APBs provided temporary housing, medical facilities, stores issue and other services afloat for naval and military personnel. The self-propelled barracks ships were fitted with diesel engines and two screws to move from place to place at a maximum speed of 11 knots. The Benewah class (APB 35–APB 48) was originally armed with two 40-mm quad guns and either eight or twelve 20-mm guns. Four of the APBs later served as riverine force flagships in Vietnam in the 1960s. They accommodated up to 900 troops and boat crewmen. Two of them—APB 39 and APB 40—are still in naval service but are now classified as non-self-propelled barracks ships [q.v.] (APL). The other APBs have been transferred, sold or scrapped.

APB 35	*Benewah*[1]	APB 41	*Wythe*[5]	APB 47	*Kingman*[11]
APB 36	*Colleton*	APB 42	*Yavapai*[6]	APB 48	*Vander-burgh*[12]
APB 37	*Echols*[2]	APB 43	*Yolo*[7]		
APB 38	*Marlboro*	APB 44	*Presque Isle*[8]	APB 48	*Accomac*[13]
APB 39	*Mercer*[3]	APB 45	*Blackford*[9]	APB 50	*Cameron*[14]
APB 40	*Nueces*[4]	APB 46	*Dorchester*[10]	APB51	*DuPage*

NOTES

1. Commissioned in March 1946 as APB, recommissioned in January 1967 for Vietnam service, decommissioned again in February 1971 and reclassified as IX 311, and transferred to the Philippines in May 1974.
2. Originally Intended as an APL but reclassified as an APB in August 1944, in service in January 1947, reclassified as IX 504 when reactivated for the use of crews of new-construction submarines in Groton, Connecticut, struck in December 1995, and sold in 2003.
3. Commissioned in September 1945 and in and out of commission between 1947 and 1968, deployed to South Vietnam in June 1968 to support mobile riverine units, reclassified as IX 502 in November 1975, reclassified as APL 39 in March 2001 and used for berthing and messing in Sasebo, Japan.
4. First commissioned in November 1945, decommissioned 1955–1968, deployed to South Vietnam in May 1968, reclassified as IX 503 in November 1975 and assigned to Sasebo, and reclassified as APL 40 and moored in Yokosuka, Japan.
5. Commissioned as LST 575 in June 1944, named *Wythe* and reclassified as APB in March 1945, struck in May 1959 and sold for scrapping in September 1959.
6. APB 42–APB 44 were formerly LST 678–LST 676, respectively.
7. Ibid.
8. Ibid.
9. APB 45–APB 48 were formerly the general stores issue ships [q.v.] AKS 16–AKS 19, respectively.
10. Laid down as LST 1114 in January 1945, renamed *Presque Isle* as general store ship [q.v.] AKS 19 in February 1945, commissioned as APB 46 in July 1945, decommissioned in January 1947, and sold for scrapping in November 1972.
11. APB 45–APB 48 were formerly the general stores issue ships [q.v.] AKS 16–AKS 19, respectively.
12. Ibid.
13. Commissioned as LST 710 in July 1944, named *Accomac* and reclassified as APB in August 1945, decommissioned in August 1946, and sold for scrapping in December 1959.
14. Commissioned as LST 928 in July 1944, named *Cameron* and reclassified as APB in July 1955, struck and sold in 1959.

Small Coastal Transports (APc)

The classification "coastal transport (small)" was created in April 1942 for a group of unnamed 103-foot wooden ships intended to carry small numbers of troops or cargo in the South Pacific. Designated APc 1–APc 111, they displaced 161 tons (light), carried two or four 20-mm guns, were manned by 21 officers and enlisted personnel, and motored at 10 knots. The small coastal transports were commissioned between October 1942 and July 1943.

APc 1–APc 50 were originally planned to be coastal minesweepers AMc 150–AMc 199, inclusively. APc 80–APc 84 were cancelled, APc 99 and APc 100 were not ordered, APc 104–APc 107 were cancelled, and APc 112–APc 115 were ordered but never built. In all, 89 APc vessels were delivered. They operated almost exclusively in the Pacific; only APc 85–APc 94 served in the Atlantic. All of the small coastal transports were disposed of, mostly through sales, in 1947 and 1948. Sixteen APc vessels were transferred to other countries (all but two to Greece) between 1947 and 1952.

3. Directory of U.S. Navy Auxiliary Ships

Anchored in San Francisco Bay near the Golden Gate Bridge in 1945–1946, USS APc 101 was sold in January 1947 to be used as a civilian freighter (U.S. Navy photograph).

Small Coastal Transports (APC)

In the summer of 1950 the Navy acquired four C1-M-AV1 cargo ships from the Army Transportation Service (ATS) for operation by the new MSTS. They were classified as small coastal transports and designated as T-APC 116–T-AP 119. Two of them later served as signals intelligence (SIGINT) ships in support of NSA requirements. USNS *Sgt. Joseph E. Muller* operated as a seagoing listening post off Cuba and USNS *Jose F. Valdez* collected signals intelligence off Africa in the 1960s. All four ships were disposed of in the 1970s.

T-APC 116	*Sgt. Jonah E. Kelley*[1]	T-APC 118	*Sgt. Joseph E. Muller*[3]
T-APC 117	*Sgt. George D. Keathley*[2]	T-APC 119	*Pvt. Jose F. Valdez*[4]

Notes

1. Commissioned in ATS in October 1947, transferred to Navy and assigned to MSTS as T-APC 116 in July 1950, removed from service in November 1969, and sold for scrapping in October 1972.
2. Assigned to ATS in July 1946, transferred to Navy and assigned to MSTS as T-APC 117 in July 1950, removed from service in December 1956, reclassified as surveying ship [q.v.] and redesignated as T-AGS 35 in December 1966, removed from service in December 1971, and transferred to Taiwan in March 1972.
3. Assigned to ATS in June 1948, transferred to Navy and assigned to MSTS as T-APC 118 in July 1950, inactive 1956–1962, converted to "research support ship" autumn of 1962 and reclassified as miscellaneous auxiliary T-AG 171, transferred to MARAD in November 1969, and sold for scrapping in October 1972.

The unusual antennas and electronics array on USNS *Sgt. Joseph E. Muller* (T-APC 118) in August 1968 reveal that she is no longer an ordinary small coastal transport. Between April 1963 and 1969 she served as a spy ship collecting signals intelligence while operating off Cuba (U.S. Navy photograph).

4. Acquired by Army in July 1945, transferred to Navy and assigned to MSTS as T-APC 119 in September 1950, removed from service in 1959, converted to spy ship in 1961 and assigned to MSTS as T-AG 169, deactivated in 1969, struck in August 1976, and sold for scrapping in July 1977.

High-Speed Transports (APD) / Small Amphibious Transports (LPR)

During World War II the Navy converted 36 old flush-deck destroyers (DDs) and some 100 destroyer escorts (DEs) into high-speed transports (APD) to deliver what would today be called special operations forces onto enemy-held beaches and water fronts. They carried four landing craft to bring the troops ashore, and were armed with either a 5-inch/38 or three 3-inch/50 guns, along with 20-mm and 40-mm AA weapons. The APDs could transport up to 200 troops and were capable of maximum speeds of 22–24 knots, much faster than the larger attack transports (APA). Nine of these ships were lost during World War II.

After the war, the APDs were no longer rated as fleet auxiliaries as they had become classified as amphibious ships. There were 92 of them on the Vessel Register in January 1950. In the 1960s, at least 30 APDs were transferred to other countries, including Chile, Colombia, Ecuador, Mexico, the Philippines, South Korea and Taiwan. Many others were either scrapped or expended as targets. Three of them—APDs 123, 130 and 135—survived long enough to serve in the Vietnam War. On January 1, 1969, the few APDs still listed on the roster were reclassified as "amphibious transports (small)" and redesignated as

3. Directory of U.S. Navy Auxiliary Ships

Commissioned in June 1945, USS *Burdo* (APD 133) served until her February 1958 decommissioning. She was sold for scrapping after nine years in mothballs (U.S. Navy photograph).

LPRs (with same hull number). The 11 such ships then remaining, all in mothballs, were struck between July 1972 and July 1975. USS *Balduck* (LPR 132) was the last ex–APD to be removed from the Naval Vessel Register. She was sold for dismantling in December 1976.

In the listing below the parenthetical designation is the vessel's original hull number prior to conversion to APD. An asterisk after the name indicates a conversion to APD that was cancelled and a "+" indicates an APD that was redesignated as a LPR in 1969. An "x" indicates an APD that was lost during World War II.

APD 1	*Manley* (AG 28)	APD 14	*Schley* (DD 103)
APD 2	*Colhoun* (DD 85)^x	APD 15	*Kilty* (DD 137)
APD 3	*Gregory* (DD 82)^x	APD 16	*Ward* (DD 139)^x
APD 4	*Little* (DD 79)^x	APD 17	*Crosby* (DD 164)
APD 5	*McKean* (DD 90)^x	APD 18	*Kane* (DD 235)
APD 6	*Stringham* (DD 83)	APD 19	*Tattnall* (DD 125)
APD 7	*Talbot* (DD 114)	APD 20	*Roper* (DD 147)
APD 8	*Waters* (DD 115)	APD 21	*Dickerson* (DD 157)^x
APD 9	*Dent* (DD 116)	APD 22	*Herbert* (DD 160)
APD 10	*Brooks* (DD 232)	APD 23	*Overton* (DD 239)
APD 11	*Gilmer* (DD 233)	APD 24	*Noa* (DD 343)^x
APD 12	*Humphreys* (DD 236)	APD 25	*Rathburne* (DD 113)
APD 13	*Sands* (DD 243)	APD 26	*McFarland* (DD 237)*

APD 27	Williamson (DD 244)*	APD 76	Schmitt (DE 676)
APD 28	Hulbert (DD 342)*	APD 77	Frament (DE 677)
APD 29	Barry (DD 248)x	APD 78	Bull (DE 693)
APD 30	Decatur (DD 341)*	APD 79	Bunch (DE 694)
APD 31	Clemson (DD 186)[1]	APD 80	Hayter (DE 212)
APD 32	Goldsborough (DD 188)[2]	APD 81	Tatum (DE 789)
APD 33	George E. Badger (DD 196)[3]	APD 82	Borum (DE 790)*
		APD 83	Maloy (DE 791)*
APD 34	Belknap (DD 251)[4]	APD 84	Haines (DE 792)
APD 35	Osmond Ingram (DD 255)[5]	APD 85	Runels (DE 793)
		APD 86	Hollis (DE 796)+
APD 36	Greene (DD 266)[6]	APD 87	Crosley (DE 226)
APD 37	Charles Lawrence (DE 53)	APD 88	Cread (DE 227)
APD 38	Daniel T. Griffin (DE 54)	APD 89	Ruchamkin (DE 228)+
APD 39	Barr (DE 576)	APD 90	Kirwin (DE 229)+
APD 40	Bowers (DE 637)	APD 91	Kinzer (DE 232)
APD 41	England (DE 635)*	APD 92	Register (DE 233)
APD 42	Gantner (DE 60)	APD 93	Brock (DE 234)
APD 43	George W. Ingram (DE 62)	APD 94	John Q. Roberts (DE 235)
APD 44	Ira Jefferey (DE 63)	APD 95	William H. Hobby (DE 236)
APD 45	Lee Fox (DE 65)		
APD 46	Amesbury (DE 66)	APD 96	Ray K. Edwards (DE 237)
APD 47	Bates (DE 68)x	APD 97	Arthur L. Bristol (DE 281)
APD 48	Blessman (DE 69)	APD 98	Truxton (DE 282)
APD 49	Joseph E. Campbell (DE 70)	APD 99	Upham (DE 283)
		APD 100	Ringness (DE 590)+
APD 50	Sims (DE 154)	APD 101	Knudson (DE 591)+
APD 51	Hopping (DE 155)	APD 102	Rednour (DE 592)
APD 52	Reeves (DE 156)	APD 103	Tollberg (DE 593)
APD 53	Hubbard (DE 211)	APD 104	William J. Pattison (DE 594)
APD 54	Chase (DE 158)		
APD 55	Lanning (DE 159)+	APD 105	Myers (DE 595)
APD 56	Lay (DE 160)	APD 106	Walter B. Cobb (DE 596)[7]
APD 57	Barber (DE 161)	APD 107	Earle B. Hall (DE 597)
APD 58	Witter (DE 636)*	APD 108	Harry L. Corl (DE 598)
APD 59	Newman (DE 205)	APD 109	Belet (DE 599)
APD 60	Liddle (DE 206)	APD 110	Julius A. Raven (DE 600)
APD 61	Kephart (DE 207)	APD 111	Walsh (DE 601)
APD 62	Cofer (DE 208)	APD 112	Hunter Marshall (DE 602)
APD 63	Lloyd (DE 209)	APD 113	Earheart (DE 603)
APD 64	Scott (DE 214)*	APD 114	Walter S. Gorka (DE 604)
APD 65	Burke (DE 215)	APD 115	Rogers Blood (DE 605)
APD 66	Enright (DE 216)	APD 116	Francovich (DE 606)
APD 67	Jenks (DE 665)*	APD 117	Joseph M. Auman (DE 674)
APD 68	Durik (DE 666)*		
APD 59	Yokes (DE 668)	APD 118	Don O. Woods (DE 721)
APD 70	Pavlic (DE 669)	APD 119	Beverly W. Reid (DE 722)+
APD 71	Odum (DE 670)	APD 120	Kline (DE 687)
APD 72	Jack C. Robinson (DE 671)	APD 121	Raymond W. Herndon (DE 688)
APD 73	Bassett (DE 672)	APD 122	Scribner (DE 689)
APD 74	John P. Gray (DE 673)	APD 123	Diachenko (DE 690)+
APD 75	Weber (DE 675)	APD 124	Horace A. Bass (DE 691)+

3. Directory of U.S. Navy Auxiliary Ships

APD 125	Wantuck (DE 692)	APD 133	Burdo
APD 126	Gosselin (DE 710)	APD 134	Kleinsmith
APD 127	Begor+	APD 135	Weiss+
APD 128	Cavallaro	APD 136	Carpellotti
APD 129	Donald W. Wolf	APD 137	DeLong (DE 684)*
APD 130	Cook	APD 138	Coates (DE 686)*
APD 131	Walter X. Young	APD 139	Bray (DE 709)
APD 132	Balduck+		

NOTES

1. Commissioned as destroyer in December 1919, converted to aircraft tender—small [q.v.] AVP 17 in November 1939, reclassified as seaplane tender-destroyer [q.v.] AVD 4 in August 1940, reclassified as destroyer DD 186 in December 1943, converted to APD in July 1944, decommissioned in October 1945, and sold for scrapping in November 1946.

2. Commissioned as destroyer in January 1920, classified as AVP 15 in November 1939, reclassified as AVD 5 in August 1940, reclassified as destroyer DD 188 in December 1943, converted to APD in March 1944, decommissioned in October 1945, and sold for scrapping in November 1946.

3. Commissioned as destroyer in July 1920, served in Coast Guard in early 1930s, classified as AVP 16 in January 1940, reclassified as AVD 3 in August 1940, classified as APD in May 1944, decommissioned in October 1945, and sold for scrapping in June 1946.

4. Commissioned as a destroyer in April 1919, converted to AVD 8 in 1940, reclassified as APD in June 1944, decommissioned in August 1945, and sold for scrapping in November 1945.

5. Commissioned as a destroyer in June 1919, converted to AVD 9 in 1940, reclassified as APD in June 1944, decommissioned in January 1946, and sold for scrapping in June 1946.

6. Commissioned as a destroyer in May 1919, converted to AVD 13 in 1941, reclassified as APD in February 1944, run aground in a typhoon on Okinawa in October 1945 and damaged beyond repair, decommissioned the next month and struck in December 1945.

7. Sank while under tow to Taiwan in April 1966.

Administrative Flagship (APF)

USS Columbia (AG 9), an early administrative flagship, is at Guantanamo Bay, Cuba, on February 22, 1922. The flag display is in honor of George Washington's birthday (U.S. Navy photograph).

In the early 1920s at least two naval vessels were used as "administrative flagships," i.e., non-combatant ships fitted with necessary berthing, office and communications facilities to enable a fleet or large unit commander and staff to direct and command his organization while afloat. The cruiser USS *Charleston* (C-22/CA 190) performed this role for the commander of the Pacific Fleet's destroyer squadrons in 1920–1923, and USS *Columbia* (AG 9) similarly served as the Atlantic Fleet administrative flagship in 1921–1922. These ships were forerunners of what were later to become amphibious force flagships [q.v.] and command ships. Neither of these two vessels nor any other appears to have been formally classified as an APF, and today the APF hull classification is listed as "inactive" on the Naval Vessel Register.

Supporting Gunnery Ship (APG)

This auxiliary ship classification dates to the World War II years but appears to have never been assigned to a specific vessel. It is today listed as "inactive" on the NVR.

Transports Fitted for Evacuation of Wounded / Wounded Evacuation Transports / Evacuation Transports (APH)

With World War II now over, USS *Pinkey* (APH 2) is approaching San Francisco on December 10, 1945, with hundreds of homecoming troops lining her rails (U.S. Navy photograph).

Three Maritime Commission C2-S1-A1 type vessels were acquired by the Navy in 1942 and provided with large berthing and messing spaces for the transport of troops. Those spaces could be readily converted into hospital facilities when needed to evacuate approximately 700 wounded personnel from forward combat areas. APH 1 was decommissioned in June 1954 and sold for scrapping in March 1958; the other two were decommissioned in December 1957 and sold for scrapping in September 1970. Two other ships were briefly classified as evacuation transports: the hospital ship [q.v.] *Haven* (AH 12), redesignated as APH 112 between June and October 1946; and *Tranquillity* (AH 14), redesignated as APH 114 between November 1945 and March 1946. Both reverted to their former classification and hull number thereafter.

| APH 1 | *Tryon* | APH 2 | *Pinkey* | APH 3 | *Rixey* |

Labor Transports / Barrack Ships / Non-Self-Propelled Barracks Craft (APL)

The barrack ship APL 55 is moored in New York on May 25, 1956 (U.S. Navy photograph).

In 1928 the Navy established the "labor transport or barrack ship" classification for an unnamed vessel (slated to be designated as APL 1) to provide housing for large numbers of workers. That acquisition was cancelled. Between 1944 and 1946, the Navy took delivery of 46 non-self-propelled barges with a multi-deck barracks structure mounted on board. These vessels, APL 2–APL 15, APL 17–APL 34 and APL 41–APL 58, could house 583 troops. (APLs 6, 7, 16, 51 and 52 were cancelled.) In August 1944, the Navy ordered six LST-type hulls fitted with a barracks structure. They were initially designated as APL 35–APL 40 but almost immediately reclassified as "barracks ships, self-propelled" (APB) [q.v.] and redesignated APB 35–APB 40. That reclassification reserved the APL classification only for non-self-propelled vessels.

Following World War II, the former USS LST 33 was reclassified as APL 59 in

September 1954 and transferred to South Korea the following year; APL 60 was added to the fleet in May 1977; APL 61 and APL 62 were placed in service in October 1977 and March 1998, respectively; APL 63 and APL 64 were cancelled; and APL 65 and APL 66 were placed in service in December and November 2000, respectively.

Almost all of the APLs now have been scrapped, transferred (Panama, South Vietnam, Turkey and U.S. Army) or sold. At this writing the following APLs are still in active service and are listed on the NVR as "barracks craft" in the "service craft" category: APLs 2, 4, 5, 42, 45, 50, 58, 61, 62, 65 and 66. Although some sources list APL 29 and 32 as active, those vessels are not now listed in the NVR.

Mechanized Artillery Transports (APM)

USS *Lakehurst* is seen here probably in late 1942 carrying a cargo of Army trucks on the main deck and other equipment stowed below from New York to North Africa. The undated photo was shot from an airship attached to Blimp Squadron ZP-12 based at Naval Air Station Lakehurst, N.J (U.S. Navy photograph).

In July 1941 the Navy reclassified eight vessels which were to have been built as mechanized artillery transports (initially designated as APM 1–APM 8) as dock landing ships (LSD 1–LSD 8), even before their keels were laid down. Those eight ships are listed below despite never serving as auxiliary vessels. The ninth vessel listed did, in fact, operate as an auxiliary, specifically as a mechanized artillery transport.

USS *Lakehurst* (APM 9) began her career in 1940 as the merchant vessel *Seatrain New Jersey* to haul railroad cars between New York and Texas. She was commissioned by the Navy, renamed, and classified as an aircraft transport [q.v.] (APV 3) in October 1942. Two months later *Lakehurst* was reclassified as a mechanized-artillery transport for the purpose of carrying Army tanks from the United States to North Africa. In August 1943, the vessel was transferred to the Army, returned to Seatrain Lines in May 1946, and scrapped in 1973.

APM 1	*Ashland*	APM 4	*Epping Forest*	APM 7	*Oak Hill*
APM 2	*Belle Grove*	APM 5	*Gunston Hall*	APM 8	*White Marsh*
APM 3	*Carter Hall*	APM 6	*Lindenwald*	APM 9	*Lakehurst*

Non-Mechanized Artillery Transport (APN)

This auxiliary ship classification dates to the early 1940s but appears to have never been assigned to a specific vessel. It is today listed as "inactive" on the NVR.

Transport Rescue Vessels / Rescue Transports (APR)

Even before the U.S. entry into World War II, the Navy considered the acquisition of specialized vessels to be used in rescuing merchant ship crews at sea. In February 1942 the hull classification symbol APR was created to designate 11 planned rescue transports. They were assigned names in August 1942. Various design options were suggested for the APRs but ultimately the Navy decided to derive the transport rescue vessel from converted PC 827-class patrol craft which would be designated as PCERs, i.e., combatants, not auxiliaries. The planned APR acquisition and ship names were cancelled in March 1943 and the 11 ships were never ordered or built.

APR 1	Adair	APR 5	Dutchess	APR 9	Montour
APR 2	Berkshire	APR 6	Lorain	APR 10	Napa
APR 3	Burleigh	APR 7	Douglas	APR 11	Westmoreland
APR 4	Cecil	APR 8	Mendocino		

Transport Submarines (APS) (APSS) (ASSP)

USS *Perch* (SSP 313) is off the Mare Island Naval Shipyard on July 17, 1948, two months after she was converted to a transport submarine. She was reclassified as APSS 313 in October 1956 and retired from active service in December 1971 (U.S. Navy photograph).

In the post-war years four diesel submarines were converted or configured during their careers to transport troops and other "passenger" personnel and their equipment, and were thus classified at one time or another as submarine transports (SSP) or transport submarines (ASSP) or submarine transports (APSS) or amphibious transport submarines (LPSS). *Perch* and *Sealion* could transport 111 troops and *Grayback* could accommodate 67 troops.

| APSS 282 | *Tunny*[1] | APSS 315 | *Sealion*[3] |
| APSS 313 | *Perch*[2] | APSS 574 | *Grayback*[4] |

NOTES

1. Originally commissioned as the submarine SS 282 in September 1942, classified as troop-carrying submarine APSS 282 from October 1966 to January 1969, designated as LPSS 282 between January 1969 and June 1969, and expended as a target in June 1970.
2. Commissioned as SS 313 in January 1944, converted to submarine transport and reclassified as SSP 313 in May 1948, redesignated as ASSP 313 in January 1950, redesignated as APSS 313 in October 1956, decommissioned in March 1960, recommissioned in November 1961, reclassified as LPSS 313 in August 1968, decommissioned and struck in December 1971, and sold for scrapping.
3. Commissioned as SS 315 in March 1944, decommissioned in February 1946, converted to submarine transport and redesignated as SSP 315 in November 1948, redesignated as ASSP 315 in January 1950, redesignated as APSS 315 in October 1956, decommissioned in June 1960, redesignated as LPSS 315 in January 1969, decommissioned in February 1970, struck in March 1977, and expended as a target in July 1978.
4. Commissioned as missile submarine SSG 574 in March 1958, converted to transport submarine and recommissioned as APSS 574 in 1968, decommissioned in June 1984, and expended as a target in April 1986.

Airplane Transport / Transport and Aircraft Ferry (APV)

On August 6, 1943, the former USS *Lakehurst* (APV 3) is anchored, probably off New York City, four days after she was transferred to the U.S. Army (National Archives Photo).

Three former Seatrain Lines railroad freight car–hauling vessels and one former passenger liner were designated by the Navy as transport and aircraft ferries (APV) during World War II to carry aircraft between ports.

APV 1	Kitty Hawk[1]	APV 3	Lakehurst[3]
APV 2	Hammondsport[2]	APV 4	Lafayette[4]

NOTES

1. Former Seatrain Lines SS *Seatrain New York* acquired by the Navy in June 1941, commissioned as *Kitty Hawk* (APV 1) in November 1941, reclassified as aircraft transport [q.v.] AKV 1 in September 1943, decommissioned in January 1946, struck in February 1946, and returned to Seatrain Lines in May 1946.
2. Former SS *Seatrain Havana* commissioned as APV 2 in December 1941, reclassified as AKV 2 in September 1943, decommissioned in March 1946, struck in April 1946, and returned to Seatrain Lines in May 1946.
3. See Mechanized Artillery Transports (APM) above.
4. Former liner SS *Normandie* acquired in December 1941 as transport [q.v.] *Lafayette* (AP 53); after a February 1942 fire, capsize and refloating in New York City, reclassified as transport and aircraft ferry APV 4 in September 1943, struck in October 1945, and sold for scrapping in October 1946.

Repair Ships (AR)

The repair ship USS *Klondike* (AR 22), a former destroyer tender, is still supporting destroyers in Subic Bay, Philippines, on November 1, 1963. Nested alongside her port side are (from inboard to outboard) are USS *Taussig* (DD 746), USS *John A. Bole* (DD 755), USS *Lofberg* (DD 759), and USS *John W. Thomason* (DD 760) (U.S. Navy photograph).

Repair ships delivered a wide variety of maintenance and repair services to the hulls, machinery and equipment of the Navy's ships in waters remote from naval shipyards. As an early example, the former civilian passenger and cargo ship *Chatham* was acquired by the Navy and commissioned as USS *Vulcan* in 1898 to provide repairs to naval vessels in Cuba during the Spanish-American War. In her first two months of service, she handled repairs on 63 ships while also furnishing various supplies to 60. That first *Vulcan* was one of the Navy's initial repair ships which had been derived from converted colliers [q.v.] and commercial vessels. The first purpose-built repair ship for naval service was USS *Medusa* (AR 1), commissioned in September 1924. Within her large shop facilities, *Medusa*'s crew could do sheet-metal, welding, boiler repairs, plating, and fixes to optical and mechanical equipment.

The Navy's first vessel built specifically as a repair ship, USS *Medusa* (AR 1), helped to down two Japanese aircraft and sink a midget submarine during the Pearl Harbor attack on December 7, 1941 (U.S. Navy photograph).

A later *Vulcan* (AR 5), commissioned in June 1941, was manned by 53 officers and 1,244 sailors, who worked in a two-deck high machine shop, a foundry of similar size, and shops that handled all manner of tasks involving, for example, pattern making, internal combustion engines, carpentry, photographic equipment, welding, and electrical gear. The ship also carried more than 3,000 tons of supplies, repair parts and provisions for its "clients." During World War II, the Navy had as many as 14 repair ships in operation. Plans for a new class of ARs were dropped in the early 1990s, and by the start of the 21st century, all of the repair ships were gone. As an alternative, the Navy relied instead on foreign shore-based repair facilities to support its deployed vessels and occasionally hired commercial heavy-lift vessels to return damaged ships back to the United States for repair, e.g., USS *Cole* (DDG 67) in 2000. The last repair ship in service was USS *Jason* (AR 8). She was decommissioned in June 1995 and dismantled in January 2008.

AR 1	*Medusa*[1]	AR 10	*Alcor*[10]	AR 19	*Xanthus*[19]
AR 2	*Bridgeport*[2]	AR 11	*Rigel*[11]	AR 20	*Laertes*[20]
AR 3	*Prometheus*[3]	AR 12	*Briareus*[12]	AR 21	*Dionysus*[21]
AR 4	*Vestal*[4]	AR 13	*Amphion*[13]	AR 22	*Klondike*[122]
AR 5	*Vulcan*[5]	AR 14	*Cadmus*[14]	AR 23	*Markab*[23]
AR 6	*Ajax*[6]	AR 15	*Deucalion*[15]	AR 28	*Grand Canyon*[24]
AR 7	*Hector*[7]	AR 16	*Mars*[16]		
AR 8	*Jason*[8]	AR 17	*Assistance*[17]		
AR 9	*Delta*[9]	AR 18	*Diligence*[18]		

NOTES

1. Decommissioned in November 1947 and sold for scrapping in August 1950.
2. The former SS *Breslau* acquired in June 1917, initially classified as a repair ship but commissioned as destroyer tender [q.v.] AD 10 in August 1917.
3. Former colliers [q.v.] AC 2 and AC 1, respectively.
4. *Ibid.*
5. Decommissioned in September 1991 and sold for scrapping in November 2007.
6. Commissioned in October 1943, decommissioned in December 1986, and sold for scrapping in May 1997.
7. Commissioned in February 1944, decommissioned in March 1987, and sold for scrapping in September 1994.
8. Commissioned as heavy-hull repair ship [q.v.] ARH 1 in June 1944, reclassified as AR 8 in September 1957, and sold for scrapping in November 2006.
9. Commissioned as cargo ship [q.v.] AK 29 in June 1941, reclassified as AR 9 in March 1943, decommissioned in December 1955, and sold for scrapping in July 1983.
10. Commissioned as miscellaneous auxiliary [q.v.] AG 34 in September 1941, reclassified as AR 10 in December 1941, reclassified as AD 34 in November 1944, and struck in August 1946.
11. Commissioned as AD 13 in February 1922, reclassified as base repair ship [q.v.] ARb 1 in April 1941, reclassified as AR 13 in December 1941, decommissioned in July 1946 and sold for scrapping in February 1948.
12. Commissioned in November 1943, struck in January 1977, and sold for scrapping in November 1980.
13. Commissioned in January 1946 and sold to Iran in March 1977.
14. Commissioned in April 1946, decommissioned in September 1971, and sold to Taiwan in April 1974.
15. Never commissioned; cancelled in August 1945.
16. *Ibid.*
17. Delivered in August 1944 but transferred to Royal Navy, returned to U.S. custody after the war, and sold for scrapping in 1974 and 1973, respectively.
18. *Ibid.*
19. Commissioned in May 1945, decommissioned in February 1947, and sold for scrapping in 1974.
20. Commissioned in March 1945, decommissioned in January 1947, and sold for scrapping in July 1972.
21. Commissioned in April 1945, decommissioned in July 1955, and sunk as artificial reef in November 1978.
22. Commissioned as AD 22 in July 1945, reclassified as AR 22 in February 1960, struck in September 1974, and sold in May 1975.
23. Commissioned as AK 31 in June 1941, reclassified as AD 21 in January 1942, decommissioned in January 1947, reclassified as AR 23 in April 1960, decommissioned in December 1969, struck in September 1976, and sold in April 1977.
24. Commissioned as AD 28 in April 1946, reclassified as AR 28 in March 1971, decommissioned in September 1978, and sold for scrapping in June 1980.

Base Repair Ship (ARb)

The former merchant ship *Edgecombe*, USS *Rigel* was commissioned as a destroyer tender [q.v.] and designated as AD 13 in February 1922. On April 10, 1941, she was reclassified as a base repair ship and redesignated as an ARb (the only naval vessel ever so classified) reflecting her role as a lesser repair ship for small combatants, such as minesweepers. *Rigel* was at Pearl Harbor undergoing a structural alteration during the Japanese attack, immediately after which she was redesignated as the repair ship AR 11 and deployed to the South Pacific armed with four 3-inch/50 mm guns. She was decom-

USS *Rigel* is seen here as a destroyer tender prior to her 1941 conversion to a base repair ship (U.S. Navy photograph).

missioned in July 1946, sold for scrapping in March 1948, and dismantled by mid–July of that year.

ARb 1   *Rigel*

Battle Damage Repair Ships (ARB)

Between 1943 and 1945 the Navy converted a dozen tank landing ships (LSTs) to battle damage repair ships (ARBs) for service in forward operating areas. Designated ARB 1–ARB 12, they carried various pieces of shop equipment, such as lathes, grinders and welding machines, enabling their 250-man crews to repair vessels damaged in combat. A key aspect of their role was the ability to patch up severely damaged combatants sufficiently to allow them to steam back to a rear-area shipyard or dry dock for heavy repairs. Eleven of the original 12 ARBs were either sold off or transferred to other navies between 1959 and 1980. The 12th, USS *Nestor* (ARB 6), was wrecked in a typhoon in October 1945. A final ARB, the former LST 50, was reclassified as an unnamed battle damage repair ship in November 1952 and transferred to Greece in September 1960. In the following list, the number in parenthesis was the vessel's hull number prior to conversion to an ARB.

ARB 1	*Aristaeus* (LST 329)[1]	ARB 5	*Midas* (LST 514)[5]
ARB 2	*Oceanus* (LST 328)[2]	ARB 6	*Nestor* (LST 518)
ARB 3	*Phaon* (LST 15)[3]	ARB 7	*Sarpedon* (LST 956)[6]
ARB 4	*Zeus* (LST 132)[4]	ARB 8	*Telamon* (LST 976)[7]

Originally planned to be built as LST 967, USS *Ulysses* (ARB 9) was commissioned in November 1944 as a battle damage repair ship. She was decommissioned in February 1947 and transferred to West Germany in June 1961 (U.S. Navy photograph).

ARB 9	*Ulysses* (LST 967)[8]		ARB 12	*Helios* (LST 1127)[11]
ARB 10	*Demeter* (LST 1121)[9]		ARB 13	(LST 50)
ARB 11	*Diomedes* (LST 1119)[10]			

Notes

1. Sold in 1962.
2. *Ibid.*
3. *Ibid.*
4. Sold in 1974.
5. Sold in 1980.
6. Sold in 1977.
7. Sold in 1974.
8. Transferred to West Germany in June 1961.
9. Sold in 1959.
10. Transferred to West Germany in June 1961.
11. Leased to Brazil in January 1962 and sold to Brazil in December 1977.

Cable Repairing or Laying Ships / Cable Repairing Ships (ARC)

See Chapter 2.

Non-Self-Propelled Auxiliary Repair Docks / Auxiliary Repair Dry Docks (ARD)

USS *Windsor* (ARD 22) was one of only five auxiliary repair dry docks to be named. Commissioned in April 1944, she is seen here in the 1950s, probably in the Philippines (U.S. Navy photograph).

In September 1934 the Navy put into service the unnamed auxiliary repair dock ARD 1. Capable of self-sustained operation after being towed to a forward area, ARD 1 could lift ships of up to 2,200 tons. Her performance while based at Pearl Harbor led the Navy to acquire another 30 such docks—ARD 2 and ARD 5–ARD 32—between May 1942 and August 1944 (ARDs 3 and 4 were cancelled). Those docks provided a nominal lifting capability of 3,500 tons (e.g., destroyers, submarines and small auxiliaries). Under certain conditions they could lift even heavier ships. ARD 12 and subsequent docks were slightly larger than the first ARDs and could handle tank landing ships (LSTs), which had a wider beam than could be accommodated by those earlier docks. ARD 33 was delivered in February 1946 but reclassified as the small auxiliary floating dry dock [q.v.] AFDL 47 (named *Reliance*), and ARDs 34 and 35 were cancelled.

Only five ARDs were named: *Waterford* (ARD 5), *West Milton* (ARD 7), *Windsor* (ARD 22), *Arco* (ARD 29) and *San Onofre* (ARD 30). ARD 18 was reclassified as medium auxiliary repair dry dock [q.v.] ARDM 3 and named *Endurance*, ARD 19 was reclassified as ARDM 1 and named *Oak Ridge*, ARD 20 was reclassified as auxiliary deep submergence support ship [q.v.] AGDS 1 *White Sands*, and ARD 26 was reclassified as ARDM 2 and named *Alamogordo*.

Twenty of the ARDs were transferred and/or sold to other countries, including Brazil, Chile, Colombia, Ecuador, Iran, Mexico, Pakistan, Peru, Taiwan, Turkey, and Venezuela. A few were scrapped. The last active ARD was *San Onofre* (ARD 30), which was removed from service in September 1996 and transferred to Mexico in 2001.

Bathyscaphe Support Auxiliary Dry Dock (ARD[BS])

USS *White Sands* (ARD[BS]) 20), the mother ship for the bathyscaph *Trieste*, is standing by as the submersible is preparing for a dive off her stern in 1972 (U.S. Navy photograph).

In October 1965 the auxiliary repair dock [q.v.] USS ARD 20 was taken out of mothballs to be converted at the Long Beach Naval Shipyard into the Navy's only bathyscaph support auxiliary repair dock. She was redesignated as the unnamed ARD(BS) 20 and recommissioned on September 14, 1966. According to her official Navy history, the dry dock was assigned to the Pacific Fleet Submarine Force "to conduct CNO research projects related to deep submergence vehicles and their operation." Named USS *White Sands* and redesignated back to ARD 20 in March 1968, the dock supported the deep submergence vehicle *Trieste* from 1968 into the early 1970s. In August 1973, *White Sands* was reclassified again—this time as an auxiliary deep submergence support ship [q.v.] and redesignated as AGDS 1. The following summer she was taken out of service and was struck from the NVR and sold in September 1974. Today the former *White Sands* is at work at the Lake Union Drydock Company in Seattle.

Auxiliary Repair Docks, Concrete / Concrete Auxiliary Repair Docks (ARDC)

See Auxiliary Floating Dry Docks—Little (Concrete) (AFDC).

Non-Self-Propelled Medium Auxiliary Repair Dry Docks / Medium Auxiliary Repair Docks (ARDM)

USS *Oak Ridge* (ARDM 1) is at the Naval Station in Rota, Spain, with the barrack ship APL 31 moored to her port side (U.S. Navy photograph).

The first three of these docks were ASD 12-class auxiliary repair dry docks [q.v.] converted in the 1960s to support nuclear-powered submarines (SSNs and SSBNs). The last two were purpose-built in 1977–1978 and 1984–1985, respectively, specifically for submarine support.

ARDM 1	*Oak Ridge*[1]		ARDM 4	*Shippingport*[4]
ARDM 2	*Alamogordo*[2]		ARDM 5	*Arco*[5]
ARDM 3	*Endurance*[3]			

Notes

1. Former ARD 19, commissioned as ARDM 1 and named in October 1963, served in New London, Conn., taken out of service in August 2001, struck November 2001, and transferred to USCG in February 2002.
2. Former ARD 26, commissioned as ARDM 2 and named in August 1965, struck in November 1993, and transferred to Ecuador in December 2000.
3. Former ARD 18, struck in July 1995.
4. Placed in service in January 1979 and currently assigned to New London.
5. Placed in service in June 1986 and currently assigned to San Diego.

Internal Combustion Engine Repair Ships (ARG)

USS *Kermit Roosevelt* (ARG 16) is barely underway in this January 1953 photo. She operated extensively in the Far East in the 1950s before her October 1959 decommissioning (U.S. Navy photograph).

With growing numbers of diesel-driven ships and craft coming into service during World War II, the Navy had to acquire several former Maritime Commission EC2-S-C1 "Liberty" ships and a few other types for conversion into tenders for diesel engine vessels in forward operating areas. Called internal combustion engine repair ships, the largest group of these wartime maintenance and support vessels (ARG 2–ARG 11, ARG 16 and ARG 17) were members of the *Luzon* (ARG 2) class commissioned between 1943 and 1945. Most of the ARGs were sold for scrapping in the 1970s. The last survivor of the type was USS *Tutuila* (ARG 4), which had been commissioned in April 1944. She was decommissioned in December 1946, recommissioned in May 1951, served in Vietnam between 1967 and 1972, and was decommissioned and transferred to Taiwan in February 1972.

ARG 1	*Oglala*[1]	ARG 8	*Leyte*[7]
ARG 2	*Luzon*[2]	ARG 9	*Mona Island*[8]
ARG 3	*Mindanao*[3]	ARG 10	*Palawan*[9]
ARG 4	*Tutuila*	ARG 11	*Samar*[10]
ARG 5	*Oahu*[4]	ARG 12	*Basilan*[11]
ARG 6	*Cebu*[5]	ARG 13	*Burias*[12]
ARG 7	*Culebra Island*[6]	ARG 14	*Dumaran*[13]

ARG 15	*Masbate*[14]	ARG 18	*Holland*[17]
ARG 16	*Kermit Roosevelt*[15]	ARG 19	*Beaver*[18]
ARG 17	*Hooper Island*[16]	ARG 20	*Otus*[19]

Notes

1. Commissioned as USS *Massachusetts* in December 1917, renamed *Shawmut* the next month, served as an aviation tender 1919–1920, reclassified as minelayer CM 4 in July 1920, renamed *Oglala* in January 1928, sunk at Pearl Harbor in December 1941, refloated in July 1942, reclassified as ARG 1 in June 1943, decommissioned and struck in July 1946, and sold for scrapping in November 1965.
2. Sold for scrapping.
3. Sunk as artificial reef.
4. Sold for scrapping.
5. Ibid.
6. Ibid.
7. Commissioned in August 1944, renamed *Maui* in May 1945, decommissioned in August 1946, and sold for scrapping in November 1972.
8. Sunk as artificial reef.
9. Ibid.
10. Sold for scrapping.
11. Originally planned as an ARG but reclassified as a miscellaneous auxiliary [q.v.] and commissioned in 1944 as AG 68 and AG 69, respectively, decommissioned in 1946, struck in 1947, and sold for scrapping in November 1970.
12. Ibid.
13. Originally planned as an ARG but reclassified as an aircraft repair ship [q.v.] and renamed and redesignated in 1944 as *Chourre* (ARV 1) and *Webster* (ARV 2), respectively.
14. Ibid.
15. Sold for scrapping.
16. Ibid.
17. Originally commissioned as submarine tender [q.v.] AS 3, AS 5 and AS 20, respectively, and reclassified as ARG in 1945. See Submarine Tender module in Chapter 2 for additional information.
18. Ibid.
19. Ibid.

Heavy-Hull Repair Ship (ARH)

The former heavy-hull repair ship USS *Jason* (ARH 1) is anchored off Vung Tau, South Vietnam, in 1968. Classified at the time as the repair ship AR 8, she has a nest of small vessels moored to her port side, while the coastal minesweeper USS *Woodpecker* (MSC 209) is refueling at her starboard side aft (U.S. Navy photograph).

In the mid–1930s the Navy identified the need for a vessel that could perform sufficient repairs on heavily damaged ships in locations very remote and distant from dry docks and shipyards to enable the damaged ship to make her way back to such facilities. This new vessel was called a heavy-hull repair ship and designated as ARH. The first and only ARH was USS *Jason* (ARH 1), laid down in March 1942, launched in April 1943, and commissioned on June 19, 1944. After serving in Asian waters during World War II and the Korean War, *Jason* was reclassified as a repair ship [q.v.] and redesignated as AR 8 in September 1957. She went on to serve during the Vietnam War and was ultimately dismantled in Texas in January 2008.

Landing Craft Repair Ship / Repair Ship, Small (ARL)

Seen underway off Louisiana shortly after her recommissioning in December 1967, USS *Sphinx* (ARL 24) served in both the Korean and Vietnam wars (U.S. Navy photograph).

In January 1943 the Navy established the ARL hull classification for the landing craft repair ship, i.e., a tank landing ship (LST)-type vessel used to repair damaged boats and small craft such as landing craft–mechanized (LCM) and landing craft–vehicles/personnel (LCVP). Some 40 LSTs were converted into ARLs and commissioned between 1943 and 1945. The ARLs were fitted with heavy hoists for lifting landing craft for servicing, and various shops and spare parts lockers were installed below the main deck in the tank hold.

During the Vietnam War *Askari* (ARL 30), *Indra* (ARL 37), *Satyr* (ARL 23) and *Sphinx* (ARL 24) provided maintenance and repair support to riverine warfare boats and small craft while USS *Krishna* (ARL 38) served as "mother ship" to Navy and Coast Guard Operation Market Time patrol boats. All of the ARLs were eventually decommissioned and sold off to commercial buyers or scrappers, or transferred to other countries. *Sphinx* was the last ARL remaining on the NVR. She was decommissioned in 1989 and sold for scrapping in November 2007.

In the following list, the number in parenthesis was the vessel's LST hull number prior to conversion to an ARL. An asterisk indicates a vessel that was disposed of by government sale.

ARL 1	Achelous (10)*	ARL 25 [9]	
ARL 2	Amycus (489)*	ARL 26	Stentor (858)*
ARL 3	Agenor (490)[1]	ARL 27	Tantalus (1117)[10]
ARL 4	Adonis (83)*	ARL 28	Typhon (1118)*
ARL 5	(81)[2]	ARL 29	Amphitrite (1124)*
ARL 6	(82)[3]	ARL 30	Askari (1131)[11]
ARL 7	Atlas (231)*	ARL 31	Bellerophon (1132)*
ARL 8	Egeria (136)*	ARL 32	Bellona (1136)[12]
ARL 9	Endymion (513)*	ARL 33	Chimaera (1137)*
ARL 10	Coronis (1003)*	ARL 34 [13]	
ARL 11	Creon (1036)*	ARL 35	Daedalus (1143)*
ARL 12	Poseidon (1037)*	ARL 36	Gordius (1145)[14]
ARL 13	Menelaus (971)*	ARL 37	Indra (1147)[15]
ARL 14	Minos (644)*	ARL 38	Krishna (1149)[16]
ARL 15	Minotaur (645)[4]	ARL 39	Quirinus (1151)[17]
ARL 16	Myrmidon (948)*	ARL 40	Remus (453)*
ARL 17	Numitor (954)*	ARL 41	Achilles (455)[18]
ARL 18	Pandemus (650)[5]	ARL 42	Aeolus (310)[19]
ARL 19	Patroclus (955)[6]	ARL 43	Cerberus (316)[20]
ARL 20	Pentheus (1115)*	ARL 44	Conus (317)[21]
ARL 21	Proserpine (1116)*	ARL 45	Feronia (332)[22]
ARL 22	Romulus (962)[7]	ARL 46	Chandra (350)[23]
ARL 23	Satyr (852)[8]	ARL 47	Minerva (374)[24]
ARL 24	Sphinx (963)		

Notes

1. Transferred to France in March 1951 and to Taiwan in September 1957.
2. Transferred to Great Britain in 1943 and returned in May 1946; sold in August 1947.
3. *Ibid.*
4. Transferred to South Korea in January 1977.
5. Expended as target in 1969.
6. Transferred to Turkey in November 1952.
7. Transferred to the Philippines in November 1961.
8. Transferred first to South Vietnam in 1971 and then to the Philippines in 1975.
9. Planned to have been LST 856 but conversion to ARL cancelled; built as LST 856.
10. Transferred to United Nations.
11. Sold to Indonesia in February 1979.
12. Wrecked and lost in December 1945.
13. Planned as LST 1141 but conversion to ARL cancelled; built as LST 1141.
14. Transferred to Iran in September 1968.
15. Sunk as reef in August 1992.

16. Transferred to Philippines in October 1971.
17. Transferred to Venezuela in December 1977.
18. Transferred to Republic of China in 1947.
19. Conversion to ARL cancelled in August 1945 and reclassification from LST to ARL and name assignment cancelled the next month.
20. *Ibid.*
21. *Ibid.*
22. *Ibid.*
23. *Ibid.*
24. *Ibid.*

Heavy-Machinery Repair Ship (ARM)

This auxiliary ship classification was established during World War II but appears to have never been assigned to a specific vessel. It is today listed as "inactive" on the NVR.

Repair and Salvage Vessels / Salvage Ships (ARS)

See Chapter 1.

Salvage Lifting Vessels (ARSD)

The salvage lifting vessels USS *Salvager* (ARSD 3) and USS *Windlass* (ARSD 4) are working together just off an unidentified beach. Both vessels assisted in moving the grounded battleship USS *Missouri* (BB 63) off a shoal in January 1950 (U.S. Navy photograph).

In 1945 the Navy converted four medium landing ships (LSM 459–LSM 552) to salvage lifting vessels ARSD 1–ARSD 4, respectively, to provide additional lifting capabilities to its salvage units. All four have since been retired and disposed of.

ARSD 1   Gypsy[1]   ARSD 3   Salvager[3]
ARSD 2   Mender[2]   ARSD 4   Windlass[4]

NOTES

1. Decommissioned in January 1948, recommissioned in 1951, decommissioned in 1955, and sold for scrapping in January 1974.
2. Ibid.
3. Decommissioned in November 1965, reclassified as salvage craft medium YMLC 3 and YMLC 4, respectively, in October 1967, and struck in August 1972.
4. Ibid.

Salvage Craft Tenders (ARST)

USS *Okala* (ARST 2) is dressed in camouflage in this mid-1945 photograph (U.S. Navy photograph).

Three new construction tank landing ships (LSTs) were converted in 1945 to tenders to support salvage vessels in the Pacific Theater. Classified as salvage craft tenders and designated as ARST 1–ARST 3, these tenders carried large equipment and materials used in salvage operations. A fourth ship, the repair and salvage vessel [q.v.] USS *Tackle* (ARS 37) was very briefly reclassified as a salvage craft tender in 1945 but was quickly redesignated again as the unclassified miscellaneous vessel IX 217.

ARST 1	*Laysan Island*[1]		ARST 3	*Palmyra*[3]
ARST 2	*Okala*[2]		ARST 4	*Tackle*[4]

NOTES

1. Laid down as LST 1098, commissioned as ARST in June 1945, decommissioned in April 1947, struck in June 1973, and sold for scrapping in January 1974.
2. Laid down as LST 1099, commissioned as ARST in February 1945, decommissioned in August 1946, and sold in June 1947.
3. Laid down as LST 1100, commissioned as ARST in July 1945, decommissioned in June 1947, and sold for scrapping in April 1974.
4. Former steamship *W.R. Chamberlain, Jr.*, commissioned as ARS 37 in August 1943, damaged by a mine in 1944, redesignated as ARST 4 in February 1945, redesignated as IX 217 the following month, decommissioned in September 1945, and sold in March 1949 for scrapping.

Aircraft Repair Ships (ARV)

USS *Chourre* (ARV 1) is anchored in the western Pacific in 1945. Among her assignments that year, she transported aviation personnel to Espiritu Santo, transferred an aviation repair unit to Saipan, and served as the station supply ship for aircraft carriers in the Philippines (U.S. Navy photograph).

In August 1943 the Navy decided to convert two Maritime Commission EC2-S-C1 type vessels into aircraft repair ships (ARVs) to perform maintenance on aircraft engines and repair airframes. The two vessels had originally been planned to be the internal combustion engine repair ships [q.v.] USS *Dumaran* (ARG 14) and USS *Masbate* (ARG 15) but were reclassified in February 1944 as aircraft repair ships and renamed in March 1944 as USS *Chourre* (ARV 1) and USS *Webster* (ARV 2), respectively. Follow on vessels to perform this work were derived from tank landing ships (LSTs) and classified as either aircraft repair ship (engine) [q.v.]—viz., ARVE 3 and ARVE 4—or aircraft repair ship (aircraft) [q.v.]—viz., ARVA 5 and ARVA 6. ARV 1 was commissioned in May 1944 and ARV 2 followed in August 1944. The hull numbers ARV 3–ARV 6 were never used.

| ARV 1 | Chourre[1] | ARV 2 | Webster[2] |

Notes

1. Decommissioned in September 1946, recommissioned in February 1952, decommissioned in September 1955, and sold for scrapping in March 1971.
2. Decommissioned in June 1946, struck in September 1962, and sunk as a reef in August 1974.

Aircraft Repair Ships (Aircraft) (ARVA)

USS *Fabius* (ARVA 5) earned one battle star for her service during the Korean War (U.S. Navy photograph).

Following the 1944 conversion of two EC2-S-C1 vessels into aircraft repair ships [q.v.], the Navy elected to split the functions of the next four ARVs into two specialized ship types. One of those types, the aircraft repair ship (aircraft), was derived from tank landing ship hulls LST 1093 and LST 1095, designated as ARVA 5 and ARVA 6, respectively, and commissioned in April 1945. The ARVAs were intended to perform repairs on airframes while beached in forward areas.

| ARVA 5 | Fabius[1] | ARVA 6 | Megara[2] |

Notes

1. Decommissioned in August 1946, recommissioned in July 1950, decommissioned in April 1952, and sold in January 1974.
2. Decommissioned in June 1946, recommissioned in January 1951, decommissioned in January 1956, and transferred to Mexico in October 1973.

Aircraft Repair Ships (Engine) (ARVE)

The second specialized ARV-type vessel was the aircraft repair ship (engine). It was derived from tank landing ship hulls LST 1092 and LST 1094, designated as ARVE 3 and ARVE 4, and commissioned in March and April 1945, respectively. The ARVEs were to focus on overhauling and repairing aircraft engines, and work in tandem with aircraft repair ships (aircraft) [q.v.] while beached in advanced bases.

ARVE 3   *Aventinus*[1]   ARVE 4   *Chloris*[2]

Notes

1. Decommissioned in August 1946, recommissioned in July 1950, Decommissioned in April 1952, and transferred to Chile in August 1963.
2. Decommissioned in June 1946, recommissioned in January 1951, decommissioned in December 1955, and sold in April 1974.

Aircraft Repair Ship (Helicopter) (ARVH)

USNS *Corpus Christi Bay* (T-ARVH 1) is moored at the Charleston Naval Shipyard in South Carolina in 1966, where she had been converted the year before from a seaplane tender into the Navy's only helicopter repair ship (U.S. Navy photograph).

The *Curtiss*-class seaplane tender [q.v.] USS *Albemarle* (AV 5) was converted in 1965 to a floating aeronautical maintenance facility for rotary-wing aircraft. Renamed USNS *Corpus Christi Bay* and redesignated as T-ARVH 1 in March 1965, she was assigned to MSC in January 1966. *Corpus Christi Bay* deployed to South Vietnam in 1966 with 308 Army aircraft technicians on board. As damaged helicopters could now be barged out to the ship and hoisted aboard for repairs in country, it was no longer necessary to transport the choppers back to the United States for refitting and overhauls. After operating in Vietnam for three years, the ship was removed from service in 1973, struck in December 1974, and sold for scrapping in July 1975.

T-ARVH 1   *Corpus Christi Bay*

Submarine Tenders (AS)

See Chapter 1.

Submarine Rescue Vessels / Submarine Rescue Ships (ASR)

The submarine rescue ship USS *Kittiwake* (ASR 13) is underway in Hampton Roads, Virginia, on December 19, 1969. During her career, she operated off the U.S. East Coast, and in the Caribbean and Mediterranean seas (U.S. Navy photograph).

These ships were intended to rescue crews trapped in sunken submarines. The first six submarine rescue vessels were derived from minesweepers of the *Lapwing* (AM 1) class (a.k.a. the "Bird" class) originally commissioned in 1918–1919 and assigned to submarine-related duties in the 1920s. In September 1929 they were reclassified as submarine rescue vessels (ASR) of the Widgeon class. The next group of ASRs—the Chanticleer class (ASR 7–ASR 11 and ASR 13–ASR 18)—were commissioned between 1942 and 1947 as replacements for the original six. Three additional ASRs—the Penguin class—were derived from fleet tugs [q.v.] in 1943 and 1945, and were designated ASRs 12, 19 and 20.

The ASRs were equipped with the McCann rescue chamber and could perform general salvage and diving operations. The final two submarine rescue ships—the Pigeon class of ASR 21 and ASR 22—were built to carry the Deep Submergence Rescue Vehicle (DSRV) and to assist in deep-ocean diving operations. They were commissioned in 1973 and decommissioned and struck in December 1998 and 1995, respectively. Both have since been dismantled.

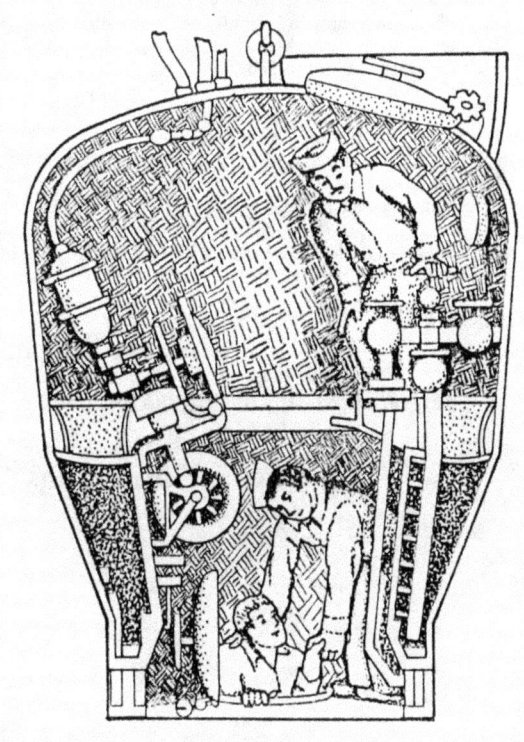

Cutaway drawing of the McCann rescue chamber used by USS *Falcon* (ASR 2) to rescue 33 crewmen from the sunken submarine USS *Squalus* (SS 192) in May 1939 (U.S. Navy photograph).

ASR 1	*Widgeon*[1]	ASR 9	*Florikan*[9]	ASR 17	*Verdin*[17]
ASR 2	*Falcon*[2]	ASR 10	*Greenlet*[10]	ASR 18	*Windover*[18]
ASR 3	*Chewink*[3]	ASR 11	*Macaw*[11]	ASR 19	*Bluebird*[19]
ASR 4	*Mallard*[4]	ASR 12	*Penguin*[12]	ASR 20	*Skylark*[20]
ASR 5	*Ortolan*[5]	ASR 13	*Kittiwake*[13]	ASR 21	*Pigeon*
ASR 6	*Pigeon*[6]	ASR 14	*Petrel*[14]	ASR 22	*Ortolan*
ASR 7	*Chanticleer*[7]	ASR 15	*Sunbird*[15]		
ASR 8	*Coucal*[8]	ASR 16	*Tringa*[16]		

Notes

1. Former minesweeper AM 22; sold in March 1948.
2. Former AM 28.
3. Former AM 39; expended as target.
4. Former AM 44; expended as target.
5. Former AM 45; sold in August 1947.
6. Former AM 47; sunk by Japanese aircraft in May 1942.
7. Sold for scrapping in June 1974.

8. Expended as target in January 1991.
9. Sold for scrapping in July 2010.
10. Sold to Turkey in February 1973.
11. Grounded and lost in February 1944.
12. Former fleet tug *Chetco* (AT 99); sold in July 1971.
13. Sunk in January 2011 as dive site and marine refuge.
14. Sold for scrapping in August 2003.
15. Sold for scrapping in July 2005.
16. Transferred to USMC in January 1983 as a target.
17. Contract cancelled in August 1945.
18. *Ibid.*
19. Laid down as fleet tug *Yurok* (ATF 164) but commissioned as ASR; transferred to Turkey in 1950.
20. Laid down as fleet tug *Yustaga* (ATF 165) but commissioned as ASR; transferred to Brazil in 1973.

Transport Submarines (ASSP)

See Transport Submarines (APS) above.

Ocean-Going Tugs / Fleet Tugs (AT)

USS *Seneca* (AT 91) was commissioned in April 1943 and served the fleet for more than a quarter-century primarily in the western Atlantic, Gulf of Mexico and the Caribbean Sea. She was decommissioned in July 1971 (U.S. Navy photograph).

Tug boats have served in the Navy since at least the Civil War. On his Shipscribe website, Stephen S. Roberts identifies 13 tugs in the Union and Confederate navies during that conflict. He names another 10 tugs acquired between 1864 and 1898 along with 17 ocean-going tugs acquired during World War I. Some 42 of these vessels were in service in the early 1920s and are listed below.

3. Directory of U.S. Navy Auxiliary Ships

Early Ocean-Going Tugs

AT 10	Patapsco	AT 26	Wandank	AT 46	Iroquois
AT 11	Patuxent	AT 27	Tatnuck	AT 47	Osceola
AT 12	Sonoma	AT 28	Sunnadin	AT 48	Peoria
AT 13	Ontario	AT 29	Mahopac	AT 49	Piscataqua
AT 14	Arapaho	AT 30	Sciota	AT 50	Potomac
AT 15	Mohave	AT 31	Koka	AT 51	Uncas
AT 16	Tillamook	AT 32	Napa[1]	AT 53	Navajo
AT 17	Wando	AT 33	Pinola	AT 53	Delaware
AT 18	Chemung	AT 34	Algorma	AT 54	Conestoga
AT 19	Allegheny	AT 35	Carrabasset	AT 55	Genesee
AT 20	Sagamore	AT 36	Contocook	AT 56	Lykens
AT 21	Bagaduce	AT 37	Iuka	AT 57	Sea Rover
AT 22	Tadousac	AT 38	Keosanqua	AT 58	Undaunted
AT 23	Kalmia	AT 39	Montcalm	AT 59	Challenge
AT 24	Kewaydin	AT 40		AT 60	Bay Spring
AT 25	Umpqua	AT 45[2]			

Later Ocean-Going Tugs

The following tugs were acquired between 1922 and 1945.

AT 61	Cahokia	AT 91	Seneca	AT 128	Caddo[9]
AT 62	Tamaroa	AT 92	Tawasa	AT 129	Cayuga[10]
AT 63	Acushnet	AT 93	Tekesta	AT 130	Missisauga[11]
AT 64	Navajo[1]	AT 94	Yuma	AT 131	Bobolink
AT 65	Seminole[2]	AT 95	Zuni	AT 132	Brant
AT 66	Cherokee	AT 96	Abnaki	AT 133	Cormorant
AT 67	Apache	AT 97	Alsea	AT 134	Grebe
AT 68	Arapaho	AT 98	Arikara	AT 135	Kingfisher
AT 69	Chippewa	AT 99	Chetco[7]	AT 136	Oriole
AT 70	Choctaw	AT 100	Chowanoc	AT 137	Owl
AT 71	Hopi	AT 101	Cocopa	AT 138	Partridge
AT 72	Kiowa	AT 102	Hidatsa	AT 139	Rail
AT 73	Menominee	AT 103	Hitchiti	AT 140	Robin
AT 74	Pawnee	AT 104	Jicarilla	AT 141	Seagull
AT 75	Sioux	AT 105	Moctobi	AT 142	Tern
AT 76	Ute	AT 106	Molala	AT 143	Turkey
AT 77	Tuscarora	AT 107	Munsee	AT 144	Vireo
AT 78	Carib[3]	AT 108	Pakana	AT 145	Woodcock
AT 79	Yuma[4]	AT 109	Potawatomi	AT 146	Maricopa
AT 80	Yaqui[5]	AT 110	Quapaw	AT 147	Esselen
AT 81	Bannock	AT 111	Sarsi	AT 148	Achomawi
AT 82	Carib	AT 112	Serrano	AT 149	Atakapa
AT 83	Chickasaw	AT 113	Takelma	AT 150	Avovel
AT 84	Cree	AT 114	Tawakoni	AT 151	Chawasha
AT 85	Lipan	AT 115	Tenino	AT 152	Cahuilla
AT 86	Mataco	AT 116	Tolowa	AT 153	Chilula
AT 87	Moreno	AT 117	Wateree	AT 154	Chimariko
AT 88	Narragansett	AT 118	Wenatchee	AT 155	Cusabo
AT 89	Nauset[6]	AT 119	–	AT 156	Luiseno
AT 90	Pinto	AT 127[8]		AT 157	Nipmuc

AT 158 –   AT 167   *Chatot*   AT 169   *Whipporwill*
AT 166[12]   AT 168   *Lark*

Reclassifications

Considerable reclassifications affected the ocean-going tug vessels, including the following: ATs 12, 13, 19, 21, 23–30, 33, 37–39, 63, 131, 133, 135–144, 147, 168 and 169 were reclassified as ocean tugs–old [q.v.] and redesignated as ATOs retaining their AT hull numbers; ATs 14, 16–18, 48, 51, 53, 58, 59, 61, 62, and 77 were reclassified as harbor tugs and redesignated as YTs with new hull numbers; ATs 66–76, 81–88, 90–98, 100–118, and 148–167 were reclassified as ocean tugs—fleet [q.v.] and redesignated as ATFs retaining their AT hull numbers; ATs 119–127 and 170–176 were reclassified as ocean tugs—rescue [q.v.] and redesignated as ATRs with new hull numbers; and ATs 128–130 were reclassified as ocean-going rescue vessels for Britain and redesignated as BAT 3–BAT 5.

Notes

1. War loss.
2. *Ibid.*
3. Cancelled.
4. *Ibid.*
5. *Ibid.*
6. War loss.
7. Completed as submarine rescue vessel [q.v.] *Penguin* (ASR 12).
8. Delivered as ocean tugs-rescue [q.v.] ATR 41–ATR 49.
9. Built as ocean-going rescue vessels BAT 3–BAT 5 for Britain.
10. *Ibid.*
11. *Ibid.*
12. Unassigned.

Ocean Tugs–Auxiliary / Auxiliary Ocean Tugs (ATA)

Auxiliary ocean tugs (ATAs) could be considered the "small" sea-going tug boats of the Navy, whereas fleet ocean tugs [q.v.] (ATFs) were the "large" ocean-going tug boats. ATAs came in two basic sizes: 143-foot former ocean tugs—rescue [q.v.] (ATRs) completed between 1943 and 1945, and 193-foot former net-laying ships [q.v.] (ANs) completed between 1944 and 1945.

ATAs 121–ATA 125 were previously designated as ATR 43–ATR 47, respectively; ATA 146 had been ATR 90; ATA 170–ATA 213 were the former ATR 97–ATR 140, respectively, and ATA 214–ATA 218 had been designated as AN 64–AN 72, inclusive. A number of auxiliary tugs were unnamed, primarily ATA 219–T-ATA 244.

After World War II, several ATAs were transferred, leased or sold to other navies, including those of Argentina, Brazil, Chile, Colombia, Dominican Republic, Mexico, Peru, South Korea, Taiwan and Turkey. Other ATAs were sold by the government to civilian buyers and put to work as commercial tug boats, as well as a fishing boat, training vessel, luxury yacht (and floating B&B inn) and a fireboat. In 1950, the Navy acquired T-AKA 239–T-AKA 244 from the U.S. Army and assigned them to service with the newly-formed Military Sea Transportation Service. They were later either returned to the Army or sold off by 1972. The Navy's last ATAs were decommissioned in the early 1970s. Ten years later, there were only five of them left—ATAs 178, 181, 190, 195 and 213—all laid up

The auxiliary tug USS *Kalmia* (ATA 184) is towing the light cruiser *Vincennes* (CL 64) out of San Diego, Calif., on October 1969. Assisting on the move are the harbor tugs *Muskegon* (YTB 763) on the cruiser's starboard bow, and *Arawak* (YTM 702) off the stern. *Vincennes* was expended as a target two weeks later (U.S. Navy photograph).

in reserve. The last remaining auxiliary ocean tug—*Keywadin* (ATA 213)—was expended as a target in June 2001.

ATA 121	*Sotoyomo*	ATA 175	*Sonoma*	ATA 193	*Stallion*
ATA 122		ATA 176	*Tonkawa*	ATA 194	*Bagaduce*
ATA 123	*Iuka*	ATA 177		ATA 195	*Tatnuck*
ATA 124		ATA 178	*Tunica*	ATA 196	*Mahopac*
ATA 125		ATA 179	*Allegheny*	ATA 197	*Sunnadin*
ATA 126[1]		ATA 180		ATA 198	*Keosanqua*
ATA 127[1]		ATA 181	*Accokeek*	ATA 199	*Undaunted*
ATA 128	*Caddo*	ATA 182	*Unadilla*	ATA 200	
ATA 129	*Cayuga*	ATA 183	*Nottoway*	ATA 201	*Challenge*
ATA 130	*Missisauga*	ATA 184	*Kalmia*	ATA 202	*Wampa-noag*
ATA 146	*Maricopa*	ATA 185	*Koka*		
ATA 166	*Chetco*	ATA 186	*Cahokia*	ATA 203	*Navigator*
ATA 167	*Chatot*	ATA 187	*Salish*	ATA 204	*Wandank*
ATA 170		ATA 188	*Penobscot*	ATA 205	*Sciota*
ATA 171[2]		ATA 189	*Reindeer*	ATA 206	*Pinola*
ATA 172		ATA 190	*Samoset*	ATA 207	*Geronimo*
ATA 173		ATA 191[3]		ATA 208	*Sagamore*
ATA 174	*Wateree*	ATA 192	*Tillamook*	ATA 209	*Umpqua*

U.S. Navy Auxiliary Vessels

ATA 210	*Catawba*	ATA 220	ATA 233[4]
ATA 211	*Navajo*	ATA 221	ATA 234
ATA 212	*Algorma*	ATA 222	ATA 238[5]
ATA 213	*Keywadin*	ATA 223	T-AKA 239
ATA 214		ATA 224	T-AKA 240
ATA 215		ATA 225	T-AKA 241
ATA 216		ATA 226	T-AKA 242
ATA 217		ATA 227	T-AKA 243
ATA 218		ATA 228	T-AKA 244
ATA 219		ATA 229	ATA 245 *Tuscarora*[6]

NOTES

1. Never served as ATA.
2. Former ATR lost in collision in April 1944.
3. Former ATR lost in grounding in October 1945.
4. Contract cancelled in August 1945.
5. Completed after the contract was cancelled in September 1945 and then subsequently sold before being placed in service.
6. Commissioned as AT 77 in December 1941, reclassified as harbor tug YT 341 in November 1942, reclassified as big harbor tug YTB 341 in May 1944, reclassified as ATA 245 in November 1958, struck in September 1961, and sold for scrapping in October 1976.

Ocean Tugs—Fleet /Fleet Ocean Tugs (ATF)

See Chapter 1.

Ocean Tugs—Old (ATO)

The ocean tug—old USS *Cormorant* (ATO 133) is underway off Norfolk, Virginia, on April 18, 1945. She was commissioned originally as a minesweeper (AM 40) and was reclassified as a tug (AT 133) in June 1942. *Cormorant* was decommissioned in March 1946 and sold the following year (U.S. Navy photograph).

3. Directory of U.S. Navy Auxiliary Ships

In May 1944 the ocean tugs listed below were reclassified as ocean tugs-old and redesignated as ATOs while retaining their former AT hull numbers. All but two of them were sold to civilian buyers after World War II.

ATO 12	Sonoma[1]	ATO 30	Sciota	ATO 137	Owl
ATO 13	Ontario	ATO 33	Pinola	ATO 138	Patridge[2]
ATO 19	Allegheny	ATO 34	Algorma	ATO 139	Rail
ATO 20	Sagamore	ATO 37	Iuka	ATO 140	Robin
ATO 21	Bagaduce	ATO 38	Keosanqua	ATO 141	Seagull
ATO 23	Kalmia	ATO 39	Montcalm	ATO 142	Tern
ATO 24	Kewaydin	ATO 58	Undaunted	ATO 143	Turkey
ATO 25	Umpqua	ATO 63	Acushnet	ATO 144	Vireo
ATO 26	Wandank	ATO 131	Bobolink	ATO 147	Esselen
ATO 27	Tatnuck	ATO 133	Cormorant	ATO 168	Lark
ATO 28	Sunnadin	ATO 135	Kingfisher	ATO 169	Whippoor-will
ATO 29	Mahopac	ATO 136	Oriole		

Notes

1. Lost in combat in October 1944.
2. Lost in combat in June 1944.

Ocean Tugs—Rescue (ATR)

Displaying her call sign of "NGAL" on the flag hoist, ATR 33 is anchored in San Francisco Bay sometime in 1945–1946 (U.S. Navy photograph).

Influenced by British experience during World War II, the U.S. Navy determined that it needed to quickly place in service several score tug boats for the purpose of towing and saving disabled vessels heavily damaged by enemy action, heavy seas or engine failures. These so-called rescue tugs (unnamed and designated as ATRs) were to be positioned in or near sea lanes adjacent to the coast where marine traffic was heaviest, and be capable of towing large merchant ships or combatant vessels shortly after they were damaged.

The construction of the first ocean tugs—rescue (ATR 1–ATR 40 and ATR 50–ATR 89) was ordered in January and August 1942. Constructed of wood, they were 165-feet long and commissioned between September 1943 and February 1945. These vessels were disposed of between October 1946 and August 1948.

In January 1942 the Navy ordered the construction of ATR 41–ATR 49 and ATR 90–ATR 100 (all but ATR 90 for the Royal Navy). These tugs were built of steel, 143-feet long and commissioned between January 1943 and April 1944. They were eliminated between December 1946 and November 1947.

Construction of the final group of ocean tugs—rescue (ATR 101–ATR 140) was ordered in April 1943. They were of steel construction and commissioned between July 1944 and June 1945. These tugs were disposed of between May 1946 and November 1974 (the former ATR 116, then *Raindeer* [ATA 189], was the last).

Among the rescue tugs sold to American civilian buyers after the war were ATRs 34, 37, 50, 55, 59, 61, 67, 69, 73, 80, and 89, which were then used in such roles as fishing boats, freighters, training ship, and, of course, commercial tug boats.

Reclassifications

ATR 17–ATR 20 were the British BATR 17–BATR 20; ATR 41 and ATR 42 were the former USN ocean-going tugs [q.v.] AT 119 and AT 120, respectively, and provided to the British; ATR 43, the former AT 121, was reclassified as the ocean tug—auxiliary [q.v.] ATA 121 and named *Sotoyamo*; ATR 44, the former AT 122, was reclassified as ATA 122; ATR 45, the former AT 123, was reclassified as ATA 123 and named *Iuka*; ATR 46 and ATR 47 were reclassified as ATA 124 and ATA 125, respectively; ATR 48 and ATR 49 were provided to the British; ATR 90 was reclassified as ATA 146; ATR 91–ATR 96 were provided to the British; ATR 97–ATR 140 were reclassified as ATA 170–ATA 213, respectively.

Salvage and Rescue Ships (ATS)

See Chapter 1.

Heavier-Than-Air Aircraft Tenders / Large Seaplane Tenders / Aircraft Tenders / Seaplane Tenders (AV)

During the first half of the last century the Navy operated numerous seaplanes and flying boats for scouting, patrol, and anti-submarine missions. These aircraft were supported in remote and forward operating areas by seaplane tenders (designated as AVs) which provided weapons, fuel and maintenance as well as spare parts, shops and accommodations for mechanics and flight personnel. The later AVs employed large cranes to

3. Directory of U.S. Navy Auxiliary Ships

In October 1944 the seaplane tenders USS *Currituck* (AV-7) (upper) and USS *Tangier* (AV-8) (lower) are anchored at Morotai, an Indonesian island, prior to the invasion of Leyte in the Philippines later that month. OS2U Kingfisher floatplanes are stowed on board both ships and small aircraft rescue boats are moored on *Tangier*'s port side (U.S. Navy photograph).

hoist seaplanes from the water to be serviced on board. As the Navy withdrew seaplanes from operation following World War II, their tenders likewise were retired and disposed of, although *Currituck* (AV 7) and *Salisbury Sound* (AV 13) served as late as the Vietnam era. By mid–1975, all of the remaining AVs had been sold off.

AV 1	*Wright*[1]	AV 10	*Chandeleur*[10]	AV 16	*St. George*[16]
AV 2	*Jason*[2]	AV 11	*Norton Sound*[11]	AV 17	*Cumberland Sound*[17]
AV 3	*Langley*[3]	AV 12	*Pine Island*[12]	AV 18	*Townsend*[18]
AV 4	*Curtiss*[4]	AV 13	*Salisbury Sound*[13]	AV 19	*Calibogue*[19]
AV 5	*Albemarle*[5]	AV 14	*Kenneth Whiting*[14]	AV 20	*Hobe Sound*[20]
AV 6	*Patoka*[6]	AV 15	*Hamlin*[15]		
AV 7	*Currituck*[7]				
AV 8	*Tangier*[8]				
AV 9	*Pocomoke*[9]				

Notes

1. Commissioned as lighter-than-air aircraft tender AZ 1 in December 1921, reclassified as heavier-than-air aircraft tender AV 1 in December 1926 (this initial nomenclature for the AV vessels was changed to seaplane tender

in the mid–1930s), reclassified as the miscellaneous auxiliary [q.v.] AG 79 in October 1944, renamed *San Clemente* in February 1945, decommissioned in June 1946, struck in July 1946, and sold for scrapping in July 1948.

2. Commissioned as Fuel Ship No. 12 in June 1913, reclassified as collier [q.v.] AC 12 in July 1920, reclassified as seaplane tender AV 2 in January 1930, decommissioned in June 1932, struck in May 1936, and sold in July 1936.

3. Commissioned as Collier No. 3 *Jupiter* in April 1913, decommissioned in March 1920, recommissioned as aircraft carrier *Langley* (CV 1) in March 1922, reclassified as seaplane tender AV 3 in April 1937, and sunk by Japanese aircraft in February 1942.

4. Commissioned in November 1940, decommissioned in September 1957, struck in July 1963, and sold for scrapping in March 1972.

5. Commissioned in December 1940, decommissioned in August 1950, recommissioned in October 1957, decommissioned in October 1960, struck in September 1962, reinstated in March 1965, converted to aircraft repair ship (helicopter) [q.v.] and placed in service as USNS *Corpus Christi Bay* (T-ARVH 1) in January 1966.

6. Commissioned as Fleet Oiler No. 9 in October 1919, designated as oiler [q.v.] AO 9 in July 1920, reclassified as AV 6 in October 1939, reclassified as AO 9 in June 1940, reclassified as AG 125 in August 1944, decommissioned and struck in January 1946, and sold for scrapping in March 1948.

7. Commissioned in June 1944, decommissioned in August 1947, recommissioned in August 1951, decommissioned in February 1958, recommissioned in August 1960, decommissioned in October 1967, struck in April 1971, and sold for scrapping in January 1972.

8. Commissioned in August 1941, decommissioned in 1947, and sold in January 1962.

9. Commissioned in July 1941, decommissioned in July 1946, struck in June 1961, and sold for scrapping in December 1961.

10. Commissioned in November 1942, decommissioned in February 1947, struck in April 1971, and sold in February 1972.

11. Commissioned in January 1945 and reclassified as guided missile ship [q.v.] AVM 1 in August 1951.

12. Commissioned in April 1945, decommissioned in May 1950, recommissioned in October 1950, decommissioned in June 1967, struck in February 1971, and sold for scrapping in March 1972.

13. Commissioned in November 1945, decommissioned in March 1967, and sold for scrapping in February 1972.

14. Commissioned in May 1944, decommissioned in May 1947, recommissioned in October 1951, decommissioned in September 1958, struck in July 1961, and sold for scrapping in February 1962.

15. Commissioned in June 1944, decommissioned in January 1947, struck in July 1963, and sold for scrapping in November 1972.

16. Commissioned in July 1944, decommissioned in August 1946, struck in July 1963, and transferred to Italy in December 1968.

17. Commissioned in August 1944, decommissioned in May 1947, struck in July 1961, and sold for scrapping in April 1962.

18. Laid down in June 1945 but cancelled two months later.

19. Cancelled in October 1944.

20. *Ibid.*

Advanced Base Ships / Aviation Logistic Support Ships (AVB)

See Chapter 2.

Catapult Lighter (AVC)

In the late 1930s the Navy was seeking to develop a long-range patrol aircraft capable of carrying large bomb loads. At the time such a heavy load could be best accommodated in a patrol aircraft if the plane were to be catapulted or launched into the air rather than in a conventional roll down a runway. To test this process, the Navy decided to install a Type XH Mark III hydraulic catapult on a 428-foot barge that was purpose-built in the Philadelphia Navy Yard. Classified as an "auxiliary vessel—catapult lighter" and designated as AVC 1 in May and June 1938, respectively, the barge was launched in August 1940. Installation of its catapult equipment was completed in May 1942. AVC 1 successfully launched the prototype XPBM-2 Mariner patrol aircraft later that year and by June 1943 its role as a catapult test platform was completed. In 1944 AVC 1 was used in evaluating various techniques for the preservation and care of inactive (i.e., mothballed) ships. The barge was placed "in commission in reserve" in March 1945, decommissioned and in service in August 1947, placed "out of service in reserve" in December 1949, and sold for scrapping in April 1956.

Seaplane Tenders—Destroyer (AVD)

The former destroyer USS *Belknap* (DD 251) was converted to the seaplane tender (AVD 8) in 1940. She is seen here three years later while operating north of the Azores in the Atlantic as part of the USS *Core* (CVE 13) hunter-killer group (U.S. Navy photograph).

Needing fast tenders to serve as mobile bases for its PBY Catalina patrol aircraft in World War II, the Navy converted two *Clemson* (DD 186)-class destroyers—*Childs* (DD 241) and *Williamson* (DD 244)—in 1938–1939 to small seaplane tenders designated as AVP 14 and AVP 15, respectively. The conversion required the removal of two forward stacks and much of the destroyers' weapons, along with installation of aviation fuel tanks in place of the two forward boilers, a light crane amidships, and added living spaces for flight and support personnel. Another five destroyer conversions were approved in 1939, followed by seven more the next year. In August 1940 the classification of the 14 converted four-stackers was changed to seaplane tender—destroyer and they were redesignated as AVDs. Each of these ships could support a 12-plane patrol squadron. Six of the AVDs were later converted in 1944 to APD high-speed transports [q.v.] and all 14 of the vessels were sold for dismantling between 1945 and 1948.

In the following listing, the number in parenthesis is the ship's original destroyer (DD) hull number. AVD 1–AVD 7 had been previously designated as AVP 14–AVP 20, respectively.

U.S. Navy Auxiliary Vessels

AVD 1	*Childs* (241)	AVD 8	*Belknap* (251)[5]
AVD 2	*Williamson* (244)[1]	AVD 9	*Osmond Ingram* (255)[6]
AVD 3	*George E. Badger* (196)[2]	AVD 10	*Ballard* (267)
AVD 4	*Clemson* (186)[3]	AVD 11	*Thornton* (270)[7]
AVD 5	*Goldsborough* (188)[4]	AVD 12	*Gillis* (260)
AVD 6	*Hulbert* (342)	AVD 13	*Greene* (266)[8]
AVD 7	*William B. Preston* (344)	AVD 14	*McFarland* (237)

Notes

1. Reclassified back to destroyer DD 244 in December 1943.
2. Reclassified as APD 33 in May 1944.
3. Reclassified as APD 31 in July 1944.
4. Reclassified as APD 32 in March 1944.
5. Reclassified as APD 34 in June 1944, decommissioned in August 1945, and sold for scrapping in November 1945.
6. Reclassified as destroyer DD 255 in November 1943 and reclassified as APD 35 in 1944.
7. Decommissioned in May 1945 as a result of heavy damage in a collision with two oilers the month before.
8. Reclassified as APD 36 in February 1944 and lost in a grounding in October 1945.

Guided Missile Ship (AVM)

Two years before she was formally reclassified as a guided missile ship, USS *Norton Sound* (AV 11) is launching a Loon missile (a copy of the German V-1 rocket) on October 12, 1949 (U.S. Navy photograph).

USS *Norton Sound* (AV 11) was a *Currituck* (AV 7)-class seaplane tender [q.v.] converted by the Philadelphia Naval Shipyard to a mobile missile launching platform in February–October 1948. Reclassified as a guided missile ship and redesignated as AVM 1 in August 1951, *Norton Sound* launched Skyhook balloons, and test fired the Loon, Terrier and Tartar guided missiles through 1962. She was decommissioned in August 1962 to be outfitted with the new Typhon anti-air weapon system and its associated AN/SPG-59 radar for testing. The Typhon program was cancelled before *Norton Sound* was recommissioned in June 1964. She then conducted tests of the SPG-59 radar (which was removed in mid–1966), Sea Sparrow surface-to-air missile and a new gun and gunfire control system. In 1974 the new Aegis weapons control system was installed on the ship and in May of that year, *Norton Sound* fired Standard-MR missiles in tests against a drone. She was decommissioned in December 1986, struck in January 1987, transferred to MARAD in October 1988 and later sold for scrapping.

Small Seaplane Tenders (AVP)

The crew of USS *Rehoboth* (AVP 50) is lining the rails on March 8, 1944, while the ship is underway off Houghton, Washington (U.S. Navy photograph).

The Navy's first small seaplane tenders were nine *Lapwing* (AM 1)-class minesweepers which had been assigned aircraft-support duties in the 1920s and early 1930s, and reclassified as AVPs on January 22, 1936. These 166-foot vessels each tended six (but sometimes more) patrol bomber seaplanes in World War II but, because their overall capabilities were somewhat limited, the Navy developed in the late 1930s a larger AVP type known as the Barnegat (AVP 10) class. Consisting of AVP 10–AVP 13 and AVP 21–AVP 67, the Barnegats were commissioned between 1941 and 1945. They were 311 feet long, supported 6–12 patrol seaplanes, and with drafts of 20 feet, and could operate in the restricted and shallow waters of forward island bases. In addition, seven former destroyers were briefly reclassified as AVP 14–AVP 20 before reclassified again as seaplane tender–destroyer (AVD) [q.v.] in 1940.

Many of the AVPs went on to interesting "second careers." For example, USS *Biscayne* became the amphibious force flagship [q.v.] AGC 18; a few were reclassified as miscellaneous auxiliaries [q.v.] in July 1945 to be converted into "press ships" as broadcast and teletype centers for war correspondents in the Pacific (but the conversions were not implemented); 18 AVPs subsequently did tours of duty in the U.S. Coast Guard; and six AVPs were transferred to South Vietnam in 1971–1972 (the former *Absecon* [AVP 23] was captured by North Vietnam in 1975; the other five escaped and were acquired by the Philippines). By 1978 all of the small seaplane tenders had either been sold or transferred; none remained on the NVR.

In the following listing, AVP 1–AVP 9 were originally the minesweepers AM 1, 10, 18, 19, 23, 27, 34, 41 and 51, respectively.

AVP 1	Lapwing[1]	AVP 30	San Pablo[30]
AVP 2	Heron[2]	AVP 31	Unimak[31]
AVP 3	Thrush[3]	AVP 32	Yakutat[32]
AVP 4	Avocet[4]	AVP 33	Barataria[33]
AVP 5	Teal[5]	AVP 34	Bering Strait[34]
AVP 6	Pelican[6]	AVP 35	Castle Rock[35]
AVP 7	Swan[7]	AVP 36	Cook Inlet[36]
AVP 8	Gannet[8]	AVP 37	Corson[37]
AVP 9	Sandpiper[9]	AVP 38	Duxbury Bay[38]
AVP 10	Barnegat[10]	AVP 39	Gardiners Bay[39]
AVP 11	Biscayne[11]	AVP 40	Floyds Bay[40]
AVP 12	Casco[12]	AVP 41	Greenwich Bay[41]
AVP 13	Mackinac[13]	AVP 42	Hatteras[42]
AVP 14	Childs[14]	AVP 43	Hempstead[43]
AVP 15	Williamson[15]	AVP 44	Kamishak[44]
AVP 16	George E. Badger[16]	AVP 45	Magothy[45]
AVP 17	Clemson[17]	AVP 46	Martanzas[46]
AVP 18	Goldsborough[18]	AVP 47	Metomkin[47]
AVP 19	Hulbert[19]	AVP 48	Onslow[49]
AVP 20	William B. Preston[20]	AVP 49	Orca[59]
AVP 21	Humbolt[21]	AVP 50	Rehoboth[51]
AVP 22	Matagorda[22]	AVP 51	San Carlos[52]
AVP 23	Absecon[23]	AVP 52	Shelikof[53]
AVP 24	Chincoteague[24]	AVP 53	Suisun[54]
AVP 25	Coos Bay[25]	AVP 54	Timbalier[55]
AVP 26	Half Moon[26]	AVP 55	Valcour[56]
AVP 27	Mobjack[27]	AVP 56	Wachapreague[57]
AVP 28	Oyster Bay[28]	AVP 57	Willoughby[58]
AVP 29	Rockaway[29]		

3. Directory of U.S. Navy Auxiliary Ships

Notes

1. Decommissioned in November 1945 and sold in August 1946.
2. Transferred to Republic of China in July 1947.
3. Decommissioned in December 1945 and sold in August 1946.
4. Sold for scrapping in December 1946.
5. Sold.
6. Operated as Q-ship *Normandie II* May 1942–April 1943, and later sold for scrapping.
7. Sold.
8. Lost in June 1942 after being torpedoed by U-653.
9. Struck in April 1946.
10. Struck in May 1958 and sold in 1962.
11. Commissioned as AVP 11 in July 1941, reclassified as amphibious force command ship [q.v.] AGC 18 in October 1944, transferred to USCG as USCGC *Dexter* (WAGC 18) in July 1946, returned to USN in July 1968, and expended as target that year.
12. Loaned to USCG in April 1949 as WAVP 370, returned to USN in March 1969, and expended as target in May 1969.
13. Loaned to USCG in April 1949 as WAVP 371, returned to USN in July 1968, and expended as target that month.
14. Former destroyer reclassified as seaplane tender—destroyer [q.v.] (AVD) in August 1940.
15. *Ibid.*
16. *Ibid.*
17. *Ibid.*
18. *Ibid.*
19. *Ibid.*
20. *Ibid.*
21. Reclassified as miscellaneous auxiliaries [q.v.] AG 121, AG 122 and AG 123, respectively, to be converted to press ship; conversion cancelled, and redesignated as AVP 21, AVP 22 and AVP 29, respectively.
22. *Ibid.*
23. Loaned to USCG in May 1949, returned to USN in May 1972, transferred to South Vietnam in June 1972, and captured by North Vietnam in May 1975.
24. Loaned to USCG in March 1947, transferred to South Vietnam in June 1972, and custody assumed by the Philippines in April 1976.
25. Loaned to USCG in May 1949, returned to USN in December 1967, and expended as target in January 1968.
26. Loaned to USCG in 1948 and sold for scrapping in May 1970.
27. First commissioned as motor torpedo boat tender (AGP) [q.v.], transferred to USC&GS in 1946.
28. First commissioned as AGP 6, struck in April 1946, reinstated on Vessel Register as AVP 28 in January 1949, and transferred to Italy in October 1957.
29. Reclassified as miscellaneous auxiliaries [q.v.] AG 121, AG 122 and AG 123, respectively, to be converted to press ship; conversion cancelled, and redesignated as AVP 21, AVP 22 and AVP 29, respectively.
30. AVP 30 and AVP 50 reclassified as surveying ships [q.v.] and redesignated as AGS 30 and AGS 50, respectively.
31. Loaned to USCG in 1948.
32. Loaned to USCG in 1948, transferred to South Vietnam in 1971, and custody subsequently assumed by the Philippines.
33. *Ibid.*
34. *Ibid.*
35. *Ibid.*
36. *Ibid.*
37. Expended as target in 1966.
38. Sold for scrapping in July 1967.
39. Transferred to Norway in May 1958.
40. Struck in March 1960 and sold in July 1960.
41. Sold for scrapping in June 1967.
42. Cancelled in April 1943.
43. *Ibid.*
44. *Ibid.*
45. *Ibid.*
46. *Ibid.*
47. *Ibid.*
48. Sold in October 1960.
49. Transferred to Ethiopia in January 1962.
50. AVP 30 and AVP 50 reclassified as surveying ships [q.v.] and redesignated as AGS 30 and AGS 50, respectively.
51. Commissioned as AVP 51 in March 1944, decommissioned in June 1947, converted to oceanographic research ship [q.v.] and renamed USNS *Josiah Willard Gibbs* (T-AGOR 1) in December 1958.
52. Struck in May 1960 and sold in 1961.
53. Expended as target in October 1966.

54. Struck in May 1960 and sold in 1960.
55. Reclassified as miscellaneous command flagship [q.v.] AGF 1 in December 1965, later employed as testbed for EMP tests, and sold for scrapping in May 1977.
56. First commissioned as motor torpedo boat tender (AGP) [q.v.], transferred to USC&GS in 1946.
57. Ibid.

Aircraft Rescue Vessel (AVR)

This auxiliary ship classification is of World War II vintage but apparently was never assigned to a specific vessel. It is today listed as "inactive" on the NVR.

Aviation Supply Ships (AVS)

On February 21, 1951, USS *Jupiter* (AVS 8) is in Korean waters coming alongside the aircraft carrier USS *Valley Forge* (CV 45) to transfer supplies to her (U.S. Navy photograph).

These vessels were used in the Pacific during World War II to store and issue aircraft equipment, material and stores in forward operating areas. The first two aviation supply ships—USS *Supply* (IX 147) and USS *Fortune* (IX 146)—were derived from former merchant freighters built in the 1920s and commissioned in February 1944. *Fortune* supported aircraft carriers and *Supply* served Marine aircraft groups and land-based units. They were soon joined by six other ships in 1945 in the new aviation supply ship designation of AVS, which was established on May 25, 1945. Other than USS *Jupiter* (AVS 8), which served as the Navy's only AVS until 1965, all of the aviation supply ships were discarded shortly after the war. *Jupiter* lasted as long as she did because she had been provided with an underway replenishment capability that allowed her to transfer at sea large aviation items such as aircraft engines and wings.

AVS 1	*Supply*[1]	AVS 5	*Gwinnett*[5]
AVS 2	*Fortune*[2]	AVS 6	*Nicollet*[6]
AVS 3	*Grumium*[3]	AVS 7	*Pontotoc*[7]
AVS 4	*Allioth*[4]	AVS 8	*Jupiter*[8]

NOTES

1. Commissioned in February 1944 as unclassified miscellaneous vessel IX 147, reclassified as AVS in May 1945, decommissioned and struck in February 1946, and sold in January 1947.
2. Commissioned in February 1944 as IX 146, reclassified as AVS in May 1945, decommissioned in October 1945, and sold for scrapping in 1946.
3. Commissioned as cargo ship [q.v.] AK 112 in October 1943, reclassified as IX 174 in June 1944, reclassified as AVS in May 1945, decommissioned in December 1945, and sold for scrapping in April 1970.
4. Commissioned as AK 109 in October 1943, reclassified as IX 204 in March 1945, reclassified as AVS in May 1945, decommissioned in May 1946, struck in May 1947, and sold in August 1964.
5. Laid down as cargo ship AK 185 but commissioned as miscellaneous auxiliary [q.v.] AG 92 in April 1945, reclassified as AVS in May 1945, decommissioned in February 1946, and delivered to General Steamship Company in November 1947.
6. Launched as cargo ship AK 199 in July 1944, commissioned as AG 93 in April 1945, reclassified as AVS in May 1945, decommissioned in June 1946, and sold to France in July 1946.
7. Launched as cargo ship AK 206 in February 1944, commissioned as AG 94 in March 1945, reclassified as AVS in May 1945, decommissioned in April 1946, and sold in June 1947.
8. Acquired in June 1941, commissioned as AK 43 in August 1942, reclassified as AVS in July 1945, decommissioned in May 1947, recommissioned in October 1950, decommissioned in June 1964, struck in August 1965, and sold for scrapping in March 1971.

Auxiliary Aircraft Transports / Auxiliary Aircraft Landing Training Ships (AVT)

The hull classification "auxiliary aircraft transport" (designated as AVT) was established in May 1959 to be applied to obsolete aircraft carriers that no longer served in a combatant role. All but the last two of the ships listed below were eventually so classified. In July 1978 the nomenclature of the AVT classification was changed to "auxiliary aircraft landing training ship" and assigned to USS *Lexington*, which had been designated as CVT 16 at the time and was then redesignated as AVT 16. The only other AVT training carrier was USS *Forrestal*, the nation's first "super carrier," which was decommissioned and struck in September 1993. There are at present no AVTs on hand, either active or in reserve (although four—AVTs 3, 4, 16 and 59—are still listed on the NVR even though they have been disposed of), and the AVT classification is not yet listed as "inactive" on the NVR. The former USS *Lexington* survives as a museum ship in Texas.

AVT 1	*Cowpens*[1]	AVT 6	*Saipan*[6]	AVT 11	*Philippine Sea*[11]
AVT 2	*Monterey*[2]	AVT 7	*Wright*[7]		
AVT 3	*Cabot*[3]	AVT 8	*Franklin*[8]	AVT 12	*Tarawa*[12]
AVT 4	*Bataan*[4]	AVT 9	*Bunker Hill*[9]	AVT 16	*Lexington*[13]
AVT 5	*San Jacinto*[5]	AVT 10	*Leyte*[10]	AVT 59	*Forrestal*[14]

The light aircraft carrier USS *Saipan* (CVL 48) has HRS (H-19) Chickasaw and HUP (H-25) Retriever helicopters on her flight deck in this mid–1950s photograph. She was reclassified as AVT 6 in 1959, converted into the major communications relay ship [q.v.] USS *Arlington* (AGMR 2) in 1963–1966, and sold for scrap in 1976 (U.S. Navy photograph).

Notes

1. Commissioned in May 1943 as aircraft carrier CV 25, reclassified as light aircraft carrier CVL 25 in July 1943, decommissioned in January 1947, reclassified as auxiliary aircraft transport AVT 1 in May 1959, struck in November 1959, and sold for scrapping in 1960.
2. Commissioned in June 1943 as CV 26, reclassified as CVL 26 in July 1943, reclassified as AVT 2 in May 1959, and sold for scrapping in May 1971.
3. Commissioned as CVL 28 in July 1943, last decommissioned in January 1955, reclassified as AVT 3 in May 1959, struck in August 1972, and sold to Spain in December 1972.
4. Was to have been CV 29 but commissioned in November 1943 as CVL 29, last decommissioned in April 1954, reclassified as AVT 4 in May 1959, struck in September 1959, and sold for scrapping in June 1961.
5. Commissioned in December 1943 as CVL 29, decommissioned in March 1947, reclassified as AVT 5 in May 1959, struck in June 1960, and scrapped.
6. Commissioned in July 1946 as light aircraft carrier USS *Saipan* (CVL 48), reclassified as AVT 6 in May 1959, converted to major communications relay ship [q.v.] AGMR 2 in 1963–1966, commissioned as USS *Arlington* in August 1966, decommissioned in January 1970, struck in August 1975, and sold for scrapping in June 1976.
7. Commissioned in February 1947 as CVL 49, decommissioned in March 1956, reclassified as AVT 7 in May 1959, reclassified as command ship and designated as CC 2 in May 1963, decommissioned in May 1970, struck in December 1977, and sold for scrapping in August 1980.
8. Commissioned in January 1944 as CV 13, decommissioned in February 1947, reclassified as attack aircraft carrier CVA 13 in October 1952, reclassified as antisubmarine warfare support carrier CVS 13 in August 1953, reclassified as AVT 8 in May 1959, struck in October 1964, and sold for scrapping in July 1966.
9. Commissioned in May 1943, decommissioned in July 1947, reclassified as CVA 17 in October 1952, reclassified as CVS 17 in August 1953, reclassified as AVT 9 in May 1959, struck in November 1966, and sold for scrapping in February 1973.
10. Commissioned as CV 32 in April 1946, reclassified as CVA 32 in July 1952, reclassified as AVT 10 and decommissioned in May 1959, and sold for scrapping in September 1970.
11. Commissioned as CV 47 in May 1946, decommissioned in December 1958, reclassified as AVT 11 in May 1959, struck in December 1969, and sold for scrapping in March 1971.
12. Commissioned as CV 40 in December 1945, decommissioned in May 1960, reclassified as AVT 12 in May 1961, struck in June 1967, and sold for scrapping in October 1968.

13. Commissioned as CV 16 in February 1943, decommissioned in April 1947, recommissioned in September 1955, reclassified as CVA 16 in October 1952, reclassified as CVS 16 in October 1962, reclassified as training carrier CVT 16 in January 1969, reclassified as auxiliary aircraft landing training ship and redesignated as AVT 16 in July 1978, decommissioned and struck in November 1991, and transferred as museum ship in Corpus Christi, Texas, in June 1992.

14. Commissioned as CVA 59 in October 1955, reclassified as a multi-purpose aircraft carrier CV 59 in June 1975, reclassified as auxiliary aircraft landing training ship AVT 59 in February 1992, decommissioned and struck in September 1993, and sold for scrapping in December 2015.

Distilling Ships (AW)

The former distilling ship USS *Abatan* (AW 4) is employed as a water storage and fuel storage hulk at the Guantanamo Bay Naval Base in Cuba on June 12, 1978. She was expended as a target two years later (U.S. Navy photograph).

Late in World War II the Navy acquired four tankers for use as distilling ships, designated as AW. These vessels were deployed in forward areas in the Pacific to convert salt water into 140,000 gallons of fresh water a day, which was then provided to naval vessels and shore facilities or stored on board for later distribution. One of the ships, USS *Abatan* (AW 4), was called back into service after 14 years in mothballs and employed briefly in late 1962 as a distilling plant at the Guantanamo Bay Naval Base and later as a water storage hulk at that facility. All four have since been disposed of. (Earlier vessels used in part as distilling ships include USS *Niagara* in 1898, USS *Iris* in 1898–1903, and USS *Rainbow* in 1898–1908.)

| AW 1 | Stag[1] | AW 3 | Pasig[3] |
| AW 2 | Wildcat[2] | AW 4 | Abatan[4] |

Notes

1. Former SS *Norman O. Pedrick*, acquired and commissioned as unclassified miscellaneous vessel [q.v.] *Stag* (IX 128) in February 1944, converted from tanker to distilling ship in mid–1944, decommissioned in April 1946 and struck the following month, used by U.S. Interior Department to supply fresh water to Virgin Islands ca. 1955, and sold for scrapping in July 1970.
2. Initially classified as IX 130, reclassified and commissioned as AW 2 in February 1944, served in the Philippines in 1945 and at the Crossroads atomic bomb tests at Bikini Atoll in 1946, decommissioned in January 1947, and sold for scrapping in January 1968.
3. Originally designated as oiler [q.v.] AO 91, commissioned as AW 3 in December 1944, decommissioned in February 1947, recommissioned in January 1948, decommissioned in June 1948, recommissioned in March 1951 and served with MSTS in Asia for 37 months, decommissioned in June 1955, struck in June 1960, and sold for scrapping in October 1975.
4. Originally designated as oiler AO 92, commissioned as AW 4 in January 1945, decommissioned in January 1947, struck in July 1960, reinstated in September 1962, struck in May 1970, and expended as target in March 1980.

Lighter-Than-Air Aircraft Tender (AZ)

An artist's drawing shows a manned balloon "flying" above the stern of USS *Wright* (AZ 1) in the early 1920s. Note the ship's deep well deck in which the balloon is stowed between flights (U.S. Navy photograph).

USS *Wright* was truly unique. She was the first and only ship ever to be formally designated as an AZ, i.e., a lighter-than-air aircraft tender. Given the kinds of aircraft she supported, it is highly unlikely that there will ever be another AZ. *Wright* was converted in 1920–1921 from a former transport hull into a tender for kite balloons. These "aircraft" were similar to blimps or non-rigid airships and used as aerial observation platforms. The "R" type kite balloons were 88 feet long with a maximum diameter of 35 feet, not free-flying but tethered to the ship, and manned by a "pilot" in a basket hanging from the balloon. The pilot communicated his observations down to the ship via a telephone line in the tether cable. *Wright* was designed to carry six knocked-down deflated stowed balloons and one inflated unit in a well deck. The ship was commissioned as AZ 1 in December 1921. Aside from her usual aircraft, she also sometimes supported 13–18 F5L patrol seaplanes. Results of the ship's kite balloon operation were disappointing so the Navy decided that *Wright* should instead be employed as heavier-than-air aircraft tender [q.v.]. She launched her last kite balloon in July 1922 and was reclassified as AV 1 in November 1923. (The initial nomenclature for the AV vessels was changed to seaplane tender in the mid–1930s.) In January 1944 *Wright* was reclassified as the miscellaneous auxiliary [q.v.] AG 79, renamed *San Clemente* in February 1945, decommissioned in June 1946, struck in July 1946, and sold for scrapping in July 1948.

Training Carrier (CVT)

USS *Lexington* (CV 16) is steaming near the Marshall Islands in the Pacific on November 12, 1943. Later that month, her aviators downed 29 Japanese aircraft. During the Cold War, the carrier was used to train Navy pilots in carrier flight operations (U.S. Navy photograph).

Between April 1957 and October 1962 the antisubmarine warfare carrier USS *Antietam* (CVS 36) was used to train new pilots in operating from a carrier flight deck. She was relieved in that role in December 1963 by the former attack aircraft carrier USS *Lexington* (CVA 16), which had been formally reclassified as a training carrier (CVT) and redesignated as CVT 16 in January 1969. In September 1970, the CVT classification, which had been previously rated as a combatant vessel, was rerated as an auxiliary ship. *Lexington* was reclassified again in July 1978 as an auxiliary aircraft landing training ship [q.v.] and redesignated at that time as AVT 16. She was decommissioned and struck in November 1991, and transferred as museum ship in Corpus Christi, Texas, in June 1992.

Utility Aircraft Carriers (CVU)

The utility aircraft carrier classification and CVU designation were established In May 1955 to encompass various Casablanca (CVE 55)-class escort carriers which were rerated as auxiliary vessels. These ships had originally been built as combatant vessels in 1943 and 1944, and were decommissioned shortly after World War II. On May 7, 1959, the classification of the remaining utility aircraft carriers was changed to "cargo ship and aircraft ferry" and redesignated as AKVs. A few CVUs were assigned to MSTS in the

Transporting a cargo of Air Force F-86D Sabre jet fighters and some Navy F9F Panther and F2H Banshee fighters, the utility aircraft carrier USNS *Windham Bay* (T-CVU 92) is passing under San Francisco's Golden Gate Bridge in 1958 (U.S. Navy photograph).

1950s as aircraft transports but all of the active and mothballed CVUs were disposed of by 1962.

T-CVU 58	*Corregidor*[1]	CVU 84	*Shamrock Bay*[13]
CVU 59	*Mission Bay*[2]	T-CVU 86	*Sitkoh Bay*[14]
CVU 60	*Guadalcanal*[3]	T-CVU 88	*Cape Esperance*[15]
CVU 61	*Manila Bay*[4]	CVU 89	*Takanis Bay*[16]
CVU 62	*Natoma Bay*[5]	CVU 91	*Makassar Strait*[17]
T-CVU 64	*Tripoli*[6]	T-CVU 92	*Windham Bay*[18]
CVU 66	*White Plains*[7]	CVU 94	*Lunga Point*[19]
CVU 74	*Nehenta Bay*[8]	CVU 97	*Hollandia*[20]
CVU 76	*Kadashan Bay*[9]	CVU 98	*Kwajalein*[21]
CVU 80	*Petrof Bay*[10]	CVU 100	*Bougainville*[22]
CVU 81	*Rudyerd Bay*[11]	CVU 104	*Munda*[23]
CVU 83	*Sargent Bay*[12]		

NOTES

1. Struck in 1958 and scrapped in 1960.
2. *Ibid.*
3. *Ibid.*
4. *Ibid.*
5. *Ibid.*

6. Struck in 1959 and scrapped in 1960.
7. Struck in 1958 and scrapped in 1959.
8. Reclassified as AKV 24, struck in August 1959, and scrapped in 1960.
9. Reclassified as AKV 26, struck in August 1959, and scrapped in 1960.
10. Struck in 1958 and scrapped in 1959.
11. Reclassified as AKV 29, struck in August 1959, and scrapped in 1960.
12. Struck in 1958 and scrapped in 1959.
13. *Ibid.*
14. Reclassified as AKV 30, struck in April 1960, and scrapped in 1961.
15. Struck in 1959 and scrapped in 1961.
16. Reclassified as AKV 31, struck in August 1959, and scrapped in 1960.
17. Struck in August 1958 and scrapped.
18. Struck in 1959 and scrapped in 1961.
19. Reclassified as AKV 32, struck in April 1960, and scrapped later that year.
20. Reclassified as AKV 33, struck in April 1960 and scrapped later that year.
21. Reclassified as AKV 34, struck in June 1960, and scrapped in 1961.
22. Reclassified as AKV 35, and scrapped in 1960.
23. Scrapped in 1960.

Fast Deployment Logistics Ship (FDL)

Proposed in 1964, the FDL program was to have included 30 vessels loaded with military supplies which could be rapidly deployed overseas or moored in proximity to anticipated trouble spots to quickly deliver equipment and cargo to U.S. ground forces abroad. Congress terminated the program before any FDL ships were built and "FDL" is listed today as an inactive hull classification symbol on the NVR.

High Speed Transport (HST)

See Chapter 2.

Unclassified Miscellaneous Vessels (IX)

In 1939 the Navy unofficially assigned the hull classification symbol "IX" and accompanying hull numbers to 36 minor or one-off vessels that had previously been listed merely as "unclassified." Official IX hull numbers for those ships along with other vessels carried in the "District Craft—Unclassified" section of the Navy list were assigned in February 1941. Among the ships classified at one time or another as "IX" are several famous and unique vessels, including the venerable "Old Ironsides," USS *Constitution*; Farragut's flagship at Mobile Bay, USS *Hartford*; the Navy's oldest steel-hulled warship still afloat, Dewey's flagship at Manila Bay, USS *Olympia*; a World War II German heavy cruiser, USS *Prinz Eugen*; and two paddle-wheel, coal-burning aircraft carriers, USS *Wolverine* and USS *Sable*. The IX vessel classification was transferred from the Navy's auxiliary ship category to the service craft category on September 23, 1970. (Individual histories and specifications for the unclassified miscellaneous vessels can be found in the IX pages of navsource.org, *Uncommon Warriors*, and DANFS—see Bibliography for full citations.)

In the listing below, note there are gaps between IX 235 and IX 300, and between IX 537 and IX 539. In addition, there are two instances in which two different vessels were assigned the same hull number, viz., IX 35 and IX 67.

IX 1	*Annapolis*	IX 4	*Cheyenne*
IX 2	*Despatch*	IX 5	*Alton*
IX 3	*Briarcliff*	IX 6	*Coast Battleship No. 4*

IX 7	Commodore	IX 60	Seaward
IX 8	Cumberland	IX 61	Geoanna
IX 9	Dubuque	IX 62	Vileehi
IX 10	Essex	IX 63	Zahma
IX 11	Gopher	IX 64	Wolverine
IX 12	Hancock	IX 65	Blue Dolphin
IX 13	Hartford	IX 66	Migrant
IX 14	Hawk	IX 67	Guinivere[1]
IX 15	Prairie State	IX 67	Burleson[2]
IX 16	Kearsarge	IX 68	Seven Seas
IX 17	Monadnock	IX 69	Puritan
IX 18	Nantucket	IX 70	Gloria Dalton
IX 19	Newport	IX 71	Kailua
IX 20	Constellation	IX 72	Liberty Belle
IX 21	Constitution	IX 73	Zaca
IX 22	Oregon	IX 74	Metha Nelson
IX 23	Paducah	IX 75	John M. Howard
IX 24	Philadelphia	IX 76	Ramona
IX 25	Reina Mercedes	IX 77	Juniata
IX 26	Southery	IX 78	Brave
IX 27	Sturgeon Bay	IX 79	El Cano
IX 28	Wheeling	IX 80	Christiana
IX 29	Wilmette	IX 81	Sable
IX 30	Dover	IX 82	Luster
IX 31	Wolverine	IX 83	Ashley
IX 32	Yantic	IX 84	Congaree
IX 33	Newton	IX 85	Euhaw
IX 34	Henry County	IX 86	Pocotagligo
IX 35	Topeka	IX 87	Saluda
IX 36	Light Target No. 2	IX 88	Wimbee
IX 37	Light Target No. 3	IX 89	Romain
IX 38	Empire State	IX 90	Forbes
IX 39	Seattle	IX 91	Palomas
IX 40	Olympia	IX 92	Liston
IX 41	America	IX 93	Irene Forsyte
IX 42	Camden	IX 94	Ronaki
IX 43	Freedom	IX 95	Echo
IX 44	Damage Control Hulk No. 1	IX 96	Richard Peck
IX 45	Favorite	IX 97	Martha's Vineyard
IX 46	Transfer	IX 98	Moosehead
IX 47	Vamarie	IX 99	Sea Cloud
IX 48	Highland Light	IX 100	Racer
IX 49	Spindrift	IX 101	Big Chief
IX 50	Bowdoin	IX 102	Majaba
IX 51	Sea Otter I	IX 103	E.A. Poe
IX 52	Chengho	IX 104	Peter H. Burnett
IX 53	Sea Otter II	IX 105	Panther
IX 54	Galaxy	IX 106	Greyhound
IX 55	Black Douglas	IX 107	Zebra
IX 56	Navajo	IX 108	Atlantida
IX 57	Araner	IX 109	Antelope
IX 58	Dwyn Wen	IX 110	Ocelot
IX 59	Volador	IX 111	Armadillo

3. Directory of U.S. Navy Auxiliary Ships

IX 112	Beagle		IX 165	Flicker
IX 113	Camel		IX 166	Linnet
IX 114	Caribou		IX 167	Leyden
IX 115	Elk		IX 168	Southland
IX 116	Gazelle		IX 169	President Warfield
IX 117	Gemsbok		IX 170	Curlew
IX 118	Giraffe		IX 171	Albatross
IX 119	Ibex		IX 172	Bluebird
IX 120	Jaguar		IX 173	Etamin
IX 121	Kangaroo		IX 174	Grumium
IX 122	Leopard		IX 175	Kestrel
IX 123	Mink		IX 176	Kingbird
IX 124	Moose		IX 177	Nightingale
IX 125	Panda		IX 178	Banshee
IX 126	Porcupine		IX 179	Kenwood
IX 127	Raccoon		IX 180	Flamingo
IX 128	Stag		IX 181	Egret
IX 129	Whippet		IX 182	Donnell
IX 130	Wildcat		IX 183	Catbird
IX 131	Abarenda		IX 184	Clifton
IX 132	Andrew Doria[3]		IX 185	Stonewall
IX 133	Antona		IX 186	Dawn
IX 134	Arayat[4]		IX 187	Belusan
IX 135	Arethusa		IX 188	Chotauk
IX 136	Carondelet[5]		IX 189	Marmora
IX 137	Celtic		IX 190	Nausett
IX 138	Malvern[6]		IX 191	Vandalia
IX 139	Octorara		IX 192	Flambeau
IX 140	Quiros[7]		IX 193	Meredosia
IX 141	Manileno[8]		IX 194	Killdeer
IX 142	Signal		IX 195	Goshawk
IX 143	Silver Cloud		IX 196	Spark
IX 144	Clyde[9]		IX 197	Mariveles
IX 145	Villalobos[10]		IX 198	Cohasset
IX 146	Fortune		IX 199	Barcelo
IX 147	Supply		IX 200	Maratanza
IX 148	North Star		IX 201	Sterling
IX 149	Midnight/Trefoil[11]		IX 202	Liberator
IX 150	Quartz		IX 203	Agile
IX 151	Silica		IX 204	Allioth
IX 152	Carmita		IX 205	Callao
IX 153	Asphalt		IX 206	Chocura
IX 154	Bauxite		IX 207	Big Horn
IX 155	Mustang		IX 208	Domino
IX 156	City of Dalhart		IX 209	Seaward
IX 157	Orvetta		IX 210	Sea Foam
IX 158	Limestone		IX 211	Castine
IX 159	Feldspar		IX 212	(no name)
IX 160	Marl		IX 213	Serapis
IX 161	Barite		IX 214	Yucca
IX 162	Lignite		IX 215	Don Marquis
IX 163	Cinnabar		IX 216	Unicoi
IX 164	Corundum		IX 217	Tackle

IX 218	*Guardoqui*	IX 512	(no name)
IX 219	(unassigned)	IX 513	(no name)
IX 220	(unassigned)	IX 514	*Baylander*
IX 221	*Eureka*	IX 515	*Sea Flyer*
IX 222	*Pegasus*	IX 516	(no name)
IX 223	*Triana*	IX 517	*Gosport*
IX 224	*Aide De Camp*	IX 518	(no name)
IX 225	*Harcourt*	IX 520	(no name)
IX 226	*Araner*	IX 521	(no name)
IX 227	*Gamage*	IX 522	(no name)
IX 228	*Justin*	IX 523	(no name)
IX 227	*Inca*	IX 524	(no name)
IX 230	*Tapacola*	IX 525	(no name)
IX 231	*Stalwart*	IX 526	(no name)
IX 232	*Summit*	IX 527	(no name)
IX 233	*Canandaigua*	IX 528	(no name)
IX 234	*Eastwind*	IX 529	*Sea Shadow*
IX 235	*Royone*	IX 530	(no name)
IX 300	*Prinz Eugen*	IX 531	(no name)
IX 301	*Dithmarschen/Conecuh*[12]	IX 532	*Joint Venture*
IX 302	(unassigned)	IX 533	(no name)
IX 303	(unassigned)	IX 534	(no name)
IX 304	*Atlanta*	IX 535	(no name)
IX 305	*Prowess*	IX 536	(no name)
IX 306	(no name)	IX 537	*Prevail*
IX 307	*Brier*	IX 538	(never assigned)
IX 308	*New Bedford*	IX 539	(no name)
IX 309	*Monob One*	IX 540	(no name)
IX 310	(no name)	IX 541	(no name)
IX 311	*Benewah*	IX 542	*White Bush*
IX 501	*Elk River*	IX 543	(no name)
IX 502	*Mercer*	IX 544	(no name)
IX 503	*Nueces*	IX 545	(no name)
IX 504	*Echols*	IX 546	(no name)
IX 505	(no name)	IX 547	(no name)
IX 506	(no name)	IX 548	(no name)
IX 507	*General Hugh J. Gaffey*	IX 549	(no name)
IX 508	(no name)	IX 550	(no name)
IX 509	(no name)	IX 551	(no name)
IX 510	*General William O. Darby*	IX 552	(no name)
		IX 1473	(no name)
IX 511	(no name)		

NOTES

1. *Guinivere*, an auxiliary schooner, was designated IX-67 sometime during her service between June 1942 and August 1945; *Burleson*, an attack transport [q.v.] (APA-67) commissioned in November 1944, was designated IX-67 on Oct. 5, 1956 and retained that designation until struck from the Navy list on September 1, 1968.
2. *Ibid.*
3. Italian tanker seized by the U.S. Government in 1941.
4. *Ibid.*
5. *Ibid.*
6. *Ibid.*
7. *Ibid.*
8. *Ibid.*

9. *Ibid.*
10. *Ibid.*
11. *Midnight* was renamed *Trefoil* and retained *Midnight*'s hull number.
12. *Dithmarshen* renamed *Conecuh* in 1946 and redesigned as the replenishment oiler [q.v.] AOR 110 in 1952.

Command Ship (LCC)

See Chapter 1.

Surface Effects Ship (SES)

On November 21, 1985, SES-200 is underway and showing off her speed for the photographer (National Archives Photo).

Developed to evaluate new hull designs for achieving higher speeds with greater stability, the BH-110 Mark 1 (later designated as SES-110BH) was delivered to the U.S. government in September 1980 for testing by the Coast Guard and Navy. She was originally constructed to ride on a "bubble" or cushion of air contained by rigid sidewalls. The Coast Guard operated the ship from 1980 to 1982 as the cutter *Dorado* (WSES 1). In January 1982, the SES was returned to builder Halter Marine, cut in half, and a 50-foot section was installed amidships to create a higher length-to-beam ratio. The modified 160-foot vessel was accepted by the Navy in September 1982 and redesignated as SES-200. In May 1987 she was instated on the NVR as the unclassified miscellaneous vessel IX 515. From 2000 to 2003 the SES air cushion system was removed and replaced by a 170-ton underwater lifting body. The rebuilt craft, known unofficially as *Sea Flyer*, began sea trials in 2004 during which she achieved speeds in excess of 30 knots. IX 515 was struck from the NVR in February 2010 and sold in September of that year.

(Other Navy SES craft included the SES-100A developed by the Aerojet-General Corporation and completed in May 1972, and the SES-100B developed by Bell Aerosystems and completed in February 1972. Both vessels exceeded 70 knots in sea trials.)

Ocean Radar Station Ships (YAGR)

The first 13 ocean radar station ships were initially designated as YAGRs but were reclassified as radar picket ships [q.v.] and redesignated as AGRs in 1958.

Bibliography

The following listing includes the many ship reference works, navy history books and magazine articles, and various Web sites which were consulted in the preparation of this book. Six of those sources were especially useful and informative, and are described below.

First, the *Dictionary of American Naval Fighting Ships* (DANFS). This nine-volume encyclopedia was originally published between 1959 and 1981, and it contains summary histories of more than 10,000 Navy ships. Fortunately for researchers and readers, the Navy's Naval History and Heritage Command (NHHC) maintains an online version of DANFS—which also includes post–1981 information—that can be easily accessed at https://www.history.navy.mil/research/histories/ship-histories/danfs.html.

Second, the "NavSource Naval History: Photographic History of the U.S. Navy" Web site. This excellent unofficial online repository provides detailed data and multiple images of all types of current and former naval ships, boats and service craft. NavSource was especially helpful to the author in compiling the all-time rosters of various auxiliary ship types, as well as in furnishing information about the pre- and post–Navy histories of some of them. Gary Priolo serves as the site's project general manager and as manager of its amphibious and auxiliary ship and yard and district craft archives. The site's pages covering auxiliaries can be accessed at http://www.navsource.org/archives/auxidx.htm.

Third, the "Shipscribe" website. Its creator, Stephen S. Roberts, has assembled an amazingly complete and detailed body of information about the Navy's auxiliary ships from 1835 to 1945. His online register of such vessels is both amply illustrated and extraordinarily rich with data. The site also lists key primary and official records enabling researchers to dive deeply into the vast sea of government information on the naval auxiliaries of the early 20th century. All this material is available at http://shipscribe.com/. Shipscribe pages devoted to specific auxiliary ship types are individually identified in the Internet section below.

Fourth, the Military Sealift Command Web site. MSC posts a great deal of information online about its ships, personnel and their activities. Of particular use to the author was the Command's current inventory of vessels. It is accessible at http://www.msc.navy.mil/inventory/.

Fifth, the *Ships and Aircraft of the U.S. Fleet* series of reference books. Launched by James C. Fahey and published in 19 editions between 1939 and 2012, *Ships and Aircraft* has evolved from a modest 48-page handbook into an authoritative encyclopedia of more than 700 pages on the Navy's ships, weapons systems, and aircraft. Each of the 19 editions are listed in the full bibliography below but six of them were particularly valuable in developing this book: Fahey's 5th and 8th editions, and Norman Polmar's 11th, 12th, 18th and 19th editions.

Sixth and last, the Naval Vessel Register (NVR). Maintained and periodically updated online by the Naval Sea Systems command, the NVR provides basic information such as specifications and current status on the Navy's ships and service craft "from the time of vessel authorization through its life cycle and disposal." This online source can be accessed at http://www.nvr.navy.mil/class.html.

In addition to these key sources, the following books, publications, articles and websites provided data, details, contextual material and background information to the author.

Books

Bauer, K. Jack, and Stephen S. Roberts. *Register of Ships of the U.S. Navy, 1775–1990: Major Combatants*. Westport, CT: Greenwood Press, 1991.

Beach, Edward L. *The United States Navy: A 200-Year History*. Boston: Houghton Mifflin Company, 1986.

Bush, Steve. *US Navy Warships & Auxiliaries including US Coast Guard*. Annapolis, MD: Naval Institute Press, 2015.

Charles, Roland W. *Troopships of World War II*. Washington, D.C.: The Army Transportation Association, 1947.

Clephane, Lewis P. *History of the Naval Overseas Transportation Service*. Washington, D.C.: Naval History Division, 1969.

Fahey, James C. *The Ships and Aircraft of the U.S. Fleet, 1939 First Edition*. Falls Church, VA: Ships and Aircraft, 1939.

_____. *The Ships and Aircraft of the U.S. Fleet, Two Ocean Fleet Edition*. New York: Ships and Aircraft, 1941 (Reprinted in 1985 by the Naval Institute Press).

_____. *The Ships and Aircraft of the U.S. Fleet, War Edition*. New York: Ships and Aircraft, 1942.

_____. *The Ships and Aircraft of the U.S. Fleet, Second War Edition*. New York: Gemsco, 1944.

_____. *The Ships and Aircraft of the U.S. Fleet, Victory Edition*. Falls Church, VA: Ships and Aircraft, 1945.

_____. *The Ships and Aircraft of the U.S. Fleet, Sixth Edition*. Falls Church, VA: Ships and Aircraft, 1950.

_____. *The Ships and Aircraft of the U.S. Fleet, Seventh Edition*. Falls Church, VA: Ships and Aircraft, 1958.

_____. *The Ships and Aircraft of the U.S. Fleet, Eighth Edition*. Annapolis, MD: U.S. Naval Institute, 1965.

Friedman, Norman. *U.S. Small Combatants*. Annapolis, MD: Naval Institute Press, 1987.

Hone, Thomas C. and Trent Hone. *Battle Line: The United States Navy, 1919–1939*. Annapolis, MD: Naval Institute Press, 2006.

Marolda, Edward J. *The U.S. Navy in the Korean War*. Annapolis, MD: Naval Institute Press, 2007.

_____. *The U.S. Navy in the Vietnam War*. Washington, D.C.: Brassey's Inc., 2002.

Marolda, Edward J. and Robert J. Schneller, Jr. *Shield and Sword: The United States Navy and the Persian Gulf War*. Washington, D.C.: Naval Historical Center, 1998.

Morison, Samuel Eliot. *History of United States Naval Operations in World War II, Supplement and General Index*. Edison, NJ: Castle Books, 2001, 75–105.

Morison, Samuel L., and John S. Rowe. *The Ships and Aircraft of the U.S. Fleet, Tenth Edition*. Annapolis, MD: Naval Institute Press, 1975.

Muir, Malcolm, Jr. *Black Shoes and Blue Water: Surface Warfare in the United States Navy, 1945–1975*. Washington, D.C.: Department of the Navy, Naval Historical Center, 1996.

Polmar, Norman. *Aircraft Carriers. A Graphic History of Carrier Aviation and Its Influence on World Events*. Garden City, N.Y.: Doubleday & Company, Inc., 1969.

_____. *The American Submarine*. Annapolis, MD: The Nautical & Aviation Publishing Company of America, 1983.

_____. *The Ships and Aircraft of the U.S. Fleet, Eleventh Edition*. Annapolis, MD: Naval Institute Press, 1978.

_____. *The Ships and Aircraft of the U.S. Fleet, Twelfth Edition*. Annapolis, MD: Naval Institute Press, 1981.

_____. *The Ships and Aircraft of the U.S. Fleet, Thirteenth Edition*. Annapolis, MD: Naval Institute Press, 1984.

_____. *The Ships and Aircraft of the U.S. Fleet, Fourteenth Edition*. Annapolis, MD: Naval Institute Press, 1987.

_____. *The Naval Institute Guide to the Ships and Aircraft of the U.S. Fleet, Fifteenth Edition*. Annapolis, MD: Naval Institute Press, 1993.

_____. *The Naval Institute Guide to the Ships and Aircraft of the U.S. Fleet, Sixteenth Edition*. Annapolis, MD: Naval Institute Press, 1997.

_____. *The Naval Institute Guide to the Ships and Aircraft of the U.S. Fleet, Seventeenth Edition*. Annapolis, MD: Naval Institute Press, 2001.

_____. *The Naval Institute Guide to the Ships and Aircraft of the U.S. Fleet, Eighteenth Edition*. Annapolis, MD: Naval Institute Press, 2005.

_____. *The Naval Institute Guide to the Ships and Aircraft of the U.S. Fleet, Nineteenth Edition*. Annapolis, MD: Naval Institute Press, 2013.

Rowe, John S., and Samuel L. Morison. *The Ships and Aircraft of the U.S. Fleet, Ninth Edition*. Annapolis, MD: Naval Institute Press, 1972.

Silverstone, Paul H. *Civil War Navies, 1855–1883*. Annapolis, MD: Naval Institute Press, 2001.

_____. *The Navy of the Nuclear Age, 1947–2007*. New York: Routledge, 2009.

_____. *The Navy of World War II, 1922-1947*. New York: Routledge, 2015.
_____. *The New Navy, 1883-1922*. Routledge, 2006.
_____. *The Sailing Navy, 1775-1854*. Annapolis, MD: Naval Institute Press, 2001.
_____. *U.S. Warships of World War I*. London: Ian Allen, Ltd., 1970.
_____. *U.S. Warships of World War II*. Garden City, NY: Doubleday & Company, 1968.
Williams, Greg H. *World War II U.S. Navy Vessels in Private Hands*. Jefferson, NC: McFarland, 2013.

Other Publications

International Logistics Program—Ship and Craft Summary (NAVSHIPS 250-574-6). Washington, D.C.: U.S. Naval Ship Systems Command, 1974.
Navy John Lewis (TAO-205) Class Oiler Shipbuilding Program: Background and Issues for Congress. Ronald O'Rourke, Congressional Research Service, December 8, 2017.
Ships' Data, U.S. Naval Vessels, Volume III, Auxiliary, District Craft and Unclassified Vessels (NAVSHIPS 250-012). Washington, D.C.: Bureau of Ships, 1945.
U.S. Navy Oilers and Tankers: Underway Replenishment and Fueling Technologies (HAER No. DC-62). Washington, D.C.: Historic American Engineering Record and U.S. Maritime Administration, 2009.

Articles

Abernethy, E.P. "The *Pecos* Died Hard." *United States Naval Institute Proceedings*, December 1969, 74–83.
Adams, W.T. "*Red Rover*: First Hospital Ship of the U.S. Navy." *United States Naval Institute Proceedings*, November 1968, 149–51.
Alden, John. "ARD-1, The *Pioneer*." *United States Naval Institute Proceedings*, July 1967, 70–8.
Baker, A. D. III. "Fraternal Sisters." *Naval History*, October 2007, 10–1.
_____. "Historic Fleets." *Naval History*, February 2001, 8.
_____. "Historic Fleets." *Naval History*, June 2001, 8.
_____. "Historic Fleets." *Naval History*, October 2001, 10.
_____. "Historic Fleets." *Naval History*, February 2004, 12.
_____. "Historic Fleets." *Naval History*, August 2005, 12–3.
_____. "The Navy's Fire God Is No More." *Naval History*, February 2007, 12–3.
_____. "USS *Melville* (AD-2). *United States Naval Institute Proceedings*," April 2005, 94.
Baker, Robert W. "USS *Sacramento* (AOE-1)." *United States Naval Institute Proceedings*, September 1964, 164–6.
Bullock, James. "USS *Compass Island*." *All Hands*, September 1975, 60–1.
Case, William. "USS *Sacramento* (AOE-1)." *United States Naval Institute Proceedings*, December 1967, 88–102.
Cordle, John P. "High Speed Is the Future." *U.S. Naval Institute Proceedings*, June 2003, 54–5.
Cressman, Robert J. "Beef Boat Extraordinaire." *Naval History*, April 2009, 10–11.
_____. "The Busy Lady." *Naval History*, August 2012, 14–5.
_____. "First of Her Breed." *Naval History*, October 2008, 12–3.
_____. "Fixer and Fighter." *Naval History*, August 2008, 12–3.
_____. "A Lady in White." *Naval History*, December 2011, 14–5.
_____. "'A Mighty Important' Makeshift Flagship." *Naval History*, February 2011, 14–5.
_____. "Ready For Any Call at Any Time." *Naval History*, April 2014, 14–5.
_____. "Sub Tender with the Spirit of a Battleship." *Naval History*, December 2014, 14–5.
_____. "The Saga of the *Williebee*." *Naval History*, December 2012, 14–5.
_____. "'This Vessel Most Successfully Accomplished Her Mission.'" *Naval History*, December 2015, 64–5.
Culver, John A. "A Time for Victories." *U.S. Naval Institute Proceedings*, February 1977, 50–6.
Cutler, Thomas J. "A Final Embrace." *United States Naval Institute Proceedings*, September 2017, 94.
Degnan, James L. "In Peril in New York." *United States Naval Institute Proceedings*, February 2002, 66–9.
Delgado, James P. "'Missing and Presumed Lost.'" *Naval History*, August 2016, 56–63.
Dolbow, Jim. "U.S. Battle Force Changes 1 January 2017–31 December 2017." *United States Naval Institute Proceedings*, May 2018, 104–13.
Eckholm, Erik. "China Complains About U.S. Surveillance Ship." *The New York Times*, September 27, 2002.
Foley, Lee M. "Yellowstone—A Classy Class of Tender." *United States Naval Institute Proceedings*, February 1980, 93–4.
Frank, Winn B. "Farewell to the Troopship." *Naval History*, February 1997, 41–5.
Froid, J.C. "The Research Catamaran T-AGOR 16." *United States Naval Institute Proceedings*, December 1968, 132–6.
Garrick, Robert M. "USNS *Range Tracker* (T-AGM-1)." *United States Naval Institute Proceedings*, June 1962, 168–9.
Gile, Chester A. "The *Mount Hood* Explosion." *United States Naval Institute Proceedings*, February 1963, 88–93.
Gillette, H. G. "USS *Waccamaw*—A New Oiler, In Part." *United States Naval Institute Proceedings*, September 1967, 141–2.
Goode, Sanchez. "Postscript to *Palomares*." *United States Naval Institute Proceedings*, December 1968, 48–53.
Gordon, Harold L. "Forward Area Air Station." *United States Naval Institute Proceedings*, April 1962, 161–3.
Hammond, James W., III, "The United States Needs Mobile Afloat Basing." *United States Naval Institute Proceedings*, November 2017, 20–5.
Harris, William R. "Market Time Mother Ship." *United States Naval Institute Proceedings*, December 1966, 148–51.
Henrizi, John T. "U.S. Navy Colliers." *United States Naval Institute Proceedings*, May 1967, 162–4.
_____. "USS *Suribachi* (AE-21)." *United States Naval Institute Proceedings*, August 1962, 152–4.
Jones, Thomas Lawton. "The Baptism of Mr. Beasley." *Naval History*, October 2003, 40–3.
Keener, Bruce, "I am the Two-Headed Ogre...." *United States Naval Institute Proceedings*, April 1976, 38–45.
Kraft, James C. "The Last Triple Expander." *United States Naval Institute Proceedings*, February 1977, 58–67.
Lademan, J. U. "USS *Gold Star*—Flagship of the Guam Navy." *U.S. Naval Institute Proceedings*, December 1973, 67–79.
Lambert, Chip. "The Hunt for the Last Mystery Shipwreck." *Naval History*, April 2003, 38–41.
Lobdell, George H. "USS *Sequoia*" (letter). *Naval History*, April 1998, pp. 12–5.

Long, E. John. "USNS *Eltanin*, Floating Laboratory." *United States Naval Institute Proceedings*, April 1963, 152–4.
Lukacs, John A. "A Century of Replenishment at Sea." *Naval History*, June 2018, 42–7.
———. "The Value of (UNREP) Time." *United States Naval Institute Proceedings*, January 2018, 68–9.
MacDonald, Donald J. "President Truman's Yacht." *Naval History*, Winter 1990, 48–9.
Marconi, James. "*Ponce* Receiving Refit for New Role as AFSB(I)." *Sealift*, March 2012, 3.
McCarty, Lindsay C. "*Proteus*—Polaris Pioneer." *United States Naval Institute Proceedings*, January 1966, 166–9.
McConnell, Jerry. "Polaris: A Success." *All Hands*, September 1960, pp. 2–8.
Meyer, Sam. "The Strange Fame of Thomas Stone." *Naval History*, Summer 1988, 46–8.
Miller, Marvin O. "Standby for *Shotline*." *United States Naval Institute Proceedings*, April 1985, 75–9.
Moeser, Robert D., and Richard N. Edwards. "USS *Repose* (AH-16)." *United States Naval Institute Proceedings*, April 1968, 80–94.
Morgan, J.R. "The U.S. Oceanographic Fleet." *United States Naval Institute Proceedings*, July 1963, 48–57.
Mulcahy, Frank S. "High-Speed Sealift Is a Joint Mission." *U.S. Naval Institute Proceedings*, January 2005, 34–7.
O'Hara, Vincent P. "A Sailor's Letters Home." *Naval History*, August 1917, 44–9.
Orias, Ely U. "You Don't See Many Like the AHLC Twins." *All Hands*, October 1967, 18–9.
Natter, Robert J. "Meeting the Need for Speed." *U.S. Naval Institute Proceedings*, June 2002, 65–7.
Nelson, Carl A. "Growing in Command in the South China Sea." *Naval History*, February 2005, 28–31.
Nervig, Conrad A. "The *Cyclops* Mystery." *United States Naval Institute Proceedings*, July 1969, 148–51.
Niblock, Robert. "USNS *Silas Bent* (T-AGS-26)." *United States Naval Institute Proceedings*, March 1966, 166–8.
Perlez, Jane, and Matthew Rosenberg. "China Agrees to Return Seized Drone, Ending Standoff, Pentagon Says." *The New York Times*, December 17, 2016.
Perlman, Benjamin. "Unknown Ship." *United States Naval Institute Proceedings*, March 1971, 78–9.
Polmar, Norman. "American Spy Ships." *United States Naval Institute Proceedings*, October 2003, 117–18.
———. "SURTASS and T-AGOS." *United States Naval Institute Proceedings*, March 1980, 122–4.
———. "Unclassified-Miscellaneous." *U.S. Naval Institute Proceedings*, July 2006, 89.
———. "USS *Norton Sound*: The Newest Old Ship." *United States Naval Institute Proceedings*, April 1979, 70–82.
Rowan, J.J. "USS *Annapolis* (AGMR-1)." *United States Naval Institute Proceedings*, May 1965, 172–4.
Scott, James M. "The Spy Ship Left Out in the Cold." *Naval History*, June 2017, 28–35.
Seal, Laura M. "MSC Accepts New OPDS Platform—Improves Ability to Support U.S. Troops Ashore." *Sealift*, November 2007.
Sharp, Erwin A. "Paddle Wheel Flattop." *All Hands*, April 1960, 10–1.
Smith, Richard K. "The Violation of the 'Liberty.'" *U.S. Naval Institute Proceedings*, June 1978, 62–70.
Stankus, Dawn. "A Perspective from the Captain's Chair." *Sealift*, May 2013, 4–5.
Stern, Robert C. "From Halifax to Singapore." *Naval History*, April 2014, 48–54.
Stillwell, Paul. "Bottom of the Pecking Order." *Naval History*, August 2013, 6.
———. "Ignominious Ends." *Naval History*, June 2012, 6.
Szostek, M. "*Sequoia*: Fitting Out the Presidential Yacht." *All Hands*, September 1975, 34–6.
Tegler, Eric. "USS *Sequoia*." *Naval History*, October 1997, 38–41.
"USS *Ponce* Returns to Homeport." *Sealift*, November 2017, 6.
Van Deurs, George. "The Year of the Fires." *United States Naval Institute Proceedings*, July 1979, 80–1.
Wertheim, Eric. "Lest We Forget." *United States Naval Institute Proceedings*, February 1998, 94.
———. "Lest We Forget." *United States Naval Institute Proceedings*, February 1999, 94.
———. "Lest We Forget." *United States Naval Institute Proceedings*, April 2002, 110.
———. "Lest We Forget." *United States Naval Institute Proceedings*, August 2002, 102.
Whitted, W.S. "The Old Naval Auxiliary Service." *United States Naval Institute Proceedings*, July 1928, 92–4.

Online Resources

"ABSD Advanced Base Sectional Drydock." http://www.sas1946.com/main/index.php?topic=24408.0 (accessed April 4, 2017).
"AC Collier." http://www.globalsecurity.org/military/systems/ship/ac.htm (accessed April 5, 2017).
"AFS—Combat Stores Ship." http://www.globalsecurity.org/military/systems/ship/afs.htm. (accessed April 20, 2017).
"AFS 1 *Mars* Combat Stores Ship." https://fas.org/man/dod-101/sys/ship/afs-1.htm. (accessed April 20, 2017).
"Aircraft Repair Ships (ARV)." http://www.shipscribe.com/usnaux/ARV/ARVtype.html (accessed June 26, 2017).
"Alternate Wars Archive, Ship's Data, U.S. Naval Vessels, Bureau of Ships, Navy Department." http://www.alternatewars.com/Archives/Ships_Data_USN/Ships_Data.htm (accessed July 11, 2017).
"Ammunition Ships (AE)." http://www.shipscribe.com/usnaux/AE/AEtype.html (accessed May 2, 2017).
"Amphibious Command Ships—LCC." http://www.navy.mil/navydata/fact_display.asp?cid=4200&tid=500&ct=4 (accessed April 21, 2017).
"Amphibious Force Flagships (AGC)." http://www.shipscribe.com/usnaux/AGC/AGCtype.html (accessed April 21, 2017).
"AP-22 *Mount Vernon* Cruise Book 1941–1946." http://www.navsource.org/archives/09/22/22022b.htm (accessed May 23, 2017).
"Attack/Amphibious Cargo Ships—AKA/LKA." http://www.navysite.de/lka/index.html (accessed May 3, 2017).
"Attack Cargo Ships (AKA)." http://www.shipscribe.com/usnaux/AKA/AKAtype.html (accessed May 3, 2017).
"Attack Transports (APA)." http://www.shipscribe.com/usnaux/APA/APAtype.html (accessed May 29, 2017).
"Auxiliary Crane Ships—T-ACS." http://www.navy.mil/navydata/fact_display.asp?cid=4800&tid=100&ct=4 (accessed October 14, 2017).
"Auxiliary General Purpose Oceanographic Research Vessel—AGOR." http://www.navy.mil/navydata/fact_display.asp?cid=4500&tid=650&ct=4 (accessed October 28, 2017).

"Auxiliary Ocean Tugs (ATA)." http://www.shipscribe.com/usnaux/ATA/ATAtype.html (accessed July 3, 2017).

"AVD Conversions." http://destroyerhistory.org/flushdeck/avd/ (accessed July 10, 2017).

"Aviation Logistics Support Ships—T-AVB." http://www.navy.mil/navydata/fact_display.asp?cid=4600&tid=400&ct=4 (accessed November 23, 2017).

"Aviation Supply Ships (AVD)." http://www.shipscribe.com/usnaux/AVS/AVStype.html (accessed July 17, 2017).

"Barracks Ships (APL)." http://www.shipscribe.com/usnaux/APL/APLtype.html (accessed June 6, 2017).

"Barracks Ships and Barges (APB, APL)." http://shipbuildinghistory.com/smallships/auxapl.htm (accessed May 30, 2017).

"Barracks Ships: Self Propelled (APB)." http://www.shipscribe.com/usnaux/APB/APBtype.html (accessed May 30, 2017).

"Battle Damage Repair Ships (ARB)." http://www.shipscribe.com/usnaux/ARB/ARBtype.html (accessed June 13, 2017).

"Building the Navy's Bases in World War II: History of the Bureau of Yards and Docks and the Civil Engineer Corps, 1940–1946, Chapter IX, Floating Dry Docks." (Washington: Department of the Navy, Bureau of Yards and Docks, n.d.). http://www.ibiblio.org/hyperwar/USN/Building_Bases/bases-9.html (accessed April 4, 2017).

"Cargo Ships (AK)." http://www.shipscribe.com/usnaux/AK/AKtype.html (accessed April 27, 2017).

"*Chouest*." https://www.globalsecurity.org/military/systems/ship/chouest.htm (accessed November 2, 2017).

"Coastal Transports (APc)." http://shipbuildinghistory.com/smallships/auxapc.htm (accessed May 30, 2017).

"Coastal Transports (Small) (APc)." http://www.shipscribe.com/usnaux/APC/APCtype.html (accessed May 30, 2017).

"Colliers (AC)." http://www.shipscribe.com/usnaux/AC/ACtype.html (accessed April 4, 2017).

"Degaussing Vessels." http://www.shipscribe.com/usnaux/ADG/ADGtype.html (accessed April 7, 2017).

"Destroyer Tenders." http://www.gyrodynehelicopters.com/destroyer_tenders.htm (accessed April 13, 2017).

"Destroyer Tenders—AD." http://www.navysite.de/ad/index.html (accessed April 13, 2017).

"Distilling Ships (AW)." http://www.shipscribe.com/usnaux/AW/AWtype.html (accessed July 24, 2017).

"Dry Cargo/Ammunition Ships—T-AKE." http://www.navy.mil/navydata/fact_display.asp?cid=4400&tid=500&ct=4 (accessed December 22, 2017).

"*Equality State*." https://www.marad.dot.gov/sh/ShipHistory/Detail/1464 (accessed October 16, 2017).

"Expeditionary Fast Transport (EPF)." http://www.navy.mil/navydata/fact_display.asp?cid=4200&tid=1100&ct=4 (accessed February 28, 2018).

"Expeditionary Transfer Dock (ESD)/Expeditionary Mobile Base (ESB)." http://www.navy.mil/navydata/fact_display.asp?cid=4600&ct=4&source=GovDelivery&tid=675 (accessed February 25, 2018).

"Fast Combat Support Ships T-AOE." http://www.navy.mil/navydata/fact_display.asp?cid=4400&tid=300&ct=4 (accessed January 11, 2018).

"Fleet Ocean Tugs (ATF)." http://shipscribe.com/usnaux/ATF/ATFtype.html (accessed February 13, 2018).

"Fleet Oilers—AO." https://www.navysite.de/ao/index.html (accessed December 30, 2017).

"Fleet Replenishment Oilers—T-AO." http://www.navy.mil/navydata/fact_display.asp?cid=4400&tid=600&ct=4 (accessed December 30, 2017).

"Floating Dry-Docks (AFDB, AFDM, AFDL, ARD, ARDM, YFD)." http://shipbuildinghistory.com/smallships/auxafd.htm (accessed April 17, 2017).

"Gasoline Tankers (AOG)." http://www.shipscribe.com/usnaux/AOG/AOGtype.html (accessed May 17, 2017).

"*Gem State*." https://www.marad.dot.gov/sh/ShipHistory/Detail/1796 (accessed October 14, 2017).

"*General Edwin D. Patrick*." https://www.marad.dot.gov/wp-content/uploads/pdf/General_Edwin_D._Patrick_HAER_Survey.pdf (accessed May 30, 2017).

"*General John Pope*." https://www.marad.dot.gov/wp-content/uploads/pdf/General_John_Pope_HAER_Survey.pdf (accessed May 30, 2017).

"General Stores–Issue Ships (AKS)." http://www.shipscribe.com/usnaux/AKS/AKStype.html (accessed May 9, 2017).

"*Green Mountain State*." https://www.marad.dot.gov/sh/ShipHistory/Detail/2014 (accessed October 16, 2017).

"Haze Gray & Underway: Naval History and Photography." http://www.hazegray.org (accessed May 12, 2018).

"High-End Warfare Requires Changes to the Combat Logistics Force." https://www.usni.org/magazines/proceedings/2017-11/high-end-warfare-requires-changes-combat-logistics-force (accessed December 4, 2017).

"Hospital Ships (AH)." http://shipscribe.com/usnaux/AH/AHtype.html (accessed November 4, 2017).

"High Speed Transports." http://www.uboat.net/allies/warships/types.html?type=High+speed+transport (accessed May 31, 2017).

"Historic American Engineering Record Surveys." https://www.marad.dot.gov/about-us/maritime-administration-history-program/vessels-of-the-maritime-administration/historic-american-engineering-record-surveys/ (accessed May 30, 2017).

"Hospital Ships—T-AH." http://www.navy.mil/navydata/fact_display.asp?cid=4625&tid=200&ct=4 (accessed November 6, 2017).

"Internal Combustion Engine Repair Ships (ARG)." http://www.shipscribe.com/usnaux/ARG/ARGtype.html (accessed June 17, 2017).

"Introduction: Troopships in World War II." https://www.skylighters.org/troopships/ (accessed May 26, 2017).

"*Keystone State*." https://www.marad.dot.gov/sh/ShipHistory/Detail/2875 (accessed October 14, 2017).

"*Kilo Moana*." http://www.soest.hawaii.edu/UMC/cms/kilo-moana/ (accessed October 27, 2017).

"Landing Craft Repair Ships (ARL)." http://www.shipscribe.com/usnaux/ARL/ARLtype.html (accessed June 19, 2017).

"List of MC Designs with Descriptions." http://shipscribe.com/shiprefs/mc/DsnList.html (accessed April 29, 2018).

"MARAD Vessel History Database." https://www.marad.dot.gov/sh/ShipHistory/ShipList?pageNumber=1&matchFromStart=True (accessed May 12, 2018).

"Marine Traffic." http://www.marinetraffic.com/en/ais/home/centerx:-12.3/centery:25.0/zoom:4 (accessed October 30, 2017).

"Maritime Digital Archive Encyclopedia, Auxiliary Vessels." http://www.ibiblio.org/maritime/media/index.php?cat=839 (accessed June 20, 2017).

"Maritime Prepositioning Ships—T-AK, T-AKR and T-AOT." http://www.navy.mil/navydata/fact_display.

asp?cid=4600&tid=200&ct=4 (accessed November 10, 2017).

"Mechanized-Artillery Transports (APM)." http://www.shipscribe.com/usnaux/APM/APMtype.html (accessed June 6, 2017).

"Military Sealift Command Reconfigures Tanker Fleet." http://www.navy.mil/submit/display.asp?story_id=56475 (accessed November 18, 2017).

"Military Sealift Command Ship inventory." http://www.msc.navy.mil/inventory/ (accessed April 6, 2017).

"Miscellaneous Auxiliaries (AG)." http://www.shipscribe.com/usnaux/AG/AGtype.html (accessed April 21, 2017).

"Motor Torpedo Boat Tenders (AGP)." http://www.shipscribe.com/usnaux/AGP/AGPtype.html (accessed April 24, 2017).

"Moving the US Troops in 1917–19." http://swansongrp.com/troopships_history.html (accessed May 26, 2017).

"MSC 2015 In Review." http://www.msc.navy.mil/annualreport/2015/pm5.htm (accessed November 18, 2017).

"National Association of Fleet Tug Sailors." www.nafts.com (accessed March 28, 2018).

"National Defense Reserve Fleet Inventory Archive." https://www.marad.dot.gov/ships-and-shipping/strategic-sealift/office-of-ship-operations/national-defense-reserve-fleet- ndrf/national-defense-reserve-fleet-inventory-archive/ (accessed May 30, 2017).

"Navigation Test Support Ship T-AGS." http://www.navy.mil/navydata/fact_display.asp?cid=4500&tid=500&ct=4 (accessed October 28, 2017).

"Net and Boom Defenses, Bureau of Ordnance, June 27, 1944." http://archive.hnsa.org/doc/netsandbooms/index.htm#pg23 (accessed May 9, 2017).

"Net Cargo Ships (AKN)." http://www.shipscribe.com/usnaux/AKN/AKNtype.html (accessed May 9, 2017).

"Net-Laying Ships (AN)." http://www.shipscribe.com/usnaux/AN/ANtype.html (accessed May 12, 2017).

"Ocean Class AGOR Names, Armstrong Class R/Vs." https://www.unols.org/sites/default/files/201403ficap04.pdf (accessed October 26, 2017).

"Ocean Surveillance Ships (AGOS)." http://shipbuildinghistory.com/smallships/auxagos.htm (accessed December 18, 2017).

"Ocean Surveillance Ships—AGOS." https://www.navysite.de/agos/index.html (accessed December 18, 2017).

"Oceanographic Survey Ships—T-AGS." http://www.navy.mil/navydata/fact_display.asp?cid=4500&tid=700&ct=4 (accessed October 28, 2017).

"Ocean-Going Tugs (AT)." http://www.shipscribe.com/usnaux/AT/ATtype.html (accessed July 1, 2017).

"Oilers (AO). http://shipscribe.com/usnaux/AO/AOtype.html (accessed December 30, 2017).

"One Hundred Years in the Making: The Birth of Military Sea Transportation Service (MSTS)." http://www.usmm.org/msts.html (accessed April 11, 2018).

"The Pacific War Online Encyclopedia, Attack Transports (APA)." http://pwencycl.kgbudge.com/A/t/Attack_Transports.htm (accessed May 29, 2017).

"The Pacific War Online Encyclopedia, Distilling Ships (AW)." http://pwencycl.kgbudge.com/D/i/Distilling_Ships.htm (accessed July 24, 2017).

"The Pacific War Online Encyclopedia, Floating Dry Docks." http://pwencycl.kgbudge.com/F/l/Floating_Dry_Docks.htm (accessed April 4, 2017).

"The Pacific War Online Encyclopedia, Internal Combustion Engine Repair Ships (ARG)." http://pwencycl.kgbudge.com/I/n/Internal_Combustion_Engine_Repair_Ships.htm (accessed June 17, 2017).

"The Pacific War Online Encyclopedia, Seaplane Tenders (AV)." http://pwencycl.kgbudge.com/S/e/Seaplane_Tenders.htm (accessed July 10, 2017).

"Prepositioning (PM3)." http://www.msc.navy.mil/PM3/ (accessed November 10, 2017).

"Repair Ships (AR)." http://www.shipscribe.com/usnaux/AR/ARtype.html (accessed June 10, 2017).

"Rescue and Salvage Ships." http://www.msc.navy.mil/inventory/ships.asp?ship=96 (accessed January 22, 2018).

"Rescue and Salvage Ships T-ARS." http://www.navy.mil/navydata/fact_display.asp?cid=4625&tid=150&ct=4 (accessed January 22, 2018).

"Rescue Tugs (ATR)." http://www.shipscribe.com/usnaux/ATR/ATRtype.html (accessed July 7, 2017).

"R/V *Atlantis*." http://www.whoi.edu/main/ships/atlantis (accessed October 27, 2017).

"R/V *Neil Armstrong*." http://www.whoi.edu/main/ships/neil-armstrong (accessed October 26, 2017).

"RV *Neil Armstrong* (AGOR-27)." http://militarynews.com/app/fleetweeknewyork/documents/rv_neil_armstrong_about.pdf (accessed October 26, 2017).

"RV *Roger Revelle*." https://scripps.ucsd.edu/ships/revelle (accessed October 27, 2017).

"RV *Sally Ride*—America's Newest Research Vessel." https://scripps.ucsd.edu/ships/sally-ride (accessed October 27, 2017).

"RV *Thomas G. Thompson*." https://www.ocean.washington.edu/story/RV+Thomas+G+Thompson (accessed October 26, 2017).

"Salvage Craft Tenders (ARST)." http://www.shipscribe.com/usnaux/ARST/ARSTtype.html (accessed June 26, 2017).

Salvage Lifting Vessels (ARSD)." http://www.shipscribe.com/usnaux/ARSD/ARSDtype.html (accessed June 20, 2017).

"Salvage Vessels (ARS)." http://shipscribe.com/usnaux/ARS/ARStype.html (accessed January 22, 2018).

"Sealift Program (PM5)." http://www.msc.navy.mil/PM5/ (accessed November 10, 2017).

"Seaplane Tenders (AV)." http://www.shipscribe.com/usnaux/AV/AVtype.html (accessed July 10, 2017).

"Ships of the U.S. Navy, 1940–1945, AE—Ammunition Ships." http://www.ibiblio.org/hyperwar/USN/ships/ships-ae.html (accessed May 2, 2017).

"Ships of the U.S. Navy, 1940–1945, AO—Fleet Oilers." https://www.ibiblio.org/hyperwar/USN/ships/ships-ao.html (accessed December 30, 2017).

"Ships of the U.S. Navy, 1940–1945, APA—Attack Transports." https://www.ibiblio.org/hyperwar/USN/ships/ships-apa.html (accessed May 29, 2017).

"Ships of the U.S. Navy, 1940–1945, APD—High Speed Transports." http://www.ibiblio.org/hyperwar/USN/ships/ships-apd.html (accessed May 31, 2017).

"Ships of the U.S. Navy, 1940–1945, AR—Repair Ships." https://www.ibiblio.org/hyperwar/USN/ships/ships-ar.html (accessed June 10, 2017).

"Ships of the U.S. Navy, 1940–1945, Auxiliaries." http://www.ibiblio.org/hyperwar/USN/ships/ships-ab.html (accessed April 4, 2017).

"Ships of the U.S. Navy's Military Sealift Command." http://www.msc.navy.mil/posters/MSC_USNavyShips.pdf (accessed April 6, 2017).

"Small Seaplane Tenders (AVP)." http://www.shipscribe.com/usnaux/AVP/AVPtype.html (accessed July 14, 2017).

"The Special Project Fleet, 1961–69, 1985–89." http://coldwar-c4i.net/SpecialProjectFleet/history.html (accessed April 22, 2017).

"Submarine Rescue Ships—ASR." http://www.navysite.de/asr/index.html (accessed June 27, 2017).

"Submarine Rescue Vessels (ASR)." http://www.shipscribe.com/usnaux/ASR/ASRtype.html (accessed June 23, 2018).

"Submarine Tender (AS)." http://www.navy.mil/navydata/fact_display.asp?cid=4625&tid=300&ct=4 (accessed February 3, 2018).

"Submarine Tenders." https://www.globalsecurity.org/military/systems/ship/as.htm (accessed February 3, 2018).

"Submarine Tenders (AS)." http://shipscribe.com/usnaux/AS/AStype.html (accessed February 3, 2018).

"T-ACS Keystone State Auxiliary Crane Ships." http://www.globalsecurity.org/military///systems/////ship/tacs.htm (accessed April 6, 2017).

T-AFS 8 Sirius Combat Stores Ships." https://fas.org/man/dod-101/sys/ship/tafs-8.htm. (accessed April 20, 2017).

T-AVB 3 *Wright*." https://fas.org/man/dod-101/sys/ship/tavb-3.htm (accessed November 34, 2017).

"Towing, Salvage, And Rescue Ships." http://seawaves.com/wp-content/uploads/2016/07/T-ATSX-Update-Brief.pdf (accessed February 20, 2018).

"Transport and Aircraft Ferries (APV)." http://www.shipscribe.com/usnaux/APV/APVtype.html (accessed May 11, 2017).

"United States Navy Fact File, Auxiliary Crane Ships—T-ACS." http://www.navy.mil/navydata/fact_display.asp?cid=4800&tid=100&ct=4 (accessed April 6, 2017).

"UNOLS Vessels." https://www.unols.org/ships-facilities/unols-vessels. (Accessed October 25, 2017).

"U.S. Navy Auxiliary Vessels, 1835–1945." http://www.shipscribe.com/usnaux/ (accessed March 30, 2017).

"U.S. Navy Radar Picket Ships 1955–1965." http://www.radomes.org/museum/ThePicketShips.php (accessed April 25, 2017).

"U.S. Navy Temporary Auxiliary Ships of World War I, 1917–1919." http://shipscribe.com/usnaux/wwl/index.htm (accessed April 16, 2018).

"U.S. Navy Temporary Auxiliary Ships, 1917–1919. World War I Era Transports—Organized by Type." http://www.shipscribe.com/usnaux/wwl/w1ap-t.htm (accessed May 23, 2017).

"U.S. Navy's Military Sealift Command History." http://www.msc.navy.mil/history/ (accessed April 12, 2018).

"U.S. Ship Force Levels, 1886–Present." https://www.history.navy.mil/research/histories/ship-histories/us-ship-force-levels.html#1917 (accessed April 6, 2018).

"USNS *Invincible* Back at Bahrain." https://www.bellingcat.com/news/mena/2016/09/28/usns-invincible-back-bahrain/ (accessed October 24, 2017).

"USNS *Vanguard* T-AG-194." http://navy.memorieshop.com/Vanguard/index.html (accessed October 24, 2017).

"USS *Annapolis*—AGR-1." http://www.agmr1-uss-annapolis.org/About-AGMR-1.html (accessed April 23, 2017).

"USS *Appalachian* (AGC-1) Amphibious Force Flagship Vessel." http://www.militaryfactory.com/ships/detail.asp?ship_id=USS-Appalachian-AGC1 (accessed April 21, 2017).

"USS *Arlington* AGMR-2 Communications Major Relay Ship." http://navy-radio.com/ships/agmr2.htm (accessed April 22, 2017).

"USS *Constitution*: America's Ship of State." https://www.history.navy.mil/browse-by-topic/ships/uss-constitution-americas-ship-of-state.html (accessed December 5, 2017).

"USS *Gage*." https://www.marad.dot.gov/wp-content/uploads/pdf/Gage_HAER_Report.pdf (accessed May 30, 2017).

"Vehicle Cargo Ships—AKR." https://www.navysite.de/akr/index.html (accessed November 14, 2017).

"Welcome to Tender Tale: Submarine Tenders of the United States Navy." http://tendertale.com/ (accessed February 3, 2018).

"Wheeler Refurbished After Purchase." http://www.msc.navy.mil/sealift/2012/December/wheeler.htm (accessed October 18, 2017).

"World Aircraft Carriers List: US Seaplane Tenders: Heavy Tenders." http://www.hazegray.org/navhist/carriers/us_sea2.htm (accessed July 10, 2017).

"World Aircraft Carriers List: US Seaplane Tenders: Miscellaneous." http://www.hazegray.org/navhist/carriers/us_sea1.htm (accessed July 10, 2017).

"World Aircraft Carriers List: US Seaplane Tenders: Small Tenders." http://www.hazegray.org/navhist/carriers/us_sea3.htm (accessed July 10, 2017).

"World War I Era Colliers—Organized By Type." http://www.ibiblio.org/hyperwar/OnlineLibrary/photos/usnshtp/ac/wlac.htm (accessed April 4, 2017).

"World War II Net Tenders." http://www.navsource.org/archives/09/18/1800001.htm (accessed May 23, 2017).

"World War II Troop Ships." http://www.ww2troopships.com/ (accessed May 26, 2017).

Index

AB 215–216
USS *Abatan* (AW 4) 331
ABD 216
USNS *Able* (T-AGOS 20) 31–32
USS *Abnaki* (ATF 96) 104–105
ABSD 216–217
AC 217–218
AD 218–220
ADG 220–221
administrative flagship 289–290
advanced aviation base ships 204–209
advanced base docks 216
advanced base sectional docks 216–217
AE 221–225
Aegir class 90
USNS *Aeolus* (T-ARC 3) 201–202
AF 223–224
AFD 225
AFDB 225
AFDC 226
AFDL 226–228
AFDL 21 226
AFDM 228–229
afloat forward staging base 24–27
AFS 229–231
AFSB 24–27
AG 231–233
AGB 233–234
AGC 130, 234–235
AGDE 236
AGDS 237
AGEH 238
AGER 238–239
AGF 238–240
AGFF 236
AGHR 240
AGM 146–152
AGMR 240–241
AGOR 152–157
AGOS 27–34

AGP 241–242
AGR 42–243
AGS 157–165
AGSC 243–245
AGSE 165–169
AGSL 245
AGSS 245–246
AGTR 246–247
AH 169–178
AHLC 247–248
aircraft cargo ships 263–265
aircraft carriers 329–331, 333–335
aircraft repair ships 309–310; aircraft 310–311; engine 311; helicopter 311–312
aircraft rescue vessel 328
aircraft tenders 320–322
aircraft transports 263–265
airplane transports 294–295
AK 248–254
AKA 254–258
AKB 257
AKD 257–258
AKE 34–41
AKF 258–259
AKI 259
AKL 259–260
AKN 260–261
AKR 186–193
AKS 261–263
AKV 263–265
USS *Alameda* (AO 10) 52
USS *Alameda County* (AVB 1) 206–207
USNS *Alan Shepard* (T-AKE 3) 34
USS *Albermarle* (AV 5) 13
USS *Albert J. Meyer* (T-ARC 6) 204
USS *Alsea* (ATF 97) 101
ammunition ships 221–225
amphibious cargo ships 254–258

amphibious command ships 234–235
amphibious force flagships 130, 234–235
amphibious transports 278–284
AN 265–268
Anchor class 77
ANL 265–268
USS *Antaeus* (AS 21) 88
AO 42–60
AOE 60–74
AOG 268–271
AOR 271–272
AOSS 272–273
AOT 193–198
AP 273–278
APA 278–284
USNS *Apache* (T-ATF 172) 109–110
APB 283–284
APc 284
APC 285–286
USS APc 101 285
APD 286–289
APF 289–290
APG 290
APH 290–291
APL 291–292
APL 55 291
APM 292
APN 292
APR 293
APS 293–294
APSS 293–294
APV 294–295
AR 295–297
Arb 297–298
ARB 298–299
ARC 198–204
USNS *Arctic* (T-AOE 8) 61, 71–72
ARD 299–300
ARD(BS) 301
ARDC 226

349

Index

ARDM 302
ARG 303–304
ARH 304–305
ARL 12, 14, 305–307
ARM 307
Armstrong class 155
USNS *Arrowhead* (T-AGSE 4) 166
ARS 74–88
ARSD 307–308
ARST 308–309
ARV 309–310
ARVA 310–311
ARVE 311
ARVH 311–312
AS 88–100
USS *Ashtabula* (AO 51) 55–56
Ashtabula class 49
ASR 312–314
ASSP 293–294
AT 314–316
ATA 316–318
ATF 100–111
USS *Atka* (AGB 3) 233
ATO 318–319
ATR 319–320
ATR 33 319
ATS 111–117
attack cargo ships 254–258
attack transports 278–284
auxiliary aircraft landing training ships 329–331
auxiliary aircraft transports 329–331
auxiliary cargo barge/lighter ship 257
auxiliary cargo float-on/float-off ship 258–259
auxiliary deep submergence support ships 237
auxiliary floating docks 225
auxiliary floating dry docks 226–228; big 225; lengthened 226–228; little (concrete) 226; medium 228–229
auxiliary general frigate 240
auxiliary ocean tugs 316–318
auxiliary repair docks—concrete 226
auxiliary repair dry docks 299–300
auxiliary research submarines 245–246
AV 320–322
AVB 204–209
AVC 322–323
AVD 323–324
aviation logistics support ships 204–209
aviation supply ships 328–329
AVM 324–325
AVP 325–328
AVR 328
AVS 328–329

AVT 329–331
AW 331–332
AZ 332–333

barracks ships 95, 283–284, 291–292
base repair ships 297–299
bathyscaphe support auxiliary dry dock 301
battle damage repair ships 298–299
USS *Beaufort* (ATS 2) 114–115
SS *Beaver State* (T-ACS 10) 144
USS *Belknap* (AVD 8) 323
USS *Benewah* (APB 35) 283
USS *Big Horn* (AO 45) 54–55
USNS *Big Horn* (T-AO 198) 48
Black Powder class 167
USS *Blue Ridge* (LCC 19) 19, 130–134
USNS *Bob Hope* (T-AKR 300) 188
Bob Hope class 189–190
Bonhomme Richard 84, 163
USNS *Bowditch* (T-AGS 62) 162–163
USNS *Bridge* (T-AOE 10) 72–73
USS *Bronx* (APA 236) 279
USNS *Bruce C. Heezen* (T-AGS 64) 164
USS *Brunswick* (ATS 3) 115–117
USNS *Brunswick* (T-EPF 6) 117
USS *Burdo* (APD 133) 287
USS *Burton Island* (AGB 1) 233

cable repairing ships 198–204
USS *Calamus* (AOG 25) 269
USS *Camden* (AOE 2) 65–66
USS *Canopus* (AS 9) 92–93
USS *Card* (ACV 11) 263
USNS *Card* (T-AKV 40) 13, 263
cargo ships 178–186, 248–254; and aircraft ferries 263–265; dock 257–258
USNS *Carl Brashear* (T-AKE 7) 39–40
MV *Carolyn Chouest* 168
catapult lighter 322–333
USNS *Catawba* (T-ATF 168) 106–107
MV *C-Champion* 167
MV *C-Commando* 167
Champion class 196
Cherokee class 102–103
China 31–33, 133, 162–163
USS *Chourre* (ARV 1) 309
USS *Cimarron* (AO 22) 53–54
Cimarron class 49
Civil War 9–10, 169
coastal surveying ships 243–245
coastal transports—small 284–285

Cobra Judy 151
colliers 10, 217–218
USS *Columbia* (AG 9) 289
combat logistics ships defined 23
combat store ships 229–231
USNS *Comet* (T-AKR 7) 190–191
USNS *Comfort* (T-AH 20) 176–178
Comfort class 171
command ships 130–138, 239–240
concrete auxiliary repair docks 226
USS *Conecuh* (AO 110) 56–57, 61, 272
Conrad class 155
USS *Consolation* (AH 15) 175–176
USS *Constitution* 9, 212–213
USS *Cormorant* (ATO 133) 318
SS *Cornhusker State* (T-ACS 6) 142–143
USNS *Corpus Christi Bay* (T-ARVH 1) 13, 311–312
MV *Cory Chouest* 33
Crandall (AHLC 2) 247–248
crane ships 139–144, 215–216
Crilley 248
USS *Currituck* (AV 7) 321
SS *Curtiss* (T-AVB 4) 205, 209
CVT 333
CVU 333–335
USS *Cyclops* (AC 4) 217

degaussing vessels and ships 220–221
USS *Deliver* (ARS 23) 74
USS *Denebola* (AF 56) 223
destroyer tenders 218–220
USS *Detroit* (AOE 4) 67–68
SS *Diamond State* (T-ACS 7) 143
distilling ships 331–332
Diver class 76–77
MV *Dolores Chouest* 167
dry cargo and ammunition ships 34–41

USNS *Eagleview* (T-AGSE 3) 168
USS *Edenton* (ATS 1) 112–114
USS *Edson* (DD 946) 229
USS *Egeria* (ARL 8) 12
Electric STREAM 16
electronic-deception hydrofoil craft 240
Elizabeth 9
USS *Emory S. Land* (AS 39) 89, 97–98
Emory S. Land class 91
MT *Empite State* (T-AOT 5193) 196

Index

environmental research ships 238–239
SS *Equality State* (T-ACS 8) 143
escort research ship 236
evacuation transports 290–291
expeditionary fast transports 117–122
expeditionary sea bases 123–130
expeditionary transfer docks 123–130
USS *Extricate* (ARS 16) 80–81

USS *Fabius* (ARVA 50) 310
Falcon class 196
USNS *Fall River* (T-EPF 4) 121–122
fast automated shuttle transfer 15–16
fast combat support ships 60–74
fast deployment logistics ship 335
USNS *Fast Tempo* 145–146
USS *Favorite* (ID-1385) 11
FDL 335
USNS *1LT Harry L. Martin* (T-AK 3015) 185–186
USS *Flamingo* (AM 32) 79
fleet ocean tugs 100–111
fleet replenishment oilers 42–60
fleet support ships defined 23
fleet tugs 100–111, 314–316
Fletcher, William B. 52
SS *Flickertail State* (T-ACS 5) 142
force levels 10–13, 20
USS *Frank Cable* (AS 40) 89, 98–99
frigate research ship 236
USS *Fulton* (AS 1) 91–92
Fulton class 90

ATB *Galveston Producer* (T-AOT 5406) 197
USS *Garrett County* (AGP 786) 241
gasoline tankers 268–271
SS *Gem State* (T-ACS 2) 141
USNS *General LeRoy Eltinge* (T-AP 154) 13
general store ship issue 259
general stores issue ships 261–263
USS *Glacier* (AGB 4) 233
USS *Glover* (AGDE 1) 236
SS *Gopher State* (T-ACS 4) 141–142
Gordon class 189
SS *Grand Canyon State* (T-ACS 3) 141
USS *Grapple* (ARS 7) 80

USNS *Grapple* (T-ARS 53) 86–87
USNS *Grasp* (T-ARS 51) 82–84
USS *Gratia* (AKS 11) 262
SS *Green Mountain State* (T-ACS 90) 143–144
USNS *Guam* (T-HST 1) 209–211
USS *Guavina* (AOSS 262) 272–273
USC&GSS *Guide* 79
guided missile ship 324–325
Gulf War 13–14

H-bomb recovery 81, 156
Haven class 171–172
heavier-than-air aircraft tenders 320–322
heavy-hull repair ship 304–305
heavy-machinery repair ship 307
heavy salvage lift craft 247–248
USNS *Henry J. Kaiser* (T-AO 187) 57–59
Henry J. Kaiser class 50
USNS *Henson* (T-AGS 63) 163—164
USNS *Hershel "Woody" Williams* (T-ESB 4) 128–129
high speed transports 209–211, 286–289
history of auxiliaries 9–14
USS *Hoist* (ARS 40) 81
SS *Hope* 176
MV *HOS Blue Water* 167
MV *HOS Dominator* 168
MV *HOS Greystone* 167
hospital ships 169–178
USS *Housatonic* (AO 35) 45
USNS *Howard O. Lorenzen* (T-AGM 25) 147, 148, 152
HST 209–211
HST 2 209–211
humanitarian assistance 37, 39–41, 73, 82, 84, 121, 134, 162, 163, 169, 176, 177, 211
USS *Hunley* (AS 31) 95–97
Hunley class 90
hydrofoil research ship 238

Ice Boat 9
ice breakers 233–234
USS *Illinois* (BB 7) 14–15
USNS *Impeccable* (T-AGOS 23) 28, 32–33
Impeccable class 30
USNS *Indomitable* (T-AGOS 7) 30
intelligence collectors 238–239, 246–247
internal combustion engine repair ships 303–304
USNS *Invincible* (T-AGM 24) 148, 151–152
IX 335–339

USS *Jason* (ARH 1) 304–305
JHSV 117–118
USNS *John Glenn* (T-ESD 2) 126–127
USS *John M. Connelly* (ID-2703) 44, 51
joint high speed vessel 117–118
USS *Jupiter* (AVS 8) 328

USS *Kalmia* (ATA 184) 317
USS *Kanawha* (AO 1) 43
USNS *Kanawha* (T-AO 196) 17
USS *Kearsarge* (BB 5) 216
MV *Kellie Chouest* 168–169
Kennedy, John F., Jr. 83
Kentucky (BB 66) 64
USS *Keokuk* (AKN 4) 261
USS *Kermit Roosevelt* (ARG 16) 303
SS *Keystone State* (T-ACS 1) 140
USS *Kidd* (DDG 100) 40
USS *Kittiwake* (ASR 13) 312
USS *Klondike* (AR 22) 295
Korean War 12–13
USS *Krishna* (ARL 38) 13–14

labor transports 291–292
USS *Lakehurst* (APM 9) 292
USS *Lakehurst* (APV 3) 294
landing craft repair ships 12, 305–307
large auxiliary floating dry docks 225; non-self-propelled 225
large seaplane tenders 320–322
laser weapons system 26
USNS *Lawrence H. Gianella* (T-AOT 1125) 195
LCC 130–138, 234–235
USNS *LCPL Roy M. Wheat* (T-AK 3016) 179
USNS *Lewis and Clark* (T-AKE 1) 36–38
USS *Lewis B. Puller* (ESB 3) 19, 25, 124, 127–128
USS *Lexington* (CV 16) 333-
USS *Liberty* (AGTR 5) 246
light cargo ships 259–260
lighter-than-air aircraft tender 332–333
USS *Lipan* (ATF 85) 103–104
USS *Littlehales* (AGSC 150) 244
LKA 254–258
USNS *Loyal* (T-AGOS 22) 28
LPA 278–284
LPR 286–289
LSMR 187
L.Y. Spear class 91
USNS *Lynch* (T-AGOR 7) 153

MT *Maersk Peary* (T-AOT 5426) 197
USS *Maine* (BB 10) 15

USNS *MAJ Stephen W. Pless* (T-AK 3007) 183–184
major communications relay ships 240–241
USS *Manna Hata* (SP-3396) 77–78
Maritime Administration 3
USNS *Mary Sears* (T-AGS 65) 164
Mattaponi class 49
USS *Maumee* (AO 2) 15, 42–43
USNS *Maury* (T-AGS 66) 158, 164
McCann rescue chamber 313
mechanized artillery transports 292
medium auxiliary floating dry docks 228–229; non-self-propelled 228–229
medium auxiliary repair docks 302
USS *Medusa* (AR 1) 296
USNS *Mercy* (T-AH 19) 169, 176
Mercy class 172
USNS *Meteor* (T-AKR 9) 191–192
MV *Mighty Servant 3* 123
USNS *Miguel Keith* (T-ESB 5) 129
Military Sea Transportation Service 3, 13, 18
Military Sealift Command 3–4, 18–19
USNS *Millinocket* (T-EPF 3) 119
USS *Milwaukee* (AOR 2) 271
miscellaneous auxiliaries 231–233
miscellaneous auxiliary submarines 245–246
miscellaneous command ships 239–240
Mispillion class 50
missile range instrumentation ships 146–152
Mission Buenaventura class 50
USNS *Mizar* (T-AGOR 11) 156
mobile landing platform 124
USS *Monitor* 83
USNS *Montford Point* (T-ESD 1) 123, 125–126
motor torpedo boat tenders 241–242
USS *Mount Whitney* (LCC 20) 19, 131, 134–137
museum ship 212–213

National Defense Reserve Fleet 4
USNS *Navajo* (T-ATF 169) 107–108
Navajo class 102–103
Naval Auxiliary Service 18

Naval Overseas Transportation Service 18
Naval Sea Systems Command 4
USS *Neches* (AO 5) 51–52
RV *Neil Armstrong* (T-AGOR 27) 156–157
Neosho class 50
USNS *Neptune* (T-ARC 2) 200–201
Neptune class 199
net cargo ships 260–261
net laying ships 265–268
net tenders 265–268
USS *Niagara Falls* (AFS 3) 230
Nimitz, Chester W. 15, 42
USS *Nitro* (AE 23) 221
non-mechanized artillery transport 292
non-self-propelled medium auxiliary repair dry docks 302
non-self-propelled repair docks 299–300
non-self-propelled barracks craft 291–292
USS *Norton Sound* (AV 11) 324

USS *Oak Ridge* (ARDM 1) 302
USNS *Observation Island* (T-AGM 23) 148, 150–151
ocean-going tugs 314–316
ocean surveillance ships 27–34
ocean tugs: auxiliary 316–318; old 318–319; rescue 319–320
oceanographic research ships 152–157
offshore petroleum distribution system 17, 144–146
USS *Okala* (ARST 2) 308
oilers 42–60, 193–198

USNS *Pathfinder* (T-AGS 60) 161
Pathfinder class 160
patrol boat tenders 241–242
USS *Paul Revere* (LPA 248) 280
USS *Peleliu* (LHA 5) 37
USS *Perch* (SSP 313) 293
USNS *PFC Eugene A. Obregon* (T-AK 3006) 182–183
USS *Picket* (AGR 7) 243
USS *Pinkey* (APH 2) 290
pirates 37
USS *Plainview* (AGEH 1) 238
USS *Pocono* (AGC 16) 234
USNS *Point Barrow* (T-AKD 1) 237, 258
USS *Point Loma* (AGDS 2) 237
USS *Ponce* (LPD 15) 24–27
USS *Portunus* (ARC 1) 200
USNS *Potomac* (T-AOT 181) 197–198
Potomac class 196

USNS *Powhatan* (T-ATF 166) 105–106
Powhatan class 103
USNS *Prevail* (T-AGOS 8) 30–31
USS *Proteus* (AS 19) 89, 93–95
USS *Pueblo* (AGER 20) 239
USNS *Puerto Rico* (T-HST 2) 209–211

Q-ship 54

radar picket ships 242–243
USNS *Rainier* (T-AOE 7) 69–71
USNS *Range Tracker* (T-AGM 1) 146–149
USS *Red Rover* 169–170
USS *Rehobeth* (AVP 50) 325
Relic 212–213
repair ships 295–297; small 14, 305–307
replenishment oilers 271–272
replenishment techniques 14–17
USS *Repose* (AH 16) 13, 172–174
Resourceful (AFDM 5) 229
rescue and salvage ships 74–88
rescue transports 293
rescues 30, 67, 71, 72, 106, 133
Revolutionary War 9
USS *Rigel* (ARb 1) 298
USNS *Robert D. Conrad* (T-AGOR 3) 155–156
USS *Robert L. Barnes* (AO 14) 52–53

USNS *Sacagawea* (T-AKE 2) 38–39
USS *Sacramento* (AOE 1) 13, 61–64
Sacramento class 63
USNS *Safeguard* (T-ARS 50) 81–82
Safeguard class 77
USS *St. Louis* (LKA 116) 255
USS *Saipan* (CVL 48) 330
RV *Sally Ride* (AGOR 28) 154
salvage and recovery operations 79–85, 87, 104, 106–107, 109, 115, 116, 156
salvage craft tenders 308–309
salvage lifting vessels 307–308
salvage ships 11, 74–88
salvage and rescue ships 111–117
salvage tugs 111–117
USS *Salvager* (ARSD 3) 307
USNS *Salvor* (T-ARS 52) 84–86
satellite launching ship 245
USS *Scorpion* (SSN 589) 156
USNS *Sealift China* (T-AOT 170) 194
Sealift class 50, 196
seaplane tenders 320–322; destroyer 323–324
USS *Seattle* (AOE 3) 16, 66–67

Index

USNS *2ND LT John P. Bobo* (T-AK 3008) 184–185
2ND LT John P. Bobo class 182
self-propelled barracks ships 283–284
USS *Seneca* (AT 91) 314
SES 339–340
SES 200 339
USNS *SGT Joseph E. Muller* (T-APC 118) 286
SGT Matej Kocak class 182
USNS *SGT William R. Button* (T-AK 3012) 180
ship types 17–18
Shugart class 189
Simon Lake class 91
USNS *Sioux* (T-ATF 171) 108–109
MT *SLNC Goodwill* (T-AOT 5419) 197
MT *SLNC Pax* (T-AOT 5356) 197
small amphibious transports 286–289
small auxiliary floating dry docks 226–228; non-self-propelled 226–228
small coastal transports 284–286
small seaplane tenders 325–328
USNS *Soderman* (T-AKR 299) 187–188
USNS *Soderman* (T-AKR 317) 187
USS *Solace* (AH 5) 174–175
Spanish-American War 10
USNS *Spearhead* (T-EPF 1) 119–121
USS *Sphinx* (ARL 24) 305
USS *Spica* (AK 16) 248
SSO 272
SSP 293–294
Stalwart class 29
standard tensioned replenishment alongside method 16
store issue ships 261–263
store ships 223–224
Suamico class 196
submarine escort ships 165–169
submarine oiler 272–273
submarine rescue vessels and ships 312–314
submarine tenders 88–100
submarines 88–89, 92–100, 245–246, 313
USNS *Sumner* (T-AGS 61) 161–162

USNS *Supply* (T-AOE 6) 68–69
Supply class 63
support ships 139–213; defined 139
supporting gunnery ship 290
surface effects ship 339–340
USS *Surfbird* (ADG 383) 220
SURTASS 27
surveying ships 157–165

T-ACS 139–144
T-AG 144–146
T-AGM 146–152
T-AGOR 152–157
T-AGOS 27–34
T-AGS 157–165
T-AGSE 165–169
T-AH 169–178
T-AK 178–186
T-AKE 34–41
T-AKR 186–193
USS *Tallahatchie County* (AVB 2) 207–208
USS *Tangier* (AV 8) 321
tankers *see* oilers
T-AO 42–60
T-AOE 60–74
T-AOT 193–198
T-ARC 198–204
T-ARS 74–88
Task Force 73 13, 64
T-ATF 100–111
T-ATS(X) 111–113
T-AVB 204–209
T-CVU 333–335
technical research ships 246–247
technologies and techniques 14–17
T-EPF 117–122
Thompson class 155
USNS *Thor* (T-ARC 4) 202–203
USS *Thresher* (SSN 593) 81, 156
T-HST 209–211
T-LSV 190–191
T-MLP 123–124
towing, salvage and rescue ships 111–117
training carriers 333
transport and aircraft ferries 294–295
transport oilers 193–198
transport rescue vessels 293
transport submarines 293–294
transports 273–278; fitted for evacuation of wounded 290–291

USNS *Trenton* (T-EPF 5) 117
Trieste II 81, 237
USS *Truckee* (AO 147) 47

USS *Ulysses* (ARB 9) 299
unclassified miscellaneous vessels 335–339
underway replenishment 15–17, 42
utility aircraft carriers 333–335

USNS *VADM K. R. Wheeler* (T-AG 5001) 144–146
USNS *Vanguard* (T-AGM 19) 148–150
vehicle cargo ships 186–193
vertical replenishment 16
USNS *Victorious* (T-AGOS 19) 31
Victorious class 29
Vietnam War 13, 173
USS *Viking* (ARS 1) 78–80
Viking class 76
USS *Vincennes* (CL 64) 317

USNS *Walter S. Diehl* (T-AO 193) 42
USS *War Hawk* (AP 168) 273
War Shipping Administration 4
USNS *Waters* (T-AGS 45) 160–161
Waters class 160
Watson class 190
USS *West Virginia* (BB 48) 216
USS *White Sands* (ARD(BS) 20) 301
USS *White Sands* (AGDS 1) 237
USNS *William McLean* (T-AKE 12) 40–41
USNS *Windham Bay* (T-CVU 92) 334
USS *Windlass* (ARSD 4) 307
USS *Windsor* (ARD 22) 300
World War I 10
World War II 11–12
wounded evacuation transports 290–291
USS *Wright* (AZ 1) 332–333
SS *Wright* (T-AVB 3) 208–209
Wright class 206

YAGR 242–243
USS *Yamacraw* (ARC 5) 203–204
USS *Yellowstone* (AD 41) 219

USNS *Zeus* (T-ARC 7) 199

www.ingramcontent.com/pod-product-compliance
Lightning Source LLC
Chambersburg PA
CBHW080803020526
44114CB00046B/2742